DIRECTORY:
ENVIRONMENT

CW00592050

DIRECTORY FOR THE ENVIRONMENT

ORGANISATIONS IN BRITAIN AND IRELAND 1986–7

COMPILED AND EDITED BY
MICHAEL J. C. BARKER, ALA

WITH A FOREWORD BY
JONATHON PORRITT

ROUTLEDGE & KEGAN PAUL
LONDON

First published in 1984
by Routledge & Kegan Paul plc

11 New Fetter Lane, London EC4P 4EE

Second edition 1986
Phototypeset in 9 on 10pt Linotron Rockwell
by Input Typesetting Ltd, London
and printed in Great Britain
by T J Press (Padstow) Ltd
Padstow, Cornwall

© *Michael J.C. Barker 1984,1986*

No part of this book may be reproduced in
any form without permission from the publisher
except for the quotation of brief passages
in criticism

British Library Cataloguing in Publication Data

Barker, Michael J. C.
  Directory for the environment:
  organisations in Britain and Ireland 1986–7
  ——2nd ed.
  1. Environmental protection——Great
  Britain——Societies, etc.
  I. Title
  333.7′06′041   TD169.6
ISBN 0–7102–0961–4

CONTENTS

FOREWORD

Over the last few years there has been a tremendous surge of interest in environmental issues. There have been similar surges in the past, but interestingly enough, this one coincides not with a time of sustained growth and prosperity, as has been the case before, but rather with a period of prolonged economic decline. And in comparison with the 'environment boom' of the early 1970s, the mood today is less utopian, less trendy, with the emphasis now more on the *causes* of the problems we face than on the symptoms, and on the determined pursuit of realistic, constructive alternatives.

The visible evidence of this surge of interest is to be found in the consistent findings of one opinion poll after another, namely that a clear majority of people consider the environment to be an area of major political concern. The less visible evidence is to be found in a whole array of often subtle political and life-style changes, by which people give substance to their theoretical concerns. Attitudes towards health, or towards diet and nutrition; an increase in the number of bicyclists and those who choose to walk; a greater readiness not to waste things, but to see them recycled and energy conserved; the accumulative impact of such small changes is difficult to quantify, but together with a growing sense of apprehension about nuclear power, acid rain, toxic wastes, the pollution of both air and water, and many desperate international problems, it is enough to put the pressure on politicians who for the most part are still indifferent or whose hearts are only in it when the votes are too.

Though the rhetorical declarations of a succession of Secretaries of State for the Environment have indicated the possibility of substantial change in this respect, nothing much has come of it. Legislation (such as the Food and Environment Protection Act or the Wildlife and Countryside Act) has usually been inadequate or implemented far too slowly.

Part II of the Control of Pollution Act was implemented ten year after it was passed in 1974, and the much heralded decision to ban the use of lead in petrol has been compromised since then by one delaying tactic after another. At the same time, the role of the Public Inquiry has come increasingly under scrutiny.

The Sizewell Inquiry into the Central Electricity Generating Board's proposal to build a Pressurised Water Reactor at Sizewell stretched the system (and many of the objectors) to breaking point. Since then, the Government's extraordinary decision to hold a *local* planning inquiry into the proposed Dounreay Reprocessing Plant, and its even more extraordinary decision to have no inquiry *at all* to consider proposals for a Channel Link (the largest civil engineering project in British history) have created further disarray amongst those who look to the planning process to resolve complex environmental issues.

For all these difficulties, most environmental organisations today are flourishing, with growing support and increased funding. In a nation which already boasts the largest number of environmental organisations per head of population, it seems impossible that yet more should somehow burgeon forth. But they do, particularly at the local level, where the true vitality of the movement is most often to be found.

And many of these environmental organisations are now beginning to broaden out, seeking common ground with those who are primarily involved in the peace movement, in the Third World, and in development groups or even in human rights issues. A new movement is taking shape: the green movement, of which today's environment groups are just one part, though still the most vocal and influential.

The make-up of this movement is often extremely confusing, even for people who are deeply involved! The *Directory for the Environment* provides an invaluable aid both for those seeking specific information on certain organisations, and for those who need to get some kind of overview of so vital and turbulent a development in British politics. It highlights both the common strands and the diversity, both the stability and the dynamic flexibility of contemporary environmentalism – and that is no mean feat!

Political commentators are referring with increasing regularity to the 'green vote', now said to number between 2 and 3 million people. The profiles of the 1400 organisations featured in this Directory demonstrate just how difficult it will be to target that vote, but few now dispute the significance of the environment movement or the fact that environmental issues have now become mainstream political concerns. The strength of people's feelings and the pressure on decision-makers fully to acknowledge our environmental responsibilities, and to change our ways accordingly, is now insurmountable.

Jonathon Porritt
November 1985

PREFACE

SECOND EDITION

The *Directory for the Environment* is not an 'alternative' directory. Time was when the term 'alternative' had a valid connotation, as being indicative of the explosion of new thought on the environment, human relations and other issues. For a while this served a valuable purpose in focusing people's attention on the fact that there were other ways of thinking about what we had so long taken for granted, such as exploiting the seemingly bottomless pit of the Earth's resources.

But time and perceptions move on. As the 'alternative scene' became more familiar in the public consciousness and as elements of it became absorbed into the mainstream, the distinction between what was alternative and what was not became blurred and less relevant. I believe it is now time to move away from this now divisive and alienating perception to an era in which ideas and advances can be considered on their own merits; too often is a concept promptly branded and stigmatised as being either outside or inside established thinking, thus blocking the channels to constructive dialogue. One can have a new vision of society, certainly, but it will not avail us to throw the baby out with the bathwater.

Hence there is a substantial number of organisations in this edition that are either statutory bodies with environment-related responsibilities or other types of organisation which are far from being alternative or radical but which nevertheless perform a key role in the subject areas covered by this Directory and may have a point of view which should not be dismissed as irrelevant by those who seek rapid change. In short, the Directory is designed to present as broad a picture as possible of current environmental activity in the British Isles.

If the future cannot accommodate all of us, it may fail to accommodate any of us.

Mike Barker
Compiler & editor
November 1985

Acknowledgments

Acknowledgment is given to the help of the British Petroleum Company plc.

Much gratitude is also due to Monica Frisch of Earthright/EGIS for her invaluable help in difficult circumstances.

Some of them were dreamers
Some of them were fools
Who were making plans and thinking of the future.
With the energy of the innocent
They were gathering the tools
They would need to make their journey back to nature. . . .

Some of them were angry
At the way the Earth was abused
By those men who learned to forge beauty into power.
In trying to protect Her from them
They only became confused
By the magnitude of their fury in the final hour. . . .

– Jackson Browne/*Before the Deluge*

© 1974 Benchmark Music
Printed by kind permission of
Benchmark Music and Warner Bros. Music Ltd.

HOW TO USE
THE DIRECTORY

Finding an organisation

If you know its name: turn straight to the main sequence 'Organisations' which is in A-Z order (remember that some organisations with particularly long names may have been listed under their acronym).

If it is not in the main sequence: try 'Organisations not based in UK or Ireland' or 'Useful addresses'.

Change of name: many organisations modify or change their name from time to time to reflect a shift of status or emphasis; recent changes will have been cross-referenced.

Ceasing to exist: if an organisation has recently ceased to function, there will be a note to that effect.

If you cannot find an organisation and you are certain that it exists and would be relevant to the Directory, do let me know (address at bottom); in the meantime, you could check with one of the organisations listed under 'Information resources' or with another body in the same field.

If you are uncertain of the name or need to find out **which organisations are active in a particular field:** turn to the Subject Index and look for the heading you think most appropriate – there are plenty of cross-references to help you. The Subject Index is based on organisations' principal concerns, but does not necessarily list a body under *all* its interests.

Journals
Journals, bulletins, newsletters, etc. are listed both under the publishing organisation, where this has an entry in the main sequence, and also in the separate Journals A-Z listing which

includes some not found in the Organisations sequence. Frequency of publication has been noted where known, but a blank space may also indicate irregular/infrequent publication. Subscription rates have not been included because of the time lag between the information being received and the Directory being in general circulation; it is better to check the latest rate with the publishing organisation.

Other publications

In this edition I have included in organisations' entries a number of items published by them or with which they are associated; I have tried to select those which might conceivably be of some interest to users of the Directory. Likewise, I have included a select bibliography of recent (1983–5) works, broadly classified and listed by author. These too are meant to be for the interest of the non-specialist, since specialists will already be familiar with the literature in their own field. I hope this new feature will prove to be a valuable addition to the Directory.

Organisations as sources of information

Although one of the main purposes of this Directory is to be a signpost to sources of information, *please remember:*
– not all the organisations listed here can be regarded as potential sources of information; those that can supply information usually indicate this;
– many organisations' primary function is to service the needs of their own membership; they are unlikely to respond very helpfully to enquiries from non-members;
– some organisations supply information only to the government and relevant statutory bodies;
– some organisations serve some other specific clientele such as the media;
– many voluntary or specialist bodies simply do not have the capacity to respond to general enquiries regarding their subject field.

Asking for information

If you are, for example, undertaking a project on a particular topic, it is worth bearing in mind a few important points:

Are you approaching the right kind of organisation for your purpose? It may seem obvious to consider this, but it is surprising how much correspondence organisations receive that is irrelevant to the work they do; careful attention should therefore be paid to the organisation's description of itself in the Directory.

Are you being specific enough? You are not likely to get much satisfaction by saying 'Please send me some information on pollution/wildlife/wind power' or whatever; if you can state in fairly precise terms what you want to find out, it will avoid time-wasting and frustration at both ends and the organisation concerned will find it easier to refer you to someone else if necessary.

Do you require existing, easily accessible, information or original research? If the latter, you will undoubtedly have to pay for it and there are special consultancies who can provide it. Don't expect anyone to involve themselves in hours of research for you out of the goodness of their hearts – people who are sufficiently motivated to be involved in organisations, particularly in a voluntary capacity, are usually very busy.

DO send a stamped addressed envelope to most kinds of organisation if you are requesting information – this will usually guarantee you at least the courtesy of a reply.

DO NOT ring up and expect instant answers – few organisations are that efficient! Also, many of the phone numbers listed for voluntary bodies are the private numbers of honorary officers who may not be entirely enthusiastic if you expect them to drop everything to help you.
In short: BE BRIEF; BE RELEVANT; BE SPECIFIC; BE PATIENT.

Criteria for inclusion in the Directory
In a subject as difficult to define as 'the environment', it is not easy to establish workable criteria by which to include or exclude organisations. In this edition the range of organisations included has been broadened a little, but on the whole I have seen no reason to depart from the original guidelines set out in the previous edition:

Activities

    (a) Organisations that are involved in activities that relate in some way to the natural, physical or human environment.

    (b) Organisations that seek to promote alternatives to the detrimental use or exploitation of the Earth and its resources and all who inhabit it.

    (c) Agencies which environmental organisations find useful to their activities.

Scope

(a) International organisations.
(b) National organisations.
(c) Regional organisations.
(d) Significant organisations, even if small or local.
(e) County- or city-wide organisations.
(f) Subsidiary organisations, if significant in their own right.
(g) Sibling organisations insofar as they are 'national' in the sense of the four home nations plus the Republic of Ireland

In apparently marginal cases, the general philosophy has been to include rather than exclude, for the greater convenience of the user.

Organisations who wish to be included should write to me directly at the address below, preferably enclosing samples of their literature.

While all efforts are made to ensure accuracy, the information contained in this Directory has been supplied by the organisations concerned, directly or indirectly, and the editor and publishers cannot accept responsibility for factual errors.

Mike Barker
PO Box 4
Hexham
Northumberland
NE46 1JT

ABBREVIATIONS

Bull.	Bulletin
HM	Her Majesty's (as in HM Inspectorate...)
HMSO	Her Majesty's Stationery Office
-L	Entry based on organisation's literature
NGO	Non-Governmental Organisation
NI	Northern Ireland
N/l	Newsletter
-NR	Entry questionnaire not returned (this edition only)
pp.	pages
Quango	Quasi-autonomous non-governmental organisation
Rev.	Revised
RI	Republic of Ireland

ORGANISATIONS

Acupuncture Information
This organisation no longer exists

Advisory Committee on Animal Experiments
c/o Home Office, Queen Anne's Gate, London
SW1H 9AT 01–213 3000
Contact The Secretary
Aims (i) To consider such matters arising
out of the administration of the Cruelty to
Animals Act 1876 as may be referred to them
by the Secretary of State, including in
particular: (a) specific proposals for experiments on living animals intended to be
carried out under the authority of the Act; (b)
trends in such experimental work; (c) questions of policy, procedure or practice; (d)
proposals for review of the law. (ii) To
propose to the Secretary of State at its discre-
tion matters arising under (b), (c) or (d)
above which in its opinion might usefully be
referred to it for its consideration. (iii) To
have regard both to the legitimate requirements of science and industry and to the
protection of animals against avoidable
suffering.
The Committee, which is constituted for
England and Wales, consists of a chairman
and 12 other members (8 scientific and 4 lay)
appointed by the Home Secretary.
Status Statutory

**Advisory Committee on Dangerous
Substances**
see HEALTH AND SAFETY EXECUTIVE *for
regional addresses*
Aims To consider and advise the Health
and Safety Commission on: (i) methods of
securing safety by controlling risks to
persons at work and related risks to the
public connected with the manufacture,
import, storage, conveyance and use of
dangerous substances (other than those dealt
with by the Advisory Committee on Toxic
Substances and the Nuclear Advisory
Standing Committee) as defined by the
Commission; (ii) other matters referred to
them by the HSC or HSE.
Status Statutory

**Advisory Committee on The Landscape
Treatment of Trunk Roads / Landscape
Advisory Committee (LAC)**
LAC Secretariat, Dept of Transport, Room
P1/033, 2 Marsham Street, London SW1P 3EB
01–212 5168
Aims To advise the Secretary of State for

Transport and the Secretary of State for
Wales upon: (i) the relative acceptability of
alternative routes and alternative standards
for proposed major new and improved trunk
roads and motorways, having regard to the
features and qualities of the landscape which
would be affected and to other related
environmental considerations; (ii) the
general landscape treatment of trunk roads
and motorways, including lighting, roadside
planting and the siting of service areas.
The Committee, which is constituted for
England and Wales, consists of a chairman,
deputy chairman and 14 other members
appointed by the Secretary of State for
Transport, including nominees of relevant
amenity and professional bodies as well as
independent members invited to serve
because of their specialist knowledge of
landscaping and amenity matters.
Status Statutory

Advisory Committee on Major Hazards
*This Committee was terminated on 31
December 1983*

Advisory Committee on Pesticides
c/o Ministry of Agriculture, Fisheries & Food,
Great Westminster House, Horseferry Road,
London SW1P 2AE 01–216 6311
Aims To keep under review all risks that
may arise from the use of: (i) pesticides; (ii)
veterinary chemicals not directly administered to animals; (iii) any other potentially
toxic chemicals specifically referred to the
Committee by Ministers; and to make
recommendations to the Ministers
concerned.
The Committee consists of an independent
chairman and 10 other independent
members, together with representatives
from the Ministry of Agriculture, Dept of
Health, Dept of the Environment, Dept of
Trade & Industry, Dept of Education &
Science, Agricultural & Food Research
Council, Medical Research Council, Natural
Environment Research Council, Nature
Conservancy Council and the Laboratory of
the Government Chemist.
Status Statutory

**Advisory Committee on Pollution of the Sea
(ACOPS)**
3 Endsleigh Street, London WC1H 0DD
01–388 2117
Secretary Dr V. Sebek

Aims To collect, evaluate and diffuse information about research into and action against the causes and effects of pollution of the sea; to identify those fields in which research and action is needed and to press for it; where appropriate, to publicise and comment on the action and research.

Formerly the Advisory Committee on Oil Pollution of the Sea, the Committee consists of a chairman, 7 other officers, 14 individual members and representatives of 26 organisations, including local authority associations, conservation and animal welfare societies; there is one observer (an association of oil companies operating in the North Sea) and representatives of 11 international organisations as overseas observers.

Activities Publishes surveys on oil pollution and studies on compensation and liability for oil pollution damage.

Status Registered company with charitable status

Publications ACOPS Newsletter (2); Yearbook & Survey (1)

Advisory Committee on the Safety of Nuclear Installations

see HEALTH AND SAFETY EXECUTIVE *for regional addresses*

Aims To advise the Health and Safety Commission and, where appropriate, Secretaries of State, on major issues affecting the safety of nuclear installations, including design, siting, operation and maintenance, which are referred to them or which they consider require attention. The Committee consists of a chairman and 18 other members.

Status Statutory

Advisory Committee on Toxic Substances

see HEALTH AND SAFETY EXECUTIVE *for regional addresses*

Aims To consider and advise the Health and Safety Commission on: (i) methods of controlling the health hazards to persons at work and related hazards to the public which may arise from toxic substances as defined by the HSC, with particular reference to those requiring notification under regulations, but excluding nuclear materials within the terms of reference of the Nuclear Advisory Standing Committee; (ii) other associated matters referred to it by the HSC or HSE.

The Committee sits under the chairmanship of the Deputy Director General and Director of Nuclear Safety of the HSE and consists of up to 14 members, including 4 members each nominated by the Confederation of British Industry and Trades Union Congress and 4 members chosen for their scientific expertise; remaining members include representatives of local authority associations.

Status Statutory

Advisory Council on Energy Conservation (ACEC)

This Council was disbanded on 31 December 1983

Advisory Council on Research & Development for Fuel and Power (ACORD)

c/o Dept of Energy, Thames House South, Millbank, London SW1P 4QJ 01–211 3000

Aims To advise the Secretary of State for Energy on the general programme of R&D of the nationalised energy industries; and to advise on such matters in the field of energy R&D as the Secretary of State may refer to it. As regards gas and coal, the Council is constituted for the whole of Great Britain; as regards electricity, for England and Wales only.

The Council consists of a chairman and 16 other members appointed by the Secretary of State for Energy; membership includes representatives from nationalised fuel industries, the Science Research Council, UK Atomic Energy Authority and independent members from private industry and the universities.

Activities The Council's advice to the Secretary of State is confidential. It meets 6–9 times a year and visits relevant research establishments.

Status Statutory

Advisory Panel on Disarmament and Non-Proliferation

c/o Foreign & Commonwealth Office (Arms Control & Disarmament Research Unit), Downing Street (East), London SW1A 2AL 01–233 5154

Aims To tap sources of ideas outside the 'official establishment', to provide specialist advice to the Minister and to provide a channel for the exchange of views on arms control and disarmament between Ministers, officials and outside bodies. Was formerly 2 bodies: the Advisory Panel on Arms Control and Disarmament and the Non-Proliferation Advisory Panel. The chairman is the Minister of State for Foreign and Commonwealth Affairs responsible for arms control and disarmament; there are 28 other members appointed by him, including parliamentarians, academics and representatives of NGOs.

Activities Meets once or twice a year, usually to discuss specific disarmament issues; its advice contributes to the formulation of official policy.

Status Statutory

Aerodyn
Meadow Farm, Greenham, Wellington,
Somerset TA21 0JW 0823 672134
> **Contact** John Shore
> **Aims** To design, make and supply small
> wind turbines which generate electricity for
> people wishing to be independent of mains
> or grid electricity. Aerodyn is related to and
> helps to fund its sister organisation Resource
> Research.
> **Activities** Design, manufacture and supply
> of low-voltage wind turbines (50W–1000W
> output). Suppliers of related equipment such
> as batteries, inverters, load controls, low-
> energy lights and fittings and light-weight
> hinged masts. Wind energy consultants.
> **Status** Commercial/manufacturing
> **Publications** The Wind User's Guide

**Agricultural and Food Research Council
(AFRC)**
160 Great Portland Street, London W1N 6DT
01–580 6655
> **Principal Information Officer** M.F.
> Goodwin
> **Aims** To advance scientific knowledge
> relevant to agriculture, horticulture and food
> supply; to exploit this knowledge to increase
> the efficiency of the agricultural, horticul-
> tural and food industries and to safeguard
> and improve the quality of food for the
> community.
> **Activities** Research into the biological and
> engineering sciences associated with agri-
> culture. This work is carried out in 28 insti-
> tutes in England, Scotland and Wales and in
> 6 AFRC Units and Groups in universities. The
> AFRC also supports research in the univer-
> sities through its Research Grants Scheme.
> The AFRC institutes and state-aided insti-
> tutes in England and Wales receive their
> funding from the Dept of Education &
> Science and from the Ministry of Agriculture,
> Fisheries & Food; in Scotland the institutes
> are funded by the Dept of Agriculture & Fish-
> eries for Scotland.
> **Status** Research council (quango)
> **Publications** Annual Report; Index of Agri-
> cultural and Food Research

**Agricultural Development & Advisory
Service (ADAS)**
see MINISTRY OF AGRICULTURE, FISH-
ERIES & FOOD

Agriculture Advisory Panel for Wales
c/o Welsh Office (Agriculture Dept, Divn 1A),
Cathays Park, Cardiff CF1 3NQ 0222 825111
> **Aims** To advise the Secretary of State on
> broad agricultural issues and problems, to
> determine possible trends and to provide
> independent and objective views of the
> industry.

The Panel consists of a chairman and 11 other
members appointed by the Secretary of
State for Wales.
> **Status** Non-statutory advisory body

**Agriculture Industry Advisory Committee
(AIAC)**
see HEALTH AND SAFETY EXECUTIVE for
regional addresses
> **Aims** To consider and advise the Health
> and Safety Commission on: i) the protection of
> people at work from hazards to health and
> safety arising from their occupation within
> the agricultural industry; and the protection
> of the public from related hazards arising
> from such activities; ii) other associated
> matters referred to them by the HSC or HSE.
> The Committee sits under the chairmanship
> of the Chief Agricultural Inspector of the
> HSE and consists of up to 12 members,
> including 6 members each nominated by
> the Confederation of British Industry and the
> Trades Union Congress.
> **Status** Statutory

Airfields Environment Federation (AEF)
17–19 Redcross Way, London SE1 1TA
01–378 6766
> **Aims** To join together amenity societies,
> local authorities, airfield operators and others
> concerned about the relationship problems
> of general aviation and the environment. To
> seek solutions through operational and tech-
> nical measures and consultation with
> government and aviation bodies for better
> planning, use and siting of airfields.
> -NR

Airfields Environment Trust (AET)
17–19 Redcross Way, London SE1 1TA
01–378 6766
> **Executive Administrator** John R. Gibbs
> **Aims** To establish the knowledge that will
> enable the promoters of general aviation to
> operate in a manner which has the minimal
> effect on the environment.
> **Activities** Sponsors research in such fields
> as: i) noise/sociological research in the
> neighbourhood of smaller airfields in the UK;
> ii) operational and technical means of
> reducing noise nuisance from smaller
> airfields. Close liaison is maintained with the
> EEC, the government, local authorities,
> airport owners and operators, commercial
> interests, amenity societies and individuals.
> The Trust works closely with the Airfields
> Environment Federation.
> **Status** Charity (membership through the
> AEF)
> **Publications** Airfields Environment Trust
> Newsletter.
> -NR

ALARM (Alert Londoners Against Radioactive Materials)

52 Acre Lane, London SW2 5SP 01–737 4144

Secretary Janice Owens

Aims To raise the level of information on the transportation of irradiated materials through populated areas, to press for a public inquiry and to reduce the dangers associated with such transport to zero.

Activities Producing a bulletin on the transport of irradiated fuels and on sea dumping of nuclear waste. Members will speak on the subject to interested groups and help in the preparation of local leaflets. Inquiries may be made by post or telephone for information held on file. An exhibition may be hired or bought. ALARM is dependent on donations to enable the unique information service to continue.

Status Voluntary

Publications Routing Out (6)

-NR

Ali-Can Recycling Scheme

Atcost Road, River Road, Barking, Essex IG11 0EQ 01–594 7141

Contact Recycling Development Manager

Aims To recycle aluminium drink cans, so as to recover and re-use the metal.

Activities Currently operating in the Greater London area. Cans may be collected from any fund raising group so long as they have accumulated 30 full sacks (provided free). We pay £400 per tonne (40p per kilo) – a useful method of fund raising for schools, clubs, charities, etc.

Status Commercial

Alliance of Small Firms and Self-Employed People Ltd

42 Vine Road, East Molesey, Surrey KT8 9LF 01–979 2293

-NR

Alternative Communities Movement (ACM)

18 Garth Road, Bangor, Gwynedd LL57 1ED, Wales

Aims To encourage people to join or build communities internationally; to help form an international federation of alternative communities; to build an alternative youth movement.

Activities Disseminating information on communal living by advertising in national publications. Running camping and courses weekends and open evenings on aspects of living in communities. Participating in exhibitions and fairs nationwide. Answering enquirers' letters from around the world. . Giving information and/or advice as requested. The ACM is organised, administered and financed by a registered charity, The Teachers. Local branches.

Status Voluntary

Publications Alternative Communities Magazine

-NR

Alternative Defence Commission (ADC)

School of Peace Studies, University of Bradford, Richmond Road, Bradford, W. Yorks. BD7 1DP 0274 733466

Co-ordinator Michael Randle

Aims To investigate defence and foreign policy for Britain if it were to give up nuclear weapons and refuse to have such weapons based on its territory.

Activities Producing reports: *Defence Without the Bomb* (subsequently updated as *Without the Bomb*); four shorter supplementary reports, including a monograph on economic conversion; a new report on foreign policy and other political implications of a British non-nuclear policy is to be published early 1986.

Status Voluntary

Publications *Defence Without the Bomb*, Taylor & Francis, 1983.
Without the Bomb, Paladin, 1985.

Alternative Energy Centres Ltd

This company is no longer trading

Alternative Photographic Library

118 Mansfield Road, Nottingham NG1 3FQ 0602 582369

Activities Provides a photographic resource with material primarily for use by women's groups, environmental organisations, anti-racist groups, trade unions, socialist and community groups.

-NR

Alternative Research

see ENERGY WORKSHOP

Alternative Research Group

Electronics Lab., University of Canterbury, Kent CT2 7ND 0227 66822

Contact Dr Ken Smith

-NR

Alternative Technology Group (Open University)

see APPROPRIATE TECHNOLOGY GROUP

Alternative Technology Information Group (ATIG)

Co-ordinators Rose Heaword, Flat 10, 85 Westbourne Terrace, London W2 6QS Charmian Larke, Hillview, Quenchwell, Carnon Downs, Truro, Cornwall TR3 6HH

Aims To enable an informal network of people to help each other in the handling and dissemination of information on alternative/appropriate technology. Originally started for librarians and information scientists, it now welcomes contact with all those who either have specific information needs or the information likely to satisfy those needs.

Activities Referral – brief enquiries free, but anything involving further research will carry a fee which will be adjusted according to the resources of the enquirer. As ATIG is a voluntary group without grant-aid of any kind, all help given by its members is subject to their current commitments. We will only handle enquiries accompanied by a stamped addressed envelope.

Status Voluntary network

Amateur Entomologists' Society (AES)

355 Hounslow Road, Hanworth, Feltham, London TW13 5JH 01–755 0325

Contact The Registrar

Aims To promote the study of entomology, particularly among amateurs and the younger generation.

Activities Study groups. Advisory Panel of experts in most Orders provides help with insect identification and other problem areas. Annual exhibition; field meetings; AGM (Spring); publications. Local groups.

Status Charity

Publications Bulletin of the Amateur Entomologists' Society (4);
Wants & Exchanges List (4);
Insect Conservation News (3/4)

Ancient Monuments and Historic Buildings Directorate

see DEPARTMENT OF THE ENVIRONMENT

Ancient Monuments Board for England

This Board was abolished (together with the Historic Buildings Council for England) by the National Heritage Act 1983 and replaced on 1 April 1984 by the Historic Buildings and Monuments Commission for England (ENGLISH HERITAGE)

Ancient Monuments Board for Scotland

3–11 Melville Street, Edinburgh EH3 7QD 031–226 2570

Secretary Iain J. MacKenzie

Aims To advise the Secretary of State for Scotland with respect to the exercise of his functions under the Ancient Monuments Consolidation and Amendment Act 1913; to report annually to the Secretary of State on the discharge of their functions. Constituted under the Ancient Monuments and Archaeological Areas Act 1979, the Board consists of a chairman and 12 members appointed by the Secretary of State for Scotland, including representatives of the Royal Commission on the Ancient and Historical Monuments of Scotland, the Royal Incorporation of Archi-

tects of Scotland and the Society of Antiquaries of Scotland.

Activities Formally meets 3–4 times a year.

Status Statutory

Publications Annual Report

Ancient Monuments Board for Wales/Bwrdd Henebion Cymru

Brunel House, 2 Fitzalan Road, Cardiff CF2 1UY 0222 465511

Secretary A. Huws.

Aims To advise the Secretary of State for Wales with respect to the exercise of his functions under the Ancient Monuments and Archaeological Areas Act 1979. The Board consists of a chairman and 6 members appointed by the Secretary of State for Wales, including members nominated by the Royal Commission on Ancient and Historical Monuments (Wales), the National Museum of Wales, the Cambrian Archaeological Association and the Royal Institute of British Architects.

Status Statutory

Publications Annual Report

Ancient Monuments Society

St Andrew-by-the-Wardrobe, Queen Victoria Street, London EC4 5DE 01–236 3934

Secretary Matthew Saunders

Aims To promote and carry out study and conservation of historic buildings of all ages and all types.

Activities Making representations to planning authorities. Organising study tours. Owns 21 disused churches through its sister society Friends of Friendless Churches.

Status Voluntary

Publications Ancient Monuments Society Newsletter (2);
Transactions (1)

Anglers' Co-operative Association (ACA)

Midland Bank Chambers, Westgate, Grantham, Lincs. NG31 6LE 0476 61008

Director Allen Edwards

Aims To fight water pollution by taking action at Common Law on behalf of members.

Activities Legal actions against polluters; fund raising activities.

Status Voluntary

Publications ACA Review (1)

Anglian Water

Information Unit: Ambury Road, Huntingdon, Cambs. PE18 6NZ 0480 56181

Chief Information Officer Jeremy Dodd

Aims To supply water to the public, industry and agriculture. To provide adequate sewerage and sewage disposal facilities. To provide land drainage and

flood protection to urban and agricultural areas. To achieve a major clean-up of rivers. To provide the use of water space for recreational and amenity purposes.
Activities Water resource conservation and development; abstraction, treatment and distribution of public water supply; sewerage, treatment and disposal of waste water; river management, land drainage and flood alleviation; control of the recreational use of water space, including fishing and navigation. Regional offices (East Anglia area).
Status Statutory
Publications Annual Report & Accounts

Anglo-European College of Chiropractic
2 Cavendish Road, Bournemouth, Dorset BH1 1QX 0202 24777
-NR

Animal Aid
7 Castle Street, Tonbridge, Kent TN9 1BH 0732 364546
Campaigns Director Mark Gold
Aims To increase public awareness of the abuse of animals generally, but particularly in vivisection laboratories and factory farms; to promote social, legal and administrative reforms in these areas; to promote vegetarianism, preventive and alternative medicine and cruelty-free cosmetics.
Activities Organising campaigns to promote the society's aims; publishing literature, posters and the journal; producing audio-visual materials, e.g. films, film strips and slide programmes for use in colleges and schools; co-ordinating local branch activities nationwide; providing speakers for public meetings and the media; organising peaceful demonstrations in opposition to animal abuse. 150 branches.
Status Charity
Publications Outrage! (6)
Ford, Martyn, *Towards Animal Rights*, Animal Aid Society, 2nd edn 1984, 16pp.

Animal Breeding Research Organisation
King's Buildings, West Mains Road, Edinburgh EH9 3JQ 031–667 6901
Secretary A.B. Totty
Aims To carry out research on the genetics of farm animals and on methods of genetic improvement of efficiency of meat production.
Activities Running experimental farms; carrying out laboratory studies; liaising with bodies responsible for national improvement programmes for farm animals; providing advice for breed societies. Research findings are published in scientific journals. The Organisation houses and liaises with the Commonwealth Bureau of Animal Breeding and Genetics.
Status Institute of the Agricultural and Food Research Council
-NR -L

Animal Defence Society Ltd/Animal Defence Trust
Field Study Centre, Laughter Hole Farm, Postbridge, Yelverton, Devon PL20 6TT 0822 88265
President Mrs Ruth R. Murray
Aims To protect animals from cruelty and suffering and to promote humane behaviour toward animals.
Activities The Trust's rescue and rehoming schemes help the injured and unwanted and take into care wild and domestic animals in need. The Society works to suppress cruelty in every form to both wild and domestic animals and to encourage young people in particular to develop a feeling of compassion and understanding for all animals. Horse & Pony and Dog Rescue mobile units are on call. The Wildlife Rescue Unit is on 24–hour call.
Status Voluntary; the Trust is a charity
-NR

Animal Disease Research Association
see MOREDUN INSTITUTE

Animal Health Trust
Lanwades Hall, Kennett, Newmarket, Suffolk CB8 7PN 0638 751030
General Secretary A.V. Payne
Aims To advance knowledge of health and disease in domesticated animals and encourage the training of future specialists in veterinary and allied sciences. To sponsor independent research with grants for Fellowships and Scholarships.
Activities Veterinary scientists study the problems of disease and investigate the contributory causes; results are published in standard veterinary works. Diagnostic, consultative, surgical and medical services are made available for the benefit of veterinary surgeons and their clients.
Status Charity
Publications Annual Report

Animal Liberation Front (ALF)
BCM 1160, London WC1N 3XX
Secretary, Supporters Group Andrea Fox
Aims To achieve total abolition of animal exploitation through a campaign of economic sabotage and disruption against anyone and everyone who denies animals their basic right of freedom.
Activities Frequent actions taken at the premises of animal abuse. These actions are illegal, taking the form of removing the animals from the establishments (and

rehoming them in responsible, caring homes) and causing damage to the property of animal abusers and to the premises of animal torture, e.g. destruction of vivisection equipment, vehicles, etc.
Status Voluntary informal network
Publications Supporters Group newsletter (variable title) (6);
Action Reports (6)

Animal Protection Alliance
91B Southwark Bridge Road, London SE1 1SG
Aims To advise the electorate on voting in relation to animal welfare reform. The Alliance is a coalition of the League Against Cruel Sports, the British Union for the Abolition of Vivisection and Compassion in World Farming.
-NR

Animal Welfare Foundation
see BRITISH VETERINARY ASSOCIATION ANIMAL WELFARE FOUNDATION

Animal Welfare Institute
London Ecology Centre, 45 Shelton Street, Covent Garden, London WC2H 9HJ 01-240 9284
Contact Angela King
-NR

Animal Welfare Trust
Tylers Way, Watford By-pass, Watford, Herts. WD2 8HQ 01-950 8215/0177
General Secretary Miss Patricia Fraser
Aims To care for unwanted, abandoned and neglected animals.
Activities Rescues and rehomes several thousand dogs and cats each year. No healthy animal coming into our care is put to sleep, no matter how long its stay. Runs Pet Concern, formed in 1979 to help provide financial assistance toward boarding fees for the pets of senior citizens and the disabled (many of whom are referred by the social services) during hospital treatment or convalescence.
Status Charity
Publications Animal Welfare Trust Bulletin (2)

Animals' Vigilantes
James Mason House, 24 Salisbury Street, Fordingbridge, Hants. SP6 1AF 0425 53663
Founder Chairman Ted Cox
Aims To fight all cruelty to animals.
Activities Campaigns against the killing of wild animals, intensive and unnatural methods of rearing animals for food, hunting and blood sports and experiments on living animals. Members raise funds, distribute literature, collect signatures for petitions and organise discussions and meetings.

Status Educational charitable trust
Publications UACTA (United Against Cruelty to Animals)

Anti-Nuclear Campaign (ANC)
This organisation is currently in abeyance

Apicultural Education Association
c/o College of Agriculture, Easton, Norwich, Norfolk NR9 5DX
Contact P. Metcalf
-NR

Applied Rural Alternatives
c/o 10 Highfield Close, Wokingham, Berks. RG11 1DG
Contact David Stafford
-NR

Appropriate Health Resources & Technologies Action Group Ltd (AHRTAG)
85 Marylebone High Street, London W1M 3DE 01-486 4175
Executive Director Dr Ken Ritchie
Aims To promote primary health care in the Third World, with particular regard to effective and affordable techniques and equipment.
Activities A resource centre provides a general information service for primary health care workers. Projects are undertaken in the identification and development of appropriate equipment – information is then disseminated through manuals and to a lesser extent through overseas consultancy work and pilot programmes. Newsletters are produced on health care issues and distributed free of charge to health care workers in the Third World.
Status Voluntary
Publications Aids for Living (3);
ARI News (3);
Dental Health Newsletter (2); Diarrhoea Dialogue (4, various languages).
Primary Health Care in Developing Countries: a guide to resources in the UK. A Cry for Health (jointly with Third World Group for Disabled People)

Appropriate Technology Exchange Between Communities (ATEC)
c/o Findhorn Foundation, The Park, Forres, Grampian IV36 0TZ, Scotland
Aims To develop links between the communities of Findhorn, Auroville (India) and Arcosanti (Arizona).
-NR

Appropriate Technology Group (ATG) [formerly Alternative Technology Group]
Faculty of Technology, Open University, Walton Hall, Milton Keynes, Bucks. MK7 6AA 0908 653716/653335

Chairman Godfrey Boyle
Aims To advance and disseminate knowledge of ecologically sound techniques and their application in socially equitable ways.
Activities Research into: wind energy conversion technology; organic and inorganic waste recycling; renewable energy technology in general; organic agriculture and permaculture; small scale production technologies; community planning and design. ATG also edits and publishes the *NATTA Newsletter* on behalf of the Network for Alternative Technology & Technology Assessment.
Status University research group
Publications NATTA Newsletter (6)
Taylor, Derek, *et al.*, *The Taylor 'V' Vertical Axis Wind Turbine: current status*, ATG 1985.

Arboricultural Association
Ampfield House, Ampfield, Romsey, Hants. SO5 9PA 0794 68717
Contact The Secretary
Aims To advance the study of arboriculture, i.e. the care, culture, management, appreciation and improvement of trees and nursery woodlands; to raise the standard of practice of arboriculture; to advance knowledge of and foster interest in trees; to assist training of students in arboriculture and to co-operate with other bodies having similar or sympathetic aims.
Activities Distribution of journal and newsletter; maintaining a directory of consultants and contractors; publishing a range of advisory booklets on trees; exhibiting at the Chelsea Show and other events. Annual Conference (September). Local branches. Membership is open to those engaged in arboricultural and allied professions, those interested in amenity trees, to students and to organisations with aims compatible with those of the Association.
Status Professional association
Publications Arboricultural Journal (4); Directory of Consultants and Contractors (free on request)

Archaeologists For Peace
67 Walton Road, Aylesbury, Bucks. HP21 7SN 0296 32356
Contact D. H. Dalwood
-NR

Architects For Peace
41 St James' Road, Sevenoaks, Kent TN13 3NG 0732 452361
-NR

Architectural Heritage Fund
17 Carlton House Terrace, London SW1Y 5AW 01-930 0914

Administrator Miss Rosemary Watt
Aims To act as a national 'revolving fund' by providing short-term low interest loans to assist local building preservation trusts and other charitable organisations to acquire and restore any buildings which merit conservation.
Activities The Fund uses its £2 million working capital to help finance the charitable restoration of old buildings. It makes loans only, not grants; these are normally offered for two years at 5% per annum interest and have so far ranged in size from £2,000 to £250,000. The Fund also encourages the growth of the building preservation trust movement by advising on the formation of new trusts and publishing a model constitution.
Status Charity
Publications Preservation in Action (2); Annual Report

Architectural Heritage Society of Scotland [formerly the Scottish Georgian Society]
43 Manor Place, Edinburgh EH3 7EB 031-225 9724
Secretary Mrs M. Gilfillan
Aims To promote the study and protection of good Scottish architecture of all periods.
Activities Examining all applications for consent to alter or demolish listed buildings and applications affecting conservation areas. Making representations to planning authorities and at public inquiries throughout Scotland. Organising lectures for members (membership open to all). Five branches.
Status Voluntary; charity
Publications Architectural Heritage Society of Scotland Journal; Annual Report

Armagh Field Naturalists Society
6 Old Road, Loughgall, Co. Armagh BT61 8JD, N. Ireland
Hon. Secretary Dr Howard Lee
Aims To promote the interest of people in County Armagh in the natural history of their county and the need for conservation.
Activities Summer field meetings are arranged in local nature reserves or other sites of interest. Winter indoor meetings are organised for lectures on natural history topics. Members are also encouraged to participate in local surveys of the distribution and abundance of plant and animal species.
Status Voluntary
Publications Annual Report
-NR

Armament and Disarmament Information Unit (ADIU)

Science Policy Research Unit, Mantell Building, University of Sussex, Falmer, Brighton, E. Sussex BN1 9RF 0273 686758

Information Officer Malcolm Spaven
Aims To be an information clearing house on defence, disarmament and arms control topics. Special emphasis on making information widely available, both through publication and through answering queries. Also aims to enable contact between people or groups with similar interests.
Activities Collecting and filing information from a wide variety of sources such as newspapers, specialist and non-specialist periodicals, commercial newsletters, conference papers and government publications. Most of the sources are from the UK or USA. We welcome requests from any groups or individuals, whether for information or for further contacts. The bi-monthly Report carries articles and lists of publications.
Status Independent; charitable (as part of University)
Publications ADIU Report (6); occasional papers; fact sheets

Arms Control and Disarmament Research Unit (ACDRU)

Foreign & Commonwealth Office, Downing Street (East), London SW1A 2AH 01-233 5154
Director Ian Soutar
Deputy Director Robert Brinkley
Aims Research into possible international measures for the limitation and reduction of armaments; to provide information on developments in the international arms control negotiations.
Activities Preparing research studies with policy recommendations; advice and support to British delegations at disarmament conferences; consultations with universities and NGOs; publication of newsletter and occasional pamphlets on arms control.
Status Statutory
Publications Arms Control and Disarmament (4)

ASH (Action on Smoking and Health)

5-11 Mortimer Street, London W1N 7RH 01-637 9843
Aims To alert the public to the dangers of smoking and to help prevent the disease and premature death which it causes.
Activities Encouraging local authorities to restrict smoking in public places; monitoring the activities of the tobacco industry; providing information; recruiting supporters and supporting local groups; publishing fact sheets, booklets and a bulletin and newspaper; campaigning for the rights of the non-smoking majority. ASH gathers a wide range of information about smoking and disseminates it to the media, health professionals, teachers and others. 12 branches, including Northern Ireland, Scotland and Wales.
Status Charity
Publications ASH Information Bulletin (24) ASH Supporters' News (4)
ASH Guide to the Hotels & Guest Houses of the British Isles 1984.

Associated Octel Company Ltd

Engine Laboratory, Watling Street, Bletchley, Milton Keynes, Bucks. MK1 1EZ
London Office: 20 Berkeley Square, London W1X 6DT 01-499 6030
Activities Activities include research into air pollution and publication of literature on the subject.
Status Research and engineering company
Publications Exhaust Gas Air Pollution Abstracts (24)
-NR

Association for the Conservation of Energy (ACE)

9 Sherlock Mews, London W1M 3RH 01-935 1495
Director Andrew Warren
Aims To encourage a positive national awareness of the benefits of and need for energy conservation and to help establish a sensible and consistent national policy and programme. ACE was formed by a number of major companies active within the energy conservation industry.
Activities Publishes detailed studies on various aspects of energy conservation.
Status Voluntary
Publications The Fifth Fuel (4)
Administering Energy Saving. ACE 1984.

Association for Holistic Medicine Ltd

Old Hall, East Bergholt, Colchester, Essex CO7 6TG
Secretary J.R. Downie
Aims To undertake and encourage education, research and other activities which will further the integration of allopathic medicine and holistic methods of health care and establish a unified medical science which considers the needs of the whole person.
Activities The Association is the governing body of the College of Holistic Medicine, which runs professional courses in holistic medicine in London and Glasgow. Courses open to the public are: i) the Diploma Course in Therapeutic Massage, a professional training course in which no previous medical experience is assumed; ii) the Professional Course in Preventive Medicine, intended primarily for existing practitioners (acupuncturists, osteopaths, nurses, etc.) but

also open to others who wish to learn how to look after their health using holistic methods. Enquiries to the Administrator of the College (J.R. Downie) at the above address, enclosing a postage stamp.
Status Charity

Association for New Approaches to Cancer (ANAC)

c/o The Seekers Trust, The Close, Addington Park, Maidstone, Kent ME19 5BL 0732 848336
Secretary June Meggitt
Aims To change the climate of cancer care toward one that pays more attention to the needs and problems of the person who has cancer and which guides the patient back to health and normal living.
Activities Promoting the formation of and providing guidance for Cancer Help Groups throughout the country with professional standards for counsellors and nutritionists; providing a telephone referral service for those in need of help and a mail order service for cassette tapes and books. Through seminars for hospital cancer departments, providing professional education in nutrition and the psychological aspects of cancer, an area mainly neglected in current orthodox medicine. ANAC is at present the only cancer charity covering the whole spectrum of cancer help, including therapy, social support, prevention and education.
Status Charity
Publications Tree of Life; Harmony (currently under review)
Forbes, Dr Alec, *The Bristol Diet.*
Pearce, Dr Ian C.B., *The Holistic Approach to Cancer.*

Association for the Protection of Rural Scotland (APRS)

14A Napier Road, Edinburgh EH10 5AY 031–229 1898
Director Robert L. Smith, OBE
Aims To stimulate and guide public opinion for the protection of the Scottish countryside; to act as a centre for advice and information on matters affecting the general welfare of rural areas; to encourage appropriate development in the countryside; to review plans prepared by District and Regional Councils for the future of their areas and to form a library of such documents and other relevant planning information; to encourage the protection of historic roads and bridges and, where appropriate, to take action to ensure it.
Activities Provides an organised channel for representations on any matter affecting rural amenity. Is in touch with planning authorities and approaches developers, private and statutory. Takes an active part in issues such as oil-related and leisure developments, quarries, sandpits, refuse disposal and litter. Examines planning proposals and makes appropriate representations. Promotes an annual award for the best new or reconstructed building in the countryside. Tries to save historic bridges by direct and indirect action. Has a number of constituent bodies and affiliated societies.
Status Voluntary; charity
Publications Annual Report

Association for the Reduction of Aircraft Noise (ARAN)

11 First Street, London SW3 2LB 01–584 1848
Secretary S. Eustace
Aims To campaign for the following reforms: i) for noise regulations to be legally enforced and operated fairly by local bodies; ii) for the Official Secrets Act to be amended so as not to apply to information concerning civil aircraft noise; iii) for aircraft to be taxed in proportion to noise, frequency of repetition and number of people disturbed; iv) for airports in densely populated areas to be closed for outgoing flights at night; v) for further airport investment resulting in noise increase to cease.
Activities Making representations to the authorities about aircraft noise; maintaining liaison with similar groups; answering requests for information.
Status Voluntary

Association for Self-Help and Community Groups

7 Chesham Terrace, Ealing, London W13 9HX 01–579 5589 (H)
Secretary H. Lobstein
Aims To help people do things for themselves.
Activities Training workshops in counselling; how to start and run self-help groups; assertiveness training; confidence building. Annual diploma courses in Humanistic Psychology methods; weekend workshops in a variety of specialised skills.
Status Voluntary
-NR

Association for Studies in the Conservation of Historic Buildings (ASCHB)

Institute of Archaeology, 31–34 Gordon Square, London WC1H 0PY
Contact Hon. Secretary
Aims To collate and disseminate knowledge of and information on all aspects of the conservation of historic buildings and sites of archaeological interest. Membership is by invitation and restricted to those professionally engaged in work related to conservation.

Activities Meetings, seminars, visits, publications; local meetings at six centres.
Status Voluntary
Publications Newsletter (4) (members & subscribers only); Transactions (1) (available to all)

Association of Agriculture
Victoria Chambers, 16–20 Strutton Ground, London SW1P 2HP 01–222 6115/6
General Secretary Miss Joan Bostock
Aims To promote understanding of farming and the countryside.
Activities Provides information and advice to teachers and students on all aspects of agriculture and the land with publications designed to meet many needs, including information sheets, bibliographical source sheets, handbooks, maps and farm studies. Also acts as intermediary in arranging farm visits for school children of 9 and over and has wide contacts in the farming community. Questionnaires sent on request.
The Association's Scottish office (Royal Highland Showground, Ingliston, Newbridge, Lothian EH28 8NB) arranges school-farm links on a continuing basis, educational demonstrations at the Agricultural Centre at Ingliston and a summer programme of Family Farm Open Days.
Status Voluntary
Publications Association of Agriculture Journal (1);
Modern Agriculture Series of booklets

Association of British Herb Growers and Producers
see BRITISH HERB TRADE ASSOCIATION

Association of British Wild Animal Keepers (ABWAK)
5 Chequers Cottages, Whipsnade, Dunstable, Beds. LU6 2LJ
-NR

Association of Community Health Councils for England and Wales
362 Euston Road, London NW1 3BL 01–388 4814
-NR

Association of Conservation Officers (ACO)
c/o The Castle, Winchester, Hants. SO23 8UJ 0962 54411 ext.670
Chairman M.S. Pearce
Aims To promote the conservation of the natural heritage. Members are conservation officers in local planning authorities.
Activities The Association has 13 regional areas and meetings are held both locally and nationally.
Status Voluntary
Publications Context (4)

Association of Consulting Engineers (ACE)
Alliance House, 12 Caxton Street, Westminster, London SW1H 0QL 01–222 6557
Secretary Major-General P.J.M. Pellereau
Aims To promote the profession of consulting engineering by associating engineers whose work is of a purely consultative nature; to provide facilities for government, public, industry, etc. to confer with consulting engineers and obtain their collective views.
Activities The secretariat provides information about the profession, its members and their work and produces publications, including a detailed brochure on overseas work undertaken by members. It also offers short lists of suitable consulting engineers for potential clients, for instance in the field of energy production and utilisation, and explains terms of engagement and related problems. It cannot arbitrate on specific matters but can assist, finding mutually acceptable independent arbitrators.
Status Voluntary; professional association
Publications Notice to Members (12) (in-house only); List of Members (1); Consulting Engineers Who's Who & Yearbook (1); Overseas Work Entrusted to Members (1)

Association of County Councils (ACC)
Eaton House, 66A Eaton Square, London SW1W 9BH 01–235 1200
Secretary John Stevenson
Aims To promote and protect the interests of member councils and of local government in general; to initiate consideration of and to take action on matters of concern to member councils generally; to disseminate information to member councils in relation to any subjects of interest to them; and to aim at the setting up of a single organisation to speak for and represent local government in England and Wales.
Activities Promoting county government policies to the public, central government, Parliament, outside interest groups, professional bodies, the EEC and the Council of Europe. Committees with environmental interests include: Agriculture, Land & Buildings; National Parks; Planning & Transportation; and Policy. In addition there are a number of county officers' societies. 45 member counties.
Publications County Councils Gazette (12); ACC Year Book (1)

Association of County Public Health Officers
Secretary (1984–5) N.J. Durnford, 1 Cloatley Road, Hankerton, Malmesbury, Wilts.SN16 9LQ 02214 3641 (B)
-NR

Association of Designer-Leatherworkers (ADL)

c/o 37 Silver Street, Tetbury, Glos. GL8 8DL
0666 52179

Co-ordinators Neil MacGregor, Valerie Michael

Aims To establish a network of communication among leatherworkers of all disciplines; to promote members' work at both collective and individual levels; to provide educational opportunities for leatherworkers to develop their work and to increase their knowledge of the material and its potential; to establish a new and productive relationship with the makers of leather, the educational institutions and organisations connected with the trade.

Activities Teaching workshops, exhibitions and other events; annual conference and establishment of regional contacts; liaising with tanners and others about the specific nature and quality of the materials required by designer-leatherworkers; production of the newsletter. 8 regional contacts, including Scotland and Wales.

Status Voluntary

Publications ADL Newsletter (3)

Association of District Councils (ADC)

9 Buckingham Gate, London SW1E 6LE
01–828 7931

Secretary Gordon McCartney

Aims To protect and further the interests of district councils as affected by legislation or otherwise and to promote a high standard of district administration; to join other local authority associations to promote the interests of local government in general; to provide central services for member districts as required.

Activities Interests include: environmental health, health and safety at work, planning and building control, transport, tourism and countryside conservation. The ADC liaises with other local authority organisations and with outside bodies and makes representations where appropriate on such matters as housing repairs, pollution by wastes and economic development, particularly where legislation is concerned. The Economic Development Unit provides advice and information to individual member authorities, who are encouraged to establish Enterprise Agencies. The ADC holds seminars and publishes papers on matters of interest to districts, e.g. community involvement in local economic development. There is a Welsh branch office in Cardiff.

Publications DCR (District Councils Review) (6); Digest (12) (to chief officers and councillors)

Association of Humanistic Psychology Practitioners (AHPP)

7 Jackson Tor Road, Matlock, Derbys. DE4 3JS
0629 4600

General Secretary Shirley Wade

Aims To establish and maintain standards of training, practice and ethics; to encourage mutual support for practitioners; to promote research and to provide an information and referral service to the general public.

Activities Meetings, conferences and workshops for practitioners of humanistic psychology and professionals in related fields; maintaining a list of practitioners who have fulfilled the membership requirements and been accepted as full members in various categories such as education, research, counselling, psychotherapy, group work, organisational development. The Association has a south-west region branch in Bath.

Status Voluntary

Association of Local Authorities of Northern Ireland (ALANI)

6 Callender Street, Belfast BT1 5BN 0232 249286

Secretary D.J. Ryan

Aims To consider and to take action on matters connected with the functions of local authorities in Northern Ireland; to protect and promote their interests, rights and privileges; to provide a centre for information.

Activities Providing, by way of meetings, conferences and papers a means of expression for local government. Representing the views of local government to central government and to various agencies. Providing a measure of administrative support for local government.

-NR

Association of Metropolitan Authorities (AMA)

36 Old Queen Street, London SW1H 9JE
01–222 8100

Secretary Alun Gronow

Aims To represent the interests of metropolitan districts, metropolitan counties, London boroughs, the Greater London Council, the Inner London Education Authority and the City of London.

Activities The Green Group Working Party has produced a report 'Green Policy' which examines local authority policies, the changing needs for open space and resources available.

Publications Municipal Review & AMA News (10)

Green Policy: report of the Green Group Working Party. AMA 1985

Association of National Parks Officers

c/o Dartmoor National Park Dept, Parke, Haytor Road, Bovey Tracey, Newton Abbott, Devon TQ13 9JQ 0626 832093
Hon. Secretary I.D. Mercer
-NR

Association of Professional Foresters (APF)

Brokerswood House, Brokerswood, Westbury, Wilts. BA13 4EH 0373 822238
National Secretary A.G. Phillips
Aims To provide a central organisation for all individuals and bodies corporate actively engaged in forestry and the suppliers of equipment and services thereto and who thereby earn their livelihood; and generally to do all such things as may be necessary to elevate the status and advance the interests of their profession; and to improve the technical and general knowledge of persons engaged in the forest industry.
Activities Information on forest industry; representations to government and to organisations in the interests of those employed in the industry. Annual conference; organising the national forest machinery demonstration as a shop window for the latest machinery in the industry; education fund for student grants; representation and exchange visits in Europe.
Status Professional association/trade association
Publications Association of Professional Foresters Newsletter (4)

Association of Public Analysts

County Offices, Matlock, Derbys. DE4 3AG 0629 3411 ext.6100
Hon. Secretary K.T. Chisnall
Aims To provide scientific advisory services to local authorities.
Activities Scientific advisory work and chemical analysis in enforcement of the Food and Drugs Act and the Agriculture Act. Other legislation includes the Trade Descriptions Act, the Consumer Safety Act, the Medicines Act and the Road Traffic Act. Analysis of pollution of land, air, water and foodstuffs; environmental problems in general; waste disposal.
Status Professional association
Publications Journal of the Association of Public Analysts (4)

Association of Railway Preservation Societies Ltd (ARPS)

Sheringham Station, Sheringham, Norfolk NR26 8RA 0263 822045
General Secretary D.P. Madden
Aims To co-ordinate the activities of over 100 societies involved in the preservation and operation of railways.
Status Voluntary

Publications Newsletter (4)
Railways Restored, Ian Allan Ltd.

Association of Veterinarians Concerned about Animal Husbandry (AVCAAH)

Alstonby, Shinfield Road, Shinfield, Reading, Berks. RG2 9BE 0734 872294
General Secretary P.G.C. Dunn
Aims To press for implementation of the recommendations of the House of Commons Agriculture Committee (1981) on animal welfare in poultry, pig and veal calf production; to establish a code for the veterinary profession, based on these recommendations, to guide and support members in their dealings with the agricultural industry.
Activities Meetings, talks, lobbying MPs.
Status Voluntary
Publications Newsletter (1)

Association of Water Officers Ltd

15 Market Place, South Shields, Tyne & Wear NE33 1JQ 0632 563882
-NR

ATindex

PO Box 450, Brighton, E. Sussex BN1 8GR
Contact John L. Noyce
Aims To provide an indexing service to the literature of appropriate technology and related fields.
Activities Producing the quarterly index; subjects covered include relevant techniques, materials and resources in: agriculture, aquaculture, forestry, energy and power (biofuels, geothermal, solar, water, wind), food, health and medicine, housing, lifestyle, rural and urban environment, small-scale business and industries, transport, waste utilisation, water. Books, monographs, reports and periodical articles are included.
Status Research institute
Publications ATindex (4)

Atomic Energy Research Establishment (AERE)

see UNITED KINGDOM ATOMIC ENERGY AUTHORITY

Avon Wildlife Trust

209 Redland Road, Bristol, Avon BS6 6YU 0272 743396
Administrative Officer Patricia Cabanas
Aims To promote conservation, enjoyment and awareness of wildlife in Avon.
Activities Establishing and managing nature reserves in the county; providing advice and assistance on wildlife conservation to public and private landowners and individuals; organising talks, nature trails, exhibitions and educational events.
Status Charity
Publications Avon Wildlife (3)
Gardening for Wildlife. 1983.

B

Baba Ltd
[formerly British Anaerobic & Biomass Association]
The White House, Little Bedwyn, Marlborough, Wilts. SN8 3JP 0672 870321
   Joint Secretary P.J. Meynell
   Aims To assist in the development of all aspects of biomass-related science and technology with an applied or commercial use. To set standards of performance, act as a co-ordinating body and represent the British biomass business in general.
   Activities Seminars and workshops; dealing with commercial and technical inquiries; identifying business opportunities for corporate members at home and abroad; consultancy and advice to public and private sector; promotion of safety standards; interaction with other biomass and energy groups at home and abroad; publication of the newsletter.
   Status Trade association
   Publications The Digest; Proceedings of workshops; fact sheets

Bach Flower Remedies Ltd
The Bach Centre, Mount Vernon, Sotwell, Wallingford, Oxon. OX10 0PZ
   Aims To continue (by legacy) and uphold the original values of the simple and natural method of establishing complete equilibrium and harmony through the personality, by means of wild flowers, discovered by Dr Edward Bach.
   Activities Supplying flower remedies, which are used, not directly for physical complaints, but for the sufferer's state of mind which can not only hinder recovery but act as a primary cause of sickness. None of the remedies, supplied in liquid form, is harmful or habit-forming. Booklets on Bach Flower Remedies can also be supplied. Names of foreign distributors available on request.
   Publications Bach Remedy Newsletter (3)

Badger Protection Society
15 Sanderstead Court Avenue, Sanderstead, Surrey CR2 9AU 01–657 4943
   Hon. Secretary Mrs H. Nowers
   Aims To encourage understanding and study of the badger; to work for its protection locally and to campaign for its general protection within the UK.
   Activities Surveying and protecting badger setts; arranging films and speakers; providing stands at fairs and fetes, for the sale of items depicting badgers. Local groups throughout the country.
   Status Voluntary
   Publications Badger Protection Society Newsletter (4)

Barbara Ward Fund
3 Endsleigh Street, London WC1H 0DD 01–388 2117
   Aims To reinforce the International Institute for Environment and Development as a centre of excellence in policy study; to raise the impact of its findings through its work in helping policy-makers, writers and broadcasters the world over to understand and promote the idea of sustainability in development. The Fund is administered in the UK by the trustees of the IIED Trust and in the United States by a separate committee of the Board.
-NR

Barge and Canal Development Association
33 Walnut Crescent, Peacock Estate, Wakefield, W. Yorks. WF2 0EU 0924 366677
   Aims To promote commercial inland waterway transport.
-NR

Barrow and District Action Group
No longer operating under this name – see CUMBRIANS OPPOSED TO A RADIOACTIVE ENVIRONMENT

Basketmakers' Association
Millfield Cottage, Little Hadham, Ware, Herts. SG11 2ED
   Secretary Mrs Olivia Elton Barratt
   Aims To ensure that this craft, which has been in danger of dying out, has a new lease of life secured by continuing supplies of tools, materials and outlets for work. To promote better standards of design and technique in the practice and teaching of basketry.
   Activities Day schools, residential courses, demonstrations, exhibitions. Information service to the public for commissions and repairs. An up-to-date index of experienced craftspeople is maintained for commercial and conservation purposes.
   Status Voluntary
   Publications Basketmakers' Association Newsletter (4)

Battery Vehicle Society
71 Ridgeway, Sherborne, Dorset DT9 6DB
Aims To encourage the development of electric vehicles and their preservation and to study their history.
Publications Battery Vehicles Review
-NR

Beauty Without Cruelty International
11 Lime Hill Road, Tunbridge Wells, Kent TN1 1LJ 0892 25587
Manager Margot Margrison
Aims To prevent the commercial exploitation of animals, especially the testing of cosmetics and the wearing of furs.
Activities 9 branches in the UK, 11 overseas. A boutique in London demonstrates alternatives by selling simulated furs and cruelty-free cosmetics.
Status Charitable trust
Publications Compassion (2)

Bedfordshire Against Nuclear Dumping (BAND)
29 The Coppins, Ampthill, Beds. MK45 2SW 0525 403909
Chairman Dr Jeremy Fitch
Aims To oppose the dumping of nuclear waste at Elstow in Bedfordshire and to campaign against the land burial of waste anywhere in the country.
Activities Petitioning and leafletting of local communities to raise consciousness of this issue in the county; liaising with similar groups throughout the country; public demonstrations; making representations to Westminster and Whitehall. 20 local groups.
Status Voluntary

Bedfordshire & Huntingdonshire Naturalists' Trust Ltd
38 Mill Street, Bedford, Beds. MK40 3HD 0234 64213
Administrative Officer David Edwards
Aims To conserve local wildlife by (i) acquiring and managing the best remaining habitats as nature reserves; (ii) providing landowners with advice and assistance on nature conservation; (iii) promoting an understanding and love of nature and the countryside in people of all ages.
Activities Management: after acquisition, management of reserves through voluntary wardens and working parties of members; approaches and advice to private landowners on conservation management; input to county/district/borough conservation planning. Services to members: admission to reserves; issue of literature; guided walks; membership participation in reserve management and fund raising. Education: Open Days; guided walks; talks to organisations and clubs; maintaing an

educational/interpretive centre with education services for schoolchildren and students. Fund raising: a wide range of activities involving members and staff.
Status Voluntary; charity
Publications Heron (4);
Annual Report
-NR

Bee Farmers Association (BFA)
Lyon View House, Fortingall, Aberfeldy, Tayside PH15 2LL, Scotland 08873 462
General Secretary Richard Rawson-Davis
Aims To further the interests of bee farmers in the UK, to promote the use of the honey bee for pollination and honey production and to maintain high standards in production and marketing of honey.
Activities Representing bee farmers within the UK; scrutiny of all aspects of the craft allied to commercial enterprise; liaising with ministerial officials and other agricultural organisations in order that our views on changes in policy on matters such as chemical spraying and bee diseases control orders are known; representation at the EEC on behalf of all commercial beekeepers; investigation into cases of spray damage, fraudulent labelling, misrepresentation and abuse of the Honey Regulations.
Status Voluntary
Publications Bee Farmers Association Newsletter (8)

Berkeley Nuclear Laboratories
see CENTRAL ELECTRICITY GENERATING BOARD

Berkshire, Buckinghamshire & Oxfordshire Naturalists' Trust (BBONT)
3 Church Cowley Road, Rose Hill, Oxford OX4 3JR 0865 775476
Administrative Officer Anthony Ziegler
Aims To establish and maintain nature reserves within the three counties on sites with valuable wildlife interest. To encourage in the general public an awareness of the need to conserve, protect and enjoy our countryside.
Activities Management of the Trust's 83 nature reserves; collection of data on plant and animal species. Fund raising of all kinds to pay for management and acquisition of reserves. 10 regional committees. Occasional publications (nature trails, etc.).
Status Voluntary
Publications BBONT Bulletin;
Diary of Events;
Annual Report

Bertrand Russell Peace Foundation (BRPF)
Bertrand Russell House, Gamble Street, Nottingham NG7 4ET 0602 784504

Secretary Ken Fleet
Aims To carry forward Russell's work for peace, human rights and social justice.
Activities Research, publications, special commissions of inquiry. Important amongst these latter have been the Russell Tribunals, numbering four to date: on Vietnam, repression in Latin America, civil liberties in the Federal Republic of Germany and the condition of the American Indians in both North and South America. After two years' preparatory work, in 1980 the Foundation joined with others in launching a new campaign for European Nuclear Disarmament; the first, highly successful, END convention was held in Brussels in 1982 and the second built on this work in Berlin in 1983. The third convention was held in Perugia in 1984 and the fourth in Amsterdam in 1985. The BRPF also undertakes an extensive publishing programme through its Spokesman imprint.
Status Voluntary
Publications ENDpapers

Berwickshire Naturalists' Club
The Hill, Coldingham, Eyemouth, Borders TD14 5QB, Scotland 03903 209
Corresponding Secretary T.D. Thomson
Aims The investigation of the natural history and antiquities of Berwickshire and its vicinage (Northumberland, Roxburghshire, East Lothian).
Activities Monthly field meetings May-September; specialised field meetings as thought fit.
Status Voluntary
Publications Annual Parts of 'The History of the Berwickshire Naturalists' Club'

BGE – Irish Gas Board
Inchera, Little Island, Co. Cork, Ireland 021 509199/963621
Secretary P. Cronin
Aims To acquire and distribute natural gas. BGE is a statutory corporation established in 1976 under the Gas Act of that year.
Activities Provides pipelines for the national distribution of natural gas. Operates natural gas transmission lines bringing gas to NET, the ESB and industries in the Cork area. In 1982 BGE commissioned a pipeline which now supplies gas from Cork to the Dublin Gas Company, the ESB in Dublin, the Carlow Sugar Factory and other industries along the route of the Cork-Dublin pipeline. BGE has two offices in Dublin.
Status Statutory
Publications Platform (4) (in-house); Annual Report & Accounts

BHRA Fluid Engineering [formerly British Hydromechanics Research Association]
Cranfield, Bedford, Beds. MK43 0AJ 0234 750422
Activities Research projects have included heat storage, solar ponds and stresses on wave power components. Organises international conferences on energy systems.
-NR

Bicycle Association of Great Britain Limited [formerly British Cycling Bureau]
Starley House, Eaton Road, Coventry, W. Mids. CV1 2FH 0203 553838
Aims To promote the interests of cyclists and to improve facilities for cycling.
Activities Acts as an information centre on behalf of the bicycle industry.

Bio-dynamic Agricultural Association (BDAA)
Woodman Lane, Clent, Stourbridge, W. Mids. DY9 9PX 0562 884933
Secretary H.A. Fynes-Clinton
Aims To foster and promote the agricultural impulse originated by Rudolf Steiner in 1924, namely to work in farming and gardening with the formative forces active within nature, using natural preparations to enhance the vitality of soil and plant.
Activities Publishing the journal and bulletin; publishing the Agriculture Course of Rudolf Steiner and other books on bio-dynamic topics; selling books on allied subjects from other publishers. Making and supplying bio-dynamic preparations and sprays for members and providing a lending library for their benefit. Annual open conference and occasional smaller local conferences. A consultant is available for advisory visits to members, for answering postal queries and for giving talks. Local groups.
Status Charity
Publications Star and Furrow (2); Members' Bulletin (2)
Soper, John. *Bio-Dynamic Gardening.* BDAA, 1983.

Birds of Prey Conservation and Falconry Centre
see RAPTOR TRUST

Birmingham Environmental Studies Association
The Bordesley Centre, Camp Hill, Stratford Road, Birmingham B11 1AR
-NR

Birmingham Peace Centre
18 Moor Street, Ringway, Birmingham B4 7UB 021–643 0996

Activities Information, books and resources on pacifism, non-violence, development and world problems. Library and meeting place.
-NR

Black Country Society
49 Victoria Road, Tipton, Staffs DY4 8SW
021-557 4662
President J. Brimble
Aims To promote interest in the past, present and future of the Black Country area.
Activities Meetings, visits, publishing material on local culture.
Status Voluntary
-NR

Blue Cross, The
[incorporating Our Dumb Friends' League]
Animals Hospital, 1 Hugh Street, Victoria, London SW1V 1QQ 01-834 4224/5556
Assistant Secretary Paul Hannon
Aims To encourage kindness to animals.
Activities Provides modern animal welfare services for animals in need and for needy owners' animals: Animals' Hospitals, Animals' Homes, Restfields for Horses and a Horse Protection Scheme. 12 local branches.
Status Charity
Publications Blue Cross Illustrated (2)

BNF Metals Technology Centre (BNF)
Grove Laboratories, Denchworth Road, Wantage, Oxon. OX12 9BJ 02357 2992
Manager, Central Services D. Boxall
Aims To provide research and development for the metals industries in all aspects from production to application; to improve the efficiency of metal manufacturing processes and the quality of metal components.
Activities Some of BNF's work is environment-related: the Process Control & Instrumentation Division carries out energy monitoring and consultancy and furnace development; the Applied Chemistry Division develops pollution measurement instruments and studies methods for reducing the nitrate content of drinking water supplies; BNF also works to reduce health hazards in the workplace and provides a consultancy service on the use of metals of all kinds in plumbing installations and various building applications.
Status Research institute

Book Action for Nuclear Disarmament (BAND)
Flat 2, 45 Trinity Rise, London SW2 2QB
Aims To act as a pressure group to oppose nuclear weapons, especially any increase in their number and the siting of any more in the UK or Europe; to encourage people in the book world to think about the realities of nuclear 'warfare' and to recognise that this is not an issue that can be separated from their professional lives; to put its members' professional skills at the disposal of other sections of the peace movement so that what they publish is presented to the public as effectively and persuasively as possible.
Activities Public actions such as reading vigils by prominent writers; bi-monthly open meetings; promoting a National Peace Book Week, a trade-wide promotion of books arguing the case for peace.
Status Voluntary
Publications BAND Newsletter (6)
-NR

Botanical Society of the British Isles (BSBI)
Dept of Botany, British Museum (Natural History), Cromwell Road, London SW7 5BD
01-589 6323
-NR

Botanical Society of Edinburgh
c/o Royal Botanic Garden, Inverleith Row, Edinburgh EH3 5LR 031-552 7171
-NR

Brecknock Naturalists' Trust
Chapel House, Llechfaen, Brecon, Powys LD3, Wales 087486 688
-NR

Brecon Beacons National Park Authority
National Park Offices, Glamorgan Street, Brecon, Powys LD3 7DP, Wales 0874 4437
National Park Officer J.H. Bradley
Activities Responsible for the National Park areas of Dyfed, Gwent, Mid-Glamorgan and Powys.
-NR

Bridge Educational Trust Ltd (BET)
Seniors, Semley, Shaftesbury, Dorset SP7 9AX
0747 3006
Aims To support educational activities in the environmental field and promote an understanding of man's relationship with the resources of nature.
Status Charity
-NR

Brighton Polytechnic
Dept of Mechanical & Production Engineering, Brighton Polytechnic, Moulsecoombe, Brighton, E. Sussex BN2 4GJ
Head of Energy Studies Dr J.C. McVeigh
Activities Specialises in solar energy studies.
Status Academic/research
-NR

British Acupuncture Association and Register (BAAR)

34 Alderney Street, London SW1V 4EU
01–834 1012/3353

Contact Dr C. Chen (Council member)

Aims To further the good practice of acupuncture in the English-speaking world and to protect the interests of both public and profession in the UK.

Activities Congresses, seminars, lectures; production of journal.

Status Professional association

Publications British Journal of Acupuncture

British Agricultural History Society (BAHS)

Institute of Agricultural History and Museum of English Rural Life, Whiteknights, PO Box 229, Reading, Berks, RG6 2AG 0734 875123 ext.475

Treasurer Dr E.J.T. Collins

Aims To further interest in and encourage research into the history of agriculture and all aspects of rural economy and society in Britain and overseas.

Activities Producing publications, including the Society's journal and various bibliographies. Two conferences yearly, normally in April (3–day residential) and December (1 day).

Status Voluntary

Publications Agricultural History Review (2)
Morgan, R., *Farm Tools, Implements and Machines in Britain, Pre-history to 1945: a bibliography*, BAHS, 1984, 275pp.
Thompson, F.M.L. (ed.), *Horses in European Economic History*, 1983, 206pp.

British Agrochemicals Association Ltd (BAA)

Alembic House, 93 Albert Embankment, London SE1 7TU 01–735 8471/2

Company Secretary Miss A.H. Buckenham

Aims To promote the responsible and safe manufacture, distribution and use of agrochemicals with due regard for the interests of the community and the environment. To represent the industry to government, consumers, media and others.

Activities Liaison with, and representation on, many bodies in the agricultural and chemical fields. The BAA has an Environmental Research Committee drawn from industry, conservation and environmental bodies, government agencies and departments, which concerns itself with the effects of pesticides on the environment; the committee is kept informed of wild-life incidents involving pesticides. The BAA deals with enquiries from the public and produces various publications, many dealing with safe use.

Status Trade association

Publications Annual Report & Handbook

Directory of Garden Chemicals (10th edn) 1985.
Directory of Sports and Amenity Turf Chemicals 1983.
Fires Involving Pesticides. 1983.
Teaching Pack.

British and European Osteopathic Association (BEOA)

133 Gatley Road, Gatley, Cheadle, Cheshire SK8 4PD 061–428 4980
-NR

British Anti-Smoking Education Society (BASES)

Now incorporated in the NATIONAL SOCIETY OF NON-SMOKERS

British Arachnological Society (BAS)

15 Newlyn Close, Bricket Wood, St Albans, Herts. AL2 3UP 09273 76451

Secretary David R. Nellist

Aims To promote the study of all Orders of Arachnida (spiders, harvestmen and pseudoscorpions).

Activities Circulation of information through the Society's publications; courses on spider identification; ecological surveys; field meetings and field study courses; lectures. Postal library available to members resident in Britain.

Status Voluntary

Publications The Bulletin (scientific journal) & Newsletter (3)
Brignoli, P.M., *A Catalogue of the Araneae Described Between 1940 and 1981* (ed. P. Merrett) (Spiders – World Species), Manchester U. Press, 1983, 755pp.

British Association for the Control of Aircraft Noise

30 Fleet Street, London EC4Y 1AA
-NR

British Association for Shooting and Conservation

Marford Mill, Rossett, Wrexham, Clwyd LL12 0HL, Wales 0244 570881
Scotland: Buchanan Home Farm, Drymen, Glasgow G63 0HU 0360 60840

Director John Anderton

Aims To promote the highest standards of safety, sportsmanship and courtesy among the shooting public and to foster a practical interest in the countryside, wildlife management and conservation.

Activities Collecting and assessing information on aspects of shooting and related matters; liaising with national and international conservation bodies where appropriate; ensuring the protection and management of sensitive and scientifically important habitats. An education programme promotes

basic levels of proficiency and sportsman-
ship. A professionally staffed Land Agency
Department helps members secure and
maintain sporting rights and negotiate
shooting tenancies with landowners.
Status Voluntary
Publications Shooting and Conservation (4)
*The Handbook of Shooting – The Sporting
Shotgun*, Pelham, 1983.

British Association of Manipulative Medicine (BAMM)

14 Wimpole Street, London W1M 7AB
01–636 9871
Hon. Secretary Dr J. Paterson
Aims To encourage postgraduate
education and research in manipulative
medicine.
Activities Weekend courses for medical
postgraduates in manipulative therapy; annual
symposium in London and various provincial
symposia; participation in congresses of the
International Federation of Manual Medicine.
Status Charity
Publications Newsletter

British Association of Nature Conservationists (BANC)

Rectory Farm, Stanton St John, Oxford OX9 1HF
086735 214
Membership Secretary Mrs Carla Stanley
Aims To provide a forum for free and
critical discussion and to enable those
concerned with conservation to exchange
views on all aspects of nature conservation,
its planning and application.
Activities Meetings and seminars on
topical issues; producing the journal and
occasional discussion papers. Membership
open to anyone interested in applied nature
conservation.
Status Voluntary
Publications Ecos (4)
Adams, W.M. *Implementing the Act.* 1984.
Grove, R.H. *Future for Forestry.* 1983.

British Association of Settlements and Social Action Centres (BASSAC)

7 Exton Street, London SE1 8UE 01–261 1919
Aims To initiate and develop work to
tackle some of the problems of individuals and
groups in urban communities.
Activities The secretariat of the London
office exists to help member organisations to:
provide each other with mutual help and
support; make their voice heard collectively
on important national and local issues;
promote the work they are doing and the
thinking behind it. BASSAC undertakes
workshops, training events, conferences
and campaigns. Publications include works
on fuel poverty and adult literacy.
Status Charity

Publications Basic (12)
-NR -L

British Beekeepers Association (BBKA)

National Agricultural Centre, Stoneleigh, Kenilworth, Warwicks. CV8 2LZ 0203 552404
General Secretary Michael H.F. Coward
Aims To promote and further the craft of
beekeeping.
Activities Education and examinations;
insurance; legal advice; protection of bees
against pesticides; publication of advisory
leaflets; encouragement of research;
promotion of honey shows, exhibitions and
conventions; maintaining a film and slide
library. 64 branches.
Status Voluntary
Publications Bee Craft (12);
BBKA News (4);
Year Book (1)

British Butterfly Conservation Society (BBCS)

Tudor House, Quorn, Loughborough, Leics.
LE12 8AD 0509 412870
General Secretary Mrs M.N. Tatham
Aims To save from extinction or protect all
species of British butterfly by conserving
them in the wild by such means as are available or by breeding numbers in captivity
and reintroducing them into natural habitats.
To sponsor further scientific study and
research in conservation of these butterflies.
To foster interest generally by educating the
public and educational establishments in
problems concerning conservation of
butterflies.
Activities Habitat surveys; establishment
of reserves; monitoring planning applications affecting established butterfly habitats. Responsible for the Butterfly Recording
Scheme previously organised by the Institute
for Terrestrial Ecology. 14 branches
improve and clear habitats, set up reserves,
etc.
Status Voluntary; charity
Publications News Bulletin (2);
conservation notes;
Habitat Survey forms;
Butterfly Monitoring Records

British Carbonisation Research Association

Wingerworth, Chesterfield, Derbys. S42 6JS
0246 76821
-NR

British Chiropractors' Association (BCA)

5 First Avenue, Chelmsford, Essex CM1 1RX
0245 358487 / 0423 870945
Executive Secretary Susan Moore
Aims To regulate the activities of
members; to promote the practice of chiro-

practic by qualified practitioners and to seek formal recognition of the profession.

Activities   Maintains a register of chiropractors who have graduated from recognised colleges and who subscribe to the Association's Code of Ethics, designed to protect the public interest. The Bye-laws and Code of Ethics regulate relationships between chiropractors, patients and other members and practitioners.

Status   Professional association

Publications   Contact (3)
-NR

British College of Acupuncture

44 New Market Square, Basingstoke, Hants. RG21 1HW 0256 465333 / 096278 261

Contact   The Registrar

Aims   To establish colleges and to award Degrees and Diplomas in Acupuncture. The College is the teaching body of the British Acupuncture Association and Register.

Activities   Provides postgraduate training to practitioners already qualified in medicine or a branch of natural therapeutics; also runs a preparatory (Ab Initio) course for potential students such as nurses. Training given includes academic lectures, practical class work and clinical experience under experienced supervision. Has a branch in Holland.

Status   Charity

British College of Naturopathy and Osteopathy (BCNO)

Frazer House, 6 Netherhall Gardens, London NW3 5RR 01-435 7830

Vice-Dean   Dr I.P. Drysdale

Aims   To provide 4-year full-time educational courses for those with the necessary entry requirements: basic science A-Levels; graduates; holistic osteopathy practitioners.

Activities   Training the above to graduation; they may then apply to the British Naturopathic and Osteopathic Association which has a strict code of ethics for its practising members.

Status   Educational

British Committee for the Prevention of Mass Destruction of Migratory Birds

c/o The Lodge, Sandy, Beds. SG19 2DL 0767 80551

Secretary   Mrs Dorothy Bashford

Aims   To raise funds, along with other Committees in northern Europe, under the Migratory Birds Programme of the International Council for Bird Preservation, to support bird protection societies in Mediterranean countries taking action to combat the large-scale (often illegal) killing of migratory birds which is so widespread in the region.

Activities   Actively seeking donations to the campaign; considering the funding of projects put forward by the Co-ordinator of ICBP's Migratory Birds Programme. Forwarding available funds to chosen projects, including campaigns for better bird protection laws and their enforcement; creation of nature reserves; education through bird books, leaflets and posters; research into the effects of hunting on bird populations; publicity for the problems of bird-killing; providing second-hand binoculars to encourage bird-watching rather than bird-killing.

Status   Voluntary committee

British Crop Protection Council (BCPC)

144-150 London Road, Croydon, Surrey CR0 2TD 01-681 6851

Aims   To promote and encourage the science and practice of pest, disease and weed control and allied subjects ('crop protection'); to disseminate and publish information on crop protection; to organise conferences and other meetings relating to crop protection and to publish reports of these; to collaborate with other organisations with similar objectives. The Council consists of 42 members, including representatives of a number of agricultural organisations.

Publications   Proceedings of Annual Conference and symposia; Weed Control Handbook; Insecticide and Fungicide Handbook; Pesticide Manual

British Cycling Bureau

see BICYCLE ASSOCIATION OF GREAT BRITAIN LIMITED

British Cycling Federation (BCF)

16 Upper Woburn Place, London WC1H 0QE 01-387 9320

Secretary   L.A. Unwin

Aims   To encourage, promote, develop and control the sport and pastime of cycling in all its forms amongst all sections of the community; to support and protect the interests of cyclists and, where necessary, their dependants.

Activities   Promotion and control of cycle racing; provision of legal aid and insurance services for pedal cyclists; provision of touring information; defence of cyclists' rights. Local branches.

Status   Voluntary

Publications   Handbook (1)
-NR

British Deer Society (BDS)

Church Farm, Lower Basildon, Reading, Berks. RG8 9NH 07357 4094

Director N.J.Foll
Aims To study and disseminate knowledge of deer; to promote proper and humane methods of management, conservation and control of deer; provision of advice on all matters relating to deer.
Activities Field meets, lectures, photography, symposia, tours of deer parks. Training courses covering all aspects of deer. An active campaign to prevent cruelty to deer. Providing the services of expert committees and panels on deer. If control is necessary the Society provides advice to ensure humane application. International tours. Local branches.
Status Voluntary
Publications Deer (3)

British Ecological Society (BES)
Burlington House, Piccadilly, London W1V 0LQ
01–434 2641
Hon. Secretary Dr J.M. Cherrett
Aims To advance the education of the public and to advance and support research in the subject of ecology as a branch of natural science and to disseminate the results of such research.
Activities Publishing; organising scientific meetings and symposia; supporting research and training; representation on other bodies. There are six specialised groups within the Society: Industrial Ecology; Production and Decomposition Ecology; Mathematical Ecology; Tropical Ecology; Mires Research; and Freshwater Ecology. There is an Ecological Affairs Committee with responsibility for dealing with topics on the interface between the science of ecology and public interest in the environment and also an Education Group aimed at teachers in secondary education.
Status Learned society
Publications Journal of Animal Ecology (3); Journal of Applied Ecology (3); Journal of Ecology (3); Members' Bulletin (4)

British Effluent and Water Association (BEWA)
[formerly British Water & Effluent Treatment Plant Association]
51 Castle Street, High Wycombe, Bucks.
HP13 6RN 0494 444544
Director & Secretary John S. Hills
Aims To provide a forum for the discussion of problems of the water and effluent treatment plant industry by its leaders; to encourage and promote expansion of business; to collect and disseminate information concerning members and the Association; to promote the standing of the Association within the industry as a whole. BEWA is the representative UK body for the water and effluent treatment plant industry.
Activities Supplying commercial and legal services to members and maintaining technical liaison; liaising with government departments, the Water Authorities Association and other public and private bodies and trade associations in the UK and overseas; work on British Standards and Codes of Practice co-ordinated; compiling statistics for the industry; preparation of BEWA Codes of Practice where needed; technical committees on a regular basis to discuss and resolve mutual problems; seminars and symposia on subjects relevant to members' interests; participation in the British Water Industries Group concerning exports.
Status Trade association
Publications Annual Report; Members' Products & Services/Buyers' Guide; Code of Practice for Salt Regenerated Ion Exchange Water Softeners for direct connection to the mains water supply

British Entomological and Natural History Society (BENHS)
c/o The Alpine Club, 74 South Audley Street, London W1Y 5FF
Hon. Secretary Dr J. Muggleton
Aims To promote and advance research in entomology and other biological sciences, including the conservation of the fauna and flora of the UK and the protection of wildlife throughout the world.
Activities Meetings, lectures and discussions; maintaining an extensive library; field meetings covering a wide range of habitats; producing reference works on entomology; annual exhibition. Members are amateur naturalists and professional biologists.
Status Voluntary
Publications Proceedings and Transactions (2)
Stubbs, Alan, *A Guide to the British Hoverflies*, BENHS, 1983.

British Foundation for Natural Therapies
Flat 9, Zetland House, Marloes Road, London W8 5LB 01–937 8405
-NR

British Gas Corporation
Rivermill House, 152 Grosvenor Road, London SW1V 3JL 01–821 1444
Aims To develop and maintain an efficient, co-ordinated and economic system of gas supply for Great Britain and to satisfy, so far as it is economic to do so, all reasonable demands for gas in Great Britain. The Corporation has powers, inter alia, to explore for natural gas; to manufacture, acquire, transmit and distribute gas; to

manufacture, treat, render saleable, supply or sell gas by-products; to manufacture, install, repair, maintain or remove plant required by the Corporation; to manufacture, sell, hire or otherwise supply gas fittings and to install, repair, maintain or remove gas fittings. The Corporation's chairman and Board are appointed by the Secretary of State for Energy.

Activities Supplying of gas to England, Scotland and Wales.

Status Statutory [N.B. It is planned to privatise British Gas in 1986]

British Geological Survey (BGS)

Keyworth, Notts. NG12 5GG 06077 6111

Director Dr G.M. Brown

Deputy Director G.I. Lumsden

Activities Conducting the Geological Survey of Great Britain and also Overseas (Aid Programme) Surveys. These include: energy and mineral resources assessment; groundwater supplies; pollution control; and natural hazards assessment. The Survey's library, open to the public for reference purposes, is based at the Geological Museum in London.

Status Statutory

British Goat Society

Lion House, Rougham, Bury St Edmunds, Suffolk IP30 9LJ 0359 70351

Secretary Mrs S. May

Aims To circulate knowledge and general information about goats.

Activities Registration and transfer of stock; circulation of information. Has affiliated societies.

Status Charity

Publications British Goat Society Journal (12);
Year Book;
Herd Book

British Grassland Society (BGS)

BGS Office, Grassland Research Institute, Hurley, Maidenhead, Berks. SL6 5LR 062882 3626/3631

Hon. Secretary A.J. Corrall

Aims To advance methods of production and utilisation of grass and forage crops for promotion of agriculture and the public benefit. To advance education and research in grass and forage crop production and utilisation and to publish the results of any research.

Activities A Summer Meeting is held at a different venue each year with visits to farms and research stations. A regular Winter Meeting has papers on a specific topic and occasional symposia are held in most years. Two major farmers' competitions are organised: the National Silage Competition and the BGS/MLC Grass-to-Meat Awards. Publications include two journals, grassland textbooks, symposia proceedings, etc. 68 local grassland societies are affiliated to the BGS.

Status Learned society

Publications Grass & Forage Science (4) (scientific);
Grass Farmer (practical)

British Hedgehog Preservation Society (BHPS)

Knowbury House, Knowbury, Ludlow, Shropshire SY8 3JT

Founder Maj. Adrian Coles

Aims To prevent cruelty to hedgehogs and protect them from unnecessary suffering; to promote education concerning wild animals and their environment, in particular concerning hedgehogs; to further the conservation and preservation of the hedgehog species.

Activities Promoting the practical welfare of the hedgehog (*Erinaceus europaeus*), including pressing for the installation of hedgehog escape ramps in all cattle/sheep grids and informing the public about avoiding other hazards to hedgehogs. Interesting the public and decision-makers in the safeguarding and conservation of the hedgehog in its natural conditions and promoting the enforcement of laws for its protection. Education, especially of young people, in appreciation and respect for natural wildlife, particularly the hedgehog. Financing serious research of benefit to *Erinaceus europaeus*. Providing promotional materials.

Status Voluntary

Publications British Hedgehog Preservation Society Newsletter

British Herb Trade Association

46 Church Street, Buckden, Huntingdon, Cambs. PE18 9SX 0480 810818

Administrator Reginald Peplow

Aims To promote knowledge of and the increased use and cultivation of herbs in Great Britain; to foster increased co-operation between all actively involved in or interested in the herb industry; to encourage improvement and maintenance of standards of products, presentation and business within the industry; to assist members to develop their skills with the profitable growth of their enterprise.

Status Trade association

British Herbal Medicine Association (BHMA)

Lane House, Cowling, Keighley, W. Yorks. BD22 0LX 0535 34487

General Secretary K.D. Robinson

Aims To defend the public's right to choose and obtain herbal remedies; to foster research and to diffuse knowledge of herbal remedies; to do everything possible to advance the science and practice of herbal medicine and further its recognition at all levels.

Activities   Liaison with the Dept of Health and other official bodies on licensing, advertising and supply of herbal remedies. Advice to members (manufacturers, suppliers, practitioners, retailers, users) on all aspects of herbal medicine, including a vetting service for advertisements, a Code of Ethics and regulations. For further information, send 9"x6" s.a.e. (no treatment by post).

Status   Trade association

Publications   BHMA Post (members) *British Herbal Pharmacopoeia* 1983 (previously available as series of monographs)

British Herbalists Union Ltd

Villa Merlynn, 18 Elgin Road, Talbot Woods, Bournemouth, Dorset BH4 9NL 0202 769297

Secretary   James Hewlett-Parsons

Status   Professional association

Publications   British Herbalists Union Newsletter

British Heritage Committee

c/o British Tourist Authority, 24 Grosvenor Gardens, London SW1W 0ET 01–846 9000

Secretary   Ms Ceri Thomas

Aims   To advise the Board of the British Tourist Authority; to represent historic properties in private ownership, in the care of the state and municipalities and those owned by the National Trust.

Activities   Advises on fiscal and environmental problems affecting historic buildings in the UK, on publicity and promotion, signposting and research; acts as the channel through which the BTA maintains contact with all heritage organisations in Britain as well as with European and international bodies.

Status   Voluntary (but secretariat supplied by the BTA, a statutory body)

British Herpetological Society

c/o Zoological Society of London, Regent's Park, London NW1 4RY

Chairman   Dr M.R.K. Lambert

Aims   To promote the study and protection, including conservation through education and captive breeding, of reptiles and amphibians, particularly the European species.

Activities   In many cases the prime interest of members is in the rearing and breeding of various species in captivity; the Society acts as a forum for the interchange of experiences in this area. Other members are concerned with the observation of animals in the wild state. Active subcommittees

include a Captive Breeding Committee, a Conservation Committee and an Education Committee (including a Junior Section). There is also a Regional Liaison Officer.

Status   Voluntary; charity

Publications   British Journal of Herpetology (2); British Herpetological Society Bulletin (4)

British Holistic Medical Association (BHMA)

179 Gloucester Place, London NW1 6DX 01–262 5299

Chairman   Dr Patrick Pietroni

Aims   To educate doctors, medical students and allied professions in the principles and practice of holistic medicine. To inform the general public; to act as a resource for likeminded bodies; to encourage research studies and publish relevant material; to provide liaison between fellow practitioners for mutual support and personal and professional development.

Activities   Regular conferences, seminars and lectures for doctors and public; producing the journal and newsletter, information leaflets and cassettes; providing an information service. 18 local groups nationwide.

Status   Professional association

Publications   Holistic Medicine (4); Holistic Health (4) (members only); the British Journal of Holistic Medicine (2) is issued under the auspices of the BHMA

British Homoeopathic Association (BHA)

27A Devonshire Street, London W1N 1RJ 01–935 2163

Aims   To spread the knowledge and use of homoeopathy among men and women of all walks of life in the UK; to encourage the study of First Aid homoeopathy; to develop the means of obtaining homoeopathic treatment and to further the cause of homoeopathy.

Activities   Deals with inquiries but does not give medical advice. Publishes a series of guides, monographs and handbooks and produces a journal; stocks and supplies books and maintains a members' library; lobbies parliament, the government, public and private bodies and the media; co-operates with other homoeopathic organisations and maintains close links with the Faculty of Homoeopathy, which trains doctors.

Status   Professional association

Publications   Homoeopathy (6)

British Humanist Association

13 Prince of Wales Terrace, London W8 5PG 01–937 2341

Administrator   Allan Shell

Aims   The mental and moral improvement of the human race by means of the advancement of Humanism, which is the moral and

social development of the community free from theistic beliefs and doctrines.
Activities The study of Humanism and the dissemination of knowledge of its principles. Local branches.
Status Charity
Publications Humanist News

British Hypnotherapy Association
67 Upper Berkeley Street, London W1H 7DH
01–723 4443
Secretary Alison Wookey
Aims To maintain a register of qualified therapists; to care for the interests of patients and members; to raise standards in therapy; to collate and disseminate information on hypnotherapy. Members are practitioners with a minimum of four years of training in psychotherapy and hypnotherapy.
Activities Referral of enquirers who want help in resolving their emotional problems, relationship difficulties, neurotic behaviour patterns or psychogenic conditions to nearest registered hypnotherapists, who help people with these problems to find and resolve the causes (prospective patients should write, stating their problems and age, enclosing £1; they are sent a 16–page pamphlet answering all the usual questions, plus details on nearest hypnotherapists on the register and with appointments available). Research into long-term results. Talks, lectures, articles, papers, books, seminars, broadcasts arranged; publications (list available on request).
Status Professional association
Publications British Hypnotherapy Association Journal
Morley, N.B., *Hypnosis in Psychotherapy.*
British Medical Hypnotists and the General Medical Council.
Choosing a Hypnotherapist.

British Institute of Agricultural Consultants (BIAC)
84 Wellingborough Road, Irthlingborough, Northants. NN9 5RF 0933 650615
Hon. Secretary Dr P.R. Sharpe
Aims To promote the science and practice of agricultural consultancy in all of its branches.
Activities Liaison with other professional organisations; annual publication of List of Members with description of their specialist services; nomination of members to advise on specific projects; participation in events and shows to promote the services of members; appointment of arbitrators. 6 regional secretaries.
Status Voluntary
Publications List of Members (1)
International Register (with CVs of consultants who work overseas).

British Isles Bee Breeders' Association (BIBBA)
11 Thomson Drive, Codnor, Derby DE5 9RU
0773 45287
Secretary Albert Knight
Aims To promote the conservation, restoration, study, selection and improvement of the honeybees of Britain and Ireland; to encourage local groups to pursue projects and research; to publish books helpful to beekeepers.
Activities Enabling beekeepers to improve their stock by selective breeding, through evaluating colonies and selecting for factors that will enable bees to perform well in their local environment, such as hardiness, resistance to disease, good temper and a low tendency to swarming. Annual conference and occasional 1–day beekeeping workshops.
Status Voluntary
Publications The Bee Breeder (1); Newsletter (2)
Cooper, Beowulf, *The Honeybees of the British Isles.*
Jenkins, Griff, *Queen Raising the Jenkins Way.*

British Lichen Society (BLS)
c/o Dept of Botany, British Museum (Natural History), Cromwell Road, London SW7 5BD
01–589 6323 ext.351
Secretary Miss F.J. Walker
Aims To stimulate and advance interest in all branches of lichenology.
Activities A Conservation Officer and committee promote the conservation of lichens and sites of lichenological importance (the increasing awareness of environmental contamination is giving lichenology a new importance because lichens can be used as pollution indicators); residential meetings; day excursions; maintaining a library; lists a panel of referees to assist members in identification of specimens; curates a herbarium and maintains collections; administers a Distribution Maps Scheme of lichens in the British Isles.
Status Voluntary
Publications The Lichenologist (3); Bulletin (2)

British Maritime League
Beaufort House, St Botolph Street, London EC3A 7DT 01–247 7325
-NR

British National Oil Corporation (BNOC)
This organisation was abolished by the government on 13 March 1985

British Naturalists' Association
23 Oak Hill Close, Woodford Green, Essex
IG8 9PH
Membership Secretary Mrs. Y.H. Griffiths
Aims To support schemes and legislation
for the protection of wildlife; to preserve
natural beauty; to promote and maintain
National Parks, nature reserves, conservation areas and sanctuaries; to extend and
popularise the study of nature.
Activities National and local meetings,
field weeks and weekends, lectures and
exhibitions. Organising observational work
and publishing literature on natural history
subjects. Producing the Association's journal,
the oldest established magazine on general
natural history in Britain, which caters both
for adults and young people; contributors
are in the main practical field naturalists who
write from first-hand knowledge. Local
branches.
Status Charity
Publications Country-Side (3)

British Naturopathic and Osteopathic Association (BNOA)
6 Netherhall Gardens, Hampstead, London
NW3 5RR 01–435 7830/8728
Secretary W.V. Copeland
Aims To promote advancement in natur-
opathy and osteopathy.
Status Professional association
[see also BRITISH COLLEGE OF NATUR-
OPATHY AND OSTEOPATHY]

British Nuclear Energy Society (BNES)
1–7 Great George Street, London SW1P 3AA
01–630 0726
Activities A society of scientific and technical bodies covering all aspects of nuclear
energy. Holds meetings, international
symposia and conferences. Affiliated to the
European Nuclear Society.
Status Learned society

British Nuclear Forum (BNF)
1 St Alban's Street, London SW1Y 4SL
01–930 6888/9
Director J.T. Corner
Aims To promote the sound and economic
development of peaceful uses of nuclear
energy.
Activities The Forum, which is an association of more than 40 member organisations,
identifies, studies and seeks solutions to
current problems affecting the nuclear
industry. It makes its views known to government and gives close support to its
members in their efforts to bring about better
public understanding of nuclear energy and
its place in society. Membership embraces
all key nuclear interests in the UK; these
cover the fields of nuclear finance and
insurance and the design and manufacture
of plant and components.
Status Trade association
Publications British Nuclear Forum Bulletin (12)

British Nuclear Fuels plc (BNFL)
Risley, Warrington, Cheshire WA3 6AS
0925 83200
Press Officer Bob Phillips (ext.2241)
Activities Provides services covering the
nuclear fuel cycle: uranium conversion,
uranium enrichment, fuel element fabrication, transport and reprocessing of spent
fuel and the manufacture of specialised fuel
element components. Manages the Sellafield reprocessing plant (formerly known as
Windscale).
Status Public limited company

British Nuclear Weapons Freeze Council (Freeze)
82 Colston Street, Bristol, Avon BS1 5BB
0272 276435
National Co-ordinator Dr Will Howard
Aims To promote a world-wide halt to the
testing, production and deployment of nuclear
weapons and their delivery systems as a first
step to meaningful reductions in nuclear
arms.
Activities Organising a national vote on
the nuclear freeze issue; giving encouragement and support to local Freeze councils;
lobbying and media work and informing
public opinion; international conference in
Geneva 1985.
Status Voluntary
Publications Freeze Update (12)

British Nutrition Foundation (BNF)
15 Belgrave Square, London SW1X 8PS
01–235 4904
Secretary P.M. Victory
Aims To advance knowledge in nutrition
and to educate the public in nutrition through
research and the dissemination of
information.
Activities Publication of the bulletin,
monographs and briefing papers; organising conferences and specialist meetings;
promotion of research.
Status Limited company recognised by the
Charities Act
Publications BNF Nutrition Bulletin (3)

British Organic Farmers (BOF)
Leggatts Park, Potters Bar, Herts. EN6 1NZ
0707 58561
Secretary Stuart Donaldson
Aims To promote contact between and
disseminate information to farmers and
others interested in organic food production,

with a view to assisting them in improving production.

Activities Farm walks; conferences; statistical information; soil analysis service; publication of journal.

Status Voluntary

Publications The New Farmer and Grower (4)

British Ornithologists' Club (BOC)

c/o British Ornithologists' Union, Zoological Society of London, Regent's Park, London NW1 4RY 01–586 4443

Aims To promote scientific discussion and facilitate publication of information connected with ornithology.

Activities Meetings at least 6 times a year; publication of journal.

Status Learned society

Publications Bulletin of the British Ornithologists' Club (4)

British Ornithologists' Union (BOU)

c/o Zoological Society of London, Regent's Park, London NW1 4RY 01–586 4443

Aims To promote the advancement of the science of ornithology.

Publications Ibis

British Osteopathic Association (BOA)

8–10 Boston Place, London NW1 6QH
01–262 5250

Hon. Secretary Dr R.S. MacDonald

Aims To train medical practitioners to become specialists in osteopathic medicine; to spread knowledge about osteopathic theory and practice to the medical profession generally; to initiate research into the application of osteopathic treatments.

Activities Association members, who are all fully trained as medical practitioners and osteopaths, administer and staff the Osteopathic Association Clinic and the London College of Osteopathic Medicine. These establishments provide respectively, subsidised treatment for patients who cannot afford private treatment, and training for doctors in osteopathic theory and practice. A list of medically qualified osteopaths is published annually (available on request to the Secretary).

Status Professional association

British Peace Assembly (BPA)

3rd Floor, 5–11 Lavington Street, London SE1 0NZ 01–928 9028

General Secretary Mrs Jean Pavett
Scotland: 42 Tweed Crescent, Dundee, Tayside 0382 642483

Secretary Ian Leggat

Aims To mobilise public opinion for an end to the arms race, for disarmament negotiations and for peaceful co-operation between all countries. To promote unilateral nuclear disarmament by Britain as a major step toward general disarmament.

Activities Meetings, conferences, exchange visits, participation in international events. Campaigning for the transfer of money and resources from arms production to socially useful goods. Over 70 affiliated organisations.

Publications British Peace Assembly Newsletter (6)
-NR

British Railways Board

Euston Square, PO Box 100, London NW1 2DZ 01–262 3232

Aims Established under the Transport Act 1962 for the provision of railway services in Great Britain. The Board has a corporate responsibility for discharging the statutory functions set out in the Transport Acts 1962 and 1968, to provide railway services and, in connection with these, such other services and facilities as appear to be expedient. In doing this, the Board must direct the affairs of the railways and its other businesses in such a way as to ensure: i) that certain standards of public service and safety are maintained; and ii) that these standards are achieved within certain financial constraints. The Board consists of a chairman, deputy chairman, 2 vice-chairmen, 5 full-time and 5 part-time members appointed by the Minister of Transport.

Status Statutory

Publications Annual Report & Accounts

British Reclamation Industries Council

Superceded by the UNITED KINGDOM RECLAMATION COUNCIL

British Rigid Urethane Foam Manufacturers' Association (BRUFMA)

206 Corn Exchange, Hanging Ditch, Manchester M4 3BQ 061–835 1031

Technical Director Dr John F. Chapman

Aims To encourage the efficiency and competitive value of the industry by providing advice, information and other services; to represent the membership to government departments and other organisations; to develop and improve standards and codes of practice relevant to the use of rigid urethane foams.

Activities Represents all the major suppliers of urethane raw materials and a substantial proportion of foam manufacturers, especially of those supplying insulation for the construction industry. Four specialist committees deal with technical and safety matters, building applications and publicity. Affiliated to the British Plastics Federation.

Status Trade association

British Road Federation (BRF)

Cowdray House, 6 Portugal Street,
London WC2A 2HG 01–242 1285
Librarian/Information Officer Ann
Hermitage
Aims To promote intelligent, balanced and
comprehensive transport planning
throughout the country, taking full account of
the industrial and social realities of life and
the way people in general wish to live; to
press for an adequate network of national
and local roads to meet economic and social
needs.
Activities Organising conferences;
producing publications, press releases and
information notes. Local groups.
Status Trade federation
Publications Basic Road Statistics (1)
Challenge and Opportunity (2 parts) 1984.

British School of Osteopathy

1–4 Suffolk Street, London SW1Y 4HG
01–930 9254
Principal Sir Norman Lindop
Aims To train students for the Diploma in
Osteopathy, a 4–year full-time course recognised by the General Council and Register
of Osteopaths.
Activities Training as above; also maintains an out-patients clinic and a sports
clinic.

British Scrap Federation

16 High Street, Brampton, Huntingdon, Cambs.
PE18 8TU 0480 55249
-NR

British Secondary Metals Association

215–216 Bedford Chambers, Covent Garden,
London WC2E 8HL 01–836 3292
Aims To promote the British non-ferrous
scrap metal industry.
Publications Bulletin (12)
-NR

British Society for Nutritional Medicine

5 Somerhill Road, Hove, E. Sussex BN3 1RP
Information Officer Dr Alan Stewart
Aims To promote the use of nutrition in
clinical medicine.
Activities Providing a forum for the
dissemination of scientific and medical information on the subject of nutrition in relation
to clinical medicine; conferences and
symposia. Full membership open to medically qualified practitioners only; associate
membership open to qualified members of
related professions (nurses, dieticians,
biochemists, etc. and academic researchers
in related fields).
Status Voluntary; academic
Publications Newsletter (2);
Conference proceedings;
information sheets

British Society for Research in Agricultural Engineering (BSRAE)

c/o National Institute of Agricultural Engin-
eering, Wrest Park, Silsoe, Beds.
MK45 4HS 0525 60000
-NR

British Society for Social Responsibility in Science (BSSRS)

9 Poland Street, London W1V 3DG 01–437 2728
Office Co-ordinator Kate Godwin
Aims To fight health hazards, particularly
in the workplace, and to provide workers with
the information to do this themselves; to draw
attention to the social significance and
responsibility of science.
Activities Dissemination of information;
conferences; publications. BSSRS co-ordinates
the activities of a number of working groups
which research and publicise in their
interest area under the BSSRS umbrella.
Local groups.
Status Voluntary
Publications Science for People (4)
Science on Our Side.

British Touch for Health Association (BTFHA)

29 Bushey Close, High Wycombe, Bucks.
HP12 3HL 0494 37409
Chairman Charles Benham
Activities Courses in Touch for Health
(based on Applied Kinesiology), a technique
to be used in conjunction with practitioners'
own skills for stress and anxiety states,
dietary and allergy testing and structural
balancing using simple muscle testing and
touch correction.
Publications Newsletter (4)
-NR

British Trust for Conservation Volunteers (BTCV)

36 St Mary's Street, Wallingford, Oxon.
OX10 0EU 0491 39766
Aims To involve people of all ages in practical conservation work throughout the UK.
Activities 1/2–week long conservation
working holidays organised throughout the
UK all year round; local group weekend
projects; regional mid-week projects;
weekend programme to enable Londoners
to do conservation work in the Home Counties; work with schools. Volunteers improve
the environment, urban or rural, by planting
trees, repairing footpaths, making nature
gardens, clearing ponds, etc. 33 regional
offices, 370 local groups.
Status Voluntary; charity
Publications The Conserver (4); Summer
Brochure (1);
Annual Report
Footpaths Handbook

D-I-Y Conservation Pack
[*See also* SCOTTISH CONSERVATION
PROJECTS TRUST]

British Trust for Ornithology (BTO)
Beech Grove, Station Road, Tring, Herts.
HP23 5NR 044282 3461
Director Dr R.J. O'Connor
Aims To promote, organise, carry on and
encourage study and research and particu-
larly fieldwork for the advancement of knowl-
edge in all branches of the science of
ornithology.
Activities Long-term monitoring schemes:
Heron (commenced 1928), Nest Record
Scheme (1939), British Ringing Scheme
(1909), Common Bird Census (1961), Birds
of Estuaries Enquiry (1969), Garden Bird
Feeding Survey (1970), Waterways Bird
Survey (1974), Raptor Research Register
(1978). Regular annual surveys, e.g. Winter
Atlas, Breeding Waders of Wet Meadows,
Wood Warblers.
Status Charity
Publications Bird Study; BTO News (6);
Ringing & Migration

British Union for the Abolition of Vivisection (BUAV)
16A Crane Grove, Islington, London N7 8LB
01–607 1545/1892
Campaigns Officer Kim Stallwood
Aims To abolish by law all vivisection
(experiments on living animals) and to
campaign for the rights of animals in this
country and internationally. We are
opposed to all cruelty to animals and advocate vegetarianism and veganism.
Activities Educating the general public by
leafletting, talks and discussions; producing a
campaigning newspaper which is sent out to
all members; organising marches, national
and local actions. We are a supporting
society of the Mobilisation for Laboratory
Animals (*see separate entry*), which is
actively campaigning against the government's proposals to update the Cruelty to
Animals Act 1876, and for its own minimum
demands to be included in any legislation to
replace the Act. Over 100 local contacts.
Status Voluntary
Publications Liberator (6)

British Urethane Contractors' Association
26 Warwick Row, Coventry, W. Mids. CV1 1EY
0203 25018
-NR

British Veterinary Association Animal Welfare Foundation
7 Mansfield Street, London W1M 0AT
01–636 6541
Secretary H.G. Bowyer

Aims To further the advancement of
education in veterinary science, medicine,
surgery and animal welfare; to relieve the
suffering of animals; any other lawful charitable purpose in connection with the
foregoing.
Activities Establishment of chairs of
learning; research in connection with animal
welfare. Two symposia to date: 'Priorities in
Animal Welfare' and 'Detection and Relief
of Pain in Animals'. General fund raising.
Status Charity

British Waste Paper Association
Highgate House, 214 High Street, Guildford,
Surrey GU1 3JB 0483 37980/9
Activities Can help with recycling
inquiries. 4 regional branches.
Status Trade association
Publications Materials Reclamation
Weekly (52)
-NR

British Water and Effluent Treatment Plant Association
see BRITISH EFFLUENT AND WATER
ASSOCIATION

British Water Industries Group
51 Castle Street, High Wycombe, Bucks.
HP13 6RN 0494 24492
-NR

British Waterfowl Association
25 Dale Street, Haltwhistle, Northumberland
NE49 9QB 0498 21176
Contact Mrs C.J. Winskill
Aims To promote the keeping, breeding
and conserving of all types of waterfowl,
including wildfowl and domestic ducks and
geese; to educate the public about waterfowl and the need for conservation.
Activities Maintaining records of breeds
and breeders in Britain and some other countries; providing help and information where
available on the keeping and raising of
waterfowl. The Association has area
representatives and access to a panel of
experts in universities and learned bodies.
Status Charity
Publications Waterfowl (2);
Waterfowl Yearbook & Buyers' Guide (1)
-NR

British Waterways Board (BWB)
Melbury House, Melbury Terrace, London
NW1 6JX 01–262 6711
Scotland: Canal House, Applecross Street,
Glasgow G4 9SP 041–332 6936
Press & Publicity Officer Peter Barnett
Aims To protect and promote the 2,000
miles of inland waterways which form an
important part of the country's landscape as

well as being living historical features; to stimulate and encourage suitable waterside planning and development. The Board consists of a chairman, vice-chairman, and 4–9 other members appointed by the Secretary of State for the Environment. **Activities** The Board's interests range from water transport and warehousing to water supply and leisure activities. The Freight Division is responsible for the promotion and development of traffic and facilities on these waterways and the running of warehouses and depots, docks and freight-carrying fleets. The Amenity Division is responsible for promoting and developing the remainder for holidays and recreation, including boating, walking, angling and the study of industrial archaeology. Local branches.
Status Public corporation
Publications Waterways News (10)
Nicholson's Guides to the Waterways (5 regional volumes)
-NR

British Wind Energy Association (BWEA)
4 Hamilton Place, London W1V 0BQ
Administrator Mr Lowe
Scotland: c/o Energy Studies Unit, University of Strathclyde, Glasgow G1 1XN 041–552 4400
Information Officer Dr John Twidell
Aims To promote discussion and to disseminate information on wind energy studies, projects and products, through publications and meetings, for the benefit of workers in the field and the general public; to encourage wind energy research and development and to promote its utilisation.
Activities Holds an annual scientific conference of technical papers covering the full spectrum of current wind energy research; at additional meetings invited speakers review progress in technical aspects, economic factors and research and development effects nationally and internationally. BWEA publishes conference proceedings and a newsletter and fosters links with similar organisations outside the UK. Special groups include a Wind Assisted Ships Working Party.
Status Professional association
Publications Windirections (4);
Proceedings of Annual Conference (1)

British Wood Turners Association
South Newton, Salisbury, Wilts. SP2 0QL
072274 2211
-NR

Buddhist Ecology Network (BecoN)
27 Devonshire Road, Bristol, Avon BS6 7NG
Membership Secretary Martin Pitt

Aims To explore and strengthen the very real links between Buddhism and the Green Movement; to act as a forum for communication between Buddhists concerned with ecology; to inform ecologists about Buddhism and *vice versa*.
Activities Twice-yearly meetings and meditations; regular internal communication discussing the role of Buddhist insights within the ecological movement. Planning to organise regular regional meetings and a national conference on the theme 'Buddhism and Ecology'.
Status Voluntary
Publications BecoN Newsletter (4)

Building and Social Housing Foundation (BSHF)
Memorial Square, Coalville, Leicester LE6 4EU
0530 39091
Director Peter Elderfield
Aims To undertake study and research into the science of the development, construction and management of residential housing; to identify ways in which residential housing will need to be adapted in a rapidly changing world; to identify a sustainable and viable way of life for the future in both the developed and developing world.
Activities Preparatory work in connection with the UN International Year of Shelter for the Homeless 1987.
Status Voluntary
Publications Alternative Communities in the UK.
Residential Housing and Nuclear Attack.

Building Conservation Trust
Apartment 39, Hampton Court Palace, East Molesey, Surrey KT8 9BS 01–943 2277
Director John Griffiths
Aims To promote the proper conservation, alteration, use and maintenance of buildings of all types and ages; to encourage sympathetic conservation of architectural heritage and correct use of craft skills, materials and products.
Status Company limited by guarantee; charity

Building Research Advisory Service
Building Research Establishment, Garston, Watford, Herts. WD2 7JR 0923 676612
Contact J.A. Fielding
Aims To provide information and advice on behalf of the Building Research Establishment, a government-funded organisation which carries out research and development, primarily for the needs of government, into a wide range of problems connected with the construction industry, the built environment, timber science and technology and the prevention and control of fire.

Activities BRE's Geotechnics & Structures Department is primarily concerned with safety and serviceability; the Materials Division with the structure and behaviour of building materials; the Environment and Design Department with providing a built environment which is better for the user, and with economic use of resources, energy conservation, noise and sound insulation. A laboratory at Princes Risborough is the centre for timber science and technology; fire research is undertaken at the Fire Research Station at Borehamwood.
Status Statutory research body of the Dept of the Environment
Publications Information Directory; BRE Digests; Defect Action Sheets; Information papers
An Economic Assessment of Some Energy Saving Measures in Housing and Other Buildings. BRE.

Building Research Energy Conservation Support Unit (BRECSU)
Building Research Establishment, Bucknalls Lane, Garston, Watford, Herts. WD2 7JR 0923 662399
Head of BRECSU J.R. Britten
Aims To manage, on behalf of the Dept of Energy, a programme of research, development and demonstration into energy conservation in buildings.
Activities Manages the Energy Efficiency Demonstration Scheme in respect of demonstrations in buildings. Selected projects, which show the benefits of novel but cost-effective energy conserving measures, are carefully monitored and the results made available to other building owners. Research and development projects are supported if they are likely to lead to new energy saving methods or to a greater understanding of the energy behaviour of buildings.
Status Statutory
Publications Project Profiles and monitoring reports (through Dept of Energy)

Buildings Energy Efficiency Confederation (BEEC)
PO Box 12, Haslemere, Surrey GU27 3AN 0428 54011
Secretary Gillian A. Allder
Aims To be a co-ordinating body for the energy efficiency industry and for liaison purposes between the Energy Efficiency Office and the industry, with the mutual aim of furthering and stimulating the market for such products and processes as used in buildings.
Activities Acting as a collective voice, when required, to put industry views to government; advising on existing EEO arrangements and studies; assisting manu-

facturers in the marketing of their products and processes; assessing possible improvements and initiating studies. Nominates a panel to provide technical expertise and other information as required by the EEO. Establishing a consumer link to follow up EEO inquiries; providing advisory and executive functions; visits, exhibitions and seminars; producing publications. The role of the Confederation is limited to the structure of the building and its components and does not include the use of heat in the production and processing industries or in power or fuel generation and production.
Status Voluntary

Business and Industry Panel for the Environment
Saxley Hill Barn, Meath Green Lane, Horley, Surrey RH6 8JA 02934 4903
Aims To promote the recognition of industry's achievements in the environment; to identify the high standards achieved by the special initiative of industry acting in a responsible way; to establish priorities for future industrial management and community co-operation. The Panel consists of a chairman and 39 other members, including representatives of industrial undertakings, commerce and professional institutions.
Activities Administers an annual awards scheme for giving premier awards and major commendations for environmental and social responsibility.
-NR

Business in the Community
227A City Road, London EC1V 1LX 01-253 3716
Director of Information Mike Garrod
Aims To help industry, commerce and the professions to contribute to the health of the community, with emphasis on local action in places where individual firms produce or sell their goods and services.
Activities Helping to create and support business-led local partnerships, principally enterprise agencies and community action programmes; working as an umbrella organisation on a wide range of issues: youth training, employment, opportunites for the handicapped and ethnic minorities, strengthening business-education links, encouraging projects for improving the local environment. Providing consultancy, publications and information for companies and local partnership initiatives; offering structured advice based on practical experience.
Status Voluntary
Publications Business in the Community (4)
[*see also* SCOTTISH BUSINESS IN THE COMMUNITY]

Byways and Bridleways Trust (BBT)
9 Queen Anne's Gate, London SW1H 9BY
024974 286
Chairman M.L. Braham
Aims To keep open, preserve, improve and develop byways and bridleways, primarily by taking appropriate action to ensure that the definitive maps compiled by the county councils and London borough councils, and other records of public rights of way, are kept accurate and up-to-date; to encourage voluntary effort and to make it effective within the framework that surrounds the whole question of enjoyment of the countryside.
Activities Representation to government about relevant legislation; advice and assistance to individual and user groups on the monitoring of definitive maps and the preparation of claims; seminars for interested parties.
Status Charitable trust
Publications Byway and Bridleway (9); seminar papers

C

Cadw: Welsh Historic Monuments
c/o Welsh Office, Brunel House, 2 Fitzalan Road, Cardiff CF2 1UY 0222 465511
Aims Similar responsibilities to English Heritage. Responsible to the Secretary of State for Wales.

CAITS (Centre for Alternative Industrial & Technological Systems)
Dept of Production Engineering, North East London Polytechnic, Longbridge Road, Dagenham. Essex RM8 2AS 01–599 5141/ 01–597 4630
Aims To develop socially useful products as a way to combat unemployment throughout the UK plants of Lucas Aerospace; to encourage the development of small-scale industrial co-operatives.
Activities Has developed, among other things, a railbus, useful for rural communities and Third World countries.
Publications CAITS Quarterly (4)

Calderdale Way Association
16 Trenance Gardens, Greetland, Halifax, W. Yorks. HX4 8NN
Secretary Margaret Rooker
-NR

Cambridge Energy Research Group (CERG)
Dept of Physics, Cavendish Laboratory, University of Cambridge, Madingley Road, Cambridge CB3 0HE 0223 66477 ext.244
Information Officer Mrs Cynthia Wilcockson
Aims An interdisciplinary group concerned with energy issues, covering industrial, UK and international energy studies.
Activities Studies include a model of the UK boiler market; modelling sector energy use; effects of structural change on fuel use; policy issues. Maintains close links with government departments and the energy industries.
Status Academic
Publications Energy Discussion Papers (series of reports)
Bending & Eden, *UK Energy: structure, outlook and policies*, CUP, 1985.
Eden & Evans, *Electricity's Contribution to UK Self-Sufficiency*, Heinemann, 1984.
Evans & Hope, *Nuclear Power*, CUP, 1984.

Cambridgeshire & Isle of Ely Naturalists' Trust Ltd (CAMBIENT)
1 Brookside, Cambridge CB2 1JF 0223 358144
Conservation Officer J.K. McNaught
Aims To acquire and maintain nature reserves; to promote an understanding of and interest in nature conservation; to liaise with all bodies concerned with the countryside.
Activities Managing 36 nature reserves: organising meetings etc. to promote the work of the Trust and to educate the general public; scientific recording of the natural history of all important sites. Local groups.
Status Voluntary; charity
Publications CAMBIENT News (3)

Campaign Against Arms Trade (CAAT)
11 Goodwin Street, London N4 3HQ 01–281 0297
Co-ordinators Steve Webster, Stephen Chappell
Aims To campaign against British involvement in the arms trade; to campaign for the conversion of military industry to socially useful production.
Activities Campaigning against arms sales; providing campaigning materials, information and publications on the connection of the arms trade with human rights issues, development issues and militarism. Local contacts.
Status Voluntary
Publications Campaign Against Arms Trade Newsletter (6)
The Arms Traders (republished 1985).

Campaign Against Farm Animal Abuse (CAFAA)
54 Allison Street, Digbeth, Birmingham B5 5TW 021–643 0469 / 021–632 6909 (Correspondence to PO Box 45, Birmingham B5)
Campaigns Officer Christopher Aston
Aims To campaign for an end to factory farming methods which are cruel and cause extreme suffering to farm animals; to promote humane livestock systems and respect for the agricultural environment; to mobilise support for free range systems and illustrate humane, healthy diet, vegetarianism and veganism; to highlight the agribusiness implications of Third World and health exploitation.
Activities Education, information, political and mainstream peaceful campaigning involving considerable media dialogue to

heighten awareness of farm animal suffering in agribusiness; circulating research findings to politicians, public and organisations promoting animal rights; specific pressure aimed at abolition of battery and broiler systems, sow units, veal, fur, live export and agridrug industries; exposure of inadequate slaughter regulations. 30 contacts nationwide.
Status Voluntary
Publications Farm Animal Campaigner (4)

Campaign Against Lead in Petrol (CALIP)
171 Barnett Wood Lane, Ashtead,
Surrey KT21 2LP 03722 75977
Organising Secretary Reg Mayes
Aims To draw public attention to the health hazard posed by exhaust fumes from motor vehicles. Originated from the Conservation Society Pollution Working Party.
Activities Informing selected MPs, MEPs, councils, journalists, etc. on the latest developments concerning lead and other vehicle exhaust emissions. The 50–odd branches of the Conservation Society act as local contacts.
Status Voluntary
Publications CALIP Newsletter (4)
Lead or Health.
Toxic Effects of Environmental Lead.

Campaign Against Lorry Menace (CALM)
62 Oakhurst Grove, London SE22 9AQ
01–693 8752
Convenor Peter Bibby
Aims To achieve the best possible system for the transport of freight, both economically and environmentally.
Activities Any activity likely to further these aims, provided it is not highly illegal.
Status Voluntary

Campaign Against Militarism
c/o Peace Pledge Union, Dick Sheppard House, 6 Endsleigh Street, London WC1H 0DX
01–387 5501
-NR

Campaign Against the Namibian Uranium Contract (CANUC)
53 Leverton Street, Kentish Town,
London NW5 2NX 01–267 1941
-NR

Campaign Against Sea Dumping (CASD)
8 Bay Road, Clevedon, Avon BS21 7BT
0272 874340
Contact Paul Glendell
Aims To oppose the disposal into the sea of all harmful or potentially harmful substances, especially in the area of the Severn estuary.
Activities Actions designed to draw the attention of the public to waste dumping issues, e.g. blockading a train carrying nuclear spent fuel (1980), carrying a mock barrel of radioactive waste by motorboat (1983); political lobbying.
Status Voluntary
Publications Seadumping News (occasional)

Campaign Atom
34A Cowley Road, Oxford OX4 1HZ 0865 726441
Activities Monitors the movements of cruise missile convoys.
-NR

Campaign for the Abolition of Angling (CAA)
PO Box 14, Romsey, Hants. SO5 9NN
Director Richard Farhall
Aims To promote public awareness of all forms of animal suffering engendered by angling; to campaign for the rights of such animals, particularly fish, with regard to their right to life, liberty and to follow the dictates of nature.
Activities Dissemination of information through press releases, publicity material and individual members. Local contacts.
Status Voluntary
Publications Information sheet (6)

Campaign for Combined Heat and Power
c/o TUSIU, Southend, Fernwood Road, Newcastle upon Tyne NE2 1PJ 091–281 6087
Contact Ken Ternent
Aims To promote combined heat and power (CHP) and district heating, i.e. using power stations to produce usable heat as well as electricity and routeing this heat to domestic homes. The campaign is run by the Trade Union Studies Information Unit (TUSIU) with the support of the Power Engineering Trade Union Committee.
-NR

Campaign for Nuclear Disarmament (CND)
22–24 Underwood Street, London N1 7JQ
01–250 4010 *071–700–2393*
General Secretary Meg Beresford
Aims To campaign for the unilateral abandonment by Britain of nuclear weapons, nuclear bases and nuclear alliances; to oppose the policies of any country which make nuclear war more likely or which hinder progress toward abolition of weapons of mass destruction.
Activities Demonstrations, public education, lobbying and other non-violent means of getting its message across. 1000 local groups throughout the country organise their own campaigns with support from national headquarters in the form of campaigning materials, speakers, etc. Has

national special interest sub-groups, e.g. Christian CND, Trade Union CND.
Status Voluntary
Publications Sanity (4); Campaign! (12)
Chalmers, Malcolm, *Trident: Britain's independent arms race*, 1984.
Dando, Malcolm & Rogers, Paul, *The Death of Deterrence: consequences of the new nuclear arms race*, 1984. 112pp.
Rogers, Paul, *A Guide to Britain's Nuclear Weapons*, 1985. 36pp.
Shelley, Diana & Jeffries, Phil. *A Legal Advice Pack for Nuclear Disarmers*, 1984 (in association with Lawyers for Nuclear Disarmament).
[N.B. CND is a prolific publisher – send s.a.e. for full listings]
[*see also* CND WALES/CYMRU; GREEN CND; IRISH CND; NORTHERN IRELAND CND; SCOTTISH CND]

Campaign for Real Ale Limited (CAMRA)
34 Alma Road, St Albans, Herts. AL1 3BW
0727 67201
Company Secretary Iain W. Dobson
Aims To protect the interests of real ale drinkers; to campaign for improvement in quality, variety and availability of real ale; to publicise where real ale can be found; to campaign for the preservation of traditional British pubs, including their public bars.
Activities Publishing the members' journal and annual Good Beer Guide; organising the annual Great British Beer Festival; lobbying government departments, the EEC, breweries and licensing authorities on behalf of real ale drinkers. 180 local branches research local guides, run local festivals and organise brewery and pub visits.
Status Company limited by guarantee
Publications What's Brewing (12); Good Beer Guide (1)

Canal Transport Marketing Board
11 Wolverton Road, Coventry,
W. Mids. CV5 7HF
-NR

Canals and Navigation Alliance
25 Victoria Street, London SW1H 0EX
-NR

Captive Animals' Protection Society (CAPS)
17 Raphael Road, Hove, E. Sussex BN3 5QP
0273 732363
Hon. Secretary Miss I.M. Heaton
Aims To promote humane education; to influence public opinion in the prevention of suffering involved in the captive and performing animals trade; to co-operate with other societies to this end and to support protective legislation and provide MPs and local authorities with relevant information.

Activities Lectures to organisations; distribution of leaflets; press and poster advertising; peaceful demonstrations; local radio broadcasts and debates; approaches to local authorities throughout the country; special correspondence with schoolchildren. Similar activities overseas. Branch at Southampton.
Status Voluntary
Publications Newsletter (occasional); Annual Report

Cardiff University
Dept of Microbiology, University College, Newport Road, Cardiff CF2 1TA
Activities Research into biofuels.
-NR

Care for the Wild
see NATIONAL SOCIETY FOR THE ABOLITION OF CRUEL SPORTS

Cartwheel
6 Crescent Road, Kingston Hill, Kingston-upon-Thames, Surrey KT2 7QR
Aims To set up a village community based on co-operation, resource-sharing and self-determination.
Activities The group's first fund-raising venture was to roll a giant cartwheel 1,000 miles around Britain.
Status Voluntary
Publications Cartwheel News

Cash-a-Can Headquarters
Alcoa of Great Britain Ltd, Goldsmith Avenue, Southsea, Hants. PO4 8QX 0705 739132
-NR

Cat Action Trust
1 Coldharbour Close, Thorpe, Egham, Surrey TW20 8TH
-NR

Cat Survival Trust
Marlind Centre, Codicote Road, Welwyn, Herts. AL6 9TU
Activities Conservation and breeding of wild species of cat, especially lesser-known types such as the margay.
-NR

Catholic Fund for Overseas Development (CAFOD)
2 Garden Close, Stockwell Road, London SW9 9TY 01–735 9041
Activities Can supply educational materials on world development issues.
-NR

Cats Protection League
17 Kings Road, Horsham. W. Sussex RH13 5PP
0403 65566

Director Group Capt. H.E. Boothby
Aims To rescue stray, unwanted and injured cats, rehabilitate them and rehome them where possible; to provide information to the public on the care of cats and kittens; to encourage the neutering of all cats not required for breeding.
Activities The League's headquarters maintains and operates 7 large animal shelters; numerous small shelters are maintained and run by local groups and branches. Branches and volunteers are dedicated to carrying out the above aims and raising funds to pay for the veterinary care and animal foods. 135 local groups and branches.
Status Voluntary; charity
Publications The Cat (6)

Cavendish Laboratory
University of Cambridge, Madingley Road, Cambridge CB3 0HE 0223 66477
Senior Technical Officer Dr D.M.A. Wilson
Activities Wind energy research.
Status Research institute

Cavity Foam Bureau
PO Box 79, Oldbury, Warley, W. Mids. 021–544 4949
-NR

Central Association of Beekeepers
c/o Long Reach, Stockbury Valley, Sittingbourne, Kent ME9
-NR

Central Board for Conscientious Objectors
6 Apollo Place, London SW10 0ET 01–703 7189
-NR

Central Council for Agricultural and Horticultural Co-operation (CCAHC)
This Council was abolished on 22 March 1983; its statutory functions were taken over by FOOD FROM BRITAIN

Central Council for Rivers Protection
This organisation no longer exists

Central Electricity Generating Board (CEGB)
20 Newgate Street, London EC1A 7AX 01–248 1202
Aims To develop and maintain an efficient, co-ordinated and economical system of supply of electricity in bulk for all parts of England and Wales, and for that purpose: (i) to generate or acquire supplies of electricity; and (ii) to provide bulk supplies of electricity for the Area Boards for distribution by them. Members of the Board are appointed by the Secretary of State for Energy.

Activities Planning, building and operating power stations and the main transmission network; its power system is one of the largest in the world under single integrated control; at the end of March 1984 it operated 90 power stations with a declared net capability of 51,028 MW. The CEGB takes an active role in international affairs concerned with electricity supply and together with other sections of the UK electricity supply industry it provides advice and assistance to many overseas electricity undertakings on a consultancy basis.
Status Statutory corporation
Publications Annual Report & Accounts
Berkeley Nuclear Laboratories
Berkeley, Glos. GL13 9PB 0453 810451
Activities The principal laboratory for nuclear power research of the CEGB.
CEGB Research Division
18 Warwick Lane, London EC4P 4EB 01–248 1202
Central Electricity Research Laboratories (CERL)
Kelvin Avenue, Leatherhead, Surrey KT22 7SE 0372 374488
Activities Research into the planning, generation and transmission of electrical power, including environmental aspects.
Publications CEGB Research (technical in-house journal)
Annual List of Published Papers
Marchwood Engineering Laboratories
Magazine Lane, Marchwood, Southampton, Hants. SO4 4ZB 0703 865711
Activities Testing of devices concerned with electrical power generation, including 'alternative' technology.
Marine Biological Laboratory
Fawley Power Station, Fawley, Southampton, Hants. SO4 1TW
Activities Research includes the effects of thermal discharges from power stations.

Central Fund for Feline Studies
see FELINE ADVISORY BUREAU

Central Rights of Way Committee
1–5 Wandsworth Road, London SW8 2LJ 01–582 6878
Secretary John Trevelyan
Aims To protect and promote rights of way in England and Wales.
Activities The Committee consists of the major national organisations which represent users of public rights of way. It meets twice a year to discuss matters of common concern and takes action as necessary.

Central Scotland Countryside Trust
Heron House, Wellside Place, Falkirk, Central FK1 5SE, Scotland 0324 37598
Aims To carry forward the initiative started

by the Central Scotland Woodlands Project, i.e. to encourage landscape improvements, particularly tree planting.

Activities Under the original project, 1.8 million trees were planted between 1979 and 1985 on a total of 500 sites, for a variety of reasons: for the commercial afforestation of large areas of unproductive moorland; for the reclamation of bings (slag heaps) and other derelict areas; for the reclamation of open-cast workings; as comprehensive tree planting schemes on the edge of villages; as projects for planting trees in village gardens; and as shelterbelt and amenity planting on farms.

Central Scotland Water Development Board (CSWDB)

Balmore, Torrance, Glasgow G64 4AJ 03602 511
Aims To develop and operate sources of supply to provide water in bulk to two or more of its constituent regional water authorities – Tayside, Fife, Lothian, Central, Strathclyde – whose limits of supply form the Board's area.
Activities Operates water schemes drawing supplies from Loch Lomond and Loch Turret.
Status Statutory

Central Scotland Woodlands Project

see CENTRAL SCOTLAND COUNTRYSIDE TRUST

Central Transport Consultative Committee (CTCC)

1st Flr, Golden Cross House, Duncannon Street, London WC2N 4JF 01–839 7338/9
Secretary L.A. Dumelow
Aims To represent the interests of British Rail's passengers at national level; to co-ordinate the work of the Area Transport Users Consultative Committees (TUCCs) with regard to British Rail's services. Constituted for the whole of Great Britain; members are appointed jointly by the Secretaries of State for Transport and for Trade and Industry.
Activities Dealing with national transport matters on behalf of rail users: has the legal right to consider and make representations on any matter affecting the services and facilities provided by the British Railways Board except fares and charges and reductions in services. Regular meetings with senior officials of the Board who supply policy papers as required. Preparing statements and reports on specific issues as necessary. Empowered to make general recommendations to the TUCCs about their procedure and functions.
Status Statutory
Publications Annual Report (1)

Central Water Planning Unit

see DEPARTMENT OF THE ENVIRONMENT

Centre for Advice on Natural Alternatives (CANA)

Tyddyn y Mynydd, Waunllapria, Llanelly Hill, Abergavenny, Gwent NP7 0PN, Wales
0873 831182
Joint Organiser Mrs A. Wilton-Jones
Aims To act as an information and referral service offering free assistance to those interested in natural alternatives, particularly in the health field.
Activities Enquirers are offered individual counselling by trained, experienced counsellors and/or referred to appropriate specialist organisations. Assistance is available by post, telephone or to individual visitors by appointment. Subjects covered include: natural and home birth; breast-feeding; home education; nutrition; alternative medicine; natural family planning; health and fitness; organic farming; alternatives to abortion; alternative technology. Address lists and information sheets available.
Status Voluntary
Publications The Canaan (4)

Centre for Agricultural Strategy

University of Reading, 1 Earley Gate, Reading, Berks. RG6 2AT 0734 68401
Secretary Mrs M.H. Baker
Aims To provide an independent and continuing assessment of agriculture (including horticulture, fisheries and forestry) with a view to developing long-term strategies for the agricultural and food industries.
Activities Organising symposia; publishing reports prepared by the Centre staff and papers which are invited contributions.
Status Academic
Publications Carruthers, S.P. & Jones, M.R., *Biofuel Production Strategies for UK Agriculture*, 1983.
Jollans, J.L., *Agriculture and Human Health (report of study and proceedings of symposium)*, 1983.
Tranter, R.B. (ed.), *Strategies for Family-Worked Farms in the UK (symposium proceedings)*, 1983.

Centre for Alternative Education and Research (CAER)

Rosemerryn, Lamorna, Penzance, Cornwall TR19 6BN 073672 530
Director Jo May
Aims To provide opportunities for people to find a fresh sense of meaning and purpose, deepen their capacity for feeling and to awaken dormant abilities and potentials; to provide training facilities to enable others to

do these things more effectively; to be part of a network of similar centres.

Activities Residential workshops and training groups in Humanistic and Transpersonal Psychology with leaders of national and international repute, including a 2–year Diploma in Humanistic Psychology sponsored by the Institute for the Development of Human Potential. Holiday periods when people can stay at the Centre without participating in a group.

Status Voluntary

Publications Programme of activities (4)

Centre for Alternative Technology (CAT)

Llwyngwern Quarry, Machynlleth, Powys SY20 9AZ, Wales 0654 2400 01654) 702400

Publicity Officer Tim Brown

Aims To demonstrate the ways in which we can live in balance with the natural systems and resources on which our lives depend and in a way which least exploits the Earth or its people.

Activities Maintaining a working demonstration of alternative technology; displaying solar panels, windmills, utilisation of water power, organic gardening, a working forge and a smallholding. Running residential courses in a variety of activities related to the above. We are a unique educational resource for visits and/or distance learning and operate the best alternative technology bookshop in the UK. Open daily (except Christmas); day visitors welcome all the year round. Postal inquiries must contain s.a.e.

Status Charity

Publications Quarry Newsletter (2)
Ten Years at the Quarry: a history of CAT, 1985.
Chop it, Cook it, Eat it: wholefood cookery guide, 1984.

Centre for the Conservation of Historic Parks and Gardens

University of York, The King's Manor, York YO1 2EP 0904 59861 ext.865/868

Contact The Secretary

Aims To promote the conservation and study of historic parks and gardens by acting as an exchange for information and by providing guidance and education.

Activities Research; collection and exchange of a wide range of information concerning the conservation, presentation and history of parks and gardens. A National Survey and Inventory of Historic Parks and Gardens in England and Wales is in progress. As part of the educational programme, events and short courses can be organised and held in York or elsewhere. Publications are produced and consultancy work can be undertaken.

Status Educational and research institute

Publications *Conservation Reading List,* 1984.
Documenting a Garden's History, 1984.

Centre for Economic and Environmental Development (CEED)

10 Belgrave Square, London SW1X 8PH 01–245 6440

Press & Information Officer Judith Abel

Aims To support, co-ordinate and monitor implementation of the Conservation and Development Programme for the UK (the UK response to the World Conservation Strategy); CEED is the only NGO in the UK specifically devoted to reconciling the needs of both economic performance and environmental protection.

Activities Assisting organisations active in the environmental and development field to relate their work to that of others and to the Conservation and Development Programme for the UK. In addition to its own staff, CEED is able to draw on the resources of a wide range of research institutions, consultants and professional and academic bodies, both in the UK and overseas, for work and advice on specific topics.

Publications CEED Bulletin (6)

Centre for Energy Studies

Polytechnic of the South Bank, Borough Road, London SE1 0AA 01–928 8989

Director Colin Sweet

Aims To bring together students, specialists and teachers from a wide variety of fields to discuss energy use and decision making.

Activities Research in energy topics, e.g. a 4–year project into small-scale Combined Heat and Power; consultancy for local authorities; short courses; community-based projects; conferences and seminars. The Centre offers an MSc. in Energy Resources Management, a part-time 2–year course.

Status Academic

Publications CES Newsletter (2)

Centre for Environmental Interpretation (CEI)

Manchester Polytechnic, John Dalton Extension, Chester Street, Manchester M1 5GD 061–228 6171 ext.2425/7

Co-Directors Gillian Binks, Graham Barrow

Aims To promote environmental interpretation through training and advice in its principles and practice ('environmental interpretation' is a broad term which encompasses the recreation services and facilities provided for tourists, day visitors and local residents which help them to understand, enjoy and care for their environment). CEI is a national centre.

Activities CEI operates in three main areas, all of which are closely related:

training; information and advice; research and consultancy. Short in-service training courses are run in Manchester and at venues throughout the country, often in conjunction with other organisations. CEI's services are available to government agencies, local authorities, trusts and charities, private companies, voluntary bodies and individuals.

Status Voluntary

Publications Environmental Interpretation(6)

Prince, David R., *Countryside Interpretation: a cognitive evaluation,* 1983.

Writing and Designing Interpretive Materials for Children (conference papers). 1983.

Centre for Environmental Management and Planning (CEMP)

Dept of Geography, University of Aberdeen, High Street, Old Aberdeen, Grampian AB9 2UF, Scotland 0224 40241 ext.5181/6515

Executive Director Brian D. Clark

Aims To encourage the use of Environmental Impact Assessment (EIA) and management for development projects, plans and policies as a means of avoiding harmful, costly and often irreversible damage to the environment; to implement and review EIAs.

Activities Research covering all areas of EIA, environmental and socio-economic impacts of oil and gas developments, open-cast mining, waste disposal, land use planning and environmental improvement. Consultancy, particularly in developing countries. Conferences and seminars in the UK and abroad on various aspects of environmental management and planning; annual seminar on EIA in Aberdeen. CEMP's training activities include manuals for UN agencies and intensive vocational training in EIA, management and planning. Numerous publications produced.

Status Research institute/consultancy

Publications Environmental Impact Assessment Worldletter (6)

Environmental Impact Assessment (edited by the Environmental Impact Assessment and Planning Unit of Project Appraisal for Development Control).

Clark, Brian D. *et al., Perspectives on Environmental Impact Assessment.*

Centre for Environmental Technology (Imperial College) (ICCET)

Imperial College of Science & Technology, University of London, 48 Princes Gardens, London SW7 1LU 01–589 5111 ext.7214

Academic Secretary Mrs D.S. Paterson-Fox

Aims To bring together teachers and researchers in Imperial College for collaborative research and consultancies and to run

a postgraduate course in Environmental Technology.

Activities Offers a 1–year postgraduate course – the MSc. in Environmental Technology – with specialist options in Ecological Management, Energy Policy, Mineral Production & the Environment, Pollution and Water Management. Postgraduate research and supervision. Inter-departmental co-ordination and in-house research, mainly in the above areas but also in Environmental Education Policy & Law and Marine Resources Assessment.

Status Academic

Publications Annual Report

Conway, G.R. (ed.), *Pesticide Resistance and World Food Production,* 1984.

Centre for European Agricultural Studies (CEAS)

Dept of Environmental Studies & Countryside Planning, Wye College (University of London), Ashford, Kent TN25 5AH 0233 812784

Acting Head of Department Dr C. Paul Burnham

-NR

Centre for Human Ecology

15 Buccleuch Place, Edinburgh EH8 9LN 031–667 1011 ext. 6696/6799

Director Dr Ulrich E. Loening

Aims To provide a forum for members of the University of Edinburgh, Napier College and the city to apply their expertise to the problems of the ecology of mankind, to conduct research and to teach and create public awareness.

Activities Lecture series: 16 lectures, open to the public, during spring and autumn provide a non-specialist approach to ecological problems and concepts. Study groups: held regularly on particular themes, including ethics and attitudes to conservation and development, ecology and economics, international conflict and arms control and controversies in land use. European workshops in human ecology: meetings of contacts with similar institutes in East and West Europe. The Centre has an extensive library and is also planning a programme of postgraduate teaching.

Status University institute

Publications Annual Report

Centre for International Peacebuilding

Wickham House, 10 Cleveland Way, London E1 4TR 01–790 2424

Director Brig. Michael N. Harbottle, OBE

Aims To undertake initiatives which can contribute to improvement in international relations and understanding; to bridge the gap between academic peace research and the activist movement; to provide a working base and resource centre so that groups can develop their own projects and studies; to establish a global network by linking with comparable centres abroad.

Activities Development of practical research and educational projects relating to international confidence building: fields of concern are the arms race and disarmament, East-West relations and collective security for the Third World. The Centre also acts as a working base for a number of professional and other groups (military, business, church, medical) whose concerns coincide with those of the Centre.

Status Voluntary

Publications *The War Games That Superpowers Play.*
Verification Technologies: the case for surveillance by consent.

Centre for Living/Fachongle Isaf

Porth Newydd, Dyfed, Wales 0239 820469

Contact John Seymour

Activities Runs a wide variety of courses in self-sufficiency skills.

-NR

Centre for Marine and Coastal Studies

University of Liverpool, PO Box 147, Liverpool L69 3BX 051–709 6022 ext.2814

Director Dr D.F. Shaw

Aims To provide multidisciplinary teams to undertake projects in the marine and coastal environment, by calling on the expertise which exists in 15 different departments of the university.

Activities Projects concerned with: fisheries management; pollution monitoring and control; coastal defence; offshore structures; estuarine studies (biology, sillation, erosion, pollution); coastal land planning. Associated staff of the Centre publish widely in the scientific and technical press.

Status University research unit

Publications 'Conservation and Development of Marine and Coastal Resources' [Chapter 4 of the *Conservation and Development Programme for the UK*], Kogan Page, 1983.

Centre for Peace Studies (CPS)

St Martin's College, Bowerham, Lancaster, Lancs. LA1 3JD 0524 37698

Director Dr David Hicks

Aims To promote awareness of peace and conflict related issues in education; to identify curriculum priorities and examine educational responses to these issues; to provide educational resources and support for development of peaceful skills for change at local and global levels; to reinforce and extend networks related to these issues.

Activities Providing an advice and inquiry service for teachers, schools and local education authorities, drawing on links and contacts with educators for peace nationally and internationally; individual lectures and workshops on world studies and education for peace; in-service training for teachers. The Centre also co-ordinates the World Studies 8–13 Project now operating in over 30 LEAs.

Status Academic

Publications Annual Report; Practical Guides, occasional papers (termly)

Centre for Population Studies

c/o London School of Hygiene & Tropical Medicine, Keppel Street, London WC1E 7HT 01–636 8636

Status A unit of the Economic and Social Research Council

-NR

Centre for Science Technology and Energy Policy

Science Policy Research Unit, Mantell Building, University of Sussex, Falmer, Brighton, E. Sussex BN1 9RF 0273 686758

Administrative Secretary, SPRU J.K. Fuller

Aims To undertake a programme of research to identify and explain the nature, determinants and economic impact of technical change in the UK, in particular the impact on: (i) international patterns of trade and growth; (ii) structural adjustment, including firms' strategies and industrial structure; (iii) level and composition of energy supply and demand. One common theme will be research aimed at understanding the preconditions and effects of the diffusion of electronics-based production technology on the strategy, structure and competitiveness of UK industry.

Status Research institute

Centre for the Study of Arms Control and International Security

University of Lancaster, University House, Bailrigg, Lancaster, Lancs. LA1 4YW 0524 65201

-NR

Centre for the Study of Rural Society/Centre for Rural Social Studies

Bishop Grosseteste College of Education, Lincoln LN1 3DY 0522 27347

Activities Research, advisory service, lectures, resource centre, courses, seminars, conferences; international links.

Publications Ruris (3)

-NR

Centre for Transpersonal Psychology

7 Pembridge Place, London W2 4XB

Director Ian Gordon-Brown

Aims To foster a spiritual worldview through educational and psychological means.

Activities Training professionals in perspectives and techniques of transpersonal (spiritual) psychology; workshop programmes for individuals who want to work seriously at their own growth; developing a counselling network.

Status Professional co-operative

Centre for Urban and Regional Development Studies (CURDS)

University of Newcastle, Newcastle upon Tyne NE1 7RU 0632 328511

Director Prof. John Goddard

-NR

Centre for Urban Ecology (BSCUE)

c/o The Birmingham Settlement, 318 Summer Lane, Birmingham B19 3RL 021–359 3562 ext.54

Project Director Gerald Dawe

Aims To encourage urban dwellers to make more energy-efficient, vegetationally diverse and productive uses of their physical and biological environment; to act as a centre of information and advice on the urban environment and its improvement through the application of ecology.

Activities Operates a demonstration site illustrating a range of options for urban planting and landscape improvement, including roof gardening, organic gardening, hydroponics, habitat creation (insect and bird gardens, grassland diversification) and plant species for difficult sites; demonstrations of alternative technology are planned. Advisory and consultancy services provided for community groups and others on landscape improvement, urban horticulture and other urban ecological topics. The Centre carries out the landscape improvement of selected inner-city sites, particularly wasteland and school grounds. Maintains a comprehensive library on urban ecology and related subjects.

Status Part of the Birmingham Settlement, a registered charity

Centre for Village Studies

Yoxford, Saxmundham, Suffolk IP17 072877 327

Aims To explore issues facing village life.

-NR

Centre for World Development Education (CWDE)

128 Buckingham Palace Road, London SW1W 9SH 01–730 8332

Director Derek Walker

Aims To increase understanding in Britain of the problems of world development and Britain's interdependence with the developing countries of Asia, Africa and Latin America.

Activities In the formal sector, provision of educational resources, conferences and other in-service activities for teachers, especially in geography, economics, religious education and for primary teachers; development of appropriate computer software for schools. In the informal sector, work with the media, voluntary organisations, parliamentarians, businessmen and trade unionists to promote and service interest in world development issues.

Status Voluntary

Publications Action for Development (12) Fyson, Nance Lui, *The Development Puzzle (sourcebook for teachers)*, 7th edn, CWDE/Hodder, 1984, 192pp. *Assemblies for Development* (compilation of 15 themes), CWDE, 1984.

Chartered Institute of Transport (CIT)

80 Portland Place, London W1N 4DP 01–636 9952

Director Leslie Aldridge

Aims To promote knowledge of the science and art of transport and to provide a source of authoritative views on transport for communication to government and the community.

Activities Acting as a forum for the presentation and discussion of information and original thought on transport; providing qualifying examinations in transport management leading to the qualification of Membership (MCIT); providing information by means of a library and a journal; commenting on matters of transport generally. 25 branches in Britain and Ireland.

Status Professional body constituted by Royal Charter

Publications Transport (6)

Chartered Institution of Building Services Engineers (CIBSE)

Delta House, 222 Balham High Road, London SW12 9BS 01–675 5211

Secretary A.V. Ramsay

Aims To promote, for the benefit of the public in general, the art, science and practice of such engineering practices as are associated with the built environment: to advance education and research in building services engineering and to publish the useful results of such research.

Activities Sets own qualifying examinations and assesses university and college courses and examinations; organises annual Conference, biennial Technical Conference, biennial National Lighting Conference and various symposia and technical meetings on all aspects of building services

(energy, heating, lighting, ventilation, air-conditioning, etc.). Liaises with government departments and other bodies (NEDO, BSI, etc.) on matters related to the built environment. Publishes wide range of technical reference works. 13 regional branches in UK, plus Republic of Ireland and Hong Kong.
Status Professional institution
Publications Building Services (12); Building Services Engineering Research & Technology (4); Lighting Research & Technology (4)
Heat Supply: the UK dilemma (conference papers). CIBSE, 1984.

Chemical Recovery Association (CRA)
Kendal, Barnhill Road, Ridge, Wareham, Dorset BH20 5BG 09295 51295
Secretary N.E. Walters
Aims To represent the Association's members, who are mainly recoverers of solvents and oils, in regular dialogue with government departments, local authorities and other relevant associations.
Activities Meetings are held by various groups within the Association with specialised interests, e.g. solvents, fuel oils, recovered lubricants.
Status Trade association
Publications Newsletter (6) (in-house)
Code of Practice for Oils and Solvents.
Specifications for Recovered Paint Thinners.

Chemical Society
9 Savile Row, London W1X 1AF 01–437 8883
Activities Concerns include hazardous chemicals.
-NR

Cheshire Conservation Trust
Marbury Country Park, Northwich, Cheshire CW9 6AT 0606 781868
Conservation Officer Michael J. Willis
Aims To help conserve the great variety of wildlife and the natural features of the Cheshire countryside: to acquire and manage as nature reserves areas of special interest in the county and to protect the wildlife in them; to record and study the chief places of natural history interest and to bring this information to the attention of county and local authorities for the purposes of planning; to advise schools and colleges about sites suitable and available for field studies and research; generally to promote the aims of conservation.
Status Voluntary; charity; limited company without share capital
Publications The Grebe (2)

Cheviot Defence Action Group (CDAG)
Amerside Law, Chatton, Alnwick, Northumberland NE66 5RF 06685 226

Joint Chairman Anthony Murray
Aims To object to any proposals to bury nuclear waste in the Cheviot area.
Activities Informing local people about nuclear waste disposal and the implications of any Cheviot dump. The group is currently in abeyance, as are the proposals, but would be reactivated if necessary.
Status Voluntary
-NR

Chickens' Lib
PO Box 2, Holmfirth, Huddersfield, W. Yorks. HD7 1QT 0484 861814/683158
Co-Founders Mrs Violet Spalding, Mrs Clare Druce
Aims To campaign for the total abolition of the battery system for egg production and to encourage humane forms of egg production; to alert the public to the true conditions behind modern egg production; to call for a boycott of broiler chicken meat.
Activities Distributing regular newsletters and factsheets to members; research (through buying live battery hens and broiler chickens) into the real conditions on factory farms, which are hidden from the public; producing information materials to let the public know the cruelty behind egg and chicken meat production; demonstrating when appropriate; providing campaign material for animal welfare groups.
Status Voluntary
Publications Chickens' Lib Newsletter (3)

Chiltern Society
Silver How, Little Hollis, Great Missenden, Bucks. HP16 9HZ
General Secretary A.G. Leighton
Aims To encourage high standards of town and country planning and architecture; to stimulate public interest in and care for the beauty, history and character of the area of the Chiltern Hills.
Activities Maintaining a full-scale operation of conservation work, with activities grouped under planning, historic works and buildings, rights of way, trees and woodlands, transport and water resources. The work ranges from footpath clearance, waymarking and stile replacement to publication of footpath maps and includes the Chiltern Society Small Woodland Project on small woodland management.
Status Voluntary
Publications Chiltern News
-NR

Chiropractic Advancement Association (CAA)
116 Purley Oaks Road, Sanderstead, Surrey CR2 0NS 01–657 2052
Hon. Secretary Mrs Joy Hawkins

Aims To provide an independent information service to the public regarding the chiropractic method of diagnosing and treating spinal dysfunction and associated neurological complaints; to advise the government and other authorities of patients' views on treatment and results.
Activities Recruitment of patients to the organisation; dissemination of information to the public; providing support for the Anglo-European College of Chiropractic; maintaining contacts with European and North American health organisations; producing the newsletter. Local branches.
Status Voluntary
Publications Back Chat (2)

CHP Bureau
Electricity Council, 30 Millbank,
London SW1P 4RD 01–834 2333
Head of Special Projects R.J.R. Budden
Aims To co-ordinate and publicise the policies and activities of the electricity supply industry in England and Wales with regard to Combined Heat and Power.
Activities Formulation and dissemination of common approach and policies on CHP; dealing with initial inquiries; provision of information, lectures, papers, brochures, etc.; maintaining an effective network of CHP managers throughout the electricity supply industry (there are designated CHP managers in all electricity boards in England and Wales); advising and assisting in development and consideration of CHP schemes.
Status Bureau of the Electricity Council, a statutory body

Christian Consultative Council for the Welfare of Animals (CCCWA)
Archbishop Tenison's School, Kennington,
London SE11 5SR 01–735 3771/2
Aims To encourage and facilitate the exchange of information between member organisations and, where necessary, to co-ordinate activities between them; to encourage the Churches and their members, in response to the insights of the Christian faith, to embrace an active concern for the wellbeing of animals; to affirm that mankind owes a duty to the animal creation neither to exploit it nor to tolerate unneccessary cruelty; to monitor, study and inquire into current practices whether relative to the exploitation or to the benefit of animals so as to take and co-ordinate action where necessary. The Council consists of representatives of 10 organisations together with 10 independent members.
-NR

Christian Ecology Group (CEG)
58 Quest Hills Road, Malvern,
Wors. WR14 1RW 06845 2630
Secretary Mrs Judith Pritchard
Aims To spread ecological insights among Christian people and churches and to spread Christian insights throughout the Green movement.
Activities Regular conferences to discuss, reflect upon and develop the relationship between the concerns of the Greens (peace, the environment, resource scarcity, work and unemployment, animal rights, nuclear power, etc.) and Christianity. Lobbying and non-violent protest; talks and discussions; publications. Local groups.
Status Voluntary
Publications Christian Ecology Group News (4)
God's Green World, 1983.

Christian Movement for Peace (CMP)
Stowford House, Bayswater Road,
Oxford OX3 9SA 0865 62866
Secretary Mrs L. Green
Aims To bring together Christians and others who share a concern for peace and justice in society; to work together toward this common goal whilst respecting differences of opinion and commitment.
Activities Organising international summer workcamps, lasting about 3 weeks, which bring together 10–15 volunteers (minimum age 17) from different countries to work on a common project of service to others. Past projects have included playschemes, work with patients in a psychiatric hospital and manual work of various kinds; some camps incorporate a study theme. CMP also places British volunteers on workcamps abroad which are organised by CMP branches in West European countries and Canada or by other workcamp organisations, e.g. in Eastern Europe.
Status Voluntary
Publications Grapevine (6)

CITES (Convention on International Trade in Endangered Species)
Administered by the INTERNATIONAL UNION FOR THE CONSERVATION OF NATURE AND NATURAL RESOURCES (*see under* Organisations Not Based in UK or Ireland)

City Farm Advisory Service
This service no longer operates

City Farms, Scotland
244 Wilton Street, Glasgow G20 6BL
041–221 9855
-NR

City Wildlife Project

1 West Street, Leicester LE1 6UU 0533 552550

Manager David Nicholls

Aims To further nature conservation in Leicester by increasing public awareness, understanding and appreciation of Leicester's wildlife heritage; to bring about a more sympathetic and responsible attitude to the environment and the natural world.

Activities Advising on ways to provide better opportunities for wildlife in our parks and open spaces, amongst houses and industry, around schools and hospitals and in private gardens; creating nature areas and wildlife gardens with schoolchildren and communities; managing wildlife habitats such as woods, wetland and grassland, to conserve wildlife for people to study and enjoy; surveying the fauna and flora of every undeveloped site in Leicester so that wildlife can be given adequate consideration in decisions affecting land use; spreading enthusiasm for nature conservation through information leaflets, illustrated talks, guided walks, exhibitions, practical conservation and community involvement.

Status Voluntary (part of Leicestershire & Rutland Trust for Nature Conservation)

Publications Leicester Wildlife News (4) *City Wildlife Project 1984.*

Civic Trust *Director, Martin Bradshaw.*

17 Carlton House Terrace, London SW1Y 5AW

~~01-830 0014~~ *071-930-8903*

Librarian Miss Saskia Hallam

Aims To stimulate interest in and action for the conservation and improvement of the environment in town and country; to foster high standards in planning, design, restoration and new building.

Activities The Trust works in close co-operation with about 1,000 local amenity societies throughout the UK. It initiates practical projects and makes annual awards for good development of all kinds. Concerns include urban wasteland, industrial dereliction, town improvement schemes and the problems of damage and disruption caused by heavy lorries. Regularly consulted by government about new legislation and regulations concerning environmental matters. Administers the Architectural Heritage Fund and runs the Heritage Education Group (*see separate entries*).

Status Charity; NGO

Publications Heritage Outlook (6); Civic Trust Awards (1)
Environmental Directory 1984.
Bypasses and the Juggernaut: fact and fiction, 1983.
see also CIVIC TRUST FOR WALES: NORTH EAST CIVIC TRUST: NORTH WEST CIVIC TRUST: SCOTTISH CIVIC TRUST

Civic Trust for Wales/Treftadaeth Cymru

St Michael's College, Llandaff, Cardiff CF5 2YJ 0222 552388

Executive Chairman T. Mervyn Jones, CBE

Aims In accordance with those for the Civic Trust.

Activities Similar to the Civic Trust. Has created and sustains over 80 Civic Societies.

Civil Aviation Authority (CAA)

CAA House, 45–59 Kingsway, London WC2B 6TE 01–379 7311

Aims To be responsible for the regulation of airlines and organisers of air travel, control of the safety of civil flying generally, the operation jointly with the Secretary of State for Defence of National Air Traffic Services and for advising on the provision of aerodromes and the management of the Scottish Highlands and Islands airports. The 6–12 members are appointed by the Secretary of State for Transport.

Status Statutory

Civil Engineers for Nuclear Disarmament (CEND)

Hillhead Cottage, Uffculme, Cullompton, Devon EX15 3EP 0884 40237

Contact Peter H. Newton
-NR

CLAWS Ltd (Community Land and Workspace Services)

61–71 Collier Street, London N1 9DF 01–833 2909

Information Officer Val Fountain

Aims To provide a high quality technical aid service on using idle land or buildings to community groups throughout Greater London.
-NR

CLEAR (The Campaign for Lead-free Air)

2 Northdown Street, London N1 9BG 01–278 9686

Administrator Judy Tavanyar

Aims To achieve the elimination of lead from petrol at the earliest possible date; to maintain surveillance on the use of lead generally and to campaign for enforcement of any measures necessary to reduce lead pollution wherever it occurs, particularly in paint and water.

Activities Lobbying Ministers, MPs and Euro-MPs; education by means of seminars, lectures, symposia, etc.; information through publications, advice, etc.

Status Voluntary

Publications CLEAR (up to 4) Wilson, Des *The Lead Scandal.*

Cleveland Nature Conservation Trust (CNCT)
Old Town Hall, Mandale Road, Thornaby, Stockton-on-Tees, Cleveland TS17 6AW 0642 608405
Administrator Dr D. Thompson
Aims To conserve within the county of Cleveland as varied a range as possible of wildlife habitats and species (both terrestrial and marine) and sites of geological interest; to foster in all sections of the community an awareness of the need for nature conservation and to promote an understanding of its principles.
Activities The Trust has 5 reserves, two of which are on ancient saltmarsh and a third an ancient regenerating oak woodland; volunteers are used for practical conservation and wildlife recordings. Close co-operation with other conservation bodies and county and district planning departments; practical advice to landowners and users; informing the general public about nature conservation and its value through exhibitions, lectures and film shows and through links with local press and broadcasting. Monitoring the effects of changes in the natural environment; using the reserves for education and research in ecology. Local groups involved in events such as guided walks; fund raising to pursue objectives.
Status Voluntary
Publications Conservation Matters (3)

Clyde River Purification Board
Rivers House, Murray Road, East Kilbride, Strathclyde G75 0LA
-NR

CND Wales/Cymru
2 Plasturton Avenue, Pontcanna, Cardiff CF1 9HH 0766 831833
Contact Bob Cole
-NR

Coal Research Establishment (CRE)
see NATIONAL COAL BOARD

Coal Utilisation Research Laboratories (CURL)
see NATIONAL COAL BOARD

Coalite Group
Buttermilk Lane, PO Box 21, Bolsover, Derbys. S44 6AB 0246 822281
-NR

Coastal Anti-Pollution Leage Ltd (CAPL)
94 Greenway Lane, Bath, Avon BA2 4LN 0225 317094
Secretary Mrs D.P. Wakefield
Aims To stop the indiscriminate pollution of Britain's beaches by sewage.

Activities Publishing the Golden List, which gives pollution ratings for beaches in England and Wales.
Status Voluntary
Publications Golden List of Beaches in England & Wales (1)

College of Health
18 Victoria Park Square, Bethnal Green, London E2 9PF 01–980 6263
Director Marianne Rigge
Aims To provide education and information about: health promotion and prevention of illness; self-care when ill; making the most effective use of the National Health Service; self-help groups and alternative medicine.
Activities Campaigning for improvements in health care and prevention of illness; distance teaching courses 'Taking Stock' and 'Fit for Life'; producing publications; free telephone information service Healthline (01–980 4848, 6pm–10pm 7 days a week: over 150 tapes on health subjects to listen to on the phone).
Status Voluntary
Publications Self-Health (4); Annual Report; Healthline Directory Guides to: Alternative medicine; Homes for Elderly People; Hospital Waiting Lists.

College of Holistic Medicine
see ASSOCIATION FOR HOLISTIC MEDICINE LTD

College of Traditional Chinese Acupuncture
Tao House, Queensway, Leamington Spa, Warwicks. CV31 3LZ 0926 22121
Registrar Mrs M.P. Postins
Aims The preservation and teaching of traditional Chinese acupuncture.
Status Training college

Combined Heat and Power Association (CHPA)
Bedford House, Stafford Road, Caterham, Surrey CR3 6JA 0883 42323
Acting Controller R.G. Sayer
Aims To promote the concept of combined heat and power/district heating, to disseminate technical information and promote excellence in CHP/DH. [Formerly the District Heating Association.]
Activities Meetings, events, technical visits, bi-annual conference, distribution of information and literature to members. 6 branches.
Status Trade association
Publications Combined Heat and Power (4); News-sheet (12); Handbook (1)

COMCOM (Community Communications)
92 Huddleston Road, London N7 0EG
Aims To be a co-ordinating body for the development of community communications services, including press, radio and television; to campaign for more funding for local services, more rights of accessibility and more local control.
-NR

COMET (Combined Organic Movement for Education and Training)
This organisation no longer exists

Committee for Nature Conservation
Hut 6, Castle Grounds, Stormont,
Belfast BT4 3SS, N. Ireland 0232 768716
Secretary W.L. Reavie
Aims To exercise the functions conferred on it by the Nature Conservation and Amenity Lands (NI) Order 1985 and to advise the Department of the Environment for Northern Ireland on matters relating to nature conservation.
Status Statutory
Publications Annual Report

Committee for the Reform of Animal Experimentation (CRAE)
10 Queensferry Street, Edinburgh EH2 4PG
031–225 6039
Secretary Clive Hollands
Aims To seek reform of the law and administration of the Cruelty to Animals Act 1876 relating to the care and use of living animals in research, experiments and other laboratory purposes. The Committee is drawn from both Houses of Parliament and from the fields of animal welfare, science and medicine.
Activities In conjunction with the British Veterinary Association and the Fund for the Replacement of Animals in Medical Experiments (FRAME), CRAE has submitted joint proposals to the Home Secretary on new legislation to govern the use of animals for research purposes. CRAE and its partners have continued regular consultation with the government leading up to the publication of the government's Bill to replace the Cruelty to Animals Act 1876.
Status Voluntary
Publications *Animal Experimentation in the United Kingdom: proposals submitted to the Home Secretary jointly by the BVA, CRAE and FRAME.* March 1983.

Committee on Analytical Requirements
c/o Health & Safety Executive, Occupational Medicine & Hygiene Laboratory, 403–405 Edgware Road, London NW2 6LN 01–450 8911
Aims To identify, within the spectrum of activities of the HSE, the needs for new or improved sampling and analytical methods for the detection and measurement of contaminants in the air. The Committee consists of a chairman and 14 other members, including representatives of the HSE, Chemical Industries Association, Chemical Society. the Departments of Health and of Trade and Industry and the Ministry of Agriculture.

Committee on Carcinogenicity of Chemicals in Food, Consumer Products and the Environment (COC)
Dept of Health & Social Security. Hannibal House, Elephant & Castle, London SE1 6TE
01–703 6380
Aims To assess and advise on the carcinogenic risk to man of substances which are: (i) used or proposed to be used as food additives, or used in such a way that they might contaminate food through their use or natural occurrence in agriculture, including horticulture and veterinary practice or in the distribution, storage, preparation, processing or packaging of food; (ii) used or proposed to be used or manufactured or produced in industry, agriculture, food storage or any other workplace; (iii) used or proposed to be used as household goods or toilet goods and preparations; (iv) used or proposed to be used as drugs; (v) used or proposed to be used or disposed of in such a way as to result in pollution of the environment. To advise on important general principles or new scientific discoveries in connection with carcinogenic risks, to co-ordinate with other bodies concerned with the assessment of carcinogenic risks and to present recommendations for carcinogenicity testing.
The Committee, which is constituted for the whole of the UK, consists of a chairman and 11 other members.

Committee on Medical Aspects of the Contamination of Air and Soil
This Committee of the DHSS is currently in abeyance. It is proposed to set up a new Committee on the Medical Aspects of the Contamination of Air, Soil and Water to replace this committee and the now disbanded Joint Committee on Medical Aspects of Water Quality.

Committee on Medical Aspects of Food Policy (COMA)
This Committee of the DHSS no longer exists

Committee on Mutagenicity of Chemicals in Food, Consumer Products and the Environment (COM)
Dept of Health & Social Security, Hannibal House, Elephant & Castle, London SE1 6TE
01–703 6380

Aims To assess and advise on the mutagenic risk to man of substances which are: (i) used or proposed to be used as food additives, or used in such a way that they might contaminate food through their use or natural occurrence in agriculture, including horticulture and veterinary practice or in the distribution, storage, preparation, processing or packaging of food; (ii) used or proposed to be used or manufactured or produced in industry, agriculture, food storage or any other workplace; (iii) used or proposed to be used as household goods or toilet goods and preparations; (iv) used or proposed to be used as drugs; (v) used or proposed to be used or disposed of in such a way as to result in pollution of the environment. To advise on important general principles or new scientific discoveries in connection with mutagenic risks, to co-ordinate with other bodies concerned with the assessment of mutagenic risks and to present recommendations for mutagenicity testing.
The Committee, which is constituted for the whole of the UK, consists of a chairman and 9 other members.

Committee on Safety of Medicines (CSM)

Dept of Health & Social Security, Market Towers, 1 Nine Elms Lane, London SW8 5NQ
01–720 2188
Aims To give advice with respect to safety, quality and efficacy in relation to human use of any substance under the Medicines Act 1968; to promote the collection and investigation of information relating to adverse reactions, for the purpose of enabling such advice to be given.
Activities Considers evidence relating to the safety, quality and efficacy of medicinal products before advising the Licensing Authority.
Status Statutory

Committee on Toxicity of Chemicals in Food, Consumer Products and the Environment (COT)

Dept of Health & Social Security, Hannibal House, Elephant & Castle, London SE1 6TE
01–703 6380
Aims To assess and advise on the toxic risk to man of substances which are: (i) used or proposed to be used as food additives, or used in such a way that they might contaminate food through their use or natural occurrence in agriculture, including horticulture and veterinary practice or in the distribution, storage, preparation, processing or packaging of food; (ii) used or proposed to be used or manufactured or produced in industry, agriculture, food storage or any other workplace; (iii) used or proposed to

be used as household goods or toilet goods and preparations; (iv) used or proposed to be used as drugs; (v) used or proposed to be used or disposed of in such a way as to result in pollution of the environment. To advise on important general principles or new scientific discoveries in connection with toxic risks, to co-ordinate with other bodies concerned with the assessment of toxic risks and to present recommendations for toxicity testing.
The Committee, which is constituted for the whole of the UK, consists of a chairman and 12 other members.

Common Ground

London Ecology Centre, 45 Shelton Street, Covent Garden, London WC2H 9HJ
01–379 3109
Co-ordinator Angela King
Aims To promote the importance of common animals, plants and familiar places; to encourage links between nature, landscape conservation and the arts to give inspiration and courage to people to help conserve their local surroundings.
Activities Research, publications, events, exhibitions, projects and general dissemination of ideas through the media. Main projects for 1985/6 are: the New Milestones Project, an attempt to encourage a new generation of sculpture involving sculptors and craftspeople with local communities in celebration of their locality; the Parish Maps Project, encouraging people to look more closely at their locality and what it contains, to express what *they* value on a map and to locate the Parish Map in a prominent place to help safeguard the features and places valued locally.
Status Limited company; charity
Publications Mabey, Richard, Clifford, Susan & King, Angela (eds), *Second Nature*, Jonathan Cape, 1985.
King, Angela & Clifford, Susan, *Holding Your Ground: an action guide to local conservation*, Temple Smith, 1985.

Common Management of Species in Zoos (Great Britain & Ireland) (CMSZ)

c/o Royal Zoological Society of Scotland, Scottish National Zoological Park, Murrayfield, Edinburgh EH12 6TS 031–334 9171
Reporter R.J. Wheater
Aims To maximise the genetic variability of animal species in captivity through scientifically co-ordinated co-operative breeding programmes.
Activities Regular meetings of participating organisations to examine the needs of species within their collections; arranging the movement of animals on a loan basis between collections in pursuit of the group's

objectives. Members of the group are major society, municipal and trust owned zoos.

Status Voluntary informal group of zoo representatives

Commons, Open Spaces and Footpaths Preservation Society
see OPEN SPACES SOCIETY

Commonweal Collection
c/o J.B. Priestley Library, University of Bradford, Bradford, W. Yorks. BD7 1DP 0274 733466
   Trustee Andrew Rigby
   Activities The Commonweal Collection is a free-loan library designed for any individual or group concerned with the creation of a peaceful, non-violent world. It contains several thousand publications, including a range of periodicals and archival material, covering the areas of non-violence, peace movements, Gandhi, non-violent social change, etc. The Collection is used by students, activists and researchers.

Commonwealth Agricultural Bureaux (CAB)
Farnham House, Farnham Royal, Slough, Berks. SL2 3BN 02814 2662
   Promotions Manager G. Philip Rimington
   Aims To provide: a world information service for agricultural scientists and other professional workers in the same and allied fields; a biological control service; and a pest and disease identification service. Has 4 institutes and 10 bureaux under its auspices (see list below). The governing body is an executive council on which 24 Commonwealth countries (as well as dependent territories) are represented.
   Activities Each institute and bureau is concerned with its own branch of agricultural science and acts as an effective clearing house for the collection, collation and dissemination of information of value to research workers. The information is published in 27 main abstract journals which have a circulation of 30,000 in 150 countries. There are also 2 primary journals and 21 journals on specialised subjects; annotated bibliographies provide information on specific topics. 3 institutes provide identification and taxonomic services and the fourth undertakes field work in biological control overseas. All data since 1973 are held on computer, accessible online; back-up services are available on request, i.e. information retrieval, photocopying, translations, etc.
   see COMMONWEALTH BUREAU OF AGRICULTURAL ECONOMICS
   COMMONWEALTH BUREAU OF ANIMAL BREEDING AND GENETICS
   COMMONWEALTH BUREAU OF ANIMAL HEALTH

COMMONWEALTH BUREAU OF DAIRY SCIENCE & TECHNOLOGY
COMMONWEALTH BUREAU OF HORTICULTURE & PLANTATION CROPS
COMMONWEALTH BUREAU OF NUTRITION
COMMONWEALTH BUREAU OF PASTURES & FIELD CROPS
COMMONWEALTH BUREAU OF PLANT BREEDING & GENETICS
COMMONWEALTH BUREAU OF SOILS
COMMONWEALTH FORESTRY BUREAU
COMMONWEALTH INSTITUTE OF BIOLOGICAL CONTROL
COMMONWEALTH INSTITUTE OF ENTOMOLOGY
COMMONWEALTH INSTITUTE OF PARASITOLOGY
COMMONWEALTH MYCOLOGICAL INSTITUTE

Commonwealth Bureau of Agricultural Economics (CBAE)
Dartington House, Little Clarendon Street, Oxford OX1 2HH 0865 59829
   Publications World Agricultural Economics and Rural Sociology Abstracts (12); Rural Development Abstracts (4); Rural Extension, Education and Training Abstracts (4); Leisure, Recreation and Tourism Abstracts (4)

Commonwelath Bureau of Animal Breeding and Genetics
Animal Breeding Research Organisation, The King's Buildings, West Mains Road, Edinburgh EH9 3JX 031-667 6901
   Publications Animal Breeding Abstracts (12); Poultry Abstracts (12)

Commonwealth Bureau of Animal Health
Central Veterinary Laboratory, New Haw, Weybridge, Surrey KT15 3NB 09323 42826
   Publications Veterinary Bulletin (12); Index Veterinarius (12); Small Animal Abstracts (4); Animal Disease Occurrence (data tables) (2)

Commonwealth Bureau of Dairy Science and Technology
Lane End House, Shinfield, Reading, Berks. RG2 9BB 0734 883895
   Publications Dairy Science Abstracts (12); Pig News and Information (4)

Commonwealth Bureau of Horticulture and Plantation Crops
East Malling Research Station, Maidstone, Kent ME19 6BJ 0732 843833
   Publications Horticultural Abstracts (12); Cotton & Tropical Fibres Abstracts (12); Ornamental Horticulture (12); Sorghum & Millets Abstracts (12); Tropical Oil Seeds Abstracts (12)

Commonwealth Bureau of Nutrition
Rowett Research Institute, Greenburn Road,
Bucksburn, Aberdeen, Grampian AB2 9SB,
Scotland 0224 712162
Publications Nutrition Abstracts and
Reviews: Series A, Human and Experimental
(12); Series B, Livestock Feeds and Feeding
(12)

**Commonwealth Bureau of Pastures and Field
Crops**
Grassland Research Institute, Hurley, Maiden-
head, Berks. SL6 5LR 062882 3457
Publications Herbage Abstracts (12); Field
Crop Abstracts (12); Crop Physiology
Abstracts (12); Weed Abstracts (12); Potato
Abstracts (12); Rice Abstracts (12); Seed
Abstracts (12); Soyabean Abstracts (12); Plant
Growth Regulator Abstracts (12); Faba Bean
Abstracts (4); Lentil Abstracts (4)

**Commonwealth Bureau of Plant Breeding
and Genetics**
Dept of Applied Biology, Pembroke Street,
Cambridge CB2 3DX 0223 358381 ext.216
Publications Plant Breeding Abstracts
(12); Maize Quality Protein Abstracts (4);
Wheat, Barley and Triticale Abstracts (4)

Commonwealth Bureau of Soils
Rothamsted Experimental Station, Harpenden,
Herts. AL5 2JQ 05827 63133 ext.271
Publications Soils and Fertilisers (12); Irri-
gation and Drainage Abstracts (4)

Commonwealth Forestry Association (CFA)
c/o Commonwealth Forestry Institute, South
Parks Road, Oxford OX1 3RB 0865 50156
Secretary M.T. Rogers
Aims To bring together all who are
concerned with conservation, development
and management of forests.
Activities Keeping members informed of
developments in forest science and practice
through its publications and meetings.
Members include foresters, forest and wood
scientists, timber merchants, ecologists,
resource managers and conservationists as
well as forest services, institutions, organisations and firms. Co-operates closely with
the CFI and is supported by the Commonwealth Forestry Bureau and the Unit of Tropical Silviculture.
Status Professional association
Publications Commonwealth Forestry
Review (4); Commonwealth Forestry
Handbook

Commonwealth Forestry Bureau
South Parks Road, Oxford OX1 3RD 0865 57185
Director W. Finlayson
Aims To facilitate collection, storage,
dissemination and retrieval of international
forestry and forest products literature.
Activities Publication of abstracts, review
articles, summaries of theses and news.
Abstracts are available online as part of the
Commonwealth Agricultural Bureaux
Abstracts Database. Other publications
include annotated bibliographies on
selected topics.
Publications Forestry Abstracts (12);
Forest Products Abstracts (12)

Commonwealth Forestry Institute
see OXFORD FORESTRY INSTITUTE

**Commonwealth Human Ecology Council
(CHEC)**
63 Cromwell Road, London SW7 5BL
01–373 6761
Executive Vice-Chairman Mrs Z.I. Daysh
Aims To encourage and promote an understanding of human ecological principles and
their application to development policies and
programmes in Commonwealth countries
and internationally. CHEC's ultimate objective is to ensure that the elementary principles of human ecology become embedded
in the values and attitudes of society.
Activities Promotion and co-ordination of
research programmes and pilot projects in
the dynamic and complex systems of human
life in various socio-cultural and economic
settings. The Council assists the formulation
of new research and applied projects in
Commonwealth countries; organises and
participates in seminars and workshops;
synthesises new research results, prepares
bibliographies and disseminates information; assists and promotes development of
curricula and educational programmes of
human ecology; assists and promotes
community self-help projects. Branches in
Commonwealth countries.
Status Voluntary; charity
Publications CHEC Journal (occasional);
CHEC Points (interim supplement to
Journal)

**Commonwealth Institute of Biological
Control**
Imperial College, Silwood Park, Ascot, Berks.
SL5 7PX 0990 28426
Publications Biocontrol News & Infor-
mation (4); Catalogue of the Parasites and
Predators of Insect Pests

Commonwealth Institute of Entomology
56 Queen's Gate, London SW7 5JR
01–581 3863/01–584 0067
Publications Review of Applied Entomology (12) (Series A, Agricultural; Series
B, Medical & Veterinary); Bulletin of Entomological Research (12)

Commonwealth Institute of Parasitology
Winches Farm, 395A Hatfield Road, St Albans,
Herts. AL4 0XU 0727 33151/5
   Publications Helminthological Abstracts:
   Series A, Animal and Human Helminthology
   (12); Series B, Plant Nematology (4); Proto-
   zoological Abstracts (12)

Commonwealth Mycological Institute
Ferry Lane, Kew, Richmond, London TW9 3AF
01–940 4086
   Publications Review of Plant Pathology
   (12); Review of Medical and Veterinary
   Mycology (4); International Biodeterioration
   (4)

Commonwork
Bore Place, Chiddingstone, Edenbridge, Kent
TN8 7AR 073277 708/255
   Centre Co-ordinator Maria English
   Aims To enable people to learn to make
   the best use of our indigenous, environmental
   and human resources and in the process
   create more opportunities for fulfilling work.
   Activities Practises a wide variety of
   farming and self-sufficiency activities; offers a
   study centre with a programme of courses
   on agriculture, ecology, personal growth,
   etc. Bookings accepted for conferences,
   tours and education projects. Linked with
   Dunamis.
   Status Commercial enterprises and charitable trusts
   Publications Mailing to Friends of
   Commonwork (2)

Communes Network
Laurieston Hall, Castle Douglas, Dumfries &
Galloway DG7 2NB, Scotland
   Aims To link people involved or interested
   in collective lifestyles.
   Activities Acting as a contact point for
   inquiries; producing a newsletter.
   Status Informal network
   Publications Communes Network (6)
   Directory of Communities 1985.

Community Design Service
The Maltings, East Tyndall Street,
Cardiff CF1 5EA 0222 494012
   Co-ordinator Neil Wallace
   Activities Work includes landscape
   design, helping groups working for the
   benefit of the community or environment.
   -NR

Community Health Foundation (CHF)
188–194 Old Street, London EC1V 9BP
01–251 4076
   Public Relations & Programme
   Manager Jill Atterton
   Aims To present practical and accessible
   means for establishing and maintaining better

health and awareness; to work in the field of
preventive health care.
   Activities Lectures, seminars and workshops for laymen and professionals; classes
   and activities open to the general public;
   consultations available with trained
   members of staff. Reflexology sessions and
   Shiatsu therapy can be arranged.
   Status Educational trust; charity
   Publications Community Health Foundation Programme Newsletter &
   Programme of Events (4)

Community Land Use (CLU)
192–6 Hanbury Street, London E1 5HU
01–247 6265
   Office Organiser Annie Donelly
   Aims To provide a landscape and building
   design service to the local community in the
   London Boroughs of Tower Hamlets,
   Hackney and Newham. (Formerly part of
   the Tower Hamlets Environment Trust.)
   Activities Feasibility studies and the
   design and contract supervision of both
   conversions and new build schemes of
   benefit to the local community, providing
   much needed services and improving the
   local environment. The Landscape Design
   team prepare and carry out under contract
   schemes ranging from allotments and nature
   gardens to estate improvements and play-
   spaces, many on vacant land, which have
   been inspired by local people's ideas and
   needs for improving their environment.
   Status Worker co-operative; member of
   the Association of Community Technical Aid

Community Projects Foundation (CPF)
60 Highbury Grove, London N5 2AG
01–226 5375
   Information Officer Frances Presley
   Aims As a national agency, to establish
   innovative community development and
   youth work projects; at local level, to explore
   new approaches to social problems of
   national concern.
   Activities The central unit in London
   supports and demonstrates the field-work
   experience and undertakes national initiatives on issues of concern through consultancy, information, publications and seminars.
   Current concerns include unemployment,
   particularly among young people, housing,
   rural community work and young offenders.
   Local branches.
   Status Voluntary; charity
   Publications Community Currents

Community Radio Association
92 Huddleston Road, London N7 0EG
   Secretary Simon Partridge
   -NR

Community Task Force (CTF)
7th Floor, Lowthian House, Market Street,
Preston, Lancs. PR1 2ES 0772 51878

Contact Information Officer
Aims To improve employment prospects of
young people by means of relevant training
and work experience; to carry out environmental improvements in urban and rural
areas; to provide temporary relief for long-
term unemployed adults.
Activities Carrying out widespread
environmental schemes under the
Manpower Services Commission's
Community Programme and Youth Training
Schemes; projects range from land clearance, building renovation and refurbish-
ment to major construction projects such as
the restoration of Bangor pier. CTF is the
largest MSC agent, handling 9,000 CP places
nationally. 16 branches.
Status Charity

Community Technical Aid Centre (CTAC)
61 Bloom Street, Manchester M1 3LY
061–236 5195

Project Director Phil Barton
Aims To provide planning, architectural
and landscape architecture aid to residents,
community groups and voluntary
organisations.
Activities Landscaping derelict sites;
project development relating to provision of
community facilities: advice on planning
problems: fund raising for community
groups; environmental education.
Status Voluntary
Publications CTAC Information Pack.

Community Transport
Keymer Street, Beswick, Manchester M11 3FY
061–273 4641

Chief Executive Norman Williams
Aims To provide transport for voluntary
and community groups and people in need.
Activities Operation of lorries and
minibuses: special dial-a-ride arrangements
for disabled people: volunteer car driver
schemes: advice and information on transport provision; community garage in Birmingham. Branches in Midlands and North
East.
Status Charity

Compassion in World Farming (CIWF)
20 Lavant Street, Petersfield, Hants. GU32 3EW
0730 64208

Educational Officer Carol Long
Aims To promote the introduction of non-
violence into our relationship with farm
animals, wildlife, the plant kingdom and the
soil itself.
Activities Concerned with the agricultural
and food aspects of the total environment;
campaigning for the abolition of factory
farming and for a ban on the export of live
food animals; educating schools and the
public on land and food management;
pressing for legislation to control the ruthless
exploitation of livestock and countryside.
The project suggestion The Place of Animals
in the Farm has been put into 30,000 schools.
Local branches.
Status Educational trust
Publications Ag

COMTECHSA (Community Technical Services Agency Ltd)
Westminster Chambers, 3 Crosshall Street,
Liverpool L1 6DQ 051–227 2204/5

Project Leader & Secretary Leslie Forsyth
Aims To provide the services of architects,
landscape architects and town planners to
community organisations in Liverpool.
Activities Providing a range of services,
including architectural, planning and landscaping, to help groups carry out feasibility
studies, funding applications, planning
permission, making drawings and arranging
and supervising the building work.
Status Non-profit-making co-operative
society
Publications Annual Report

Confederation of British Industry (Environmental Division) (CBI)
Centre Point, 103 New Oxford Street, London
WC1A 1DU 01–379 7400

**Secretary, Environmental & Technical
Legislation Committee** Dr E.F. Thairs
Aims To recommend industrial policy as it
concerns environmental matters and related
technical legislation and to take any
necessary action.
Activities Monitoring proposals for
environmental legislation from government
departments and the EEC and commenting
as appropriate; keeping under review all
legislation and matters arising therefrom
affecting use of land by industry; providing
industrial opinion to authoritative studies (e.g.
Royal Commission on Environmental
Pollution) on environmental issues; proffering
advice to CBI members on environmental
matters, including proposed legislation.
Status Voluntary
Publications Newsletter (6)
*Control of Water Pollution: a practical guide
for industry.*
*Guidelines on the Responsible Disposal of
Waste.*
*Mineral Operations: a practical guide for the
extractive and water industries.*

Conference on Training Architects in Conservation (COTAC)
19 West Eaton Place, Eaton Square, London SW1X 8LT 01–245 9888

Hon. Secretary Donald Insall

Aims To encourage the establishment of better facilities for specialist training for architects wishing to devote particular attention to the conservation of historic areas, buildings and monuments.

Activities Encouragement, co-ordination and advice on all matters in connection with specialist training in conservation.

Status Voluntary

Connections (New Travel)
7–8 Lyme Street, London NW1 0EH 01–485 2337

Contact Julie Elwick

Aims To promote and provide information on 'alternative' opportunities for travel and leisure, bearing in mind the negative effects on the environment, local population and cultures of mass tourism and also the limited scope of most package holidays for self-development, education and communication.

Activities Publishing a regular bulletin plus factsheets on 'environmental' holidays, voluntary work opportunities worldwide, exchange schemes, etc.

Status Voluntary

Publications New Travel Bulletin (4)

Conservation Bureau
Rosebery House, Haymarket Terrace. Edinburgh EH12 5EZ 031–337 9595

Conservation Officer Nic Allen

Aims To provide help to all those concerned with conservation of historic buildings and objects in Scotland.

Activities Collecting and making available information regarding all aspects of conservation, especially the location of conservation skills and materials; publication of information; provision of grants for short-term training for conservators. Funded by central government through the Scottish Development Agency.

Publications *Scottish Conservation Directory 1985/6.*

Conservation Education Services
c/o WWF/IUCN Education Project, Greenfield House, Guiting Power, Cheltenham, Glos. GL54 5TZ

-NR

Conservation Foundation
11A West Halkin Street, London SW1X 8JL
0171 591 3111
1, Kensington Gove
SW7 2AR

Directors Dr David Bellamy, David Shreeve

Aims To encourage industry and the business community to support conservation by helping to publicise the efforts of those involved in practical conservation work and, when requested, seek sponsorship for them; to produce publications and media support material.

Activities Organises annual European Conservation Awards in the UK, France, Spain, Belgium, Switzerland, Holland and Austria, sponsored by Ford Motor Company; Community Chest sponsored by Trusthouse Forte making monthly financial donations; Special Awards financed by the Electricity Council. Publishes annual Conservation Review and bi-annual Conservation Catalogue in association with Friends of the Earth, Council for the Protection of Rural England and other conservation organisations; produces a variety of material in association with sponsors. Contracted associates in Europe.

Status Charity

Publications Conservation Review (1); Conservation Catalogue (2) First Conservation Annual. Second Conservation Annual.

Conservation Society (ConSoc)
12A Guildford Street, Chertsey, Surrey KT16 9BQ 09328 60975

Director Dr John Davoll

Aims To work for a sustainable and equitable society; to press for policies to reduce the rapid depletion of resources and degradation of the environment.

Activities Campaigns by seeking to influence both public opinion and official policies to achieve its aims. Among past and current campaigns have been ones for the provision of family planning advice on the National Health Service; against the dumping of poisonous wastes; for a rational transport policy to economise on energy and protect the environment; for energy policies based on conservation and greater efficiency of use, rather than increased production; and for the removal of lead from petrol. Local branches.

Status Voluntary

Publications Conservation News (3)

Conservation Society of the Yorkshire Derwent (CONSYDER)
The Elms, East Cottingwith, York, N. Yorks. YO4 4TT 07593 296

Secretary Mrs J.M. Burnett

Aims To protect the river system and its life; to maintain its cleanliness and minimise pollution; to preserve the river habitat; to support and improve the natural amenities of the river and promote a greater awareness of the river system.

Activities Publicising and commenting on any developments or activities concerning the

river; collating information and undertaking an annual census of river usage. Educating the public and seeking to influence decisions by statutory bodies. The Society has produced a book, The Yorkshire Derwent: a case for conservation.
Status Voluntary
Publications Newsletter (4)

Conservation Tools and Technology
143 Maple Road, Surbiton, Surrey KT6 4BH
-NR

Conservation Trust (CT)
George Palmer School, Northumberland Avenue, Reading, Berks. RG2 0EN 0734 868442
Hon. Director Peter S. Berry
Aims To encourage greater environmental awareness amongst people of all ages.
Activities Information service on environmental topics; resource bank of teaching materials, including books, slides, posters, etc., available on free loan to members. Maintains comprehensive computerised database (Resource Bank 1: teaching materials; Resource Bank 2: articles; Resource Bank 3: 1400 entries on statutory and voluntary organisations). Publications, mainly relating to environmental education, include series of study notes, guides and packs (send large s.a.e. with inquiries). 6 regional display centres.
Status Educational charity
Publications Conservation Trust Newsletter (3)
Environmental Education Enquiries (4th edn) 1985.
Guide to Resources in Environmental Education (10th edn) 1985.
Resource Bank Index (4th edn) 1985.

Conservative Ecology Group
51 Stakes Hill Road, Waterlooville, Hants. PO7 7LD
-NR

Consultative Panel on Badgers and Tuberculosis
c/o Ministry of Agriculture, Fisheries & Food, 10th Floor, Tolworth Tower, Surbiton, Surrey KT6 7DX 01–399 5191
Aims To keep under review: (i) the evidence relating to bovine tuberculosis in badgers, including its incidence and its relationship to bovine tuberculosis in cattle; (ii) the operations to be undertaken by the Ministry in order to eradicate bovine tuberculosis from badgers and to monitor its existence in the badger population. The Panel, which is constituted for England only, consists of a chairman and 14 other members, including representatives of agricultural employers and employees, animal

welfare societies, scientific societies and environmental conservation interests.
Publications Bovine Tuberculosis in Badgers (1) (free)

Consumer Campaign
11 Forth Street, Edinburgh EH1 3LE
031–557 4283
Contact Linda Hendry
Aims To encourage electricity consumers to withold the 'nuclear' portion (about 12%) of their electricity bill in protest against the nuclear power programme.
Activities Research, education, publications. Receiving and holding witheld monies, then repaying the electricity board at consumers' request; publicising the campaign and collecting donations to forward the above aims.
Status Voluntary
Publications Consumer Campaign Newsletter

Convention of Scottish Local Authorities (COSLA)
16 Moray Place, Edinburgh EH3 6BL
031–225 1626
Secretary Graham H. Speirs
Aims To watch over, protect and promote the respective interests, rights, powers and duties of its member authorities as these may be affected by legislation or otherwise; to provide a forum for the discussion of matters of concern to its member authorities and to obtain, consider and disseminate information on matters of importance and interest to them; to provide such essential services for them as it may consider appropriate.
Activities Considers legislation before Parliament on matters of local government interest and is usually consulted beforehand; negotiates and consults with other national bodies whose work affects local authorities or who look to local government for financial support; negotiates on annual Exchequer grant; submits evidence to Royal Commissions and committees of inquiry. Available to guide member authorities on any matter where a uniform approach by authorities is desirable.
Status Voluntary

Convention on International Trade in Endangered Species
see CITES

Co-operative Advisory Group
272–276 Pentonville Road, London N1 9JY
01–833 3915
Administrator Ruth Goodwin
Aims To provide business advisory services to co-operatives, community businesses and employment projects; to provide

training to people who work in them and who are involved in their promotion; to provide consultancy services to economic and employment initiatives in the UK and elsewhere.

Activities Assistance offered includes: feasibility studies; business planning and strategy; preparation of funding proposals; marketing studies and product evaluation; organisational development and employment issues; business monitoring and information systems. Emphasis is on democratically controlled businesses. Training courses are tailored to reflect the needs of the participants.

Status Co-operative company limited by guarantee

Publications *Marketing in Worker Co-operatives in the UK.* 1984. *Alternative Economic Initiatives, Job Creation and Democratic Control in the Local Economy.* 1983.

Co-operative Development Agency (CDA)

Broadmead House, 21 Panton Street, London SW1Y 4DR 01–839 2988

Contact Development Officer

Aims To identify and recommend ways in which the establishment, development and evolution of co-operatives might be facilitated.

Activities Representing and promoting the interests of the co-operative sector with government, local authorities and other organisations; providing advice to anyone who seeks it on the co-operative form of enterprise; identifying, appraising and promoting projects; providing a forum for debate within the co-operative movement. Branch in Manchester.

Status Statutory

Publications CDA News (occasional); Annual Report *How to Set Up a Co-operative Business. The New Co-operatives: a directory and resource guide.*

Co-operative Union Ltd

Holyoake House, Hanover Street, Manchester M4 4AH 061–832 4300

Aims To co-ordinate, inform and advise co-operatives and to act as a national voice for the co-operative movement.
-NR

Co-operatives Research Unit (CRU)

Faculty of Technology, Open University, Milton Keynes, Bucks. MK7 6AA 0908 652102

Secretary Doreen Pendlebury

Aims To increase understanding of the process of co-operative organisation; to develop education and training materials for workers' co-operatives; to search for meth-

odologies appropriate to policy-oriented studies and action research.

Activities Current areas of interest include: co-operative development; worker-oriented information systems; commitment in co-operatives; biographies of co-operative activists; value systems in co-operatives. Research reports and information leaflets produced.

Status Academic

Co-ordinating Animal Welfare (CAW)

PO Box 61, Camberley, Surrey GU15 3HA

Aims To unite activists from the various animal liberation/welfare groups.

Publications CAW Bulletin (6)
-NR

Cornwall Trust for Nature Conservation Ltd (CTNC) [formerly Cornwall Naturalists' Trust]

Trendrine, Zennor, St Ives, Cornwall TR26 3BW 0736 796926

Administrative Officer W.F.H. Ansell

Aims To safeguard wildlife and natural habitats throughout Cornwall.

Activities Acquisition and management of nature reserves. which are owned, leased or held on agreement; liaison with planning bodies, other societies, the Farming and Wildlife Advisory Group and similar organis-ations; education in nature conservation (especially in schools); surveying, recording and monitoring conservation sites. 7 branches.

Status Voluntary; charity

Publications Cornwall Trust for Nature Conservation Newsletter (2)

Council for British Archaeology (CBA)

112 Kennington Road, London SE11 6RE 01–582 0494

Director Dr H.F. Cleere

Aims To advance the study and practice of archaeology pertaining to Great Britain and Northern Ireland; in particular to promote the education of the public in British archae-ology and to conduct and publish the results of research therein.

Activities Conferences and meetings; publication of research reports, handbooks, abstracts, etc. Formulation of policies for research and preservation through specialist committees; encouragement of archaeology in education; general public relations for archaeology. Representational role in relation to central and local govern-ment, statutory bodies, business and industry and environmental organisations. 14 regional groups.

Status Voluntary

Publications CBA Newsletter (9); British Archaeological Abstracts (2); CBA Churches & Schools Bulletins (2); Archaeology in Britain (1)

Council for Education in World Citizenship (CEWC)
19–21 Tudor Street, London EC4Y 0DJ
01–353 3353

Director Margaret Quass
Aims To create a global perspective and to promote education for international understanding in schools and colleges throughout the UK.
Activities Services to members include: Newsletters and current affairs broadsheets; conferences and seminars for teachers and students on national and international issues; provision of speakers; use of the resource centre; UN and world affairs literature. Members include 2,000 schools and colleges. Local branches.
Status Voluntary
Publications CEWC Broadsheets (6)
World Studies Resource Guide 1984 (biennial).
Environment and Development Pack 1984.
Peace and Disarmament Pack 1984.
United Nations Pack 1984.

Council for Environmental Conservation (CoEnCo)
Zoological Gardens, Regent's Park, London NW1 4RY 01–722 7111

Information Officer Tom Cairns
Aims To co-ordinate the activities of the voluntary conservation movement at national level in Britain. With regard to major environmental issues, to provide a forum for discussion and promote a unified response on matters of concern.
Activities Providing secretariat services for environmental campaigns such as the World Conservation Strategy and the Council of Europe's Water's Edge campaign. Providing an information service on conservation issues (but does not handle educational inquiries). Producing reports on major issues of environmental concern; producing handbooks and leaflets (publications list available – s.a.e. with all inquiries).
Status Voluntary; charity
Publications Habitat (12)
-NR

Council for Environmental Education (CEE)
School of Education, University of Reading, London Road, Reading, Berks. RG1 5AQ
0734 875234 ext.218

Director John Baines
Aims To encourage and promote environmental education through co-ordination and support programmes, especially in school and youth sectors. The Council, which is constituted for England and Wales, brings together representatives of about 60 national organisations with interests in the fields of education and environmental management and conservation.
Activities Providing an Information Centre and information services on all aspects of environmental education; producing publications, especially bibliographies of educational materials available from all sources. Conferences and meetings, including twice-yearly meetings for all member organisations and Associates. Has an office in London.
Status Voluntary; charity
Publications CEE Newsheet (10); REED (Review of Environmental Education Developments) (3)
Education for Commitment (*in* The Conservation and Development Programme for the UK: response to the World Conservation Strategy), Kogan Page, 1983.

Council for Environmental Science and Engineering (CESE)
20 Queensberry Place, London SW7 2DZ
01–581 8333

Aims To anticipate and evaluate environmental problems and to represent, co-ordinate and promote the activities of engineers and scientists in solving these problems for the benefit of mankind; to seek and promote the adoption of realistic solutions to environmental problems, particularly where technological works are concerned to minimise any adverse consequences; to encourage and co-ordinate initiatives by member bodies in the arranging of conferences and in undertaking the study of problems in environmental science and engineering. CESE consists of 21 members who are representatives of the member institutions of the Council of Science and Technology Institutes and the Council of Engineering Institutions.

Council for Justice to Animals/Humane Slaughter Association
34 Blanche Lane, Potters Bar, Herts. EN6 3PA
0707 59040

Aims To minimise the suffering of animals to be slaughtered.
-NR

Council for National Parks (CNP)
London Ecology Centre, 45 Shelton Street, Covent Garden, London WC2H 9HJ
01–240 3603

Publicity/Information Officer Francesca Fraser Darling
Aims To uphold and promote the purposes for which the ten National Parks of England and Wales were designated: namely the conservation and enhancement of their

[handwritten: Local N'for Mrs Jim Larkater (01280) 703556 Vice chair: Helena Alsop 01536771308]

natural beauty and the promotion of their *[handwritten]* enjoyment by the public. Membership *[handwritten]* consists of 36 national and local organisations which include amenity, recreation and conservation interests.
Activities Acts as a forum for discussion of National Park issues, problems and policies; undertakes research; publishes reports; makes representations to government, local authorities and others; holds conferences and seminars to further public awareness and understanding of National Parks. Increasingly the Council has a growing educational and publicity role to play, as with the publication of an education pack on National Parks. Individuals support the Council's work by becoming a Friend of National Parks.
Status Voluntary
Publications Tarn and Tor (2); Annual Report
Know Your National Parks. 1984.
New Life For The Hills. 1983 *[handwritten]*

Council for the Protection of Rural England (CPRE)
[handwritten: 0171 976 6433]
4 Hobart Place, London SW1W 0HY.
~~01-235 9481~~ *[handwritten: Andrew Burkiss]*
Director ~~Robin Grove-White~~
Aims To promote and encourage the improvement and protection of the countryside and of rural amenities; to act as a centre for advice and information upon matters affecting the protection of amenities; to arouse, form and educate public opinion in order to ensure the promotion of these aims.
Activities Campaigns inside and outside Parliament, for example on: motorways; new towns; regional plans; afforestation; energy policy; water strategy. Local branches seek to influence planning and development control policies of public authorities and private developers. Individual membership of more than 30,000; 42 county branches.
Status Voluntary; charity
Publications Countryside Campaigner (3); Yearbook

Council for the Protection of Rural Wales/ Cymdeithas Diogelu Cymru Wledig (CPRW)
Ty Gwyn, 31 High Street, Welshpool, Powys SY21 7JP, Wales 0938 2525
Director Simon Meade
Aims To organise concerted action to secure the protection and improvement of rural scenery and of the amenities of the countryside and towns and villages of Wales; to act as a centre for furnishing or procuring advice and information upon any matters affecting such protection and improvement; to arouse, form and educate opinion in order to ensure the promotion of these aims.
Activities Represents the interests of all

who appreciate the Welsh countryside; provides expert argument against undesirable development; balances the demands of commercial interest with environmental desirability; provides opportunity for personal involvement through 13 local branches.
Status Voluntary
Publications Rural Wales (3)

Council for Science and Society (CSS)
3–4 St Andrew's Hill, London EC4V 5BY
01–236 6723
Executive Secretary Barbara Farah
Aims To assist society in using science and technology for the greatest good and to ensure that possible ill effects are minimised.
Activities A project to investigate *in vitro* fertilisation, allied technologies and their social and ethical implications was completed in 1984. Current work in progress includes projects on: military research and development; urban movement options; the rationale of wildlife conservation; the role of companion animals in society; openness and secrecy in science; duration and quality of lives; and private health care.
Status Charity
Publications Annual Report
Human Procreation. 1984.
Expensive Medical Techniques. 1983.

Council for Small Industries in Rural Areas (CoSIRA)
141 Castle Street, Salisbury, Wilts. SP1 3TP
0722 336255
Head of Information Henry Clark
Aims To help regenerate the rural areas of England by providing consultancy, training and finance services to small businesses.
Activities Action in support of the above. 32 local offices.
Status Agency of the Development Commission
[*For similar services in the remainder of the UK, see* LOCAL ENTERPRISE DEVELOPMENT UNIT (NI); SCOTTISH DEVELOPMENT AGENCY; WELSH DEVELOPMENT AGENCY]

Council for Urban Studies Centres (CUSC)
c/o Notting Dale Urban Studies Centre, 189 Freston Road, London W10 6TH 01–968 5440
Contact Anne Armstrong
Aims To promote and encourage urban studies, to support existing USCs and to promote the setting up of proposed USCs.
Activities Publicising the activities of Urban Studies Centres; holding workshops and conferences on aspects of urban studies; supporting research into areas of curriculum development relevant to urban studies.

Status Voluntary
Publications Journal (11); Newsletter
Urban Studies in the 80s.

Council of National Beekeeping Associations of the UK (CONBA)
12–27 Ethel Terrace, Edinburgh EH10 5NA
031–447 5332
Activities Has the authority to negotiate with national and international official bodies. The Council consists of a chairman and 11 other members nominated by the British Beekeepers' Association, the Scottish Beekeepers' Association, the Welsh Beekeepers' Association and the Ulster Beekeepers' Association.

Counter Information Services (CIS)
9 Poland Street, London W1V 3DG
Activities Issues reports revealing information that has been suppressed or distorted in official versions.

Country Landowners Association (CLA)
16 Belgrave Square, London SW1X 8PQ
01–235 0511
Aims To promote and protect the interests of rural and agricultural land-owners.
Activities Providing advice for members on taxation, legal matters, land use and water resources; making representations on behalf of members.
-NR

Countryside Commission
John Dower House, Crescent Place, Cheltenham, Glos. GL50 3RA 0242 521381
Head of Communications Branch Calvin Pugsley
Aims To conserve the landscape beauty of the countryside; to develop and improve facilities for recreation and access in the countryside; to advise government on matters of countryside interest in England and Wales.
Activities The Commission is an advisory and promotional body, not an executive one. It achieves its objectives through collaboration with public authorities, voluntary bodies and private individuals and organisations. Main areas of work include promoting understanding of the countryside; research; experiment; policy advice; technical advice; designating areas of outstanding landscape; encouraging conservation and recreation by local authorities, voluntary bodies, landowners and farmers. 8 local branches.
Status Statutory
Publications Countryside Commission News (6)
Countryside Access Charter.

Countryside Commission for Scotland (CCS)
Battleby, Redgorton, Perth PH1 3EW
0738 27921
Public Relations Officer Malcolm Payne
Aims To provide for the better enjoyment of the Scottish countryside and the conservation of its natural beauty and amenities.
Activities Planning advice to central and local government; grants to local authorities and others; research and development; design; environmental education and training; policy review functions. Providing information and publicity relating to the countryside; production of a wide range of publications.
Status Statutory
Publications Annual Report
Directory of Outdoor Education Centres in Scotland.
Providing for Children's Play in the Countryside.

Countryside Commission Office for Wales
8 Broad Street, Newtown, Powys SY16 2LU
0686 26799
Aims and activities as per Countryside Commission.

Countryside Management
Yew Tree Cottage, Salperton, Cheltenham, Glos. GL54 4EE 04515 361
Activities Providing expertise and services in conservation work for landowners on a consultancy basis.
-NR

Countryside Recreation Research Advisory Group (CRRAG)
16 Upper Woburn Place, London WC1H 0QP
01–388 1277
Secretary Nicola Lloyd (ext.250)
Aims To co-ordinate and harmonise research carried out by statutory bodies concerning countryside recreation. Serviced by the Sports Council, the Group's membership includes Countryside Commissions, the Forestry Commission, the British Waterways Board, local authority bodies, etc.
Publications Countryside Recreation Research: the programmes of the CRRAG agencies (1)
-NR

County Planning Officers' Society
c/o East Cliff County Offices, Preston, Lancs. PR1 3EX 0772 54868
Hon. Secretary D. Tattersall (County Planning Officer)
-NR

Crafts Commission
1 St Michael's Church Road, St Michael's Hamlet, Liverpool L17 7BD

Aims To promote and preserve traditional skills. Evolved from the former Amalgamated Institute of Antiquarian Craftsmen.
Activities Include provision of environmental and architectural services.
-NR

Crafts Council
12 Waterloo Place, London SW1Y 4AU 01–930 4811
Aims To promote and support contemporary craft work.
Activities Operates a grants scheme for craftspeople and special projects. Facilities include: a large gallery featuring a changing programme of exhibitions; information service; register of craftspeople; slide index and loan service; education department.
Status Charity incorporated under Royal Charter
Publications Crafts Magazine (6)
Science for Conservators.

Craftsmen Potters Association of Great Britain
William Blake House, Marshall Street, London W1V 01–437 7605
-NR

Cranfield Institute of Technology
Cranfield, Bedford MK43 0AL 0234 750111
Head of Applied Energy (School of Mechanical Engineering) Prof. Douglas Probert (ext.2302)
Activities Within the university sector, the Institute is Britain's largest centre of applied research and development in industrial technology. Energy forms a large part of the total research and includes thermal insulation, heat recovery, design of thermal systems, solar energy and wind power.
Status Charity
Publications Applied Energy (12)

Crofters Commission
4–6 Castle Wynd, Inverness, Highlands IV2 3EQ, Scotland 0463 237231
Aims To promote the interests of crofters in the seven crofting counties of Scotland.

Cruelty to Animals Inspectorate
Home Office, 50 Queen Anne's Gate, London SW1H 9AT 01–213 3000
Aims To visit registered places to ensure compliance with the provisions of the Cruelty to Animals Act 1876; to advise the Secretary of State on technical and scientific matters relating to administration of the above Act and to advise on suitability of premises to be registered; to ensure that experiments are carried out only in registered places, by persons holding necessary authorisation and acquaint all such licensees with the requirements of the Act; to advise responsible authorities on required standards of accommodation and inspect registered premises to ensure maintenance of required conditions for experimental animals.
Status Statutory

Cumbria Trust for Nature Conservation Ltd
Church Street, Ambleside, Cumbria LA22 0BU 0966 32476
Senior Officer Joy Ketchen
Aims To protect wildlife species and their habitats through management of nature reserves; to educate the young and old in the need for conservation; to provide sound advice to all involved in the use of land.
Activities Setting up and managing nature reserves; providing practical advice on conservation matters to local and water authorities, landowners and farmers; conducting and promoting wildlife surveys. Nature trails, lectures, discussions and WATCH junior branch. Organising activities through 16 support groups; regular management tasks on Trust reserves; seeking to ensure that variety of wildlife is maintained throughout the countryside. Local branches.
Status Voluntary; charity
Publications Cumbria Trust for Nature Conservation Newsletter (3)

Cumbrians for Peace (C for P)
17 Sneckyeat Court, Hensingham, Whitehaven, Cumbria CA28 8PQ 0946 62626
Convenor Charles Searle
Aims To provide a vehicle in Cumbria for the opposition to all weapons of mass destruction and all policies that obstruct the long-term objective of European and world disarmament; and to operate non-violently and through education in a non-sectarian, non-party political manner.
Activities As an affiliated organisation of the Campaign for Nuclear Disarmament (CND), promoting the national campaign's issues at local level; raising public awareness of the threat to this country's security posed by the installation of cruise missiles and the development of the Trident programme; holding public meetings, organising street canvasses and petitions, lobbying local MPs. Also, focusing on local nuclear installations by staging marches and setting up peace camps at RNAD Broughton Moor, the NATO bombing range at Spadeadam and at CAD Longtown which regularly serves as a stopping-off point for the Polaris warheads convoy. Have campaigned successfully for Cumbria to be declared a Nuclear-Free Zone. 10 local groups and a number of affiliates.
Status Voluntary

Publications Cumbrian Campaigner (bulletin of the NFZ Support Group)

Cumbrians Opposed to a Radioactive Environment (CORE)

3A Slater Street, Barrow-in-Furness, Cumbria LA14 1SJ 0229 33851

Activities Has submitted evidence on radioactive waste to the House of Commons Environment Committee. Formerly known as the Barrow and District Action Group.
-NR

Cyclebag

35 King Street, Bristol, Avon BS1 4DZ 0272 28893
Secretary Chris Hutt
Aims To bring about the acceptance of cycling as a safe and valuable means of urban transport, backed by public policy and public funding.
Activities Urban Campaign: pressing for cycle facilities and routes and for all new highway schemes to take account of the needs and safety of cyclists; persuading the county council to make a positive commitment to the promotion of safer cycling. Cyclepaths: promoting, constructing and managing routes for cyclists and pedestrians on disused railways, canal towpaths and riverbank paths, including the Bristol & Bath Railway Path.
Status Voluntary
Publications Cyclebag News (4)

Cyclists' Association

Cotterell House, 69 Meadrow, Godalming, Surrey GU7 3HS 04868 7217
-NR

Cyclists' Touring Club (CTC)

Cotterell House, 69 Meadrow, Godalming, Surrey GU7 3HS 04868 7217
Contact National Secretary
Aims To encourage recreational cycling and to protect cyclists' interests; to promote everyday urban cycling as well as access to and preservation of the countryside.
Activities As a national association, lobbying central and local government and other bodies. Services to members include cycle touring advice, cycle touring holidays, insurance and technical advice. 200 local branches organise rides and social events.
Status Voluntary
Publications Cycletouring (6)
Cycling Accidents: final report of a survey of cycling accidents.

D

Dag Hammarskjold Information Centre (on the Study of Violence and Peace)
110 Eton Place, Eton College Road, London NW3 2DS 01–722 3008
Aims To provide a comprehensive and accurate information service, primarily for the mass media but also for decision makers and community leaders; to advance the education of the public by study and research into the causes of violence and the means of avoiding conflict.
Status Educational trust; charity
Publications Chronicle (12)
-NR -L

Dartington Hall Trust
The Elmhirst Centre, Dartington Hall, Totnes, Devon TQ9 6EL 0803 862271
Contact John Lane (trustee)
Aims To provide a focus and support for a wide range of activities in the arts, education, farming, research and business; to offer a rural alternative to the concentration of resources in metropolitan areas.
Activities The Trust is a unique organisation which incorporates many different bodies. Those of environmental interest include:
– Dartington Institute which pursues research and innovatory action in the field of local development, including a Land Resources team, a Rural Development team, a New Communities team, the Bridge Community Programme agency and the Devon Energy Project;
– Yarner Trust (*see separate entry*)
– Dartington Hall Farms Ltd;
– Land Forum which deals with such topics as hedgerow removal and crop spraying;
– Grounds & Gardens Department, including a Horticultural Training Workshop;
– Dartington Trading which operates from the Cider Press Centre, one of the leading craft shops in the country;
– Dartington Farm Foods
Status Charity
Publications Dartington Voice (12); Friends of Dartington Newsletter (2); Annual Report

Dartmoor Badgers Protection League (DBPL)
Riverside Cottage, Poundsgate, Ashburton, Devon TQ13 7NV 03643 231
Secretary Brenda Charlesworth
Aims To promote a greater knowledge, love and understanding of the badger; to oppose all badger slaughter, either by government or by the illegal bloodsports of badger-digging and badger-baiting. DBPL is a national badger group.
Activities Organising patrols and camps to protect threatened badgers and setts; political campaign to strengthen and improve legislation affecting the badger.
Status Voluntary
Publications DBPL Newsletter (6)

Dartmoor National Park Authority (DNPA)
Parke, Haytor Road, Bovey Tracey, Newton Abbott, Devon TQ13 9JQ 0626 832093
Information Officer John W.H. Weir
Aims Under the National Parks & Access to the Countryside Act 1949, to conserve and enhance landscape, promote the enjoyment of National Park areas and to have due regard for the socio-economic wellbeing of local communities.
Activities Development control; consultation and production of National Park plans, local plans and other management plans; processing of agricultural grant notifications; providing for informal recreation; providing information and interpretation. Work relating to farmed landscapes, common land management, archaeological and ecological interests and woodland management; provision of a ranger service.
Status Statutory
Publications Annual Report
National Park Plan, 1st review. 1983.

Dartmoor Preservation Association (DPA)
c/o Town Hall, Princetown, Yelverton, Devon PL20 082289 288
Hon. Secretary Kate Ashbrook
Aims To preserve the wildness and natural beauty of the Dartmoor landscape and traditional rights of access.
-NR

Department of Agriculture and Fisheries for Scotland (DAFS)
HQ: Chesser House, 500 Gorgie Road, Edinburgh EH11 3AW 031–443 4020
London Office: Dover House, Whitehall, London SW1A 2AU 01–233 3000
Activities Responsible for the promotion of agriculture and the fishing industry in Scotland. On the agricultural side, this includes participation in EEC negotiations on agricultural policy, the provision of technical and financial help to farmers, the supervision of

educational, advisory and research services, the administration of a variety of schemes for the improvement of land, farm stock and crops, the development of crofting and the management of a large area of agricultural land which is in public ownership. As regards fisheries, duties include participation in international arrangements for conservation and other aspects of fishing and in EEC negotiations on fisheries policy, financial support for the fishing industry, assistance for fishery harbours, scientific research and the protection of Scottish fisheries by the Department's fleet of fishery cruisers.

Research, education and advisory services Agricultural Reseach Institutes; commissioning of research; liaison with Agricultural and Food Research Council; Royal Botanic Gardens, Edinburgh; Agricultural Colleges; education; advisory services; development work; secretariat of Scottish Agricultural Development Council. [*Enquiries:* 031–443 4020 ext. 2074]

Scientific Adviser's Unit Advises the Department on research and development programmes undertaken by Scottish Agricultural Reasearch Institutes and Colleges and on the educational and advisory services provided by the Colleges; also has responsibility for liaison with AFRC and MAFF. [*Enquiries:* 031–443 4020 ext. 2080]

Royal Botanic Garden Inverleith Row, Edinburgh EH3 5LR (also Younger Botanic Garden, Benmore; Logan Botanic Garden, Stranraer; and Dawyck Arboretum, Peebles). The Gardens maintain a scientific display of plants for the public; investigate the classification of plants; and operate a training scheme for student horticulturists. [*Enquiries:* 031–552 7171 ext. 206]

Land tenure, land use and forestry; crofting development; emergencies planning (a) Agricultural land tenure; general land use questions; proposals to use agricultural land for non-agricultural development; impact of taxation and rating policies on agriculture; (b) Scottish Office interest in forestry policy; liaison with Forestry Commission, with Nature Conservancy Council (on notification of scientific sites) and with Red Deer Commission; (c) administration of crofting legislation, including grants and loans; livestock improvement schemes for crofters; effect of transport policy on agriculture; (d) emergencies planning. [*Enquiries:* 031–443 4020 ext. (a) 2654; (b) 2602; (c) 2764; (d) 2797]

Crops, plant health, pests and pollution Production and first stage marketing of agricultural and horticultural crops; plant health; control of seeds and planting materials; pest control; pollution. [*Enquiries:* 031–443 4020 ext. 2527]

Livestock products Beef, sheep, pigs, poultry, eggs policy; beef and sheep market support measures; milk and milk products, wool; slaughterhouses and meat hygiene; milk and dairy hygiene. [*Enquiries:* 031–443 4020 ext. 2420]

Agricultural scientific services East Craigs, Edinburgh EH12 8NJ. Scientific executive, consultative and research functions in relation to statutory or regulatory aspects of plant health, the quality of planting materials, pests and the use of pesticides. [*Enquiries:* 031–339 2355]

Agricultural structures and animal health and welfare a) Farm Capital grants; arterial drainage; agricultural credit; b) animal health and welfare. [*Enquiries:* 031–443 4020 ext. a) 2736; b) 2282]

Fisheries I EEC Common Fisheries Policy, with respect particularly to conservation, sharing of resources, access to waters and arrangements with third countries; Law of the Sea matters; pelagic and whitefish quota management; marketing policy and international trade; fisheries harbours. [*Enquiries:* 031–443 4020 ext. 2576]

Fisheries II Salmon and freshwater fisheries; liaison on fish research; marine pollution; fishing and offshore oil; fish and shellfish farming; seals. [*Enquiries:* 031–443 4020 ext. 2185]

Fisheries III Fishing industry structure and financial arrangements; protection and enforcement policy; DAFS fishery protection and research fleet; fisheries economics and statistics unit. [*Enquiries:* 031–443 4020 ext. 2580]

Marine Laboratory PO Box 101, Victoria Road, Aberdeen AB9 8DB. Research into marine fisheries; enviromental pollution; efficiency of fishing gear. [*Enquiries:* 0224 876544]

Freshwater Fisheries Laboratory Faskally, Pitlochry, Tayside PH16 5LB. Studies principally of salmonid fisheries; investigation of the chemical constituents and pollutants in the freshwater environment. [*Enquiries:* 0796 2060]

Department of Agriculture for Northern Ireland
Dundonald House, Upper Newtownards Road, Belfast BT4 3SB 0232 650111

Activities Responsible for the development of the agricultural, forestry and fishing industries in Northern Ireland; the provision of an advisory service for farmers, agricultural research and education; agent of the Ministry of Agriculture, Fisheries and Food in the administration in Northern Ireland of schemes affecting the whole of the UK;

involvement with the application to Northern Ireland of the EEC agricultural policy.

Agricultural Improvement Division   Magnet House, 81–93 York Street, Belfast BT15 1AB. Agricultural and Horticultural Grants Scheme; Agricultural and Horticultural Development Schemes; Northern Ireland Agricultural Development Programme; farm structure; hill livestock compensatory allowances; non-marketing of milk and conversion of dairy herds premium schemes; land use; conservation; planning and pollution; housing on farms; EEC policy in relation to farm structure and capital investment. [*Enquiries:* 0232 224681]

Fisheries Division   Hut 5, Castle Buildings, Stormont, Belfast BT4. Administration of sea and inland fisheries in Northern Ireland. [*Enquiries:* 0232 63939 ext. 2372]

Animal Health Division   Diseases of animals, including eradication of brucellosis and bovine tuberculosis; welfare of animals; animal and poultry importations; Medicines Act; thereapeutic substances; dog control; importation of endangered species. [*Enquiries:* ext.660]

Milk Division   Administration of legislation relating to milk, milk products and milk quotas. [*Enquiries:* ext. 773]

Cereals, Horticulture and Farm Safety Division   Cereals; eggs and poultry; horticulture; plant varieties and seeds; farm safety; pesticides; agricultural credit; bee pest prevention. [*Enquiries:* ext. 493]

Potatoes, Plant Health and Marketing Division   Seed and ware potatoes; plant health; agricultural co-operation; agricultural marketing legislation. [*Enquiries:* ext. 496]

Drainage Division   Hydebank, 4 Hospital Road, Belfast BT8 8JP. Arterial drainage; Lough Neagh levels; water recreation; water management. [*Enquiries:* 0232 647161]

Forest Service   All forest operations in Northern Ireland, including acquisition and planting of land; nursery, arboricultural and advisory work; education and training; recreational and educational uses of forests; wildlife conservation and management. [*Enquiries:* ext. 463]

Agricultural Inspectorate   Advisory, education and training services in agriculture and food technology; development and quality control in food production and marketing; technical services. [*Enquiries:* ext. 604]

Department of Education and Science (DES)
Elizabeth House, York Road, London SE1 7PH 01-928 9222
   Activities   Environmental responsibilities include safety arrangements in the use of toxic chemicals in educational establish-

ments and the non-agricultural uses of pesticides, including domestic use.

Department of Employment (DE)
Caxton House, Tothill Street, London SW1H 9NF 01-213 3000
   Activities   Concerns include the health of workers in relation to noise and air pollution in factories. The Department issues a series of booklets, The Detection of Toxic Substances in Air, each devoted to a specific substance.

Department of Energy (DEn)
Thames House South, Millbank, London SW1P 4QJ 01-211 3000
   Activities   Responsible for the development of national policies in relation to all forms of energy, including energy efficiency and the development of new sources of energy; it is also responsible for the international aspects of energy policy. The Department's responsibilities include the government's relationships with the nationalised energy industries (coal, gas and electricity) as well as the Atomic Energy Authority. It is the sponsoring Department for the nuclear power construction industry and the oil industry. It is responsible for the government interest in the development of the oil and gas resources on the British sector of the Continental Shelf and for the Offshore Supplies Office in its role of developing the ability of UK suppliers to meet the needs of the offshore operators on the UK continental shelf and world wide.

Information Division   01-211 7374

Coal Division   Financial matters relating to the coal industry; supply, distribution and demand for solid fuels; European Coal and Steel Community and other international organisations; imports and exports of solid fuels; environmental matters; opencast coal working; mining subsidence; defence planning and civil emergencies; NCB appointments. [*Enquiries:* 01-211 3197]

Electricity Division   General energy policy and organisational aspects of the electricity supply industry; industrial relations; emergency planning; Board appointments; consumer questions; Code of Practice for payment of electricity bills; international matters; private generation; combined heat and power; consents for power stations and overhead lines. Electricity investment programmes (E&W): financial aspects of the electricity industry; divisional financial interest in nuclear matters. [*Enquiries:* 01-211 5861]

Atomic Energy Division   British Nuclear Fuels plc; Centrifuge enrichment project and policy; uranium procurement policy; energy aspects of Nuclear Installations Act 1965;

relations with Health and Safety Executive; environmental questions; physical security. Overseas aspects of atomic energy policy, including EURATOM, International Atomic Energy Agency, Nuclear Energy Agency and International Energy Agency; nuclear exports; nuclear non-proliferation policy. UK Atomic Energy Authority and the National Nuclear Corporation; nuclear reactor policy and monitoring of programmes; public debate on nuclear energy; nuclear aspects of energy policy. IAEA safeguards policy and implementation in the UK; EURATOM safeguards; safeguards aspects of nuclear trade. [*Enquiries:* 01–211 6248]

Energy Policy Division Nationalised industries policy; policy co-ordination and studies; environmental aspects of energy; international energy policy. [*Enquiries:* 01–211 4991]

Energy Efficiency Office (see separate entry)

Gas Division Financial aspects of the gas industry; consumer issues; DEn interests in gas safety; energy conservation; security; emergency planning; environmental issues, planning and land matters. National gas supply and disposal; gas aspects of energy policy; gas field development programmes; gas gathering projects; international gas issues; gas research and development. [*Enquiries:* 01–211 5028]

Petroleum Engineering Division Exploration; development; projects; environmental aspects; protection of offshore installations; operations and safety inspectorial advisory functions; accident investigations; Pipelines Inspectorate; Diving Inspectorate; research and development related to safety, exploration and exploitation. [*Enquiries:* 01–211 3691]

Oil Division Co-ordination of policy on UK continental shelf development; oil depletion policy; oil field financing; security of onshore terminals; civil liability for offshore oil pollution; abandonment of offshore installations. [*Enquiries:* 01–211 4229] NATO and home defence oil planning; civil contingency planning, including oil emergency aspects of the IEA and EEC; UK oil stocks policy. Disposal of North Sea oil, including policy on participation; supply and marketing in the UK of oil products, including Liquefied Petroleum Gas and other natural gas liquids; UK oil refining and distribution; environmental and quality aspects of oil products; private and government oil pipelines and government oil storage system. [*Enquiries:* 01–211 4459]

Energy Technology Division Electricity, coal and gas supply technologies; environmental aspects of non-nuclear energy sources. Departmental R&D programmes on

technology of geothermal, wind, tidal, solar, biofuels and wave energy sources. Energy R&D strategy and co-ordination; secretariat of the Advisory Council on Research and Development for Fuel and Power (ACORD); international aspects of energy R&D. [*Enquiries:* 01–211 5801]

Department of Energy/An Roinn Fuinnimh (Republic of Ireland)
Clare Street, Dublin 2, Ireland 0001–71 5233
Activities Established in 1980, the Department of Energy has responsibility for national policy in relation to the supply and use of energy in all its forms and to exploration and development of minerals and petroleum.

Department of the Environment (DoE)
2 Marsham Street, London SW1P 3EB
01–212 3434
Activities Responsible for: planning; local government; new towns; housing; construction; inner city matters; environmental protection; water; countryside affairs; sport and recreation; conservation; royal parks and palaces; historic buildings and ancient monuments. The Property Services Agency is responsible for government buildings, land and property holdings and associated supplies and transport services.
Information Enquiries 01–212 4693
Inner Cities Division 1: Economic and employment aspects of inner city programmes and policies; Inner Urban Areas Act; private sector involvement in inner cities; Urban Development Grant. [*Enquiries:* 01–212 8119]

Division 2: Inner city policy; partnership arrangements; programme authorities; traditional urban programme; liaison with voluntary sector. [*Enquiries:* 01–212 4018]

Division 3: Enterprise zones; planning; land and the environmental aspects of inner cities; race apects of DoE responsibilities; garden festivals; research and information. [*Enquiries:* 01–212 8440]

Division 4: Compulsory purchase, land transaction and land compensation policy; registers of under-used public land, derelict land grants. [*Enquiries:* 01–212 8172]

Regional Policy DoE interest in regional affairs; local authority assistance to industry; small firms; rural economic and social problems; Development Commission. [*Enquiries:* 01–212 0310]

Regional Development National and regional land resource structure issues; industrial, energy and infrastructure developments; distribution of populations; regional strategic guidance. [*Enquiries:* 01–212 3666]

New Towns All matters concerning new towns in England, expanding towns, Letchworth Garden City Corporation, London Housing Staff Commission. [*Enquiries:* 01–212 3252]

Greater London Housing Housing for the Greater London Area. [*Enquiries;* 01–212 4350]

Greater London Planning Statutory functions under the Planning Acts and the related legislation applicable to the Greater London area, including Section 36 Planning Appeals; London Docklands Development Corporation. [*Enquiries:* 01–212 3184]

Greater London Professional Planning Professional planning and research, advice on general economic and social matters in Greater London. [*Enquiries:* 01–212 3528]

Policy and Procedures on Development Plans Development plan policies and procedures; Green Belt; housing land availability. [*Enquiries:* 01–212 4019]

Specialist Planning Appeals Tollgate House, Houlton Street, Bristol, Avon BS2 9DJ. Enforcement and Land Compensation Act appeals; purchase notices; planning control of outdoor advertising, advertisement appeals. [*Enquiries:* 0272 218574]

Development Control Development control policies and procedures. [*Enquiries:* 01–212 0798]

Public Inquiry Procedures and Costs Public inquiry procedures and award of costs; liaison with the Council on Tribunals; hazardous development; environmental assessment; Planning Redvelopment Grant; planning legislation. [*Enquiries:* 01–212 8561]

Planning Information and Research Planning practice, information systems and management of Planning Research Programme. [*Enquiries:* 01–212 3129] International work in the planning field, including UN(ECE), OECD and Council of Europe. [*Enquiries:* 01–212 4003]

Minerals Planning Policy, legislation and casework on planning control over mineral working, including guidelines for aggregates working, policy on coal and onshore oil and gas advice to local authorities and mineral operators. [*Enquiries:* 01–212 3521] Professional advice and research management on minerals planning, geology and land reclamation. [*Enquiries:* 01–212 8489]

Cartographic Services Map library; air photos unit; drawing offices. [*Enquiries:* 01–212 4950]

Rural Affairs Tollgate House, Houlton Street, Bristol, Avon BS2 9DJ.
Division 1 (Countryside Division): Countryside conservation policy; Countryside Commission; National Park policy; trees; public paths; access to open country; common land; village greens; allotments; tent and caravan camping. [*Enquiries:* 0272 218178] Planning and research advice related to countryside and coast; recreation; sport; tourism; rural socio-economic and environmental issues. [*Enquiries:* 0272 218159]
Division 2 (Wildlife Divison): Nature and wildlife conservation; Nature Conservancy Council; international trade in endangered species; species conservation, including birds; registration of scheduled birds; licensing under Endangered Species (Import and Export) Act and Wildlife and Countryside Act; habitat protection policy; zoos policy; Dangerous Wild Animals Act; environmental education. [*Enquiries:* 0272 218233]

Waste Disposal Romney House, 43 Marsham Street, London SW1P 3PY. Radioactive Waste (Administration): Policy on radioactive waste management. [*Enquiries:* 01–212 4764] Secretariat, Radioactive Waste Management Advisory Committee. [*Enquiries:* 01–212 5988] Radioactive Waste (Professional): Radioactive waste management planning; research management and co-ordination; international aspects of radioactive waste management; assessment of potential disposal sites. [*Enquiries:* 01–212 8804]
Radiochemical Inspectorate: Inspection of premises and assessment of plant under Radioactive Substances Act 1960. [*Enquiries:* 01–212 8088] Land Wastes: Collection, treatment, disposal and reclamation of domestic, commercial and industrial wastes. [*Enquiries:* 01–212 6216] Technical aspects of household and commercial waste management; research. [*Enquiries:* 01–212 6287] Technical aspects of industrial waste management. [*Enquiries:* 01–212 8666] Hazardous Wastes Inspectorate. [*Enquiries:* 01–212 6086]

Central Directorate of Environmental Protection Romney House, 43 Marsham Street, London SW1P 3PY
Toxic Substances Division: Scientific aspects of domestic and international policy for environmental protection; environmental assessment of toxic substances; liaison with Scientific Counsellors and attachés in the UK and overseas on environmental matters. [*Enquiries:* 01–212 0991] Notification scheme for new chemicals; OECD Chemicals Programme; indoor air quality (including asbestos); contaminated land; toxic metals; co-ordination of UK input to EEC environmental research programme. [*Enquiries:* 01–212 0991]
Policy Planning and Co-ordination Division: Policy planning for pollution control; co-ordination of UK policy on domestic pollution control; liaison with Royal Commission on

Environmental Pollution; planning and pollution; lead pollution; marine pollution. [*Enquiries:* 01–212 8881]
International Division: Co-ordination of DoE interests in EEC business; co-ordination of UK involvement in environmental protection matters in other international bodies, including UN and OECD. [*Enquiries:* 01–212 0140]
Environmental Protection Statistics and Economics: Statistical and economic support to environmental protection divisions; environmental pollution trends and forecasts; liaison with international bodies on environmental statistical and economic issues; pollution control standards and charging policies; financial instruments for pollution control. [*Enquiries:* 01–212 5984]
Air and Noise Division: Domestic smoke control; industrial air pollution; environmental effects of air pollution from all resources; scientific assessment and domestic and international policy; research and monitoring; noise policy; scientific aspects of noise; statutory nuisance and offensive trades; control of dogs. [*Enquiries:* 01–212 0611]

Water Directorate   Romney House, 43 Marsham Street, London SW1P 3PY
Water Administration Division: Organisation and administration of water services in England; Regional Water Authority powers, duties and appointments; affairs of British Waterways Board and Inland Waterways Amenity Advisory Council; inland navigation and water recreation; EEC and Exchequer grants for water supplies and sewerage; coast protection; casework on bills, orders and appeals under Water Acts, Drought Act, Public Health Acts, Drainage of Trade Premises Act and Water Resources Act; safety of reservoirs. [*Enquiries:* 01–212 6871]
Water Technical Division: Water industry operations, including in emergencies; water industry procurement; export promotion; overseas visitors; WHO Fellowships; home defence; water byelaws; sludge disposal policy and research; formulation and administration of DoE water research programme. [*Enquiries:* 01–212 6071]
Water Quality Division: Policy and related legislative, chemical, biological, health and research questions on the quality of water supplies and the quality of rivers, estuaries, coastal and underground waters; policy and legislative questions on sewerage, sewage disposal and sewer adoption; chemical and biological matters on sewage and on trade effluent reception, treatment and disposal; international aspects of all these matters, including negotiation and implementation of EEC directives. [*Enquiries:* 01–212 5778]
Housing and Construction   2 Marsham Street, London SW1P 3EB

Division HB7: Energy conservation; quality in construction/building defects; Housing Design Awards; Homes Insulation Act. [*Enquiries:* 01–212 3508]
Construction Industry   Romney House, 43 Marsham Street, London SW1P 3PY
Building Regulations Division: Policy, preparation and amendment of building regulations; Building Regulations Advisory Committee. [*Enquiries:* 01–212 4040]
Construction Industry Research Unit: Co-ordination of the construction industry directorate's responsibilities for building and construction research in support of health and safety, energy conservation in buildings and sponsorship of the construction industry. [*Enquiries:* 01–212 7631]
Ancient Monuments and Historic Buildings   2 Marsham Street, London SW1P 3EB
Heritage Sponsorship   2 Marsham Street, London SW1P 3EB
Branch 1: Heritage policy; sponsorship of heritage bodies; European and international heritage matters. [*Enquiries:* 01–212 8343]
Branch 2, Lambeth Bridge House, Albert Embankment, London SE1 7SB: Preparation of lists of buildings of special architectural or historic interest. [*Enquiries:* 01–211 7334]
Branch 3, Lambeth Bridge House, Albert Embankment, London SE1 7SB: Scheduled monument and listed building consent casework and policy; conservation areas policy. [*Enquiries:* 01–211 5004]
Environmental Protection Statistics and Economics   Romney House, 43 Marsham Street, London SW1P 3PY. Statistical and economic support to Environmental Protection Divisions; environmental pollution trends and forecasts; macroeconomic implications of environmental policies; water quality, pollution and supply; waterways industry and recreation; air pollution; oil pollution; heavy metals; toxic substances; waste management, collection, disposal, reclamation and recycling; radioactivity; noise; pollution control costs; liaison with international bodies on environmental statistical and economic issues; pollution control standards and charging policies; financial instruments for pollution control. [*Enquiries:* 01–212 5984]
Environmental Science Policy Unit   2 Marsham Street, London SW1P 3EB. Advice on scientific issues; scientific and technical reviews and tasks; research audits; scientific liaison with Cabinet Office and other government departments; briefing for Chief Scientists and DoE representatives on relevant government, international and other committees. [*Enquiries:* 01–212 6958]
Building Research Establishment   Building Research Station, Garston, Watford, Herts.

WD2 7JR 0923 674040 [*see also entries for*
BUILDING RESEARCH ADVISORY SERVICE
and BUILDING RESEARCH ENERGY
CONSERVATION SUPPORT UNIT]

Department of the Environment for Northern Ireland
Stormont, Belfast BT4 3SS 0232 63210
Activities Has direct responsibility for, or
exercises certain controls over, a wide range
of functions. These include: planning; roads;
water; works services; housing and transport policies; collection of Regional and
District rates: mapping of Northern Ireland.
Additional responsibilities include certain
controls over local government, the creation
and management of country parks and the
designation of nature reserves and areas of
outstanding natural beauty, environmental
public health, Clean Air and Alkali Acts, the
listing and preservation of historic buildings,
ancient monuments and an archaeological
survey, conservation and safe-keeping of the
records of government departments.
Conservation Division Conservation,
historic monuments and buildings, environmental services. [*Enquiries:* ext. 2043]
Planning Division Commonwealth House,
Castle Street, Belfast BT1 1GH 0232 221212
Policy and legislation; development plans;
development control; landscape; Preservation Orders; Planning Appeals
Commission; purchase notices; enforcement; major planning applications; land
values.
Roads Service Commonwealth House,
Castle Street, Belfast BT1 1GH 0232 221212
Planning, maintenance and operation of the
road system; street lighting; car parks;
private streets; traffic management.
Water Service Water and sewerage
services, water resources; programmes and
quality control; central design. [*Enquiries:*
ext.2104]
Transport Division Hampden House,
Royal Avenue, Belfast BT1 1FX 0232 221212
Transport policy and legislation, including
airports, buses, railways and shipping;
motor taxation; road safety; vehicle inspection; driving tests; vehicle and driver
licensing; enforcement of Road Transport
Law, Fire Precautions and Fire Service.
Land Registry River House, 48 High Street,
Belfast BT1 2PT 0232 233552

Department of the Environment (Republic of Ireland)
Custom House, Dublin 1, Ireland 0001-74 2961
Activities Responsible for the development of policies in areas such as housing,
roads, water and sewerage services; co-ordinating the implementation of these policies
by local authorities; issuing reports on
environmental policy and pollution control.

Department of Health and Social Security (DHSS)
Alexander Fleming House, Elephant and
Castle, London SE1 6BY 01-407 5522
Activities Responsible in England for the
administration of the National Health
Service; for the social services provided by
local authorities for the elderly and handicapped, socially deprived families and children in care; and for certain aspects of
public health. Throughout Great Britain it is
responsible for the payment of social
security benefits and allied services. The
Department also makes reciprocal social
security and health arrangements with other
countries; represents the UK in the World
Health Organisation and in other international fora; and is responsible for pensions
and welfare services for UK war pensioners
and war widows throughout the world.
Health Services Division Hannibal House,
Elephant & Castle, London SE1 6TE
Branch 1: Hospital scientific and technical
services; hospital pharmaceutical services;
blood transfusion services; laboratory
services; safety; toxicology and chemical
health hazards; cancer services; terminal
care; radiological protection. [*Enquiries:*
01-703 6380 ext. 3536]
Branch 2: Hospital medical and surgical
services; accident and outpatient services;
ambulance services; hospital transport; unorthodox medicine; Standing Medical
Advisory Committee and Standing Nursing
and Midwifery Advisory Committee –
secretariat. [*Enquiries:* 01-703 6380 ext. 3212]
Branch 3: Private practice in NHS hospitals;
private sector of medicine; treatment of
overseas visitors; health services for ethnic
minorities; patient welfare; voluntary work
for health services; linen and laundry
services; catering and domestic services;
use of contractors by NHS. [*Enquiries:* 01-703
6380 ext. 3537]
Branch 4: Alexander Fleming House,
Elephant & Castle, London SE1 6BY: Food
hygiene and safety; rehabilitation and
remedial services; aids for the physically
handicapped. [*Enquiries:* 01-407 5522 ext.
6644]
Community Services Alexander Fleming
House, Elephant & Castle, London SE1 6BY
Branch 1: Local authority social services
(legislation, organisation, development,
manpower); voluntary sector; general social
policy issues. [*Enquiries:* 01-407 5522
ext.6341]
Branch 2: Alcohol misusers; drug and solvent
misusers; the homeless. [*Enquiries:* 01-407
5522 ext. 6960/7265]

Branch 3: a) Elderly people; b) physically disabled people. [*Enquiries:* 01–407 5522 ext. a) 6292, b) 6015]

Medicines Division   Market Towers, 1 Nine Elms Lane, London SW8 5NQ 01–720 2188 Medicines Commission; Committee on Safety of Medicines; Committee on Review of Medicines; Committee on Dental and Surgical Materials; licensing and enforcement; British Pharmacopoeia Commission; implementation of the Medicines Acts 1968 and 1971 and the Biological Standards Act 1975; medicines control and its international aspects.

Medical TEP Toxicology, Environmental health, Prevention) Division   Market Towers, 1 Nine Elms Lane, London SW8 5NQ Toxicity, mutagenesis, carcinogenesis of chemicals in food, consumer products and the environment, including soil, air and water; smoking; toxic waste disposal; hazards from radiation and noise; prevention of ill health; health education; liaison with Health & Safety Executive and other departments. [*Enquiries:* 01–720 2188 ext. 3533] [*see also* COMMITTEE ON CARCINOGENICITY OF CHEMICALS etc.; COMMITTEE ON MEDICAL ASPECTS OF THE CONTAMINATION OF AIR AND SOIL: COMMITTEE ON MUTAGENICITY OF CHEMICALS etc.; COMMITTEE ON SAFETY OF MEDICINES]

Department of Health and Social Services (Northern Ireland)
Dundonald House, Upper Newtownards Road, Belfast BT4 3SF 0232 650111

Activities   Responsible in Northern Ireland for all aspects of the health and personal social services and the administration of the social security schemes.

Health and Personal Social Services
Division A: Community health; general health services; medicines; food control; Social Services Branch. [*Enquiries:* 0232 650111 ext. 359] Planning Division: Long-term development and strategic planning of health and personal social services; central secretariat. [*Enquiries:* ext. 656]

Medical and Allied Services   General hospital services, including laboratory radiology and other scientific and technical services; services for the physically handicapped; orthopaedics; rehabilitation; paramedical services; ambulance services. [*Enquiries:* 0232 650111 ext. 373] Health education and preventive medicine; environmental medicine and communicable disease control; information services and research. [*Enquiries:* 0232 650111 ext. 758) Employment Medical Advisory Service: 0232 245888

Department of Trade and Industry (DTI)
1 Victoria Street, London SW1H 0ET
01–215 7877

Activities   Responsible for: international trade policy; promotion of UK exports and assistance to exporters (under the direction of the British Overseas Trade Board); policy in relation to industry; competition policy and consumer protection, including relations with the Office of Fair Trading and the Monopolies and Mergers Commission and the National Weights and Measures Laboratory; policy on science and technology and research and development matters; standards and designs; support for innovation; administration of the National Physical Laboratory, National Engineering Laboratory, Warren Spring Laboratory and the Laboratory of the Government Chemist; administration of company legislation and the Companies Registration Office; the Insolvency Service; regulation of the insurance industry; regulation of radio frequencies; the Patent Office; the Business Statistics Office.

Regional Policy Division   Kingsgate House, 66–74 Victoria Street, London SW1E 6SJ

Research and Technology Policy Division   Ashdown House, 123 Victoria Street, London SW1E 6RB

Air Division   20 Victoria Street, London SW1H 0NF 01–215 5545 Branch 3: Environmental aspects of aircraft operations; technical aspects of national and international aircraft noise legislation.

DTI Small Firms Information Centres   Free advice and information to small firms, or those about to start up, on finance, tax, planning, importing, exporting, etc.; free publications. [*Enquiries:* contact the Department for regional Freephone numbers] [*see also* LABORATORY OF THE GOVERNMENT CHEMIST; NATIONAL ENGINEERING LABORATORY; NATIONAL PHYSICAL LABORATORY; WARREN SPRING LABORATORY]

Department of Transport (DTp)
2 Marsham Street, London SW1P 3EB
01–212 3434

Activities   Responsible for land, sea and air transport, including sponsorship of the nationalised airline, rail and bus industries; airports; domestic and international civil aviation; shipping and the ports industry; navigational lights, pilotage, HM Coastguard and marine pollution; motorways and trunk roads; oversight of road transport, including vehicle standards, registration and licensing, driver testing and licensing, bus and road freight licensing, regulation of taxis and private hire cars, road safety; oversight of local authorities' transport planning, including payment of Transport Supplementary Grant.

Information Enquiries 01–212 4693

Railways Directorate

Division A: General government/BR relations; matters affecting BR's corporate plan, investment programme and investment appraisal; BR's subsidiary activities, including BREL; rail research; EEC Infrastructure Committee and Regional Development Fund. [*Enquiries:* 01–212 4470]
Division B: Matters affecting BR's Provincial and London & South East sectors; the PSO and level crossing grant; closures; transport consumer matters. [*Enquiries:* 01–212 7947]
Division C: Freight facilities grants; rail aspects of civil emergencies; BR sponsored legislation; light railway orders; BR (and other nationalised industries') land and property; British Transport Police; railway exports liaison; co-ordination of EEC matters affecting railways. [*Enquiries:* 01–212 6530]
Division D: General questions on longer-term railway policy; matters affecting BR's Inter-City, Freight, Parcels and Freightliner businesses; main-line electrification; fares; appointments to the British Railways Board. [*Enquiries:* 01–212 8397]
Railway Inspectorate: Railway safety; inspection of new railway works, level crossings, etc.; investigation of accidents; enforcement of health and safety legislation. [*Enquiries:* 01–212 8132]

Freight and Local Transport Local Transport Division: a) Passenger Transport Executives; plans, guidance, revenue support, effects of abolition and rate capping; shire counties; concessionary and children's bus fares; b) co-ordination of DTp interests in abolition of the GLC and Metropolitan County Councils. [*Enquiries:* a) 01–212 5611, b) 01–212 8460]
Freight Policy and Road Haulage Division: Inland freight policy; lorries and the environment; goods vehicle operator licensing; Transport Tribunal; carriage of dangerous goods (non-radioactive); international road haulage agreements; drivers' hours and tachographs. [*Enquiries:* 01–212 0153] Radioactive Materials Transport Division: UK Competent authority for transport of radioactive materials by all modes. Co-ordination of policy on UK and international legislation; assessment and certification of compliance for package designs and transport operations. [*Enquiries:* 01–212 7249]

Shipping Policy Directorate

Division 1: UK shipping industry, including implications for shipping of economic industrial competition and other government policies; general relations with the GCBS and the maritime unions; departmental interests

in shipbuilding; shipping interest in UN Law of the Sea Convention and other law of the sea issues. [*Enquiries:* 01–212 5468] Policy on legal questions affecting the liabilities of ship owners; policy toward the International Maritime Organisation, including financial matters; International Oil Pollution Compensation Fund Directorate estimates. [*Enquiries:* 01–212 4542]
Division 2, Parliament Square House, 34–36 Parliament Street, London SW1A 2ND: Plans for emergency and wartime use of merchant shipping for defence purposes; advice on the charter, purchase and use of shipping for defence and government purposes; sale of government ships and Department-owned wrecks; security questions concerning shipping; UK role in NATO planning for merchant shipping; war risks insurance; shipping intelligence. [*Enquiries:* 01–233 8889]

Marine and Ports Directorate Sunley House, 90–93 High Holborn, London WC1V 6LP 01–405 6911

Division 2: Pilotage; civil hydrography works in tidal waters; safety of navigation and traffic systems; wreck clearance. [*Enquiries:* ext. 436]
Marine Emergency Operations and Marine Pollution Control Unit: Marine pollution contingency planning; operational control and co-ordination; infringements of anti-pollution regulations; HM Coastguard, Search and Rescue. [*Enquiries:* ext. 378]
Marine Survey Service: Marine survey and examination work, including the setting and enforcement of appropriate standards of construction, equipment and navigation of ships; professional work on marine pollution and hazardous cargoes; inquiries into ship casualties; representation at the International Maritime Organisation. [*Enquiries:* ext. 494]

Road and Vehicle Safety 2 Marsham Street, London SW1P 3EB

Road Safety Division: (a) Planning; legislation; education policy; economic appraisal of safety measures; medical aspects; pedestrian safety; (b) Traffic signs and signals; road speed limits, motorway regulations; safety aspects of highway engineering; rallies and racing on highways; publicity; highway code. [*Enquiries:* (a) 01–212 4143, (b) 01–212 4112]
Vehicle Standards and Engineering Division: Policy and legislation on vehicle safety and environmental standards; vehicle speed limits; vehicle testing requirements. [*Enquiries:* 01–212 3048]

Highway Engineering St Christopher House, Southwark Street, London SE1 0TE

Structure Approvals, Signs and Lighting: Technical approval of structures; Severn Crossing; traffic signals; traffic signs; road lighting. [*Enquiries:* 01–928 7999 ext. 4595]
Bridge Engineering Standards: Standards for

design, construction and maintenance of all highway structures. [*Enquiries:* 01–928 7999 ext. 2506]

Engineering Intelligence: Pavement design and materials; highway data bank and information systems; pavement performance monitoring; geotechnical and drainage aspects; engineering aspects of contract management; quality assurance testing; safety fences; geometric layout design of roads and junctions; traffic flow and capacity standards. [*Enquiries:* 01–928 7999 ext. 4575]

Highway Policy and Programme 2 Marsham Street, London SW1P 3EB

Road Programme and Highways Policy: Trunk road policy planning and management and control of expenditure; progress of trunk road schemes. [*Enquiries:* 01–212 7113]

Assessment Policy and Methods: Highways investment appraisal; traffic, economic and environmental appraisal of trunk road schemes; economic advice on overall programme. [*Enquiries:* 01–212 8365]

Local Roads: (a) Local authority roads, construction and improvements, policy; administration of Transport Supplementary Grant and IDA and specific grants; (b) policy on tolls and application for tolls increases. [*Enquiries:* (a) 01–212 3539, (b) 01–212 7505]

Traffic and Greater London Roads 2 Marsham Street, London SW1P 3EB

Traffic Policy: (a) Urban traffic policy, including traffic regulation, parking control and enforcement; (b) Orange Badge Scheme for disabled drivers; (c) cycling policy, pedestrianisation and walkways; inner urban areas policy; Traffic Advisory Unit; (d) specialist advice on traffic management matters; (e) development and demonstration of provision for cyclists. [*Enquiries:* (a) 01–212 7482, (b) 01–212 5252, (c) 01–212 7470, (d) and (e) 01–212 7942

Greater London Roads and Traffic: Planning, construction and maintenance of trunk road schemes in London; other London highways policies and traffic issues. [*Enquiries:* 01–212 4669]

Civil Aviation Policy Directorate 2 Marsham Street, London SW1P 3EB

Division 5: Policy on reduction at source of aircraft noise and engine emissions; implementation through certification; international discussion on such matters. [*Enquiries:* 01–212 8083] Environmental aspects of civil aviation in the UK. [*Enquiries:* 01–212 8957] Complaints about aircraft noise. [*Enquiries:* 01–212 7068]

Transport Policy Review Unit 2 Marsham Street, London SW1P 3EB

Central policy work on transport; transport

for disabled people. [*Enquiries:* 01–212 5022]

[*see also* ADVISORY COMMITTEE ON THE LANDSCAPE TREATMENT OF TRUNK ROADS: TRANSPORT AND ROAD RESEARCH LABORATORY]

Derbyshire Naturalists' Trust (DNT)
Elvaston Castle Country Park, Derby DE7 3EP 0332 756610

Development Officer N. Brown

Aims To conserve wildlife throughout Derbyshire; to establish nature reserves; to provide advice to individuals, landowners and organisations; to defend threatened species, e.g. the badger, rare plants and animals.

Activities Acquisition and management of nature reserves; carrying out wildlife surveys; maintaining interest in 44 nature reserves covering over 1,000 acres. The Trust has documented over 300 sites of biological importance; it checks on proposals for development and actively opposes plans which threaten areas of wildlife interest. Advice to local authorities, other bodies and private individuals on nature conservation; expanding educational role in schools and colleges; talks, advice on educational reserves, field meetings, surveys, management work. 7 local groups.

Status Voluntary; charity

Publications Ring Ouzel (3) *Derbyshire Dragonflies.*

Derry Anti-Nuclear Group
6 Shipquay Street, Derry BT48 6DN, N. Ireland 0504 61159/61616

Contact Peter McKenzie

Aims To maintain the island as a nuclear-free zone; to educate locally on the dangers of nuclear weapons and to support diversion of military funds to socially useful purposes. -NR

Derwent Valley Protection Society (DVPS)
18 Glamis Crescent, Rowlands Gill, Tyne & Wear NE39 1AT 02074 2377

Hon. Secretary G.K. Wilson

Aims To protect the Derwent Valley from all forms of development or change of use of land, woodland or buildings considered by the Society to be undesirable or intrusive upon the natural landscape and a threat to flora and fauna.

Activities Examining and assessing the need and purpose of any proposed development within the Derwent Valley, whether by private individual or body or local or statutory authority. Assistance and co-operation with other organisations, including local authorities, to protect and enhance the landscape in general, but in particular wood-

lands, hedgerows and all forms of flora and fauna. Encouraging authorities to support these objectives; making representations on any proposals contrary to the Society's aims.
Status Voluntary
-NR

Development Commission (DC)
11 Cowley Street, London SW1P 3NA
01–222 9134
Chief Executive John Williams
Aims To tackle economic and social problems, particularly unemployment, in rural areas of England.
Activities Construction of small factories and workshops, through English Industrial Estates. Technical and management advice, training and loans, through the Council for Small Industries in Rural Areas (CoSIRA) [see separate entry]. Promotion of some local housing schemes; aid to rural communities with services and facilities; support for voluntary organisations which promote local activity; assistance for the conversion of some redundant buildings to light industrial use.
Status Statutory
Publications Rural Focus (6)

Development Education Resource Centre
see SCOTTISH EDUCATION AND ACTION FOR DEVELOPMENT (SEAD)

Development Techniques Ltd
see INTERMEDIATE TECHNOLOGY DEVELOPMENT GROUP (ITDG)

Devon Trust for Nature Conservation
35 New Bridge Street, Exeter, Devon EX4 3AH
0392 79244
Executive Secretary Sally Newton
Aims To protect and cherish the natural environment of Devon.
Activities Management of nature reserves; advice on the management of land for conservation; running educational programmes for adults and children. Headquarters acts as co-ordinator of central, area and reserve committees and local groups. Area committees and local groups organise conservation, fund raising and social activities for members in their area; reserve committees direct the day-to-day running of their reserves. The Trust has a Manpower Services Commission team engaged in habitat mapping, general reserve management and provision of information. The Devon Tree Bank, a scheme to encourage the growing of trees and the restoration of woodlands, is run jointly with the county council. Local branches.
Status Charity

Dharma Therapy Trust
49 Caerau Court Road, Caerau, Cardiff CF5 5JD
0222 598112
Director T. Zangmo
Aims To help build a new society by creating rural communities based on principles of self-sufficiency, ecology, understanding and peace; to promote psycho-physical health through the understanding and practice of complementary therapies and Tibetan medicine.
Activities Meetings in Cardiff and Bristol; counselling, therapy and courses in Tibetan medicine at various venues. Local branches.
Status Charity

District Heating Association (DHA)
see COMBINED HEAT AND POWER ASSOCIATION

Ditchley Foundation
Ditchley Park, Enstone, Oxon. OX7 4ER
060872 346
Director Sir Reginald Hibbert, GCMG
Aims To promote, carry out or advance any charitable objectives, and in particular any branches or aspects of education, likely to be for the common benefit both of British subjects and citizens of the USA.
Activities Organising high-level residential conferences at Ditchley Park to promote the discussion, study and better understanding of matters of common interest to the British and American peoples, with the participation of other nationalities as is judged useful in relation to particular topics. Conference themes are frequently on environment-related issues. Reports of the conferences are published.
Status Non-profit organisation
Publications The Ditchley Newsletter (3)

Domestic Coal Consumers' Council
Gavrelle House, 2 Bunhill Row, London EC1Y 8LL 01–638 8914
-NR

Dorset Naturalists' Trust (DNT)
39 Christchurch Road, Bournemouth, Dorset BH1 3NS 0202 24241
Administrative Officer Mrs M. Pike
Aims To protect the Dorset heritage of wild nature by guiding the forces of change.
Activities Establishing nature reserves and other specially protected and managed areas; collaboration with landowners, farmers and local authorities to preserve the quality and variety of landscape and hence its wildlife; supporting research into conservation problems and carrying out surveys. Education in its broadest sense: a varied programme of meetings, films, excursions and visits to schools. Local branches.

Status Voluntary; charity
Publications DNT Newsletter

Dr Hadwen Trust for Humane Research
46 Kings Road, Hitchin, Herts. SG5 1RD
0462 36819
General Secretary Dr Gill Langley
Aims To promote the development of
humane, non-vivisectionist techniques of
research which do not use living animals, in
order to replace animal experiments and to
further essential biomedical research.
Activities Provides research grants to
scientists working to develop scientific
methods which do not involve living animals;
grants may be used to pursue research,
purchase equipment or prepare written or
filmed material relevant to our aims. Publi-
cises the need for and the potential of
humane research techniques; educates
people, including scientists, by means of a
newsletter, leaflets, articles in national
publications, talks, debates, press releases
and letters to the media. 9 branches.
Status Charity
Publications Alternative News (4); catalogue of mail order goods

Draughtproofing Advisory Association Ltd (DPAA)
PO Box 12, Haslemere, Surrey GU27 3AN 0428
54011
Secretary Gillian A. Allder
Aims To uphold standards, promote
draughtproofing and liaise with government;
to represent the interests of draughtproofing
manufacturers and contractors throughout
the UK.
Status Trade association

Dry Material Cavity Insulation Council
43 Church End, Walkern, Stevenage, Herts.
SG2 7PB 0438 86347
  -NR

Dry Stone Walling Association (DSWA)
c/o YFC Centre, National Agricultural Centre,
Kenilworth, Warwicks. CV8 2LG 0203 56131
Secretary J.D. Murray
Aims To foster the craft of walling by
increasing public knowledge, organising
training and recommending approved
craftsmen.
Activities Advice and help to professional
craftsmen; encouragement of apprentice-
ships; organisation of beginners' courses;
competitions and demonstrations; general
advisory service. 10 local branches.
Status voluntary
Publications Dry Stone Walling Association Newsletter (3)
A Beginner's Guide to Dry Stone Walling
(reprinted 1985)

Dunamis
St James' Church, 197 Piccadilly, London W1V
9LF 01-437 6851
Secretary Nigel Pearce
Aims To create a forum to explore
traditional and alternative approaches to
international security; to examine the psychological, moral and spiritual links between
personal and international security; to look
beyond East and West and build bridges
between the world's rich North and poor
South.
Activities Public lectures and discussions
at St James' Church, many of which are
recorded on cassettes and sold; private
supper/seminars with people in positions of
power and responsibility; publications and
research projects; co-ordination of
ecumenical working parties on The Theology
of Peacemaking; setting up Dunamis groups
around the country; residential workshops on
personal security at the Commonwork
Centre in Kent. Local groups.
Status Educational foundation

Dunters, The (Orkney Environmental Concern Society)
Dyke End, South Ronaldsay, Orkney KW15 2TJ
Contact Ross Flett
Aims To promote and encourage the
protection of the environment in Orkney and
surrounding areas.
Activities Campaigning against the culling
of grey seals; against the proposal to mine
uranium in Orkney; against the proposal to
dump nuclear waste off the coast of Orkney;
and against the proposed Dounreay nuclear
reprocessing plant.
Status Voluntary

Durham County Conservation Trust (DCCT)
52 Old Elvet, Durham DH1 3HN 0385 69797
Administrative Officer Julie Gaman
Aims To promote the conservation of
wildlife and the natural environment in those
parts of the counties of Durham and Tyne &
Wear which lie between the rivers Tyne
and Tees.
Activities Establishing and managing 17
nature reserves, either purchased or
leased; liaising with local authorities and
other organisations and individuals about
habitat protection for other sites; educational
work with schoolchildren and the general
public. Membership of over 2,000, many of
whom are active in fund raising, reserve
management or conservation of certain
groups, e.g. bats, reptiles and amphibians.
Local groups.
Status Voluntary
Publications Durham County Conservation
Trust Bulletin (3)

E

Earth Resources Research (ERR)
258 Pentonville Road, London N1 9JY
01–278 3833
Executive Director David Baldock
Aims To provide thorough, challenging research directly applicable to current policy in the fields of energy, agriculture, transport and wildlife; to disseminate the results to decision makers.
Activities Original research, technical and economic surveys and desk studies; commissioning of outside consultants to prepare reports; providing evidence to parliamentary committees, public inquiries and government bodies; providing back-ground papers and speakers for conferences and seminars; information and advice for voluntary bodies, pressure groups, consumer councils and the media. The results of research projects are usually published.
Status Charitable company
Publications
Timber! an investigation of the UK tropical timber industry. Friends of the Earth, 1985.
Accidents Will Happen . . . an inquiry into the social and economic consequences of a nuclear accident at Sizewell B. 1984.
Alternatives to Factory Farming. 1983.
Energy-Efficient Futures: opening the solar option. 1983.

Earth's Survival Secretariat
see CENTRE FOR ECONOMIC AND ENVIRONMENTAL DEVELOPMENT

Earthlife
37 Bedford Square, London WC1B 3HW
01–631 1790
Director Nigel Tuersley
Aims To improve living quality and social and economic productivity through resource-efficient, environmentally sensitive design and development; to accelerate innovation in mainstream areas of economic activity through pioneering and publicising projects that demonstrate the commercial logic of a socially and environmentally inte-grated approach.
Activities Earthlife's activities embrace both urban and rural contexts, focusing initially on urban renewal (proposals for London's docklands) and tropical forest conservation and sustainable development.
Status International non-profit group headed by registered foundation.
-NR

Earthscan
3 Endsleigh Street, London WC1H 0DD
01–388 9541
Contact John McCormick
Aims To provide a global news and infor-mation service for the world's media and NGOs on development and environment issues.
Activities Twice-weekly news feature service; publication of press briefing docu-ments and paperback books; bi-monthly bulletin for NGOs and broadcasters; convening of press briefing seminars and training workshops; comprehensive photo library. Subject areas include: desertification; energy; acid pollution; human settlements; wild genetic resources; environment and conflict; appropriate technology; wetlands; nuclear winter. Branches in Paris and Wash-ington DC.
Status NGO operated by the International Institute for Environment and Development (IIED)
Publications Earthscan Bulletin (6)

East Anglian Alliance Against Nuclear Power (EAANP)
2 St Helens Street, Ipswich, Suffolk IP4 1HJ
0473 214308
Secretary Roy Thompson
Aims To oppose nuclear power, particu-larly throughout East Anglia; to promote safe, sensible energy policies; to raise public awareness on the energy debate.
Activities Submitted evidence to the public inquiry into the proposal to site a Press-urised Water Reactor at Sizewell. Talks to schools, community groups, etc.; production of leaflets and books and a newsletter.
Status Voluntary
Publications Sizewell Reactions

East Malling Research Station
see COMMONWEALTH BUREAU OF HORTI-CULTURE AND PLANTATION CROPS

East-West Peace People (EWPP)
3 Hinchinbrook House, Greville Road, London NW6 5UP 01–328 3709
Secretary Peter Cadogan
Aims As set out in the Peace Charter 1978: the settling of international differences by negotiation; the renunciation of war by popular action; the essential complemen-tarity of peace and human rights across all frontiers; ending the official arms trade.

Activities   Feeding internationalist ideas, information and contacts into the wider peace movement; initiating and supporting international projects and activities; hosting visitors from overseas; propagating the Peace Charter in many languages; producing the newsletter, leaflets and press information. Involved with the National Peace Council, the Human Rights Network and European Nuclear Disarmament (END).

Status   Voluntary

Publications   East-West Peace People Newsletter (3/4)

ECD Partnership, The (ECD)
[Formerly Energy Conscious Design]
11–15 Emerald Street, London WC1N 3QL
01–405 3121

Contact   David Turrent (Partner)

Aims   To combine the highest standards in building design with efficient and cost-effective energy saving measures.

Activities   ECD is a multi-disciplinary practice offering a range of professional services, including architecture, energy consultancy and mechanical and electrical engineering; clients include government departments, local authorities, housing associations and private organisations. From 1980 to 1984 we were also involved in co-ordinating a major programme of solar energy research and development for the Commission of the European Communities.

Status   Professional partnership

Publications   Turrent, D. & Baker, N., *Solar Thermal Energy for Europe: an assessment study*, Reidel.

ECO Communications
16 Stanley Gardens, London W11 2NE
01–221 2153

Managing Director   Thomas Schultze-Westrum

Aims   To promote and increase awareness of the need for conservation and the need to balance its aims with the requirements of local people; to encourage the integration and maintenance of traditional skills and new technology for sustainable development.

Activities   Making television documentaries on ecology and traditional lifestyles in Europe and in developing countries.

Status   Film production company

Ecoculture
16 Stanley Gardens, London W11 2NE
01–221 2153

Contact   The Co-ordinator

Aims   To ensure that conservation and development policies benefit indigenous people and make use of those aspects of traditional land use and management which

are ecologically sound. Set up by IUCN in 1981.
-NR

Ecological Life Style Ltd
see ENVIRONMENTAL BUILDING DEVELOPMENTS LTD

Ecological Parks Trust (EPT)
c/o Linnean Society, Burlington House, Piccadilly, London W1V 0LQ 01–734 5170

Director   E. Willoughby Ward

Aims   To advance the education of the public in, and to further knowledge of, the ecology of urban areas; to develop, conserve, protect and restore the natural resources and animal and plant life of such areas.

Activities   Establishment and maintenance of demonstration ecology/nature parks; environmental education on own sites and training and advice to teachers using similar sites; research into urban ecology and production of advisory publications; advice to other voluntary groups on the establishment and maintenance of sites. 5 ecological/nature parks.

Status   Voluntary; charity

Publications   Annual Report
New Life for Old Space
Natural History Teaching Resources

Ecological Physics Research Group
Cranfield Institute of Technology, Cranfield, Bedford MK43 0AL 0234 750993

Director   Prof. G.W. Schaefer

Aims   To integrate physics and zoology, within research contracts and postgraduate studies, in order to achieve a deeper understanding of the natural processes occurring in major ecological problems, for the benefit of man and nature.

Activities   Consultancies to governement environmental bodies with regard to crop protection on several continents (agricultural, riverain, cotton, forestry); the physics of crop spraying with chemicals and biologicals; quantified population dynamics of crop 'pests' and natural enemies; remote sensing of insect migration by radar and infra-red; the structure of atmospheric turbulence; natural aerodynamics (wind, insect, bird). Research papers and journals.

Status   Research institute department
-NR

Ecological Research Consultants (ERC)
Binswood Croft, Binswood End, Harbury, Leamington Spa, Warwicks. CV33 9LN
0926 613273

Principal   Dr A. Tasker

Aims   To provide consultancy advice on all aspects of ecology: land management, pollution monitoring, wildlife conservation, land reclamation, fish farming, forestry, environmental impact assessment.

Activities We have facilities for chemical analysis of soil and water, for field surveys and for accurate identification of plants and animals. The most appropriate methods are integrated into a programme tailored to the client's needs.

Status Private company

Ecology Building Society
43 Main Street, Cross Hills, Keighley, W. Yorks. BD20 8TT 0535 35933

Aims To make loans secured on property, in order to promote the saving of non-renewable resources, the promotion of self-sufficiency in individuals or communities and the most ecologically efficient use of land.

Activities Loans on ecological properties or on other properties to finance ecological activities. Mortgages to date include smallholdings, small workshops, sound inner city housing and a village shop.

Status Registered under the Building Societies Act 1962

Ecology Party (The Green Party of the UK)
36–38 Clapham Road, London SW9 0JQ
01–735 2485

Press & Campaigns Director Tony Jones
Office Manager John Bishop

Aims To campaign as a democratic political party whose policies are based on the principle that people must live in harmony with nature within the limitations of the Earth's finite supply of resources.

Activities Fighting elections at local, national and European level; campaigning on environmental, peace and economic issues; raising public consciousness of 'green politics' and the need for a sustainable, no-growth economy. 257 branches throughout the UK (as at 11.04.85).

Status Political party

Publications Econews (4)
Towards a Green Europe (European Election Manifesto 1984).
Politics for Life (General Election Manifesto 1983).

Ecoman Trust
The Bothy & Forge, Ightham Court, Ightham, Sevenoaks, Kent TN15 9JF

Activities Research and education in ecology.
-NR

Economic and Social Research Council (ESRC)
[Formerly the Social Science Research Council]
1 Temple Avenue, London EC4Y 0BD
01–353 5252

Director of Information David Wainwright (ext. 208)

Aims To encourage and support research in the social sciences; to provide and operate services for common use in carrying on such research; to make grants to students for postgraduate training in the social sciences; and to provide advice and disseminate knowledge on the social sciences.

Activities The Council fulfils this remit by research in its own research units in universities and by supporting other research centres; by providing funds for research programmes and projects conducted by academics in British universities, polytechnics and recognised research institutes; by identifying and encouraging research into topics of social and economic concern; and by replenishing the country's stock of well qualified academic minds by funding the research and training of outstanding postgraduate students in the social sciences. The Council has an Environment and Planning Committee which studies land use and planning, housing and residential location, urban and regional development, environmental pollution and conservation and industrial location and infrastructure; the analysis of the effects of development and of economic and technological change on the environment provides a major focus for the Committee's work. A paper on the Committee's research policy and priorities is available free.

Status Research council

Publications ESRC Newsletter (3)
Research Supported by the ESRC (1)
Annual Report

Ecoropa
Crickhowell, Powys NP8 1TA, Wales
0873 810758

Contact Sue Taplin

Aims To alert the wider public to the threats to survival (our own and that of the natural systems on which we depend) and to promote environmentally responsible ways of living; to campaign for institutional and political reforms that encourage liberty, true democracy and self-reliance; to encourage a decentralised and regionalised Europe; to define the characteristics of an ecological society; to emphasise the global dimension of local or national ecological issues; to facilitate the flow of information between 'green' groups in Europe.

Activities Widespread distribution of literature across Europe; campaigns on specific issues; conferences; fund raising.

Status Non-profit-making limited company

Publications Ecoropa Newsletter (2)

Edinburgh School of Agriculture
West Mains Road, Edinburgh EH9 3JG
031–667 1041
Secretary & Treasurer D.S. Land
Aims To sustain a programme of high
quality teaching, advisory, research and
development activity for the promotion of
agricultural and rural development; to
benefit the farming and food industries
locally, nationally and internationally.
Activities Teaching; research and development; advisory work.
Status Statutory
Publications Annual Report

Education for Neighbourhood Change
School of Education, University of Nottingham,
Nottingham NG7 2RD 0602 56101 ext. 2730
Aims To encourage and promote neigh-
bourhood development.
Activities Producing fact banks, feasibility
packs, unemployment materials, planning
packs and schools project packs.
-NR

Effluent and Water Treatment Advisory Committee
This Committee no longer exists

EGIS Environmental Information Service/EGIS Education
North Lodge, Elswick Road Cemetery, Newcastle upon Tyne NE4 8DL
Secretary Monica Frisch (091–413 7972)
(H)
Aims EGIS Environmental Information
Service aims to increase awareness of
environmental issues by collecting, classi-
fying and making available information on
environmental topics. EGIS Education, its
sister organisation, seeks to advance
environmental education.
Activities Maintaining a library of reports
and periodicals on alternative technology,
conservation, ecology, energy, food,
pollution, resources, transport, wildlife and
related subjects; material is obtained from a
wide range of bodies in this country and
abroad. Dealing with written requests for
information on specific topics; callers are
welcome by prior arrangement. EGIS
Education publishes information packages,
slide packs and work cards; to date these
include water pollution, energy resources
and world food prospects.
Status Voluntary; EGIS Education is a registered charity
Publications
*Energy Resources: Britain and the future of
energy supply.* (pack) 1985.

Eigenwelt Studies
4 Market Place West, Morpeth, Northumberland NE61 1HE 0670 57434
Contact Jenny Biancardi
Aims To provide courses in counselling,
groupwork, psychotherapy, psychodrama,
communication and human relations skills
and personal growth and development.
Activities A full programme of short
(mostly 2–day) courses is held throughout the
year on the above topics; students are able
to enroll for a longer programme leading to
a Diploma in counselling or in groupwork.
Some courses are held in the Midlands or
Scotland. Eigenwelt Books (contact David
Brazier) holds a stock of about 500 titles on
body, mind and spirit topics, available for
sale; a mobile bookshop is provided on
courses.
Status Independent training agency
Publications Course programme (2) (free
on request)

Electric Vehicle Association of Great Britain Limited (EVA)
13 Golden Square, Piccadilly, London
W1R 3AG 01–734 7873
Director D.C. Gribble
Aims To promote electric transportation,
primarily battery-powered.
Activities Organising exhibitions and
conferences; publishing.
Status Trade association
Publications Electric Truck and Vehicle
World (3)

Electric Vehicle Development Group Ltd (EVDG)
City University, 10 Northampton Square,
London EC1V 0HB 01–253 2432
Activities Research into all aspects of
development of electric and hybrid
vehicles.
Publications Electric Vehicle
Developments
-NR

Electricity Consumers' Council (ECC)
Brook House, 2–16 Torrington Place, London
WC1E 7LL 01–636 5703
Director Jennifer Kirkpatrick
Aims To represent the interests of electricity consumers in England and Wales at
national level; concerned with a wide range
of issues covering all the activities of the
electricity supply industry and many other
matters that affect users of electricity.
Activities Through its Council and committees, the ECC considers: electricity pricing;
electricity generation; the legal position of
consumers; social policy; consumer information; and energy conservation issues.
The ECC also has a small programme of

commissioned research. It makes representations to government and the electricity supply industry and publishes a wide range of research, information and discussion documents, free consumer leaflets and a newsletter. There are 14 independent statutory Area Electricity Consultative Councils, one for each Area Electricity Board in England, Scotland and Wales.
Status Statutory
Publications Electricity Newsletter (4)
A Guide to Questions of Law and Practice in Relation to Electricity Consumers in England and Wales. 3rd edn, 1984.
Series of 8 Proofs of Evidence to the Sizewell B Power Station Public Inquiry. 1983.

Electricity Council
30 Millbank, London SW1P 4RD 01–834 2333
   Aims To advise the Secretary of State for Energy on questions affecting the electricity supply industry and matters relating thereto; and to provide and assist the maintenance and development by Area Electricity Boards in England and Wales of an efficient, co-ordinated and economical system of electricity supply. The Council consists of a chairman, 2 deputy chairmen and up to 3 other members appointed by the Secretary of State for Energy, together with the chairman of the Central Electricity Generating Board, 2 other members of that Board designated by the Board, and the chairmen of the Area Electricity Boards.
   Activities The Council has power, if so authorised by all the Area Boards in England and Wales, or by any group of them, to perform services for them or act on their behalf in matters of common interest. It is responsible for the general programme of research for the electricity supply industry and is itself empowered to carry out research.
Electricity Council Research Centre: Capenhurst, Chester, Cheshire CH1 6ES 051–339 4181
   Status Statutory
   Publications Annual Report; Statement of accounts and statistics

Electricity Supply Board (Republic of Ireland)
Lower Fitzwilliam Street, Dublin 2, Ireland 0001–76 5831
   -NR

Electronics for Peace (EfP)
Townsend House, Green Lane, Marshfield, Chippenham, Wilts. SN14 8JW 0225 891710
   Co-ordinator Tony Wilson
   Aims To link and support people in computing and electronics who share a common concern about the militarisation of their profession; to promote awareness, provide technical information, co-ordinate action, encourage plans for arms conversion and develop positive, socially appropriate, applications of electronics.
   Activities Providing technical information to the media and peace groups; research with other groups; providing a network and newsletter for members; speaking and debating; peace education; arms conversion; maintaining a jobs/skills register. 12 branches.
   Status Voluntary network
   Publications Electronics for Peace Newsletter (6)
Williams, Tim, *The Ground Launched Cruise Missile: a technical assessment.*

Elms Across Europe
c/o Pitney Bowes plc, The Pinnacles, Harlow, Essex CM19 5BD 0279 37756
   General Secretary Jacqueline Barrett
   Aims To reintroduce the elm into the English countryside (following the loss of over 15 million elm trees in Britain and millions more across Europe) by encouraging industry and commerce to plant new trees specially developed for their resistance to Dutch Elm Disease.
   Activities The scheme was launched by Pitney Bowes in 1979. A Propagation Centre is in operation at the company's premises, growing large numbers of disease-resistant elms which are only available for purchase directly from the company. There are two despatching periods, during the spring and autumn tree planting seasons (March/April and October/November); elms will be despatched by post in any required quantity to anywhere in the UK. An educational pack, which includes a disease-resistant elm and has been specially designed for schools, may also be purchased from the company.
   Status Pitney Bowes is a public limited company

Employment Medical Advisory Service (EMAS)
c/o Health & Safety Executive, St Hugh's House, Stanley Precinct, Bootle, Merseyside L20 3QY 051–951 4381
Scottish Regional Office: Belford House, 59 Belford Road, Edinburgh EH4 3UE 031–225 1313
Welsh Regional Office: 13th Floor, Brunel House, 2 Fitzalan Road, Cardiff CF2 1SH 0222 497777
Northern Ireland: c/o DHSS, Dundonald House, Upper Newtownards Road, Belfast BT4 3SF 0232 245888
   Aims To provide advice to employed or self-employed workers, trade union representatives, employers and medical practitioners on the effects of work on health

and to provide guidance on the placement and return to work of people with health problems; to prevent ill health caused by work; to carry out investigations which help the HSE develop policies for improving occupational health.

Activities Ensuring the regular health supervision of persons working on processes known to be hazardous; carrying out other medical examinations of workers and investigations to help safeguard health at work; giving advice on provision of company or group occupational health services; approving and monitoring the training of workplace first-aiders; giving specialist advice on the medical aspects of fitness for work and occupational rehabilitation; giving specialist advice on the occupational health aspects of poisonous substances, allergic disorders, dust, noise, vibration, ionising radiations and mental stress. EMAS does not provide medical treatment: people are referred to their own doctor or to hospital. EMAS is part of the HSE's Medical Division and has offices in 8 English regions in addition to the above addresses.

Energy Advice Unit
see ENERGY INFORMATION CENTRE

Energy Business Centre
211 Regent Street, London W1R 5DE
01-439 9021
  -NR

Energy Conscious Design
see ECD PARTNERSHIP

Energy Conservation and Solar Centre (ECSC)
99 Midland Road, London NW1 2AH
01-380 1002
  Company Secretary R.P. MacPhail
  Aims To advance public education in energy conservation and to promote the take-up of energy efficiency measures in local authority and private housing.
  Activities Energy audit service for local authorities and private householders; courses in energy efficiency awareness for local authority housing officers, housing associations and tenants' groups; tenants' energy advice service (heating surveys and temperature monitoring for DHSS claims and discussions with local authorities on improved heating and insulation) aimed particularly at low-income groups.
  Status Educational charity

Energy Conservation Group (of the Energy Technology Support Unit)
This group was formed to promote ENCORD (the Energy Conservation Demonstration

Projects Scheme). ENCORD has now been superceded by the Energy Efficiency Demonstration Scheme which is sponsored by the Energy Efficiency Office and managed on its behalf by the Energy Technology Support Unit (ETSU) and the Building Research Energy Conservation Support Unit (BRECSU).

Energy Efficiency Centre
London Building Centre, 26 Store Street, London WC1E 7BS 01-636 3202
  -NR

Energy Efficiency Office (EEO)
Dept of Energy, Thames House South, Millbank, London SW1P 4QJ 01-211 3850
EEO Northern Ireland: Dept of Economic Development, Netherleigh, Massey Avenue, Belfast BT4 2JP 0232 63244
EEO Scotland: Scottish Economic Planning Dept, Energy Division, New St Andrews House, Edinburgh EH1 3TA 031-556 8400
EEO Wales: Welsh Office, Industry Dept, Cathays Park, Cardiff CF1 3NQ 0222 823126
  Directorate 1 (Domestic, Local Authority & Education): Energy efficiency measures in the domestic sector; energy labelling of domestic non-heat appliances; local authority and education sectors; the voluntary sector scheme. [*Enquiries:* 01-211 3845]
  Directorate 2 (Industry & Commerce): Energy efficiency in industry and commerce, general policy campaigns; energy managers movement; training; Regional Energy Efficiency Officers; relations with specific sectors; monitoring and targetting programme; Energy Efficiency Survey Scheme. [*Enquiries:* 01-211 4825]
  Directorate 3 (Technology & Innovation): Energy efficiency technology; research and development; Energy Efficiency Demonstration Scheme; Combined Heat and Power (including district heating); plant efficiency; energy conservation industry. [*Enquiries:* 01-211 4660]
  Directorate 4 (Marketing, Publicity & Promotion): Energy efficiency programme of advertising and publicity campaigns, information and advice directed at all energy consumers. [*Enquiries:* 01-211 7336]
  Directorate 5 (General Policy & Co-ordination): Development of general energy efficiency policy; market advisers; efficiency measures in the public sector and transport; role of nationalised fuel industries; international aspects of energy efficiency; finance. [*Enquiries:* 01-211 6381]

Energy Industries Council
178-202 Great Portland Street, London W1N 6DU 01-637 8841
  Aims To promote the sale of British-made

equipment for the oil and petrochemical industries.
Activities Meetings, exhibitions, export promotion, information. 5 branches in the UK and 1 in Holland.
Status Trade association

Energy Inform
Energy Projects Office, 2nd Floor, Sunlight Chambers, 2–4 Bigg Market, Newcastle upon Tyne NE1 1UW 0632 615677
Co-ordinator Aileen Calligan
Aims To provide consultancy services in the area of domestic energy issues, including energy conservation.
Activities Full consultancy services available covering the production of publicity and promotional work, publications and training in the field of energy use; comprehensive library and audio-visual services, including an extensive slide library.
Status Co-operative company
Publications
The Energy Advice Guide.
Heating Help.
Heating Help in Retirement (published by Age Concern England).
The Heating Action Pack (for the Energy Efficiency Office).

Energy Information Centre
43 Grainger Street, Newcastle upon Tyne NE1 5JE 0632 618428
Information Manager Linda Pickering
Aims To provide a walk-in information service offering help and advice to domestic energy users on ways to reduce fuel bills and increase levels of comfort; also to work with industrial and commercial energy users to improve energy efficiency and generate additional job opportunities.
Activities Exhibitions; comparative advice on heating systems, choice of insulation materials, etc.; register of grants, loans and other assistance; Energy Counselling Scheme for small businesses; seminars and briefing sessions; literature bank. The Centre was established by Newcastle City Council and is supported by the Energy Efficiency Office and the fuel industries.

Energy Research Group (ERG)
[*formerly* Energy Research Support Unit (ERSU)]
Rutherford Appleton Laboratory, Chilton, Didcot, Oxon. OX11 0QX 0235 21900
Head of ERG Prof. N.H. Lipman
Aims To undertake energy research in collaboration with universities and polytechnics and to co-ordinate energy research funded by the Science and Engineering Research Council (SERC) in universities and polytechnics; to provide central research

facilities and to advise SERC on energy strategy.
Activities Current work includes: wind energy studies and experiments, particularly wind/diesel systems; energy storage; measurement of meteorological characteristics at wind turbine sites; computer modelling of wind energy systems.
Status Statutory
Publications Energy News (2)

Energy Research Support Unit (ERSU)
see ENERGY RESEARCH GROUP

Energy Studies Unit
University of Strathclyde, 100 Montrose Street, Glasgow G4 0LZ 041–552 4400 ext. 3307
Activities An interdisciplinary research unit specialising in energy analysis, dynamic modelling and the role of energy in the economy.
-NR

Energy Study Unit (ESU)
Physics Dept, University of Exeter, Stocker Road, Exeter, Devon EX4 4QL 0392 77911 ext. 751
Director Prof. A.F.G. Wyatt
Aims To understand the use of energy in the built environment in order to conserve energy and harness renewable resources.
Activities Solar water heating and passive solar heating of buildings; thermal response of buildings for energy targetting and design; mesoscale meteorology relevant to energy conservation and renewable resources; energy management in local authority buildings; heating plant commissioning; combined heat and power; heat recovery; ventilation in buildings; regional energy supply; publication of reports and papers.
Status Research unit

Energy Systems Trade Association (ESTA)
PO Box 16, Stroud, Glos. GL5 5EB 0453 873568
Status Trade association
-NR

Energy Technology Support Unit (ETSU)
Energy Efficiency Branch, Building 156, AERE Harwell, Didcot, Oxon. OX11 ORA 0235 834621
Head of Branch Dr W.M. Currie
Aims To promote the development and adoption of new or improved technology for the efficient use of energy; through demonstrations, to stimulate £5 per year of energy saving for each £1 spent on the programme.
Activities Management of the Energy Efficiency Office's Demonstration Scheme and a parallel R&D programme; the Demonstration Scheme is normally open only to non-nationalised companies and organis-

ations in industry, commerce and local authorities. Eligible projects must contain innovative features and be economically attractive to other users in order to encourage replication; to this end applicants are required to co-operate fully in the publication and promotion of information in journals, seminars and conferences which the EEO consider is necessary to publicise the particular novel technique which is being demonstrated. The EEO's R&D programme provides financial support for feasibility studies, investigatory work, research and development in new energy efficiency areas which have strong national energy saving and market potential. A Renewables Energy Branch and a Strategic Study Group are also based at ETSU.

Status Statutory

Publications RE News (for Dept of Energy); Demonstration Monitoring Reports; project profiles and R&D reports; Energy Efficiency Series (HMSO)

Energy Users' Research Association (EURA)

PO Box 97, Altrincham, Cheshire WA14 5HT
061–928 3538

Aims To promote all aspects of efficient energy utilisation in commerce and industry.

Activities Information service to members; education and training; research; statistics; energy surveys and plant performance evaluation.

Status Trade association

Publications Engineering Bulletin (12); Management Bulletin (12)
Energy Users' Databook. (pub. Graham & Trotman)
-NR

Energy Workshop

Dept of Physical Sciences, Sunderland Polytechnic, Ryhope Road, Sunderland, Tyne & Wear SR2 7EE 0783 76191 ext. 3

Research Associate Dr N.D. Mortimer

Aims To conduct technical and economic assessments of new energy technologies.

Activities Contract research for national and international agencies; advice and research services to trade unions, campaigning organisations and pressure groups.

Status Academic

Publications

Crowther, S. & Mortimer, N.D. *Social Costs of a Nuclear Power Programme: proof of evidence on behalf of the Town & Country Planning Association at the Sizewell B Public Inquiry.* 1983.

Engineers for Nuclear Disarmament (EngND)

115 Riversdale Road, Highbury, London N5 2SU
01–359 7476

Secretary P.S. Woods

Aims To work for the abolition of nuclear weapons; to awaken the engineering profession and the public to the catastrophic effects of nuclear war; to publicise the diversion of resources from much-needed public works to expenditure on nuclear weapons.

Activities EngND doubts the adequacy of current civil defence programmes and is conducting independent research into the effects of nuclear weapons on engineering structures and systems such as water supplies; the state of the engineering infrastructure is causing concern and we seek to draw attention to the effect of diverting funds to nuclear weapons production. We are also concerned that much of the world faces unnecessary hardship as a result of a lack of engineering infrastructure. Have held several public meetings on these issues and have been in correspondence with our professional bodies. 2 branches.

Status Voluntary

Publications EngND Newsletter (4)

English Heritage (Historic Buildings & Monuments Commission for England)

Fortress House, 23 Savile Row, London
W1X 2HE 01–734 6010

Aims To secure the preservation of ancient monuments and historic buildings situated in England; to promote the preservation and enhancement of the character and appearance of conservation areas; to promote the public's enjoyment of, and advance their knowledge of, ancient monuments and historic buildings and their preservation. The Commission, which assumed its responsibilities on 1 April 1984, replacing the Ancient Monuments Board for England and the Historic Buildings Council for England, consists of 8–17 members appointed by the Secretary of State for the Environment; members are persons with relevant knowledge such as history, archaeology, architecture, preservation of monuments, town and country planning, tourism, commerce, finance and local government; the Commission reports annually to the Secretary of State for the Environment. Education Service: 15 Great Marlborough Street, London W1V 1AF

English Woodlands Ltd

The Old Barn, Roke Lane, Witley, Godalming, Surrey GU8 5NT 04868 2125

Activities Operating a biological control service to eliminate garden pests without resorting to harmful chemicals; supplies

natural enemies (e.g. *Encarsia formosa* for glasshouse whitefly) and biological sprays.
-NR

Environment Centre
[formerly Environmental Resource Centre]
Drummond High School, Cochran Terrace, Edinburgh EH7 4QP 031–557 2135

Co-ordinator Graham White

Aims To promote environmental awareness through education and practical action with schools, youth and community groups; to foster direct action, self-help environmental improvement and conservation in town and countryside.

Activities Publishes a wide range of environmental education packs oriented toward learning by direct experience and investigation; local guides and trails. Acts as a Community Technical Aid Centre which helps community groups plan, design and carry out small-scale environmental improvements.
A practical projects team called Lothian Action works with young unemployed people on projects such as garden creation, the building of substantial play structures and painting of murals. The Centre loans out tools free of charge to schools and community groups.

Status Voluntary

Publications Newsletter (4)
Children's Flower Pack.
Tree Games Pack.
Water of Leith Trails.

Environment Committee (House of Commons)
Committee Office, House of Commons, London SW1A 0AA 01–219 3289/5462

Clerk to the Committee Clive Bennett

Aims To enable the House of Commons to investigate environmental matters of national concern. The Committee consists of MPs from both sides of the House of Commons; it ceases to exist when Parliament is dissolved and is reconstituted following the return of the new Parliament.

Activities In 1984 the Committee's concerns included: the Green Belt and land for housing, and acid rain; it also provided the basis for a private member's bill to close the loopholes in the Wildlife and Countryside Act 1981. Activities in 1985 included: reporting on the operation and effectiveness of Part 2 of the Wildlife and Countryside Act; and conducting an inquiry into radioactive waste, focusing on the options available for storage and disposal. In 1986 activities will include an inquiry into the operation of the planning appeals system, including public inquiries into major development proposals, and an enquiry into historic buildings and ancient monuments.

Publications
Green Belt and Land for Housing (HC 275). 1984.
Acid Rain (HC 446). 1984.
The Problems of Management of Urban Renewal (234). 1984.

Environment Council (Republic of Ireland)
This Council no longer exists

Environment for Hypersensitives (EH)
c/o 5 Kilham, Orton Goldhay, Peterborough, Cambs. PE2 0SU

Secretary/Organiser Rayne Harvey

Aims To assist those who suffer as a result of various forms of pollution found in the air, in food and in buildings.

Activities The first phase is to plan and build a peaceful holiday village in a safe, pollution-free environment; currently still searching for a suitable 20–acre site and funding; disseminating information to members.

Status Voluntary

Environment Foundation O71-
Ibex House, Minories, London EC3N 1HJ

Executive Director/Trustee T.C.M. O'Donovan

Aims To advance knowledge in the field of environmental protection and enhancement through the provision of support for scientific, technical and socio-economic activities for the benefit of society at large.

Activities Sponsoring the Pollution Abatement Technology Award which is promoted by the Confederation of British Industry, the Department of the Environment and the Royal Society of Arts; financing a study by Reading University on silage pollution; sponsoring a book on Symbiotic Technology which is being produced in conjunction with the Conservation Foundation.

Status Charitable trust

Publications Pollution Abatement Technology Award (1)

Environment Information Group
27 Canadian Avenue, Gillingham, Kent ME7 2DW 0634 575981

Activities Providing environmental and anti-nuclear information for the area of Kent, Sussex and Surrey.
-NR

Environment Resource
c/o School of Creative Arts & Design, Leeds Polytechnic, Calverley Street, Leeds, W. Yorks. LS1 3HE
-NR

Environmental Analysis Ltd
Commercial Road, Bromborough, Wirral,
Cheshire L62 3PF 051–334 2643
-NR

Environmental Building Developments Ltd (EBD)
[*formerly* Ecological Life Style Ltd]
Tirmorgan, Pontyberem, Dyfed SA15 4HP,
Wales 0269 871014
Secretary David Stephens
Aims To develop techniques and to market products for reducing energy and resource consumption of buildings; to create ecological villages designed to conserve resources in every way.
Activities Constructing solar heated housing; installing energy-saving equipment in housing; developing an ecological village; developing Tirmorgan Farm on permaculture principles, in association with Lifestyle 2000 Ltd. Information and news about EBD's activities is published in Practical Alternatives journal.
Status Private company limited by shares.

Environmental Communicators' Organisation (ECOjournalists)
8 Hooks Cross, Watton-at-Stone, Hertford,
Herts. SG14 3RY 0920 830527
Chairman Alan Massam
Aims To spread information about world ecological problems among professional journalists and broadcasters.
Activities Pursuing the above aims through telephone contact.
Status Voluntary
Publications Newsletter (occasional)

Environmental Conservation and Development Group
Dept of Environmental Science, University of Stirling, Stirling, Central FK9 4LA, Scotland 0786 73171 ext. 2262
Convenor P.H. Selman
Aims To promote the principles of the Conservation and Development Programme for the UK (response to the World Conservation Strategy) amongst town planners and those involved in the planning process.
Activities Regular meetings on topics related to the CDP; co-ordination of working groups on key issues, e.g. urban fringe, integrated rural development, etc.
Status Voluntary

Environmental Consortium
31 Clerkenwell Close, London EC1R 0AT
01–251 4818
Activities Identification and investigation of environmental problems; providing and implementing workable answers to these problems. Works in temporary association with amenity groups, local and national authorities, private business, artists, scientists, sociologists, etc.
-NR

Environmental Data Services Ltd (ENDS)
Unit 24, 40 Bowling Green Lane, London EC1R 0BJ 01–278 4745/7624
Aims To provide accurate, unbiased, authoritative information on the impact of industrial and commercial activities on the environment.
Activities ENDS is an independent research and information centre providing a service for management. Industry and company reports review the environmental problems facing the business community and report in detail on the policies, programmes and projects adopted in response. Central interests are energy management, resource conservation and waste management.
Status Commercial consultants
Publications ENDS Report (12)
-NR -L

Environmental Education Advisers' Association (EEAA)
Pendower Hall Teachers' Centre, West Road, Newcastle upon Tyne NE15 6PP 091–274 3620
Secretary Cliff Winlow
-NR

Environmental Forum (ENFORM)
12A Ennis Road, London N4 3HD 01–263 8505
Director/Hon. President Criton Tomazos
Aims To increase individual awareness on all environmental issues; to create new possibilities in a multi-racial, multi-ethnic society of participatory involvement in different inter-related socio-cultural activities and to promote new ideas on the subject; to make effective change possible.
Activities Lectures, open discussions, poetry and play readings, art exhibitions; research; publication of texts from lectures and poetry collections; participation in public forums and open forums on environmental and cultural issues; creating international contacts; creating links with similar organisations.
Status Voluntary
Publications Environmental Forum Magazine

Environmental Information Centre
182 Mansfield Road, Nottingham NG1 3HW
0602 582561
Secretary P. Smith
Aims To inform people of every facet of the environmental movement; to bring together people and ideas; to publicise campaigns, both local and national, and

generally to be an information and resource centre.

Activities Provides a library and research facilities and houses various local groups; runs a number of projects, including a self-help bicycle workshop, recycling schemes and home insulation. Trades in ecologically sound goods (e.g. recycled paper) under the name Earthwise and is itself a project of Environmental Factshop Ltd.

Status Educational charity

Publications Earthwise Magazine (4) (jointly with Nottingham FoE)

Environmental Institute
Greaves School, Bolton Road, Swinton, Manchester M27 2UX 061–736 5843 ext. 235
Deputy Director Dr M. Pugh Thomas
Aims To promote and provide facilities for the study of the man-made and natural environment.
Activities Postgraduate degree courses and diplomas; research; seminars; conferences; maintaining an environmental library; publishing a journal. Houses the North West Civic Trust.
Status Institute of the University of Salford
Publications Journal of Environmental Education and Information (4)

Environmental Resource Centre
see ENVIRONMENT CENTRE

Environmental Resources Limited (ERL)
106 Gloucester Place, London W1H 3DB
01–486 1211
Managing Director Dr. Robin Bidwell
Status Commercial consultants
Publications Perspectives

Environmental Trust
31 Clerkenwell Close, London EC1R 0AT
01–251 4818
-NR

ERA Technology Ltd
Cleeve Road, Leatherhead, Surrey KT22 7SA
0372 374151
Activities An independent contract research and development organisation offering services in initial planning for the use of wind turbine generators, site selection, wind measurement, machine selection, testing and evaluation, design of electrical systems, network integration and analysis and market and economic assessments.
Status Commercial

Essex Naturalists' Trust Ltd
Fingringhoe Wick Nature Reserve, South Green Road, Fingringhoe, Colchester, Essex CO5 7DN 020628 678
Secretary Miss V.G. Beckett

Aims To conserve Essex wildlife by establishing nature reserves; to oppose or comment on measures which would adversely affect wildlife, such as building development and land drainage; to educate the general public and children on the need for wildlife conservation.
Activities The Trust has established 60 nature reserves, 27 of which it owns; these are maintained by locally recruited conservation workers. Planning applications and other proposals are monitored and, where necessary, opposed. The Trust maintains a public display centre and nature trails at its Fingringhoe Wick reserve; frequently mounts displays and open days at its other reserves; and provides speakers on conservation topics. Local branches.
Status Voluntary; charity
Publications Watch Over Essex (2)

Esso Petroleum Company
Esso House, 94–98 Victoria Street, London SW1E 5JW 01–834 6677
-NR

Estuarine and Brackish-Water Sciences Association (EBSA)
Dept of Zoology, University of Cambridge, Downing Street, Cambridge CB2 3EJ
0223 358717 ext. 506
General Secretary Dr R.S.K. Barnes
Aims To promote the production and dissemination of scientific knowledge and understanding concerning estuaries and other brackish waters.
Activities Meetings, symposia, workshops and training courses; publication of bulletin and journal; production of handbooks of methodology and organismal identification and of symposium volumes.
Status Learned society; charity
Publications Estuarine, Coastal and Shelf Science (12); Bulletin (3)

Eurisol-UK (Association of British Manufacturers of Mineral Insulating Fibres)
St Paul's House, Edison Road, Bromley, Kent BR2 0EP 01–466 6719
Director General Ian Knight
Aims To further the cause of energy conservation by promoting improvement of thermal insulation standards.
Activities Making available the technical expertise of the mineral insulating fibre industry through publications, seminars and Insulation Fact Sheets.
Status Trade association

European Atomic Forum (FORATOM)
1 St Alban's Street, London SW1Y 4SL
01–930 6888/9
Secretary-General J.T. Corner

Aims To group together the national atomic forums of 14 European countries for the purpose of promoting the peaceful development of nuclear energy.
Publications Status Report on Nuclear Power in Western Europe (1)

European Foundation for the Improvement of Living and Working Conditions
Loughlinstown House, Shankill, Co. Dublin, Ireland 0001–82 6888
Director Clive Purkiss
Aims To contribute to the planning and establishment of better living and working conditions through action designed to increase and disseminate knowledge.
Activities The Foundation is a European Community institute which contracts out research and publishes the findings. It also compiles bibliographies on the themes of its work programme and, where possible, provides information in response to demands; it produces numerous research reports on such topics as shiftwork, work organisation, new technology, work/leisure time, transport and commuting, physical and psychological stress, etc.
Status Statutory
Publications Annual Report; Annual Programme of Work

European Nuclear Disarmament (END)
11 Goodwin Street, London N4 3HQ 01–272 9092
Organising Secretary Fiona Weir
Aims To achieve a nuclear-free Europe and the dissolution of the two great power alliances; to defend the right of all citizens, East and West, to take part in this common movement and to engage in every kind of exchange, to work for disarmament and detente 'from below'.

Activities Campaigning mainly by means of meetings, conferences, dayschools, publications and sometimes vigils; arranging exchanges of speakers; encouraging British participation in other European peace movement events and co-operating closely with like-minded movements throughout Europe, East and West. Regional groups.
Status Voluntary
Publications END Journal (6); END Churches Register (4)

European Proliferation Information Centre (EPIC)
258 Pentonville Road, London N1 9JY
Contact R.V. Hesketh or David Lowry
-NR

Exmoor National Park Authority
Exmoor House, Dulverton, Somerset TA22 9HL 0398 23665
National Park Officer Dr L.F. Curtis
Aims To conserve and enhance the natural beauty and amenity of the National Park and to promote its enjoyment by the public; to prepare National Park plans and to review such plans at intervals of not more than 5 years. The NPA has 21 members, including 7 appointed by the Secretary of State for the Environment, 8 by Somerset County Council, 4 by Devon County Council and 2 by district councils.
-NR

External Wall Insulation Association (EWIA)
PO Box 12, Haslemere, Surrey GU27 3AN 0428 54011
Secretary Gillian A. Allder
Aims To promote external wall insulation, uphold standards of practice and liaise with government.
Status Trade association

F

Fachongle Isaf
see CENTRE FOR LIVING

Faculty of Herbal Medicine
Villa Merlynn, 18 Elgin Road, Talbot Woods,
Bournemouth, Dorset BH4 9NL 0202 769297
Secretary James Hewlett-Parsons
Activities Offers complete training to the
qualifying standard for admission to the
General Council and Register of Consultant
Herbalists and the British Herbalists' Union.
Status Company limited by guarantee
Publications Prospectus

Faculty of Homoeopathy
Royal London Homoeopathic Hospital,
Great Ormond Street, London WC1N 3HR
01–837 3091
[Scottish Faculty of Homoeopathy, 1000 Great
Western Road, Glasgow G12 0NR]
Aims To advance the principles and prac-
tice of homoeopathy.
Activities Biennial conference; meetings;
education and training; examinations;
research; study groups; information; library.
Publications British Homoeopathic Journal
(4)

Falconaide
Slackwood Farm House, Silverdale, Carnforth,
Lancs. LA5 0UF 0524 701353
Chairman Allan Oswald
Aims To promote the care and conservation of birds of prey and their environment; to educate the general public to an
awareness of and respect for such birds.
Activities Maintaining and operating a
hospital and care facility for injured birds of
prey; ensuring that birds of prey in need of
care and attention are looked after by suitably qualified persons with proper facilities
and then, if capable of fending for themselves, returned to the wild in a manner that
as far as possible ensures their survival.
Lectures on the history of falconry and
conservation of birds of prey; displays at
fetes, etc. Concerned with improving
existing legislation and above all pressing
for the introduction of a possession licence
scheme for all birds of prey.
Status Voluntary

Families Against the Bomb (FAB)
124A North View Road, Hornsey,
London N8 7LP
-NR

Farm and Food Society (FAFS)
4 Willifield Way, London NW11 7XT
01–455 0634
Hon. Secretary Joanne Bower
Aims To promote farming methods that are
humane to animals, wholesome for consumers
and fair to farmers, involving sustainable
methods on ecological principles.
Activities Producing a newsletter
reporting the latest developments in agriculture and related subjects; pressing the
government for improved livestock welfare,
a national food policy and a fair deal for
farmers not involved in agribusiness, and
also for development of farming benign to
the environment. Annual General Meeting
at which a speaker gives a lecture on livestock, nutrition or farming. FAFS is an
educational and pressure group affiliated to
the International Federation of Organic
Agriculture Movements (IFOAM); it is
represented on the British Organic Standards Committee and other bodies, including
specialist committees of the Farm Animal
Welfare Co-ordinating Executive and the
National Council of Women.
Status Voluntary NGO
Publications Farm and Food Society
Newsletter (3)
*The Long Way Ahead: new concepts of
agriculture.*

Farm Animal Care Trust
34 Holland Park Road, Kensington,
London W14 8LZ 01–602 3164
Contact Mrs R. Harrison
-NR

**Farm Animal Welfare Co-ordinating
Executive**
Dolphin House, Charlton Park Gate, Chel-
tenham, Glos. GL53 9DJ
-NR

Farm Animal Welfare Council (FAWC)
Government Buildings, Hook Rise South,
Tolworth, Surbiton, Surrey KT6 7NF
01–337 6611 ext.435
Secretary Miss A. Dennis
Aims To keep under review the welfare of
farm animals on agricultural land, at markets,
in transit and at the place of slaughter and to
advise Agriculture Ministers of any legislative or other changes that it considers
necessary.
Activities Drafting and revision of Welfare

Codes for all farm species; consideration of proposals for regulations under the provisions of Section 2 of the Agriculture (Miscellaneous Provisions) Act 1969: reviews of welfare of livestock (including poultry) at slaughter; reviews of welfare of farmed deer and of livestock at markets; consideration of research and development programmes relating to the welfare of farm animals; advising on legislative proposals and codes of practice relating to the transit of livestock.
Status Independent advisory body appointed by Agriculture Ministers

Farmers for a Nuclear-Free Future (FFANFF)
Lower Westcott Farm, Doccombe, Moretonhampstead, Devon TQ13 8SU
0647 40323
Chairman Brendan Butler
Aims To create an awareness in the farming community of the vital importance of the role that farmers would be expected to play after the holocaust.
Activities Publication of well researched guides to the effects on agriculture of a nuclear disaster; distribution of the video 'Nuclear Harvest' outlining the above in visual format; lectures.
Status Voluntary (independent, nonpolitical)
Publications *Would Farming Survive a Nuclear Disaster?* 1984.

Farming and Wildlife Advisory Group (FWAG)
The Lodge, Sandy, Beds. SG19 2DL 0767 80551
Adviser E.S. Carter
Aims To identify the problems of reconciling the needs of modern farming with the conservation of nature and the landscape which supports it; to explore areas of compromise and to disseminate the results as widely as possible.
Activities Publicity, promotion, conferences, practical demonstrations and any other means of stimulating understanding between farming and conservation interests; providing a forum for informal liaison and exchange of ideas, information and experience; advice on wildlife conservation integrated with practical farming; collection, exchange and dissemination of information on research, experience and techniques relating to wildlife conservation on farmland. County groups.
Status Voluntary

Farming and Wildlife Trust (FWT)
The Lodge, Sandy, Beds. SG19 2DL 0767 80551
Director W.H.F. Dawson
Aims To promote conservation of landscape and wildlife in relation to modern agriculture; in particular, to promote and support the Farming and Wildlife Advisory Groups throughout the country.
Activities Through the appointment of Farm Conservation Advisers on a county basis, providing practical on-farm advice to farmers and landowners on landscape and wildlife conservation and the integration of conservation and agriculture on a whole farm basis.
Status Company limited by guarantee; charity

Fauna and Flora Preservation Society (FFPS)
c/o Zoological Society of London, Regent's Park, London NW1 4RY 01–586 0872
Executive Secretary John A. Burton
Aims To ensure the international conservation of wild animals and plants, especially those that are considered endangered or threatened.
Activities Interesting the public and decision makers in the safeguarding and conservation of wild animals and plants in their natural conditions; promoting the establishment and proper management of National Parks and reserves and the enforcement of laws for the protection and conservation of wild animals and plants; establishing relations with societies throughout the world having similar interests; and, for the purposes of the above, promoting and undertaking publications, especially *Oryx* magazine; meetings, exhibitions, symposia and other informative activities. 3 branches in the UK, 1 in the USA.
Status Charity
Publications Oryx (4)
Bat News (4)

Federation of British Craft Societies
8 High Street, Ditchling, E. Sussex BN6 8TA
Aims To represent and protect the wellbeing of the craft movement.
Activities Meetings; research; exhibitions; information.
Publications Newsletter (4)
-NR

Federation of Energy Co-ops
Energy Conservation and Solar Centre, 99 Midland Road, London NW1 2AH 01–380 1002
-NR

Federation of Environmental Trade Associations (FETA)
Unit 3, Phoenix House, Phoenix Way, Heston, London TW5 9ND 01–897 2848
Aims Common action concerning environmental activities.
-NR

Feline Advisory Bureau & Central Fund for Feline Studies

350 Upper Richmond Road, Putney, London SW15 6TH 01–789 9553

Hon. Secretary Julia May

Aims To promote humane behaviour toward the cat; to establish funds to promote investigations into feline diseases.

Activities Conferences and meetings; research; information and production of leaflets.

Publications Bulletin (4)

Fellowship of Cycling Old-Timers

2 Westwood Road, Marlow, Bucks. SL7 2AT 06284 3235

Hon. Secretary Jim Shaw

Aims To enable all cyclists to keep in touch with one another and the world of cycling even if their days of active cycling are over.

Activities Production of the magazine which consists mainly of members' contributions; annual luncheon and meeting.

Status Voluntary network

Publications Fellowship News (4)
-NR

Fellowship Party

141 Woolacombe Road, Blackheath, London SE3 8QP 01–856 6249

Activities Formed in 1955 to oppose military conscription and the manufacture of atomic bombs. Was the first British group to start a petition against atomic weapons testing. Its philosophy goes beyond pacifism to common ownership, decentralisation and alternative forms of energy.
-NR

Feminists Against Nuclear Power

This organisation no longer exists

Field Studies Council (FSC)

Preston Montford, Montford Bridge, Shrewsbury, Shropshire SY4 1HW 0743 850674

Education Officer Paul Croft

Aims To increase environmental understanding for all.

Activities Courses in biology, geography, geology, natural history, art, archaeology, etc. for people of all ages. Studies the ecological effects of marine pollution, particularly in tidal areas. 10 field centres, 9 of which are residential.

Status Company limited by guarantee; charity

Publications Field Studies (1); programme of courses (1)

Findhorn Foundation

The Park, Forres, Grampian IV36 0TZ, Scotland 0309 30311

Aims To foster a deeper understanding of our relationship to nature and society through spiritually-oriented educational programmes and work projects.

Activities Educational and practical projects, including all aspects of horticulture, building and maintaining community, the arts, inter-personal relations and philosophy. Residential and guest facilities.

Status Voluntary; charity

Publications One Earth Magazine (6)

Fisheries Society of the British Isles (FSBI)

Marine Biology Unit, CEGB, Fawley, Southampton, Hants. SO4 1TW

Hon. Secretary Dr A.W.H. Turnpenny

Aims To further knowledge of all aspects of fish and fisheries science.

Activities Sponsoring national and international scientific meetings; publishing the journal. International society.

Status Voluntary

Publications Journal of Fish Biology (12); Newsletter (3)

Food Additives and Contaminants Committee

This committee was merged with the Food Standards Committee on 1.11.83 to form the FOOD ADVISORY COMMITTEE

Food Advisory Committee (FAC)

Ministry of Agriculture, Fisheries & Food, Great Westminster House, Horseferry Road, London SW1P 2AE 01–216 6113

Aims To advise the Minister of Agriculture, the Secretary of State for Social Services, the Secretaries of State for Scotland and Wales and the Head of the Department of Health and Social Services for Northern Ireland on matters referred to it by Ministers relating to: the composition, labelling and advertising of food; additives, contaminants and other substances which are or may be present in food or used in its preparation, with particular reference to the Food and Drugs Act 1955 and corresponding legislation in Scotland and Northern Ireland. The Committee consists of a chairman and 14 other members appointed by appropriate Ministers in a personal capacity on the basis of individual expertise, with an industry, enforcement, academic or consumer background.

Food and Energy Research Centre

Evesham Road, Cleeve Prior, Evesham, Worcs. WR11 5JX
-NR

Food Education Society (FES)

160 Piccadilly, London W1 0NQ 0223 248825/ 0223 44014 ext.465

Chairman & Secretary Dr Alan N. Howard

Aims To raise the standard of national health and reduction of preventable disease by promoting knowledge in the choice and preparation of food and the relationship between food quality and human health.
Activities Conferences; research; information.
-NR

Food from Britain
[incorporating the Central Council for Agricultural & Horticultural Co-operation]
301–344 Market Towers, New Covent Garden Market, Nine Elms Lane, London SW8 5NQ
01–720 2144
Aims To identify marketing opportunities for British food and drink in the home and overseas markets; to encourage producers and manufacturers to meet those opportunities with produce of the appropriate quality and grade; to increase the amount of home-produced food and drink consumed in the UK; to increase the amount of British food and drink we export; to improve agricultural and horticultural marketing in the co-operative sector; over-all, to change how British food and drink is perceived. The Council, which is constituted for the whole of the UK, consists of a chairman and 13 members appointed by the Agriculture Ministers for their expertise in food and agricultural marketing – not directly representing sectors of the industry. Within the Council are 2 Boards; the British Food Board, dealing with the marketing and promotion of British food; and the Co-operative Development Board, incorporating the work of the CCAHC, including the administration of grants under the Agricultural and Horticultural Scheme 1971.
Publications Farming Business (4); Food From Britain News (occasional)

Food Hygiene Advisory Council
This Council was disbanded on 15 August 1983

Food Research Institute
Colney Lane, Norwich, Norfolk NR4 7UA 0603 56122
Aims To support the broad national interest of consumers in quality, e.g. safety, nutritive value and acceptability, of the food supply in the UK; in collaboration with the research associations, to assist the food manufacturing industry in maximising its efficiency and effectiveness.
Activities Nutrition and Food Quality Division: concerned with the nutritional value and acceptability of foodstuffs for human consumption.
Microbiology Division (*Head* Dr B.H. Kirsop): concerned with gaining information about organisms producing methane from wastes;

improving methods of achieving high concentrations of methanogenic organisms in fermenters; obtaining organisms specially adapted for this purpose by genetic manipulation and selection; hence developing improved systems for conversion of waste to methane.
Status Research institute grant-aided by the Agricultural and Food Research Council
Publications Newsletter (4); Biennial Report

Food Standards Committee
This committee was merged with the Food Additives and Contaminants Committee on 1.11.83 to form the FOOD ADVISORY COMMITTEE

Forestry Commission
231 Corstorphine Road, Edinburgh EH12 7AT
031–334 0303
Aims To promote the interests of forestry, the development of afforestation and the production and supply of timber and other forest products in Great Britain; to administer forestry legislation, including that relating to private forestry and plant health, and to undertake forestry research. Has permissive powers to make provision for public recreation in its forests and is required to pay due regard to the maintenance of the beauty of the countryside. The Commission consists of a chairman and up to 10 other members appointed by the Crown; responsible to, and subject to directions by, the forestry ministers, who are the Minister of Agriculture in England and the Secretaries of State for Scotland and Wales.
Activities Collection and dissemination of forestry information; development of education and training in forestry; the conduct of forestry research; provision of advice and financial aid to private forestry; the regulation of felling; control of tree pests and diseases. Also concerned with the effects of pollution on forest trees and works in close co-operation with the Natural Environment Research Council and its institutes. Regional offices and research stations.
Status Statutory
Publications Annual Report; Report on Forest Research (1); guides, etc.

Forth River Purification Board (FRPB)
Colinton Dell House, West Mill Road, Colinton, Edinburgh EH13 0PH 031–441 4691
Director W. Halcrow
Aims To control pollution of the aquatic environment in all streams draining to the Firth of Forth and in Firth itself.
Activities Biological, chemical and physical monitoring of all surface waters, fresh, brackish and saline, within the Board's

designated area; issue of consents to discharge of effluents or other liquids; investigation of complaints and incidents of pollution, fish kills, etc.; advice on planning, solid waste disposal, fishery management and research. Use of specialist staff and equipment on behalf of other authorities on repayment basis, e.g. chemical analysis, bathymetric surveys, geological reports. Estuary Survey Section at Port Edgar and other branches at Stirling and Glenrothes.
Status Statutory
Publications Annual Report

Foundation for Alternatives
The Rookery, Adderbury, Banbury, Oxon. OX17 3NA 0295 810993
Director Stan Windass
Aims To promote pilot projects in alternative forms of social and political organisation which incorporate the values of local and community responsibility and good husbandry of the Earth's resources.
Activities Projects have been fostered in the areas of education, employment, health, housing and rural resettlement; operates a residential centre for meetings; publishes working papers on various topics.
Status Charity
-NR

Foundation for Holistic Consciousness (FHC)
19 Goddington Chase, Goddington Lane, Orpington, Kent BR6 9EA 0689 32648
General Secretary Mrs P. Restall
Aims To engage in the study, teaching and practice of spiritual, psychological and esoteric disciplines, both ancient and modern, which promote the concept of man as a holistic being (having a spiritual origin and nature made manifest through a physical body and states of consciousness commonly referred to as thought, feeling and psyche).
Activities Natural therapies; healing; spiritual healing; correspondence course in self-development and esoteric studies allied to healing and backed up by student classes in various places. 4 branches.
Status Voluntary, non-profit-making

Foundation Seven
This organisation no longer exists

Fourth World Movement
24 Abercorn Place, London NW8 9XP 01-286 4366
Editor, *Fourth World Review* John Papworth
Aims To secure peace and economic stability as well as a sound concern for the environment by the break-up of all giant states and empires into units of no more than

around five million and the localisation of most forms of decision-making power in communities of around five thousand people.
Activities Seminars, lectures, annual assembly, Academic Inn dinner discussions; publishing the journal.
Status Voluntary
Publications Fourth World Review (6) Albery, N., *How to Save the World: a Fourth World guide to the politics of scale*, Turnstone Press, 1984, 318pp.

FRAME (Fund for the Replacement of Animals in Medical Experiments)
5B The Poultry, Bank Place, St Peter's Gate, Nottingham NG1 2JR 0602 584740
Secretary Mrs Carole Taylor
Aims To promote the development of alternatives to the use of live animals in research and the safety evaluation of substances; to hasten better protection of laboratory animals via the legislation and the testing regulations.
Activities Research programme to develop and validate cell culture alternatives, funded by individuals and commercial bodies. Toxicity Committee, set up to assess animal-based tests and the alternatives (Final Report 1983). FRAME All-Party Parliamentary Group. Local branches.
Status Charity
Publications ATLA (4); FRAME News (4) *Report of the FRAME Toxicity Committee* 1983.
Animals and Alternatives in Toxicity Testing Academic Press.
Animal Experimentation.

Freight Transport Association (FTA)
Hermes House, St John's Road, Tunbridge Wells, Kent TN4 9UZ 0892 26171
Manager: Press and Information Geoff Dossetter
Aims To represent the interests of, and to provide services for, users of all forms of freight transport; recognised in this capacity by both central and local government.
Activities Maintains a continuous interest in the effect of freight transport on the environment: roads, amenity, lorry controls, traffic, planning, pedestrianisation, etc. Seeking adequate provision for industrial operation of freight transport with due care for the environment; care and concern regarding operation of vehicles, legislation, noise, pollution, etc. 4 branches.
Status Trade Association
Publications Freight (12); Yearbook (1)

Freshwater Biological Association (FBA)
The Ferry House, Far Sawrey, Ambleside, Cumbria LA22 0LP 09662 2468
Director Dr R.T. Clarke

Aims To promote research into the biology (in the widest sense) and environmental physics and chemistry of fresh waters.
Activities Basic and strategic research into: the environmental physics and chemistry of freshwaters; the ecology and biology of microbes, algae, macrophytes, invertebrates and fish of freshwaters; freshwater ecosystems. HQ laboratory at Windermere; river laboratory near Wareham, Dorset.
Status Non-profit-making limited liability company without share capital
Publications Annual Report; current awareness service: Scientific Publication series (keys and handbooks on methods); Occasional Publication series (bibliographies, environmental data and user manuals)

Friends of Animals League (FOAL)
FOAL Farm, Jail Lane, Biggin Hill, Kent TN16 3AX 0959 72386
Hon. Secretary Mrs E. Lambert
Aims To take in as many animals as possible, restore them to health and place them in vetted caring and permanent homes; no healthy animal is ever destroyed – if no home is found, the animal remains at our Rescue Centre.
Activities Maintaining the Rescue Centre; fund raising activities (sales, bazaars, etc.); annual Gala Day, including a parade of ex-FOAL dogs.
Status Voluntary
Publications FOAL Newsletter (3)

Friends of the Earth (FoE)
377 City Road, London EC1V 1NA 01-837 0731
Information Officer Adam Markham
Aims To promote policies to protect the natural environment; to change government policies on the environment through direct lobbying and public education.
Activities FoE has four full-time campaigners working on safe energy, pollution, transport and wildlife and countryside issues from its London office. In addition there are 250 local FoE groups throughout England and Wales (FoE Scotland is a separate organisation) who run both local campaigns and national ones such as the Save Our Swans and recycling campaigns. Friends of the Earth Trust undertakes the research and educational work of the organisation and provides an information service which produces free information sheets for teachers, students and members of the public as well as providing more detailed information for journalists, researchers, etc.
Status Voluntary; British arm of Friends of the Earth International
Publications FoE Newspaper (3)

Chudleigh, Renee & Cannell, William. *The Gravedigger's Dilemma: radioactive waste management in Britain.*
Strawburning: you'd think farmers had money to burn . . .
SSSIs '84: the failure of the Wildlife & Countryside Act 1981.
Nectoux, Francois & Cannell, William. *Accidents Will Happen. . . (a study of the consequences of an accident at a British nuclear power station).*
[N.B. FoE officers also publish books through mainstream publishers]

Friends of the Earth (Scotland)
53 George IV Bridge, Edinburgh EH1 1EJ 031–225 6906
Joint National Co-ordinators Andy Kerr and Donald McPhillimy
Aims To promote the conservation, restoration and rational use of the environment.
Activities Campaigns actively on a broad range of environmental issues as part of the FoE international network. Campaigns include energy, recycling, transport, employment, bicycles and whales, but all promote more sustainable and socially useful systems with the minimum of wastage and pollution. A local group network campaigning on recycling, wildlife habitats and other local issues, together with national campaigns on Scottish countryside and acid rain, ensures a strong Scottish angle. 15 local branches.
Status Voluntary; charity
Publications Newsletter (3)
-NR

Friends of Herbalism
6 Ronald Close, Eden Park, Beckenham, Kent BR3 3HX
Aims To preserve the right to use herbal medicine and receive natural treatment; to support the work of the National Institute of Medical Herbalists.
-NR

Friends of the Lake District
Gowan Knott, Kendal Road, Staveley, Kendal, Cumbria LA8 9LP 0539 821201
Secretary J.M. Houston
Aims To protect and cherish the landscape and natural beauty of the Lake District and the county of Cumbria as a whole; to unite those who share these aims; to take common action with other societies when need arises.
Activities Conservation, footpaths, tree planting, hedge laying, dry stone walling; campaigning against power boating, inappropriate development, heavy vehicles, commercial conifer planting and water abstraction from the lakes. Represents the

Council for the Protection of Rural England in Cumbria.
Status Voluntary; charity
Publications Conserving Lakeland (2); Report & Newsletter (2)

Fulmer Research Institute Ltd

Hollybush Hill, Stoke Poges, Slough, Berks. SL2 4QD 02816 2181
Managing Director Dr W.E. Duckworth
Activities Contract research in the field of materials, including analysis, testing, consultancy, failure analysis, corrosion, fire testing and air pollution. Study of domestic solar energy systems; also economic factors governing the choice of alternative energy systems and energy audits of material processing and fabrication methods.
Status Limited company

Future in Our Hands (FIOH-UK)

UK Information Centre: 120 York Road, Swindon, Wilts. SN1 2JP 0793 32353
Information Officer Michael Thomas
Aims To attain international social justice through a movement of individuals committed to personal change; the movement exists to help and encourage us to change our lives by reassessing our personal values, goals and lifestyles.
Activities Participants are encouraged to: learn more about the true causes of poverty; live more simply and resourcefully; give a proportion of their income on a regular basis to help the poor help themselves; campaign peacefully with others to change unjust policies. Has instigated a network to research for a set of guidelines on non-exploitative lifestyles. FIOH (Ireland): 15 William Street, Wexford, Co. Wexford, Ireland.
Status Voluntary
Publications FIOH Newsletter (4)
Dammann, Erik, *Revolution in the Affluent Society*, Heretic Pubs.

Future Studies Centre (FSC)

Birmingham Settlement, 318 Summer Lane, Birmingham B19 3RL 021–359 3562/2113
Administrator Christian Kunz
Aims To provide a contact point for an international network of people interested in present trends and developments and alternative options for the future; to assemble and disseminate information in various areas of future studies, particularly on social and environmental issues.
Activities Running a research centre which contains a wide range of up-to-date information, publications and contact addresses; maintaining the library which is open to anybody on a self-help basis; developing research or action projects and projecting them to the public for discussion; producing a newsletter which co-ordinates research and enables readers to keep in touch with the state of knowledge and with each other; newsletter available either by subscription or in exchange for other relevant publications.
Status Charity (part of the Birmingham Settlement)
Publications Common Futures (4)

Futures Network

316A Prescot Road, Aughton, Ormskirk, Lancs. L39 6RR
Secretary Denis Loveridge
Aims To act as an informal association of people interested in the study of futures, i.e. longer-term developments and their implications regarding some or all aspects of our society.
Status Voluntary
Publications Futures Network Newsletter (4)
-NR

Press Dept
0171 566 1649

FOE
26-28 Underwood St
London
N1 7JQ
071 - 490 - 1555 Tel.
0171 - 490 0881 Fax.
Tony Bosworth (Atmos & Transport

G

Game Conservancy
Burgate Manor, Fordingbridge, Hants. SP6 1EF
0425 52381
Activities Research into conservation, breeding and rearing of game of all descriptions in the UK, for the benefit of those concerned with agriculture, forestry, breeding and sale of game birds, manufacture of feedstuffs, agricultural chemicals, guns and ammunition.
-NR

Gandhi Foundation
68 Downlands Road, Purley, Surrey CR2 4JF
01-668 3161
General Secretary Surur Hoda
Aims To relate the message of the life and teachings of Mahatma Gandhi to the problems of Britain and the world today.
Activities Publication of the newsletter and other material; meetings and summer schools; promoting the showing of the film 'Gandhi' in schools, colleges and groups of various kinds.
Status Voluntary
Publications Gandhi Foundation Newsletter (4)

Garden History Society (GHS)
66 Granville Park, London SE13 7DX
Hon. Membership Secretary Mrs Anne Richards
Aims To preserve our historic parks and gardens; to study various aspects of garden history, including landscape design, botany, horticulture, architecture and forestry.
Activities Lectures, symposia, visits and tours are arranged, including at least one tour abroad each year; a Summer Conference of visits and lectures, lasting two or three days, is held each year in a different part of the country. A Conservation Committee deals with threats to historic gardens and gives advice on restoration.
Status Charity
Publications Garden History

GEC Energy Systems Limited
Cambridge Road, Whetstone, Leicester
LE8 3LH 0533 863434
-NR

General Council and Register of Consultant Herbalists Ltd
Villa Merlynn, 18 Elgin Road, Talbot Woods, Bournemouth, Dorset BH4 9NL 0202 769297

Secretary/Director James Hewlett-Parsons
Aims To provide training through the Faculty of Herbal Medicine to the qualifying standard of entry to the Register as a Registered Medical Herbalist with DBTh (Diploma in Botano-Therapy).
Activities Conferences, lectures, AGM. 5 clinical training centres.
Status Company limited by guarantee
Publications Newsletter (4); Prospectus

General Council and Register of Osteopaths (GCRO)
1–4 Suffolk Street, London SW1Y 4HG
01-839 2060
Aims To establish and maintain standards of education for practitioners of osteopathy for the protection and benefit of the public; to liaise with other bodies conforming with the Register's standards in osteopathic education; to keep a register of persons suitably qualified to practise osteopathy; to supervise the ethical behaviour and professional conduct of persons on the Register; to promote the progress of the healing arts, particularly osteopathy. The General Council consists of 12 elected members of the Register.
Activities Inspecting approved osteopathic schools and clinics; opposing legal restrictions on the freedom of members to practise under common law; advice and guidance to members; liaising with government departments.
Publications Annual Report; Directory of Members (1)

Generals for Peace and Disarmament
Centre for International Peacebuilding,
Wickham House, 10 Cleveland Way,
London E1 4TR 01-790 2424
Administrator Brig. Michael N. Harbottle, OBE
Aims To influence public thinking and appreciation of the dangerous threat to humanity created by the present East-West arms race.
Activities Periodic workshop sessions and subsequent publication of the group's reaction to developing issues concerned with East-West relations, European security and the arms race, with particular reference to nuclear deterrence strategy.
Status Voluntary
Publications Bulletin (1)

Arms Race to Armageddon. 1983. (also available in German)

Geological Society
Burlington House, Piccadilly, London W1V 0JU
01–734 2356
Executive Secretary R.M. Bateman
Aims To represent the geological sciences in Britain by providing advice on all geological matters to government commissions of inquiry and educational bodies, etc.; to provide a national centre for the geological sciences.
Activities Maintains a major national library with over 300,000 monographs, periodicals, books, text books, rare books, the Murchison letters and diaries and over 35,000 maps. Holds over 60 scientific meetings a year in the Society's lecture theatre and other centres; organises courses, workshops and field excursions; awards medals and funds to those who have made outstanding contributions to the science; publishes journals and many occasional papers on all aspects of geology.
Status Charity
Publications Journal of the Geological Society (6);
Quarterly Journal of Engineering Geology (4);
Annual Report

Georgian Group
37 Spital Square, London E1 6DY 01–377 1722
Secretary Roger White
Aims To save from destruction or disfigurement Georgian buildings, monuments, parks and gardens of architectural and historic interest and to encourage their appropriate repair where necessary; to stimulate public knowledge and appreciation of Georgian architecture and town planning.
Activities Makes representations to government and local authorities about threatened Georgian buildings, as one of the national amenity societies to whom listed building consent applications are required to be notified. Organises visits to Georgian buildings to stimulate members' interest; lectures and discussions; reports and publications.
Status Voluntary
Publications The Georgian Group News;
Annual Report

Geothermal Energy Project (Camborne School of Mines)
Rosemanowes Quarry, Herniss, Penryn, Cornwall TR10 9DU 0209 860141
Publications Co-ordinator Ms J. Pye
Aims To demonstrate the viability of electricity generation by utilising the heat of the Earth's rock at depth.

Activities Energy exploration research into exploitation of the thermal properties of granitic rocks at depths of over 2,100m, with a view toward electricity generation; this involves detailed investigations into the nature of local granite and hence includes studies in rock mechanics, *in situ* stress and permeability enhancement. The project is funded by the Dept of Energy and the EEC.
Publications Newsletter; Information Series

Glamorgan Trust for Nature Conservation (GLAMNATS)
[formerly Glamorgan Naturalists' Trust]
Ivy Cottage, Cwmpennar, Mountain Ash, Merthyr Tydfil, Mid-Glam. CF45, Wales
0443 472736
Aims To study, record and protect wildlife and its habitats as well as geological features and to promote education in these subjects.
Activities Managing nature reserves which are owned or leased by the Trust or are subject to management agreements; seminars, lectures and courses on wildlife conservation; walks and field study outings. Local branches.
Status Voluntary
Publications GNAT

Glasgow Environmental Education – Urban Projects (GEE-UP)
c/o Victoria Drive Secondary School, Larchfield Avenue, Glasgow G14 9BZ 041–954 2291
Chairman L.K. Hazra
Aims To promote interest in practical environmental education and stimulate teachers to undertake conservation projects in Glasgow.
Activities Co-ordinating projects via committee; publication of newsletter and bulletins; conferences on project work; liaison with voluntary and statutory bodies; teacher in-service courses (day/residential).
Status Voluntary
Publications GEE-UP Newsletter (2)
-NR

Glass and Glazing Federation (GGF)
6 Mount Row, London W1Y 6DY 01–409 0545
Public Relations Officer I.D. Muir
Aims To set technical and trading standards for the industry; to provide advice on the use of the industry's products and particularly to put enquirers in touch with members who can handle their specialist needs.
Activities Promoting energy conservation through multiple glazing; promoting the safer use of glass; industrial relations and training.
Status Trade association
Publications Glass and Glazing News (6)

Glass Manufacturers Federation (GMF)
19 Portland Place, London W1N 4BH
01–580 6952

Environmental Officer Peter Mansfield

Aims The main concern of the Environmental Department within the GMF is to promote the environmental benefits of glass containers as a packaging material, by encouraging the re-use or recycling thereof when appropriate or economic.

Activities Establishing a national recycling scheme, involving the setting up of Bottle Bank schemes in district council areas and encouraging the collection of cullet (waste glass) from commercial. catering and industrial sources.

Status Trade association

Publications Glass Recycling Bulletin; Glass Gazette; Glass View; Bottle Bank statistics (4)

Glasshouse Crops Research Institute
Worthing Road, Rustington, Littlehampton. W. Sussex BN16 3PU 09064 6123

Secretary R.K. Arthur

Activities Crop protection and microbiology: crop science. physiology and chemistry.
-NR

Glastonbury Green Gathering Collective
see GREEN COLLECTIVE

Gloucestershire Trust for Nature Conservation
Church House, Standish, Stonehouse, Glos. GL10 3EU 045382 2761

Director Dr Gordon McGlone

Aims To protect and conserve Gloucestershire's wildlife and countryside.

Activities Has established over 60 nature reserves, which include old woodland, downland, gravel pits, flood meadows, disused railway lines and quarries; they contain most of the habitats and many of the plants and animals to be found in the county. Free advice on nature conservation to members, county and district councils, water authorities and many other organisations; liaison with farmers and landowners through the Farming and Wildlife Advisory Group; talks, lectures, exhibitions. nature fairs and open days. The Trust has a membership of over 4,500 and various area committees.

Status Voluntary

Publications Gloucestershire Trust for Nature Conservation Newsletter (3): Annual Report

Good Gardeners' Association
Arkley Manor Farm, Rowley Lane. Arkley. Barnet, London EN5 3HS 01–449 7944

Hon. Director C.R.G. Shewell-Cooper

Aims To further the growing of fruit, flowers and vegetables the organic way, which are healthy, edible and sweet flavoured.

Activities Training students in the art of practical horticulture; arranging courses; holding demonstration days. The Director is willing to deliver lectures throughout the country.

Status Charity

Publications Good Gardeners' Association Newsletter (6)

Grapevine
BBCtv, Television Centre, Wood Lane, London W12 8QT

Activities Grapevine is a TV magazine which encourages community action by means of providing an exchange of information and experience. Information sheets are available on rural initiatives, fund raising and other aspects of community enterprise.
-NR

Grassland Research Institute
Hurley, Maidenhead. Berks. SL6 5LR 062882 3631

Aims To promote research and other scientific work bearing on grassland husbandry, including the establishment, productivity. quality and management of grassland herbage, and on the management of crops and livestock in relation to grassland husbandry.

Activities Research on most aspects of grass and forage (crops which the animals consume whole, apart from the root), with the exception of plant breeding and seed production. The Institute's divisions and departments include: Animal Nutrition & Production; Permanent Grassland; Biomathematics; Soils & Plant Nutrition; Plant & Crop Physiology; and the Agronomy Group. The library stocks over 10,000 books and 1,200 current periodicals on agriculture and allied subjects. The Institute houses the Commonwealth Bureau of Pastures and Field Crops (which is financially and administratively independent).

Status Research institute grant-aided by the Agricultural and Food Research Council (AFRC)
-NR – L

Greater London Council (GLC)
The GLC, which carried out a wide variety of environmental functions, was due to be abolished in April 1986; the devolution or transference of these functions is uncertain at time of going to press.

Greater London Enterprise Board (GLEB)
63–67 Newington Causeway, London SE1 6BD
01–403 0300
Information Officer   Marian Conry
Aims   To generate employment in London
and strengthen the capital's industrial base.
Activities   Investment in industry with the
aim of creating and saving jobs; operating
Technology Networks to develop new, socially useful products; special interest in
workers' co-operatives, projects of benefit to
women and ethnic minorities, new technology that will create rather than destroy
jobs; development of industrial workspaces.
Status   Local government agency
Publications   Enterprising London (4)

Green Alliance
60 Chandos Place, London WC2N 4HG
01–836 0341
Director   Tom Burke
Aims   To build a constituency inside each
political party to promote an ecological
perspective; to further understanding of
political processes among ecological
groups; to further development of Green
ideas and analysis of their political
dimension.
Activities   Debates, seminars, publications,
lobbying.
Status   Association, with limited
membership
Publications   Green Alliance Parliamentary Newsletter (fortnightly while Parliament
is in session)
Ash, Maurice. *Green Politics – The New
Paradigm.*
Skolimowski, Henryk. *Economics Today –
What Do We Need?*

**Green Alliance/Comhaontas Glas (Republic
of Ireland)**
15 Upper Stephen Street, Dublin 8, Ireland
0001–78 4380
Co-ordinator   Janice Spalding
Activities   Ireland's Green Party; formerly
the Ecology Party of Ireland.
-NR

Green Cars
11 Church Green Road, Bletchley, Milton
Keynes, Bucks. MK3 6BJ
0908 641548 (after 6pm)
Secretary   Steve Cousins
Aims   To promote shared ownership of
vehicles between households.
Activities   Supplying a guide to shared car
ownership; helping with the few problems that
may arise; information on electronic car-
sharing meters.
Status   Voluntary

Green CND
23 Lower Street, Stroud, Glos. GL5 2HT
04536 70962
Secretary   John Marjoram
Aims   To promote CND within the wider
Green movement, showing the links between
the two, and also 'greening' CND in the
process by developing the Green view of
peace.
Activities   Providing speakers on CND-
Green links and on the Green view of peace;
highlighting the links between nuclear
energy and nuclear weapons; producing
literature to assist our aims.
Status   Voluntary, specialist section within
the Campaign for Nuclear Disarmament
Publications   Green CND Newsletter
Embrace the Earth: a Green view of peace.
1984. 44pp.

Green Collective
4 Bridge House. St Ives, Huntingdon, Cambs.
PE17 0480 63054
Contact   Richard Oldfield
Aims   To promote ecology, feminism, non-
violence, direct democracy, social justice, co-
operation and personal development as
interlinked Green principles; to help facilitate the growth of an independent Green
movement based on such principles.
Activities   Organises annual gatherings of
people who are sympathetic to the above
principles; sponsors a Green Roadshow
offering workshops, literature, theatre,
music, cafe and creche to fairs, gatherings
and demonstrations; organises a special
'Greenfield' at the annual Glastonbury CND
festival; helps to link over 100 local Green
groups plus individuals.
Status   Voluntary informal network
Publications   Green Collective Mailing (6)
The Green Pack (assorted material)
Green Gathering Advice Pack (on staging
large outdoor gatherings)

Green Deserts (GD)
Geoff's House, Rougham, Bury St Edmunds,
Suffolk IP30 9LY 0359 70265
Company Secretary   Mrs N. Pepin
Aims   To promote and take part in desert
reclamation schemes in arid zones or
wasted areas; to conduct research into
systems of reclaiming desert and under-
used land; to bring the facts about desertification to the awareness of the general public.
Activities   Maintaining an audio-visual
library on deserts and their problems, for
general information and education;
producing Green Papers – prints of technical
papers on specific subjects; engaged in an
afforestation project in the Sudan; organising
a Tree Fair which aims to combine a
traditional country fair with a central theme

of trees and their importance to our environment. Woodland management; recycled products; manufacture of wood-burning stoves; four charity auctions per year. Local branches.
Status Charity
Publications Green Deserts (4)

Greencure Trust
Grosvenor Lodge, Gordon Road, Clifton, Bristol, Avon BS8 1AW
Aims To promote the constructive use of wasteland and disused buildings as a positive contribution to community life and useful work.
-NR

Greenham Common Peace Camp
London Office: 52–54 Featherstone Street, London EC1Y 8RT 01–608 0244
Activities Providing a focus for support action for the Greenham women's peace camp.

Greenham Women Against Cruise
PO Box 165, Hackney. London E8
Activities Involved in legal action against the US government over the deployment of cruise missiles in Britain.
-NR

Greenpeace Ltd
36 Graham Street, London N1 8LL 01–608 1461
Campaign Director Pete Wilkinson
Aims To campaign on specific issues of environmental abuse, through lobbying, scientific presentations, public education and non-violent direct actions.
Activities Monitoring activities likely to adversely affect the environment, such as the discharging of radioactive effluent into the sea from nuclear reprocessing plants or toxic wastes from chemical plants; direct actions include physically obstructing whaling, seal culling and the dumping of radioactive waste at sea. British branch of Greenpeace International [Temple House, 25–26 High Street, Lewes, E. Sussex BN7 2LU 07916 78787] which has 15 offices around the world.
Status Voluntary
Publications Greenpeace News (4)

Greenpeace (London)
6 Endsleigh Street, London WC1H 0DX 01–387 5370
Contact G. Price
Aims To promote decentralisation, freedom, sharing, co-operation and respect for individual diversity; to oppose animal exploitation, mass industrialisation, state institutions, militarism and capitalism.
Activities Meetings; campaigning on specific issues; encouraging people individually and collectively to oppose the various forms of militarism, environmental pollution, exploitation of animals and human oppression. No formal membership or branch structure. (No connection with Greenpeace Ltd or Greenpeace International)
Publications *Energy For All: a look at centralised energy systems and the practical alternatives.*
Wildlife and the Atom.

Groundwork Foundation
27 Mawdsley Street, Bolton, Lancs. BL1 1LN 0204 35155
Office Manager Barbara Bryson
Aims To promote conservation, protection and improvement of the physical and natural environment; to provide facilities in the interest of social welfare for recreation and leisure time occupation; to advance public education in environmental matters; to raise voluntary funds and receive donations in order to carry out the above.
Activities Groundwork, set up by the Countryside Commission, is the first national programme to link public, private and voluntary interests to improve the environment around towns and cities and is a different way of tackling environmental problems in the remnant countryside of these areas. It tries to harness the experience and powers of public bodies, the knowledge and skills of local people and voluntary bodies and the technical and practical expertise and resources of industry and commerce; this is achieved in practice by creating a clear focus in the form of a charitable Trust for the commitment of resources offered by the different sectors.
Status Voluntary
Publications Groundwork Newsletter (occasional)

Groundwork Trust (Operation Groundwork)
32–34 Claughton Street, St Helens, Merseyside WA10 1SN 0744 39396
Executive Director Dr J.F. Handley
Aims To make the most of the countryside and restore damaged and neglected land to beneficial use in St Helens and Knowsley.
Activities The Trust undertakes the following roles within Operation Groundwork: communication – raising expectations about the environment in the area; co-ordination – working with local authorities to establish through them a programme of major land reclamation schemes and countryside projects; implementation – developing a projects programme with the private sector, voluntary organisations and community groups; environmental education;

research and development, including
research into landscape management.
Status Charitable Trust
Publications Operation Groundwork (4);
Annual Report

Gwent Trust for Nature Conservation (GTNC)

16 White Swan Court, Church Street,
Monmouth, Gwent NP5 3BR, Wales 0600 5501
Hon. Secretary I.T. Stone
Aims To establish and manage nature
reserves; to survey wildlife habitats and
provide advice on nature conservation.
Activities Managing 20 nature reserves in
Gwent; acquiring wildlife habitats as
reserves; carrying out conservation work on
the reserves and at other sites of importance
to nature conservation; liaising with statutory
and voluntary bodies; providing advice and
holding talks, outings and film shows. Local
branches.

Status Voluntary; charity
Publications Gwent Trust for Nature
Conservation Newsletter

Gwynedd Grassroutes

Greenhouse, Trevelyan Terrace, Bangor,
Gwynedd LL57 1AX, Wales 0248 355821
Hon. Planner R. Mike Chown
Aims To connect local minor routes by
building and restoring old tracks; to provide
a safe system of access for local people in
each area; to satisfy the needs of access for
the disabled, safety for children and conti-
nuity for cyclists; to create new confidence
through a sustainable environmental project.
Activities Surveying disused railways,
seeking approval and undertaking construction work; liaising with various bodies such
as the Forestry Commission. Branches at
Caernarfon, Bangor and Dolgellau.
Status Voluntary
-NR

HMIP Tel: 01-276-8149/8589

021-236-6599
Dr. Martin Biggs.

Le BATNEECS.

H

Hahneman Society For The Promotion of Homoeopathy
217 Coldharbour Lane, London SW9 8RU
01–737 3979
-NR

Hampshire & Isle of Wight Naturalists' Trust
8 Market Place, Romsey, Hants. SO5 8NB
0794 513786
General Secretary G. Duncan
Aims To promote nature conservation by acquiring and managing nature reserves; to offer advice to landowners and authorities on conservation; to inform members and the public on wildlife, the countryside and conservation; to encourage involvement in nature conservation.
Activities Reserve acquisition; conservation and management work; field survey and monitoring exercises; wardening of wildlife sites; publishing journals, booklets and leaflets; organising guided walks, talks, lectures, exhibitions, displays, reserve Open Days, etc.; recruiting support through membership and subscription; fund raising.
Status Voluntary; charity
Publications Hampshire & IOW Naturalists' Trust Newsletter (3)

Hannah Research Institute (HRI)
Ayr, Strathclyde KA6 5HL, Scotland
0292 76013/7
Information Officer P.D. Wilson
Aims To conduct fundamental research into nutritional and physiological factors that, in the cow, influence milk production and milk composition and into the chemical and physical characteristics of milk and milk products; to apply this knowledge to the agricultural and dairy industries.
Activities Research topics include: milk utilisation; limits to milk production; feeding for milk production. The Institute's programme of research is agreed in consultation with the Agricultural and Food Research Council (AFRC) and the Department of Agriculture and Fisheries for Scotland.
Status Research institute
Publications Journal of Dairy Research (4); Hannah Research (1)

Hawk Trust
c/o Birds of Prey Section, Zoological Society of London, Regent's Park, London NW1 4RY
Aims To conserve, and encourage the appreciation of, birds of prey, particularly our native species.
Activities Organising exhibitions, lectures, meetings, film shows and stands at country and agricultural shows; carrying out research on a wide range of subjects, mostly of relevance to free-living populations; studying the problems of captive breeding, rehabilitation and reintroduction to the wild; conducting a nation-wide survey of the status of the Barn Owl. The Trust manages a forest reserve and provides volunteer wardens at vulnerable nesting sites. Works with other conservation organisations and can call upon the services of skilled veterinary surgeons; assists with bird hospital work all over the country.
Status Charity
Publications Hawk Trust News; Annual Report
-NR

Hazardous Waste Inspectorate
see DEPARTMENT OF THE ENVIRONMENT

Health and Safety Agency for Northern Ireland (HSA)
Canada House, 22 North Street, Belfast BT1 1NW 0232 243249
Secretary D.M. Darragh
Aims To make recommendations to government on enforcement policies and on the making of health and safety regulations; to arrange for and encourage others in research, training and information; to issue codes of practice; to promote health and safety at work.
Activities In the course of pursuing the above aims, the Agency undertakes considerable promotion work by way of the publication of leaflets, codes of practice and the mounting of exhibitions, conferences, etc. relating to health and safety at work.
Status Statutory
Publications Health, Safety and You

Health and Safety Commission (HSC)
Regina House, 259–269 Old Marylebone Road, London NW1 5RR 01–723 1262
Secretary Miss C. Johnson
Aims To take appropriate steps to secure the health, safety and welfare of people at work; to protect the public generally against risk to health and safety arising out of the work situation. Responsible to the Secretary of State for Employment; membership

includes representatives of employers, trade unions and local authorities.

Activities Provides a forum for the development of policies in the field of health and safety at work; organises widespread consultation on all aspects of health and safety and is advised by a number of advisory committees and working parties as well as by the expertise and committees of its task force and executive arm, the Health and Safety Executive; responsible for legislation and codes of practice.

Status Statutory

Publications Health and Safety Commission Newsletter (6)

Health and Safety Executive (HSE)
Public Enquiry Points based on the Library and Information Service:
Broad Lane, Sheffield, S. Yorks. S3 7HQ
0742 752539
Baynards House, 1 Chepstow Place, Westbourne Grove, London W2 4TF
01-229 3456 ext.6721/2
St Hugh's House, Stanley Precinct, Trinity Road, Bootle, Merseyside L20 3QY 051-951 4381

Head of Library & Information Services Mrs Sheila Pantry

Aims To exercise on behalf of the Health and Safety Commission such of its functions as the Commission directs and to make adequate arrangements for the enforcement of relevant health and safety legislation under the 1974 Act; to achieve a corpus of standardised and integrated law, codes of practice and guidance to meet all current and foreseeable needs.

Activities Provides inspection, guidance and advice; promotes the furtherance of safety training, working closely to this end with the Manpower Services Commission and industrial training boards, in association with the HSC's industry advisory committees; represents British interests in health and safety matters in the international field, particularly the EEC, and is represented on working groups establishing common standards and practices. Operates in England, Scotland and Wales through 21 area offices and several specialist Inspectorates [listed below].

Status Statutory

Publications Health and Safety Executive News Bulletin Service (press releases issued weekly); Publications in Series; Toxic Substances Bulletin (occasional)

see also HM AGRICULTURAL INSPECTORATE
HM ALKALI AND CLEAN AIR INSPECTORATE
HM FACTORY INSPECTORATE
HM INSPECTORATE OF MINES AND QUARRIES

HM NUCLEAR INSTALLATIONS INSPECTORATE

Health Education Advisory Committee For Wales
Welsh Office, Cathays Park, Cardiff CF1 3NQ
0222 823925

Aims To assist in improving the relevance, accessibility and impact of health education activities in Wales. Established in 1984, the Committee consists of a chairman and 19 members appointed by the Welsh Office and drawn from various sectors of the community with an interest in health education.

Health Education Bureau (Republic of Ireland)
34 Upper Mount Street, Dublin 2, Ireland
0001-76 1116

Public Relations Officer Ms Harriet Duffin

Aims To act as a national centre of expertise and knowledge in all aspects of health education; to advise the Minister on the aspects of health education which should have priority; to draw up and carry out programmes of health education for promotion at national and local level; to promote and conduct research to evaluate health education activities.

Activities Research; training and education; support for voluntary organisations; community health education programme; information service; public health promotion; general health education.

Status Statutory

Publications HEB News (4)
Health in Rural Ireland: a study of selected aspects. (In association with the North Western Health Board)

Health Education Council (HEC)
78 New Oxford Street, London WC1A 1AH
01-637 1881

Contact Information Officer

Aims To act as the national centre of expertise and knowledge in all aspects of health education in its broadest sense; to encourage and promote health education.

Activities Campaigning for good health through the media, the health-related professions and schools; producing materials and helping with national and local initiatives; training and promoting training in health education work; liaising with the Health Education Units of local health authorities. Publications include source lists (including one on Environmental Health), leaflets, posters, film catalogue and current awareness lists. Information also available on Prestel key no.544.

Status Statutory

Publications   Health Education News (6);
Health Education Journal (4)

Health Information Centre
Greenhouse, 1 Trevelyan Terrace, Bangor,
Gwynedd LL57 1AX, Wales 0248 355821
Co-ordinators   Sarah Andrews, Chris
Walker
Aims   To help people improve and maintain their health on a physical, mental and
spiritual level by promoting a holistic understanding of health and sickness; to increase
public awareness of the value of preventive
health care, natural therapies, complementary medicine and healing.
Activities   Staffing an information desk 10–5
Monday-Friday; maintaining a reference
library on complementary medicine,
nutrition and natural childbirth; providing a
healing room for use by practitioners of
natural therapies; regular public meetings,
lectures, classes and demonstrations. We try
to work in co-operation with the existing
health service to ensure the most appropriate
route to health for each individual and seek
a free health service on these lines for all.
Status   Voluntary
Publications   Health Information Centre
Newsletter (12)
-NR

**Heat Pump and Air Conditioning Advisory
Bureau**
Electricity Council, 30 Millbank,
London SW1P 4RD 01–834 8827
Aims   To ensure that the heat pump market
in Britain is not undermined by poor products.
Status   Trade association

Heat Pump Manufacturers' Association
Nicholson House, High Street, Maidenhead,
Berks. SL6 0628 34667/8
Status   Trade association
-NR

**Heating and Ventilating Contractors' Associ-
ation (HVCA)**
ESCA House, 34 Palace Court, Bayswater,
London W2 4JG 01–229 2488
Secretary   Brian Peck
Status   Trade association
Publications   HVCA Yearbook

Heavy Horse Preservation Society
Old Rectory, Whitchurch, Shropshire ST13 1LF
Activities   Operating a fund to buy and
care for farm horses that have been ousted
by mechanisation and would otherwise be
slaughtered.
-NR

**Henry Doubleday Research Association
(HDRA)**
National Centre for Organic Gardening,
Ryton-on-Dunsmore, Coventry, W.Mids. CV8
Executive Director   Alan Gear
Aims   To encourage improved methods of
agriculture, and especially small-scale horticulture, along organic (i.e. non-chemical)
lines.
Activities   Running a 22–acre centre which
is open to the public; conducting scientific
experiments to improve the practice of
organic growing; publishing books and
booklets; maintaining a specialist library;
providing advice to members; encouraging
the cultivation of endangered vegetable
varieties, especially through the establishment of vegetable sanctuaries and a
vegetable seed library. 10 local groups.
Status   Charitable research organisation
Publications   HDRA Newsletter (4)
Gear, Alan, *The Organic Food Guide*.
Hills, Lawrence D., *The Good Fruit Guide*.

Herb Society
34 Boscobel Place, London SW1W 9PE 01–235
1530
Publications   Herbal Review (4)
-NR

**Herefordshire and Radnorshire Nature Trust
Ltd**
25 Castle Street, Hereford HR1 2NW 0432 56872
Aims   To preserve and encourage the
breeding of rare species of plants, birds and
other wildlife, mainly through the acquisition
of nature reserves.
Activities   Managing the 30 nature
reserves owned by the Trust; when
requested, assisting private landowners to
manage their own land. Local branches.
Status   Voluntary
Publications   Herefordshire & Radnorshire
Nature Trust Newsletter (2)
-NR

Heritage Co-ordination Group
Conewood House, Crawley Ridge, Camberley,
Surrey GU15 2AN 0276 22034
Hon. Secretary   Mrs. J.V. Cowen
Aims   To encourage communication
between heritage preservation organisations, particularly at regional level; to co-
ordinate activities when mutually advan-
tageous; to encourage the training of
professional and voluntary conservators in
order to preserve our cultural heritage.
Activities   The committee meets three
times a year to exchange information and
further the aims of the Group; the Group
holds annual conferences at which anyone
interested in heritage can listen to and question experts in conservation, meet with

others working in similar fields, appeal for help with projects, learn how volunteers can be trained in simple conservation techniques and hear the latest developments in preserving the cultural heritage. News of the Group goes 3–4 times a year to the organisations in the Group
Status Voluntary
Publications Report of the Annual Conference

Heritage Education Group
Civic Trust, 17 Carlton House Terrace, London SW1Y 5AW 01–930 0914
Secretary Brian Lymbery
Aims To promote a wider awareness of the opportunities for environmental education, especially relating to the built environment and the heritage.
Activities Conferences, seminars, publications and other activities to promote environmental education and bring about closer co-operation between education authorities, schools, planning departments, other professionals and local amenity societies. The Group is administered by the Civic Trust and its educational concerns cover the whole field of interests of the Trust.
Status Voluntary
Publications Heritage Education News (2)

Heritage Holidays Ltd
10 Highfield Close, Wokingham, Berks. RG11 1DG 0734 783204
Chairman D.S. Stafford
Aims To promote understanding among the general public of Third World development in particular and rural development world-wide in general; respect for the environment and indigenous cultures is a particular concern.
Activities Organising study tours in the UK, conferences, lectures, day schools and similar occasions in association, wherever possible, with like-minded bodies.
Status Voluntary co-operative

Hertfordshire and Middlesex Trust For Nature Conservation
Grebe House, St Michael's Street, St Albans, Herts. AL3 4LZ 0727 58901
Hon. Secretary Col. P.E. Gerahty, CBE
Aims To promote nature conservation within Hertfordshire and the former county of Middlesex.
Activities Promoting the establishment of nature reserves and assisting in their maintenance; managing 42 reserves; ensuring that nature conservation receives due attention in the planned development of the area; helping to reconcile pressure on the countryside with the continued survival of wildlife; educating the younger generation

to appreciate and respect wildlife. The Trust has a Wildlife Interpretive Centre, Garden and Shop at Grebe House open to the public 7 days a week from 1 March to Christmas. Local branches.
Status Voluntary
Publications Herts & Middlesex Trust for Nature Conservation Newsletter (3)

Hertfordshire Society
29A Mill Lane, Welwyn, Herts. AL6 9EU 043871 7587
Hon. Director Brig. F.M. De Butts
Aims To promote the preservation and improvement of the county for the benefit of the public generally and especially the inhabitants of the county; to promote the protection and preservation of lands, buildings and scenery of beauty or historic or local interest; to prevent harmful disfigurement and to assist in the control of future development by reconciling preservation with necessary development; to promote co-operation between local authorities, other societies, property owners and other interested parties.
Activities Organising an annual Best Kept Village competition in the summer; monitoring planning applications and acting to preserve the local component of the Metropolitan Green Belt and listed buildings. Incorporates the Hertfordshire branch of the Council for the Protection of Rural England.
Status Charity
Publications Hertfordshire Society Newsletter (2); Yearbook

Highland Anti-Nuclear Group (HANG)
2 Wester Raddery, Fortrose, Highland IV10, Scotland 0381 20869
Secretary Ance Karlsson
Aims To oppose nuclear power on economic, safety and sociological grounds and because of its unavoidable links with nuclear weapons technology; to campaign for substantial research and development of renewable energy resources and for the conservation and more efficient usage of energy supplies.
Activities Campaigns to date have been in connection with: test bores for the possible dumping of nuclear waste; developments at the Dounreay Fast Breeder Reactor; plutonium nitrate shipments between Dounreay and Sellafield (Windscale) along the west coast of Scotland; trying to persuade the Highland Health Board to sell its shares in Rio Tinto Zinc which mines uranium in Namibia; supporting alternative energy initiatives in the area.
Status Voluntary
Publications HANG Newsletter

Highland River Purification Board
Strathpeffer Road, Dingwall, Highland
IV15 9QY, Scotland 0349 62021
Director & River Inspector D. Buchanan
Aims To prevent river pollution.
Activities Controlling the quality of
discharges to rivers; monitoring water
quality; measuring river flow and rainfall.
Local branches.
Status Statutory
Publications Annual Report

**Highlands & Islands Development Board
(HIDB)**
Bridge House, 27 Bank Street, Inverness, Highland IV1 1QR, Scotland 0463 234171
Aims To keep under review all matters
relating to the economic and social wellbeing and development of the Highlands &
Islands; to prepare proposals for development for approval by the Secretary of State
for Scotland and to concert, promote, assist
or undertake measures to implement any
proposals so approved; to advise the
Secretary of State on such matters relating to
their functions as he may refer to the Board
or as the Board may think fit.
Activities The Board has powers to
acquire land and erect buildings; to carry
out works; to set up and carry on businesses;
to provide advisory, training and management services; and to promote publicity. It
provides financial assistance by way of
loans, grants and share investment to businesses, including industrial, commercial,
agricultural, tourism and fisheries enterprises; provides financial, legal and practical help for setting up community co-
operatives.
Publications Annual Report & Accounts

Hill Farming Research Organisation (HFRO)
Bush Estate, Penicuik, Lothian EH26 0PY, Scot-
land 031–445 3401
Director J. Eadie
Aims To improve the economic viability of
meat production from the hills and uplands
of the UK.
Activities Research into animal production
and nutrition, grazing ecology and pasture
production in hills and uplands.
Status Research institute
Publications Biennial Report

**Historic Buildings and Monuments
Commission For England**
see ENGLISH HERITAGE

**Historic Buildings and Monuments Direc-
torate (Scotland)**
see SCOTTISH DEVELOPMENT
DEPARTMENT

Historic Buildings Bureau for England
*The functions of this Bureau have been
absorbed into* ENGLISH HERITAGE

Historic Buildings Bureau (Scotland)
Scottish Development Department, New St
Andrew's House, St James Centre, Edinburgh
EH1 3SZ 031–556 8400 ext.4618
Aims To assist in the sale or lease of
historic buildings by maintaining registers
both of buildings and of prospective tenants
or purchasers (but does not advise on ques-
tions of price or rent).
Publications List of available properties (4)

Historic Buildings Bureau (Wales)
New Crown Buildings, Cathays Park, Cardiff
CF1 0222 823864
Contact Chief Estates Officer
Aims To provide a service to owners of
buildings listed as being of historical or architectural interest whereby such buildings on
offer for sale or to let are included in lists
circulated to interested parties.

Historic Buildings Council for England
*This Council was abolished (together with the
Ancient Monuments Board for England) by the
National Heritage Act 1983 and replaced on 1
April 1984 by the Historic Buildings and Monu-
ments Commission for England* (ENGLISH
HERITAGE)

Historic Buildings Council For Scotland
25 Drumsheugh Gardens, Edinburgh EH3 7RN
031–226 3611
Secretary D.J. Christie
Aims To advise the Secretary of State for
Scotland on matters relating to buildings of
historic or architectural interest.
Activities Making representations to the
Secretary of State under the terms of the
Historic Buildings and Ancient Monuments
Act 1953; advising and reporting to the
Secretary of State on the exercise of functions
and powers relevant to the Act, on the
general state of preservation of relevant
buildings, on ways of finding new uses for
historic buildings and on grants or loans
toward the costs incurred in the promotion,
preservation or enhancement of the
character or appearance of an outstanding
conservation area or any part thereof.
Status Statutory
Publications Annual Report

**Historic Buildings Council for Wales/Cyngor
Adeiladau Hanesyddol Cymru**
Brunel House, 2 Fitzalan Road, Cardiff CF2 1UY
0222 465511
Secretary R.J. Bolus
Aims To advise the Secretary of State for
Wales on the exercise of his powers with

regard to historic buildings and conservation areas, especially in respect of the making of grants for repair or restoration works.
Status Statutory
Publications Annual Report

HM Agricultural Inspectorate
Health & Safety Executive, Magdalen House, Stanley Precinct, Bootle, Merseyside L20 3QZ 051–951 4000
Activities Concerned with agricultural health and safety matters. 34 offices nationwide.
Status Statutory (part of the Health and Safety Executive)

HM Alkali and Clean Air Inspectorate
Health & Safety Executive, Becket House, 1 Lambeth Palace Road, London SE1 7ER 01–928 7855
Activities Concerned with control of air pollution from scheduled industrial processes, relative to public health and amenity.
-NR

HM Factory Inspectorate
Health & Safety Executive, Magdalen House, Stanley Precinct, Bootle, Merseyside L20 3QZ 051–951 4000
Activities Concerned with safety of factory machinery and work activities under the Health and Safety at Work 1974 Act.

HM Industrial Pollution Inspectorate (Scotland)
Pentland House, 47 Robb's Loan, Edinburgh EH14 1TY 031–443 8681
Activities A unit of the Scottish Development Department, performing similar functions to HM Alkali and Clean Air Inspectorate in England.
-NR

HM Inspectorate of Mines and Quarries
Health & Safety Executive, Regina House, 259 Old Marylebone Road, London NW1 5RR 01–723 1262
Activities Concerned with the health and safety of workers in mines and quarries.
-NR

HM Nuclear Installations Inspectorate (NII)
Health & Safety Executive, Thames House North, Millbank, London SW1P 4QL 01–211 6790
Activities Responsible for site licensing, safety assessments and inspections of nuclear power stations and other civil nuclear installations.
Publications Quarterly Statement on Nuclear Incidents (4)
-NR

Home Energy Audit Advice and Treatment (HEAT)
26 Store Street, London WC1E 7BS 01–637 1022
-NR

Homoeopathic Development Foundation Ltd
Harcourt House, 19A Cavendish Square, London W1M 9AD 01–629 3204/5
General Administrator Charlotte Reynolds
Aims To promote effectively a knowledge and appreciation of homoeopathy among the general public and to encourage and initiate research in support of this aim.
Activities Providing an information service, reference library and book order service. The Directors of the Foundation are those prominent in the field of homoeopathy; when setting up the Foundation in 1980, they emphasised that it would not duplicate activities already undertaken by other bodies.
Status Charity
Publications
Homoeopathy for the Family.
Homoeopathy for Pets.
Homoeopathic Treatment of Dogs.

Hooves (The Campaign for Horses)
2A West Preston Street, Newington, Edinburgh EH8 9PX 031–667 6488
Aims To make the roads a safer place for horses, ridden or driven; to encourage the provision of livery stables and parking for horses in cities.
Activities Encouraging representation to local councils on provision for horses and inclusion of horse transport in structural plans; raising public awareness and educating as to the needs of horses; fund raising.
Status Voluntary
-NR

HOPE (Help Organise Peaceful Energy)
The Anchor, Bantry, Co. Cork, Ireland
Secretary Jeremy Wates
Aims To further the development of alternative technology, locally and globally; to oppose environmentally harmful practices and industries; to promote political and personal peace; to secure the psychic and physical health of all people by evolving wholesome, non-exploitative lifestyles.
Activities Providing a library and information centre on matters relevant to our aims; co-ordinating a national campaign against the dumping of nuclear waste in the Atlantic.
Status Voluntary
Publications HOPE Newsletter (6)
-NR

Horse and Pony Lovers Against Bloodsports
23 Levernside Crescent, Glasgow G53 5JY
Contact Margaret Smith
-NR

Horses and Ponies Protection Association (HAPPA)
Greenbank Farm, Greenbank Drive, Fence, Burnley, Lancs. BB12 9QJ 0282 65909
Public Relations Officer Mrs L. Jennings
Aims To obtain reforms and improve conditions in slaughter, in transit and at sales and pony fairs and to protect horses and ponies from cruelty and ill-treatment, whether deliberate or caused through callousness, neglect or ignorance.
Activities Maintains 3 rest homes/rescue centres; has 4 field officers nation-wide who investigate reports of cruelty; takes in ill-treated equines, restores them to health and prosecutes the people responsible where possible. Many animals are then put on loan to suitable homes and checked regularly but never sold; those unable to go into a home are offered for adoption and visited by members; the rest homes are open to visitors; membership available.
Status Charity
Publications HAPPA Newsletter (3); Annual Report

Horticultural Education Association (HEA)
see INSTITUTE OF HORTICULTURE

Howey Foundation
2A Lebanon Road, Croydon, Surrey CR0 6UR 01–654 5817
Activities Concerned with environmental health.
Status Charity
-NR

Humane Education Centre (Crusade Against Cruelty to Animals)
Avenue Lodge, Bounds Green Road, London N22 4EU 01–889 1595
-NR

Humane Education Council
39 Bramber Way, Burgess Hill, W. Sussex RH15 8ER
-NR

Humane Research Trust
Brook House, 29 Bramhall Lane South, Bramhall, Cheshire SK7 2DN 061–439 8041
National Organiser Mrs Pamela Brown
Aims To promote essential medical and scientific research in which the use of animals for testing will be replaced by advanced techniques.
Activities Continuously promoting studies in a wide field of illnesses, such as cancer, blindness, nervous diseases, diabetes and rheumatism. Supported by Groups throughout the British Isles who raise money and disseminate literature; this money can be used to supply researchers with equipment that will replace animals (e.g. a scintillation spectrometer given to the Christie Hospital for Cancer Research). The Trust also manufactures stationery and other items for sale (catalogue on request). Local branches.
Status Charity
Publications Humane Research Trust Journal (3)

Humane Slaughter Association
see COUNCIL FOR JUSTICE TO ANIMALS

Humanist Party
261 Archway Road, London N6 5BS
Contact Steve Konrad
-NR

Hunt Saboteurs Association (HSA)
PO Box 19, London SE22 9LR 0392 219581
Joint Secretaries Maggi Sheehy, Harry Cross
Aims To save the lives of hunted animals until such time as hunting ceases.
Activities Taking direct action to sabotage fox hunts, beagle hunts, stag hunts, harrier hunts, hare coursing and mink hunting; some groups also sabotage fishing and shooting. Nation-wide network of groups.
Status Voluntary
Publications Howl (3)

Huntingdon Greens
4 Bridge House, St Ives, Huntingdon, Cambs. PE17 0480 63054
Contact David Taylor
Aims To encourage greater public and political airing and acceptance of the Green philosophy throughout the area of West Cambridgeshire; this philosophy is based on the need for a sustainable and environmentally sound society and economy through the practices of resource conservation, co-operation rather than competition, equality of opportunity and non-violence.
Activities Collection and presentation to the public and to politicians of data on: unsound environmental and social practices in the area; positive alternatives to current environmental and social problems, such as pollution, straw burning and structure plan policies; publicising the Green philosophy through the media and through public meetings throughout the area.
Status Voluntary

Huntingdon Research Centre plc (HRC)
Huntingdon, Cambs. PE18 6ES 0480 890431
Director, Sales & Marketing R. Ridler

Aims To undertake contracted research in the field of biological safety evaluation.
Activities Areas of research include: industrial and environmental studies, including ecology, mutagenicity and industrial toxicology; agrochemicals, industrial chemicals, carcinogenicity and evaluation of environmental pollutants, insecticides and smokes. Liaison offices in USA, France and Japan.
Publications HRC News (2)

Hydraulics Research Limited
Wallingford, Oxon. OX10 8BA 0491 35381

Activities Making predictions of the performance of civil engineering works, including tidal power and wave power devices, and of their consequences to the environment; researching into such matters as wave transformation in shallow water, mooring forces and sediment transport by tidal currents.

Hypnotherapy Centre
see INSTITUTE OF CURATIVE HYPNOTHERAPISTS

I

ICOF (Industrial Common Ownership Finance Ltd)
4 St Giles Street. Northampton, Northants. NN1 1AA 0604 37563
Company Secretary David Ralley
Aims To provide common ownership and co-operative enterprises with financial assistance, particularly at time of start-up.
Activities Administers a revolving loan fund for common ownership and co-operative enterprises: loans average £7,500 and are made over a 5–year period to viable activities which are registered. ICOF also works with local authorities in its promotion of co-operatives and provision of funds.
Publications ICOF Newsletter (1)

ICOM (Industrial Common Ownership Movement Limited)
7–8 The Corn Exchange, Leeds, W. Yorks. LS1 7BP 0532 461737/8
Organising Secretary Mike Campbell
Aims To achieve democratic control of work by people at work.
Activities Assists new worker co-operatives in starting up and registering under the most suitable model rules; advises new co-ops, promotional agencies, local agencies, local councils. government, academics and trade unions on the relevance of common ownership to their environment. Has a network of voluntary workers and consultants around the country in addition to its full-time staff and a branch in London.
Status Voluntary
Publications The New Co-operator (4)
Cockerton, Peter & Whyatt, Anna. *The Workers Co-operative Handbook.* 1984.
Berry, John & Roberts, Mark. *Co-op Management and Employment.* 1984.

Impact
39 Northumberland Road, Old Trafford, Manchester M16 9AN 061–872 5583
Activities A local authority support unit for community self-help groups concerned with local environmental problems.
-NR

Imperial College of Science and Technology
Prince Consort Road, South Kensington, London SW7 2AZ 01–589 5111
-NR

In Business for the Community
c/o Billiton (UK) Ltd, 3 Lincolns Inn Fields, London WC2A 3AA 01–831 7252
Chairman N.J. Bower
Aims To offer the business and managerial expertise of members of the British Institute of Management to local councils, organisers of voluntary and community projects and all non-profit-making organisations.
Activities Responding to approaches for skilled help by putting the organisation concerned in contact, through a committee member, with volunteers from BIM's Central London branch who have the relevant skills; members work with organisations in their free time and no charge is made. The skills offered range from general management feasibility studies to finance and planning; members also undertake legal, accounting and company secretarial practice responsibilities. The Committee can quickly put together teams to study the feasibility of a scheme or give a professional view on organisational problems; confidence is respected and no obligation incurred. Preliminary informal discussion with a committee member can be arranged.
Status Voluntary
-NR

In the Making (ITM)
44 Albion Road, Sutton, Surrey SM2 5TF
Activities Collecting information and producing a directory of co-operatives, alternative technology groups, etc.
Publications In The Making (1)
-NR

Incorporated Society of Registered Naturopaths (ISRN)
Kingston Clinic, 291 Gilmerton Road, Liberton, Edinburgh EH16 5UQ 031–664 3435
General Secretary Peter Fenton
Aims To maintain a register of qualified naturopaths; to promote the practice of naturopathy and to disseminate nature cure ideas in society at large; to train students in naturopathy; to produce literature on nature cures.
Activities Maintaining residential nature cure clinics; practice of nature cure in outpatient practices through the membership. In therapy the emphasis is on fasting and corrective nutrition, hydrotherapy, manipulation, light therapy, psychotherapy and exercise therapy: it totally excludes homoeopathic, herbal and biochemical remedies,

vitamin concentrates, pharmaceuticals or hypnosis. Some members form local health societies. Reading list available.
Status Limited company
-NR

Independent Scientific Committee on Smoking and Health

Dept of Health & Social Security, Hannibal House, Elephant & Castle, London SE1 6TE
01–703 6380

Aims To advise the Health Ministers and, where appropriate, the tobacco companies on the scientific aspects of matters concerning smoking and health, in particular: (i) to receive in confidence full data about the constituents of smoking materials and their smoke and changes in these; (ii) to release to *bona fide* research workers for approved subjects such of the above as is agreed by the suppliers of it. To review the research into less dangerous smoking and to consider whether further such research, including clinical trials and epidemiological studies, needs to be carried out; and to advise on the validity of research results and of systems of testing the health effects of tobacco and tobacco substitutes and on their predictive value to human health. The Committee, appointed by Health Ministers, consists of a chairman, a chief scientific adviser, a chemistry adviser and 11 other members.
Publications Third Report of the Committee, 1983.

Independent Waste Paper Processors Association

25 High Street, Daventry, Northants. NN11 4BG
03272 3223
Status Trade association
-NR

Industry Committee for Packaging and the Environment (INCPEN)

161–166 Fleet Street, London EC4A 2DP
01–353 4353/4
Secretary General Michael Mitchell
Aims To provide a forum in which packaging manufacturers and producers and distributors of packaged consumer goods formulate and co-ordinate their views on the economic, social and environmental aspects of packaging; to present facts and rational argument to government, consumer organisations, environmentalists and the general public about the function and benefits of packaging.
Activities Explaining the purpose and benefits of packaging in a free competitive society; providing information and argument on the social and economic reasons for packaging; keeping members up-to-date with developments; working groups and panels consider current issues affecting packaging and recommend policies and action to members; conducting research, producing reports, discussion papers and articles on various aspects of packaging, including litter, recycling, solid waste, energy, raw materials, benefits of packaging and legislation; producing a journal. INCPEN is a member of the European Union for Packaging and the Environment (EUPE), the EEC-wide packaging forum.
Status Trade/industrial
Publications INCPEN (4)
A Background to Packaging and Food Hygiene. 6pp.
Degradability and Plastics Packaging. 10pp.

Information Centre

Greenhouse, Trevelyan Terrace, Bangor, Gwynedd LL57 1AX, Wales 0248 355821
Contacts Paul Fletcher, Huw Roberts, Sue Snowball
Aims To support and aid local and national initiatives to deal with the crisis facing this culture, whilst seeing it as an opportunity for change for humankind; to reach out to the general public, heightening awareness and creating the conditions for a shift in consciousness.
Activities Maintaining a fully-staffed office 10–5 Monday-Saturday; maintaining over 100 files on topics such as human rights, ecology, animal welfare, the 'new age', peace, Third and Fourth World; acting as a networking centre both for local people and to connect wider networks.
Status Voluntary
-NR

Information for Energy Group

Institute of Petroleum, 61 New Cavendish Street, London W1M 8AR 01–636 1004
-NR

Information Service on Energy (ISE)

69 Gilmore Place, Edinburgh EH3 9NU
Aims To counter pro-nuclear propaganda, especially in schools, libraries, etc.
-NR

Inland Shipping Group (ISG)

Inland Waterways Association, 114 Regent's Park Road, London NW1 8UQ
01–586 2510/2556
General Secretary, IWA J. Taunton
Aims To campaign for the greater use and development of the commercial waterways of this country for the transport of freight.
Activities Compiling fact sheets, publishing articles, addressing meetings and staging exhibitions; monitoring commercial traffic on waterways and giving advice to the relevant sections of industry wishing

to make greater use of commercial water transport. 7 regional committees.
Status Voluntary

Inland Waterways Amenity Advisory Council (IWAAC)
122 Cleveland Street, London W1P 5DN
01–387 7973

Secretary Miss Frances Moon
Aims To advise the Secretary of State for the Environment and the British Waterways Board on the use and development of 2,000 miles of inland waterways for recreation and amenity, including provision of facilities and additions to the protected network. The Council consists of a chairman and 14 members appointed by the Secretary of State.
Activities Required by law to consider any representation relating to the above; duties entail discussion and analysis of views of interested authorities, private firms and user interests in England, Scotland and Wales. Publishes advice on current trends and issues to stimulate discussion.
Status Statutory
Publications Summary of matters considered (5/6)
Waterway Ecology and the Design of Recreational Craft. 1983.

Inland Waterways Association (IWA)
114 Regent's Park Road, London NW1 8UQ
01–586 2510/2556

General Secretary John Taunton
Aims To promote the restoration, retention and development of inland waterways in the British Isles and their fullest commercial and recreational use.
Activities Lobbying government to implement a policy of improvement and development of the waterway system; supporting local restoration work and providing volunteer labour and finance for projects. To date over 200 miles of inland waterways have been restored. 7 regional branches; membership of over 19,000.
Status Voluntary; charity
Publications IWA Waterways (3)

Inland Waterways Protection Society Ltd
The Cottage, 69 Ivy Road, Macclesfield, Cheshire SK11 8QN 0625 23595 (evenings)

Chairman Ian Edgar
Aims To ensure the preservation, restoration and well-being of the inland waterways of the UK; to promote their use for multi-purpose commercial and/or amenity use as appropriate.
Activities Restoring and developing Bugsworth Basin at the head of the Peak Forest Canal for multi-purpose use commensurate with its ancient monument status;

establishment on the site of a museum to the limestone extractive industry; giving support to other voluntary groups looking after their local waterways; campaigning on a national level for the canal system as a whole.
Status Voluntary
Publications Onward (3)

INLAW (International Law Against War)
90 Gladstone Street, Bedford. Beds. MK41 7RT -NR

Institute for Complementary Medicine (ICM)
21 Portland Place. London W1N 3AF
01–636 9543

Contact Information Section
Aims To improve the quality and range of health care by extending the use of complementary medicine.
Activities Maintaining a computerised library and information service; running a national volunteer-manned information network; has founded an Association to create contacts between individuals and provide channels for information; practitioners' Education and Advisory Committees examine and encourage standards of training; programme of sponsoring pure research; running special courses for medical students, nurses and adult education authorities.
Status Charity
Publications Newsletter (4): Journal (1)
Davies, P., *Report on Trends in Complementary Medicine*, 1984.

Institute for European Environmental Policy (IEEP)
3 Endsleigh Street, London WC1H 0DD
01–388 2117

Head of London Office Nigel Haigh
Aims To facilitate contact between the various institutions, particularly parliaments, concerned with environmental policy in a European context and to advance environmental policy-making in Europe.
Activities Critical analysis of strategies for dealing with environmental problems that need attention at European level; studies. mostly of a comparative nature, relating to subject matter relevant to European policy-making, particularly in terms of the European Community. The Institute, which is a part of the European Cultural Foundation, is an independent non-profit centre with its head office in Bonn (*see* Organisations Not Based in UK. . .) and another office in Paris.
Status Voluntary
Publications The Environment in Europe (5)
Haigh, Nigel, *EEC Environmental Policy and*

Britain: an essay and handbook, Environmental Data Services Ltd, 1984.
Baldock, David, *Wetland Drainage in Europe: the effects of agricultural policy in four EEC countries,* IEEP, 1984.
Baldock, David. *The CAP Price Policy and the Environment: an exploratory essay,* IEEP, 1985.

Institute for Marine Environmental Research (IMER)

Prospect Place, The Hoe. Plymouth, Devon PL1 3DH 0752 21371
Director Dr B.L. Bayne
Aims To study the processes which determine the performance of marine and estuarine ecosystems; this is treated as the essential basis for the detection and prediction of any effects that man's activities might have on marine ecosystems.
Activities The principal programmes deal with estuarine ecosystems and the pelagic system of the open seas. IMER studies ecotoxicology, environmental radioactivity and plankton distribution; other work includes the formulation of simulation models for detection and prediction; research cruises; development of new equipment for on-site experimentation; nutrient cycling; contract research related to the above programmes.
Status Research institute of the Natural Environment Research Council

Institute for Research on Animal Diseases

Compton, Newbury, Berks. RG16 0NN 063522 411
Information Officer Miss D.M. Northall
Aims To research economically important diseases of farm animals, particularly cattle and pigs.
Activities Operates COSREEL, a computer-based system for recording information on individual farm animals, with particular emphasis on veterinary aspects.
Status Grant-aided institute of the Agricultural and Food Research Council
-NR

Institute for Transport Studies (ITS)

University of Leeds, Leeds, W. Yorks. LS2 9JT 0532 431751
Assistant Director of Research H.R. Kirby
Aims To conduct research that can help guide and inform decision-makers as to the consequences of their transport decisions.
Activities Research and postgraduate training in transport studies; research is sponsored by many agencies and is concerned with methods and assessing the effects of changes in the transport system or in policies. Current work includes the environmental impact of railways and bus lanes;

studies of shopping behaviour; and hospital access. Working papers are published.
Status Academic
Publications Annual Report
-NR

Institute of Animal Physiology

Babraham, Cambridge CB2 4AT 0223 832312
Secretary B.E. Faulkner, OBE
Aims To extend knowledge of the basic physiology and biochemistry of farm livestock as a foundation for improved animal production.
Status Grant-aided institute of the Agricultural and Food Research Council
-NR

Institute of Antiquarian Craftsmen

see CRAFTS COMMISSION

Institute of Biology

20 Queensberry Place, London SW7 2DZ 01-581 8333
-NR

Institute of Botanic Medicine Ltd

538 Forest Road, London E17 4NB 01-520 3811
-NR

Institute of Chartered Foresters (ICF) [formerly Institute of Foresters of Great Britain]

22 Walker Street, Edinburgh EH3 7HR 031-225 2705
Secretary Mrs M.W. Dick
Aims To maintain and improve the standards of practice of forestry; to advance, spread and promote all aspects of forestry, especially in the UK, and to encourage the study of forestry.
Activities Publishes a Code of Ethics to which all members subscribe; keeps under review the needs of education, research and training; offers examinations for professional qualifications; reviews the status of forestry and of the profession and makes representations when necessary; annual study tour of forests in the UK; weekend discussion meetings annually on forestry and allied subjects of current interest; overseas tours. 6 regional groups.
Status Professional institute
Publications Forestry (2); Newsletter (4) *Broadleaves in Britain.* ICF/Forestry Commission conference proceedings, 1982.

Institute of Curative Hypnotherapists (ICH)

Equity House, 49–51 London Road, Waterlooville, Hants. PO7 7EX 07014 65880
Aims To promote and protect the good name of hypnotherapy and its practitioners throughout the UK; to maintain a high standard of ethics and procedures and to

provide a pool of information and assistance for its members' convenience.

Activities Runs the Hypnotherapy Centre which offers treatment to people troubled by alcohol, smoking, asthma, depression, etc.

Status Non-profit organisation

-NR – L

Institute of Development Studies (IDS)

University of Sussex, Falmer, Brighton, E. Sussex BN1 9RE 0273 606261

Academic Secretary Zoë Mars

Aims To promote development and the alleviation of material poverty in the Third World and to enhance the relationships between rich and poor countries. Established as a national centre in 1966 by the Ministry of Overseas Development.

Activities Research, training and operational assignments directed to a wide range of development problems, particularly those relating to poverty, employment and income distribution within Third World countries and to the unequal realtionships between the Third World and the rest of the world economy. The IDS has an extensive programme of publications, conferences and workshops to disseminate the results of its work in ways which make an impact on policy-making; the IDS library is a national centre of documentation on Third World development and is an official depository for UN publications; the collection now exceeds 100,000 non-serial titles and can be used by scholars by arrangement.

Status Research institute

Publications IDS Bulletin (4); Annual Report & Handbook

Institute of Energy (IE)

18 Devonshire Street, London W1N 2AU 01–580 7124

Aims To bring together energy engineers and others concerned with the economic selection, production and utilisation of all forms of energy with minimum pollution of the environment.

Activities The Institute is an international organisation recognised by the Privy Council as the senior body for energy and fuels. Publications include journals, conference proceedings and the findings of working parties.

Status Professional association

Publications Energy World (12); Fuel and Energy Abstracts (6); Journal of the Institute of Energy (4)

Institute of Estuarine and Coastal Studies

University of Hull, Cottingham Road, Hull, Humberside HU6 7RX 0482 46311 ext.7511

Director Dr N.V. Jones

Aims To encourage multi-disciplinary

research and teaching in estuarine and coastal studies within the university; to foster links between the university and outside bodies with interests in the same field.

Activities Organising meetings within the university and with outside organisations; execution of contract research within and between different disciplines; exploring the possibility of postgraduate teaching across disciplinary boundaries.

Status Academic

-NR

Institute of Geological Sciences (IGS)

Keyworth, Notts. NG12 5GG 06077 6111

Principal Secretary D. Hackett

Activities Incorporates the British Geological Survey. Research includes: energy and mineral resources assessment; groundwater supplies; pollution control; natural hazards assessment. The Institute's library, open to the public for reference purposes, is based at the Geological Museum in South Kensington, London.

Status Statutory

Institute of Horticulture (IoH)

PO Box 313, 80 Vincent Square, London SW1P 2PE 01–834 4333

Secretary P.A. Johns

Aims To promote horticulture as a distinct and credible profession and to confer status on its members; to act as an authoritative body and to encourage the interests and developments of all branches and associated disciplines; to promote conferences, lectures and tours of inspection. The Institute now incorporates the Horticultural Education Association.

Activities Three national seminars/conferences per year; regular branch meetings to discuss relevant topics and visit places of interest; providing information and literature for members. 8 branches in UK and Ireland.

Status Professional institute

Publications Institute of Horticulture News (4); Scientific Horticulture (1)

Institute of Hydrology

Maclean Building, Crowmarsh Gifford, Wallingford, Oxon. OX10 8BB 0491 38800 Telex 849365

Information Officer ext.264 *Librarian* ext.266

Aims To carry out fundamental studies of the behaviour of water in its main phases in the hydrological cycle and of the manner of its movement between these phases.

Activities Subjects studied include hydrology, meteorology, climatology, geomorphology, soil science, water

resources and water quality. Reference library available to visitors.
Status Institute of the Natural Environment Research Council

Institute of Marine Biochemistry (IMB)
St Fittick's Road, Torry, Aberdeen, Grampian AB1 3RA, Scotland 0224 875695
    Publicity Officer A. Mitchell
    Aims To study at the biochemical level the basic life forces within the marine environment.
    Activities Research includes: fish nutrition; lipids in the marine ecosystem; trace metal accumulation and pollutant detoxification in marine organisms; chemical ecology and chemoreception; defence mechanisms in fish.
    Status Institute of the Natural Environment Research Council
    Publications Research Report 1980–84

Institute of Marine Studies
University College of Swansea, Singleton Park, Swansea, W. Glam. SA2 8PP, Wales 0792 205678
    Director Prof. J.A. Beardmore
    Aims To co-ordinate the marine studies carried out by various departments of the University College.
    Activities Investigating the marine environment, particularly around south-west Wales, and the various problems arising therein, both in relation to human activities and from natural processes. Research papers are published and listed annually.
    Status Academic/scientific research institute

Institute of Oceanographic Sciences (IOS)
Brook Road, Wormley, Godalming, Surrey GU8 5UB 042879 4141
    Aims To advance the science of oceanography, with emphasis on the long-term research required to improve understanding of the basic physical, geological, chemical and biological processes in the ocean and the application of the research to practical problems.
    Activities Studies include: ocean circulation; temperature; salinity; exchange processes at the air-sea boundary; waves and currents; response of the sea surface to wind and pressure changes; the physics of tides and surges; chemistry and organic production of the oceans; geology and geophysics of the continental shelf and deep ocean basins; dynamics of sediment transport; engineering oceanography; design and development of oceanographic equipment. Specialist advice and consultancy is provided by IOS scientists through the

Marine Information and Advisory Service (MIAS). Reports are published.
    Status Institute of the Natural Environment Research Council
    Publications MIAS News Bulletin; Annual Report

Institute of Offshore Engineering (IOE)
Heriot-Watt University, Riccarton, Edinburgh EH14 4AS 031–449 3393/3794
    Information Officer Arnold Myers
    Aims To provide support to industries involved in offshore engineering and related activities.
    Activities Current research activity centres mainly on: environmental pollution studies; marine fouling; underwater systems and operations; instrumentation; pipeline engineering; topside processing, including effluent treatment; safety and risk assessment; decommissioning/abandonment strategy; bioresource exploitation. The Institute manages the university Marine Technology Programme and operates a specialist information service in the marine technology field as well as running seminars and short courses and offering contract and consultancy services, including environmental impact assessment.
    Status Research institute
    Publications IOE Library Bulletin (12); IOE Newsletter (occasional)
Current Research in Environmental Sciences and Bioresources at Heriot-Watt University Marine Technology Centre 1984. 70pp.
Offshore Information Conference Papers 1984. 166pp.

Institute of Petroleum (IP)
61 New Cavendish Street, London W1M 8AR 01–636 1004
    Head of Library/Information Dept Mrs J. Etherton
    Aims To give objective consideration to the science, technology and economics of petroleum and its products and their uses and to express an independent viewpoint and provide a forum for discussion and exchange of ideas; to co-ordinate expertise between its own committees, between the Institute and other organisations and with appropriate government departments; to promote a flow of factual information about petroleum and about the work of the Institute and the petroleum industry; to provide appropriate services to members, both individual and collective.
    Activities There are 14 main committees, including environmental committees on the protection of the atmosphere, ground and freshwater, the marine environment and research into these and other fields. The Institute disseminates a considerable

volume of information about oil matters each year through publications, meetings, conferences and seminars; it is represented at selected international exhibitions and sponsors major conferences associated with such exhibitions; publications include abstracts, books and technical papers; members have access to a library of 15,000 volumes. 15 branches.

Status Professional institute

Publications Petroleum Review (12) Know More About Oil (series of booklets) Oil Data Sheets (facts and figures)

Institute of Psychosynthesis

1 Cambridge Gate, London NW1 4JN
01–486 2588

Co-ordinator Judy Sender

Aims To provide in-depth experience in the principles and practice of psychosynthesis which is an inclusive approach to human growth guided by the higher self.

Activities Introductory evenings and weekends; counselling and other on-going groups; low-cost individual counselling; annual 2–week summer school; 7–day intensive course in Fundamentals: professional education and training; diploma courses. 1 branch in Ireland (Eckhart House, 5 Pembroke Park, Dublin 4) and 1 in Holland.

Status Educational/psychotherapeutic institute

Publications Yearbook (no.4 available August 1985)

Institute of Rural Life at Home and Overseas (IRL)

This organisation was disbanded in 1985

Institute of Terrestrial Ecology (ITE)

HQ: 68 Hills Road, Cambridge CB2 1LA
0223 69745
Outstations: Banchory Research Station, Hill of Brathens, Glassel, Banchory, Grampian AB3 4BY, Scotland 03302 3434
Bangor Research Station, Penrhos Road, Bangor, Gwynedd LL57 2LQ, Wales
0248 364001
Culture Centre of Algae & Protozoa, 36 Storey's Way, Cambridge CB3 0DT 0223 61378
Edinburgh Research Station, Bush Estate, Penicuik Lothian EH26 0QB, Scotland
031–445 4343
Furzebrook Research Station, Wareham, Dorset BH20 5AS 0929 51518
Merlewood Research Station, Grange-over-Sands, Cumbria LA11 6JU 04484 2264
Monks Wood Experimental Station, Abbots Ripton, Huntingdon, Cambs. PE17 2LS
04873 381

Aims To extend our knowledge about the structure, composition and processes in terrestrial ecosystems, to provide a scientific basis for predicting and modelling environmental changes and to carry out investigations, under contract where appropriate, on matters of environmental concern.

Activities Research in 1985 included: national and regional surveys of vegetation and land use; growth and management of trees and their effects on soil, associated vegetation and wildlife; mutual effects of acid rain and forest trees, soils and mycorrhizal fungi; the distribution and behaviour of pollutant radionuclides in terrestrial environments; fungi and their role in plant decomposition and nutrient availability; plant nutrient diagnostic techniques with emphasis on phosphorus and nitrogen; effect of clear felling forests on soil stability and chemistry; provision of specialist chemistry and computing support service. About 30 scientific papers, books and reports are produced each year, details of which are given in the Annual Report.

Status Research institute of the Natural Environment Research Council

Publications Annual Report

Institute of Transport Administration (IoTA)

32 Palmerston Road, Southampton, Hants. SO1 1LL 0703 31380

National Secretary P.F. Green

Aims To improve the knowledge and skills of its membership, whether as employers, managers or employees, in the many aspects and sectors of the transport industry; to improve the standards of transport administration within the industry both at home and overseas.

Activities Conducting examinations and awarding recognised certificates and diplomas; electing members to the various grades of Institute membership; bringing members together by meetings, seminars, conferences and social events through the medium of the 34 established centres throughout the UK. Monitoring transport policy, activities and developments; providing professional advice to government, local government and other institutions on transport matters; making known to the relevant authorities the views of the membership on major transport issues. 34 branches in the UK and 3 overseas.

Status Professional association

Publications Transport Management (4)

Institute of Waste Management

3 Albion Place, Northampton, Northants. NN1 1UD 0604 20426

Aims To provide information and expert advice to local authorities, industrial companies and others on problems of refuse and industrial waste storage and collection, transport, treatment and disposal; to train and qualify professional staff in this field.

Activities Carrying out the above objectives; conferences, symposia, publications; providing the secretariat for the International Solid Waste Association.

Status Professional association

Publications Solid Wastes (12)

-NR – L

Institute of Water Pollution Control

Ledson House, 53 London Road, Maidstone, Kent ME16 8JH 0622 62034

Executive Secretary H.R. Evans

Aims To promote the advancement of the science and practice of the treatment of waste waters, both domestic and industrial, of the management of rivers and of the prevention of water pollution.

Activities Annual conference and exhibition; symposia; publishing a journal and Manuals of British Practice in Water Pollution Control. 16 branches.

Status Voluntary

Publications Water Pollution Control (4)

Institution of Environmental Health Officers

Chadwick House, 48 Rushworth Street, London SE1 0QT 01–928 6006

Secretary K.J. Tyler

Aims To promote education and training in environmental health, ensuring the effectiveness of environmental health officers and their usefulness to the community; to promote the dissemination of knowledge of environmental health for the benefit of the public and to maintain high standards of practice and professional conduct by all its members.

Activities Areas of concern include: food hygiene and inspection; health and safety at work; pollution control; housing; caravanning and camping; environmental health protection; port health; solid wastes; and legislation in all the relevant fields. Most of the Institution's members work for local authorities.

Status Professional institution

Publications Environmental Health (12); Environmental Health Report (1)

Johnson, Reginald. *A Century of Progress.* 1983.

Institution of Environmental Sciences (IES)

14 Princes Gate, Hyde Park, London SW7 1PU

Hon. Secretary Dr John F. Potter

Aims To function as a learned, professional and corporate body at national and international level for persons possessing responsibilities for environmental matters; and for consultation and co-ordination of matters of public and professional interest concerning environmental sciences.

Activities National and international seminars and conferences; publications on environmental science; promotional and advisory services. Local branches.

Status Professional association; charity

Publications Institution of Environmental Sciences Journal; Newssheet (6)

-NR

Institution of Gas Engineers

17 Grosvenor Crescent, London SW1X 7ES 01–245 9811

-NR

Institution of Mining Engineers

Hobart House, Grosvenor Place, London SW1X 7AE 01–235 3691

-NR

Institution of Nuclear Engineers (INucE)

Allan House, 1 Penerley Road, London SE6 2LQ 01–698 1500

Secretary Mrs S.M. Blackburn

Aims To promote and advance nuclear engineering and allied branches of science and engineering; to improve and widen the understanding of nuclear engineering and its supporting scientific and technological bases; to promote contact between nuclear engineers throughout the world.

Activities Lectures, meetings, specialist conferences; has founded an Educational Trust Fund and promotes scholarships and prizes; fostering international contacts by the encouragement of overseas branches and through being one of the constituent bodies of the European Nuclear Society; speaks for the profession in consultations with government and other statutory bodies; publishes a journal and occasional monographs. 4 branches.

Status Professional association

Publications The Nuclear Engineer (6)

-NR

Institution of Occupational Safety and Health (IOSH)

222 Uppingham Road, Leicester LE5 0QG 0533 768424

Activities Concerns include industrial health and safety, occupational hygiene and health hazards and environmental problems.

Publications Protection (11)

-NR

Institution of Public Health Engineers (IPHE)

Grosvenor Gardens House, 35–37 Grosvenor Gardens, London SW1W 0BS 01–834 8785/6

Secretary D.J. Dacam, OBE

Aims To promote, for the benefit of the public in general, the art, science, technology, profession and practice of public health engineering; to advance education in these.

Activities Meetings, lectures, symposia, conferences and training periods on subjects relating to public health engineering; encouraging students in the subject with prizes, etc.; providing a library and information service for members; publishing a journal, newsletter and other literature. 12 District Centres.
Status Professional institution
Publications The Public Health Engineer (4)

Institution of Water Engineers and Scientists
31–33 High Holborn, London WC1V 6AX
01–831 6578
Status Professional institution
Publications Journal of the Institution of Water Engineers and Scientists (6)
-NR

Insulating Jacket Manufacturers' Federation
c/o Ideal Insulations (Burton) Ltd, Little Burton West, Derby Street, Burton-on-Trent, Staffs. DE14 1PP 0283 63815/6
Chairman C.C. Smith
Aims To further fuel conservation by producing quality insulation jackets.
Status Trade association

Interchange Trust
[formerly Inter-Action Trust Ltd]
15 Wilkin Street, Kentish Town, London NW5 3NG 01–267 9421
Activities The Trust's Environmental Advisory Service uses an integrated approach to help groups whose primary purposes are not environmental but who wish to use the environment as an element of their programme; it offers advice and information about a range of issues concerned with urban/rural interchange, urban food production, networking and legal issues affecting proposed environmental activities.
Status Charity
-NR – L

Inter-Departmental Environment Committee (Republic of Ireland)
c/o Dept of the Environment, Custom House, Dublin 1, Ireland 0001–74 2961
Aims To co-ordinate the activities of 13 relevant departments.
Activities Has particular responsibilities for assessing the impact of actions proposed by the European Commission and developments at international level.
Status Statutory

Interhelp
20 Landsdowne Close, Kendal, Cumbria LA9 7BS 0539 29256
Aims To help people develop a response to threats to our collective survival – allowing them to remain sane and take charge of their future.
Activities Operating as a network of individuals and groups expanding throughout the UK and Europe from its origins in the USA. Work is focused primarily on the nuclear situation which is recognised as the most immediate of many global threats; Interhelp offers guest speakers, a newsletter and workshops in which people can explore their personal response to planetary threats, moving beyond feelings of powerlessness toward effective action; training is available for workshop leaders.
Status Informal network
Publications Threads (6)
-NR – L

Intermediate Technology Development Group (ITDG)
Myson House, Railway Terrace, Rugby, Warwicks. CV21 3HT 0788 60631
Information Officer David Collins
Aims To help the Third World poor to work themselves out of poverty, using their own skills and resources, through the development or adaptation of tools, equipment and methods which are appropriate to local conditions, both environmental and socio-economic; IT concentrates on increasing production of food, water, building materials, renewable energy supplies and goods needed in rural areas and minimising demands on scarce and imported resources.
Activities Providing a free technical enquiry service for field workers; publishing a wide range of buyer's guides, bibliographies, manuals, case studies and reviews; undertaking consultancies on behalf of charities, UN agencies and governmental aid organisations; assisting in the establishment of local Appropriate Technology centres; undertaking research and development, field trials and implementation of new or adapted small-scale technologies in collaboration with local groups or institutions; advising aid institutions, ministries and government agencies on policy development to encourage small-scale, decentralised local production. Operates in 10 main areas of endeavour: food production; food processing; sugar processing; textiles; fuel-efficient cooking stoves; small-scale hydro-electricity; fishing boat building; rural transportation; wood and metal working equipment; and mining and building materials. Two companies within the Group, Development Techniques Ltd and IT Products Ltd, are wholly-owned subsidiaries for licensing the Group's 'intellectual property' and are located at the above address; IT Publications Ltd is the Group's bookshop and Communications Division, situated at 9 King Street,

Covent Garden, London WC2E 8HW
(01–836 9434). [*Other component companies
listed below*]
Status Charity
Publications Appropriate Technology (4);
Waterlines (4); Intermediate Technology
News (2)
Tools for Agriculture, 3rd edn. IT Pubs, 1985,
200pp. (buyer's guide)
Stern, Peter *et al.* (eds), *Field Engineering:
a guide to construction and development
work in rural areas*, IT Pubs, 1983, 288pp.
Stewart, W. *et al., Improved Wood, Waste
and Charcoal Burning Stoves: a prac-
titioner's manual*, IT Pubs, 1985, 144pp.
Bollard, Alan, *Just for Starters: a handbook of
small-scale business opportunities*, IT Pubs,
1984, 208pp.
*Appropriate Technology Institutions: a direc-
tory*, IT Pubs, 1985, 38pp.
Sinclair, Angela, *A Guide to Appropriate
Technology Institutions*, IT Pubs, 1985,
124pp.
see also INTERMEDIATE TECHNOLOGY
POWER; INTERMEDIATE TECHNOLOGY
TRANSPORT; INTERMEDIATE TECH-
NOLOGY WORKSHOPS

Intermediate Technology Power
Mortimer Hill, Mortimer, Reading, Berks.
RG7 3PG 0734 333231
Activities Associate company of ITDG
specialising in renewable energy consult-
ancies, including solar, wind, micro hydro,
biomass and small engines.
Status Professional consultancy

Intermediate Technology Transport
Home Farm, Ardington, Oxon. OX12 8PN
Activities Associate company of ITDG
specialising in low-cost transportation
consultancies.
Status Professional consultancy

Intermediate Technology Workshops
Corngreaves Estate, Overend Road, Warley,
W. Mids. B64 7DD
Activities Associate company of ITDG
specialising in low-cost building materials and
techniques.
Status Professional consultancy

**International Association against Painful
Experiments on Animals (IAAPEA)**
51 Harley Street, London W1N 1DD 01–580 4943
General Secretary Colin Smith
Aims To ensure that the use of living
animals for experimental purposes becomes
prohibited; to promote co-operation between
member societies and to assist in the formation of societies in countries where there is
no opposition to animal experimentation.
Activities Supplying expert speakers to

international conferences; establishing
humane research groups for the development of techniques not requiring the use of
live animals; distributing films, publications
and display material relating to the use of
animals in science; sponsored an International Conference on Religious Perspectives on the Use of Animals in Science (1984).
58 member societies in 27 countries.
Status Voluntary
Publications International Animal Action

**International Association for Ecology
(INTECOL)**
Harvest House, 62 London Road, Reading,
Berks. RG1 5AS
Aims To promote the science and practice
of ecology.
-NR

**International Association of Hydrological
Sciences (IAHS)**
c/o Institute of Hydrology, Maclean Building,
Crowmarsh Gifford, Wallingford, Oxon.
OX10 8BB 0491 38800
Secretary General Dr John C. Rodda
Aims To promote the study of hydrology as
an earth science and in relation to water
resources.
Activities Organising symposia and
publishing the proceedings of these;
publishing the journal.
Status Voluntary
Publications Hydrological Sciences
Journal (4)
Rodier, J.A. & Roche, M. (eds), *World Cata-
logue of Maximum Observed Floods*, 1984,
384pp.

**International Association of Organic
Gardeners**
see GOOD GARDENERS' ASSOCIATION

**International Association on Water Pollution
Research and Control (IAWPRC)**
Alliance House, 29–30 High Holborn, London
WC1V 6BA 01–405 4552
Publications Manager Ms Elizabeth Izod
Aims To facilitate the exchange of high
quality information, on an international basis,
on all aspects of water pollution control,
scientific and theoretical.
Activities Biennial international conferences; 8–10 regional and specialised conferences per year involving the world's leading
experts; specialist Study Groups and Task
Groups on topics of importance in water
pollution control; liaison with other international organisations in the form of co-operation on relevant activities; publication of
two journals, a newsletter, a yearbook and a
range of books.
Status Charity; NGO

Publications Water Research (12); Water Science and Technology (12); IAWPRC Newsletter (4); Directory of Members (1)
Bannink, B.A. *et al.* (eds), *Integration of Ecological Aspects in Coastal Engineering Projects* (Rotterdam Seminar 1983), 820pp.
Jenkins, S.H. & Schjodtz Hansen, P. (eds), *Airborne Pollutants from Coal-Fired Power Plants: water pollution problems* (Copenhagen Conf. 1983), 128pp.

International Bee Research Association (IBRA)

Hill House, Chalfont St Peter, Gerrards Cross, Bucks. SL9 0NR 0753 885011
   Director Dr Margaret Adey
   Aims To advance research on bees and beekeeping.
   Activities Acting as an international clearing house for scientific and technical information about honeybees and closely related insects, their biology and role in the environment and their products; maintaining close contact with research and educational establishments and beekeeping associations worldwide; publishing scientific papers, authoritative texts, reports, directories, bibliographies, dictionaries, etc.; maintaining one of the most comprehensive apicultural libraries in the world. The Association's work is funded by grants, subscriptions, donations and the sale of services and publications; it has members and subscribers in over 100 countries.
   Status Limited company; charity
   Publications Apicultural Abstracts (4); Bee World (4); Journal of Apicultural Research (4)
   Crane, Eva & Walker, Penelope, *Directory of Important World Honey Sources*, 1984.
   Crane, Eva & Walker, Penelope, *Pollination Directory for World Crops*, 1984.
   Crane, Eva, *World Perspectives in Apiculture*, 1985.

International Centre for Conservation Education (ICCE)

Greenfield House, Guiting Power, Cheltenham, Glos. GL54 5TZ 04515 549
   Director Mark Boulton
   Aims To promote greater understanding of conservation and the environment, with particular emphasis on developing countries.
   Activities Provides consultancy and advisory services and specialist photographic and technical services; runs an annual training course for conservation educators from developing countries; operates an environmental photolibrary; prepares and publishes audiovisual programmes (catalogue on request) and prepares teaching materials (filmstrips,

posters, booklets, etc.) to order. Has a subsidiary trading company, Conservation Education Services Ltd.
   Status Charity
   Publications Africa Link (2) (for conservation educators in Africa)
   A/V programmes: Acid Rain – the silent crisis; Introducing British Mammals; Planning for Survival – the World Conservation Strategy.

International College of Oriental Medicine (UK) Ltd

Green Hedges House, Green Hedges Avenue, East Grinstead, W. Sussex RH19 1DZ
0342 28567
   Contact The Administrator
   Aims To provide a course in Traditional Chinese Medicine to the highest possible standard; to contribute toward the maintenance of a high degree of professionalism in acupuncture throughout the world.
   Activities Providing a 4–year course in Traditional Chinese Medicine, culminating in a B.Ac. degree; practical experience is available in our adjoining clinic three days per week, in which only members of the International Register of Oriental Medicine practise.
   Status Charity
   -NR

International Commission on Radiological Protection (ICRP)

Clifton Avenue, Sutton, Surrey SM2 5PU
01–642 4680
   Scientific Secretary Dr M.C. Thorne
   Aims To give general guidance on the more widespread use of radiation sources caused by the rapid developments in the field of nuclear energy; to make recommendations on basic radiation protection.
   Activities The policy adopted by the Commission in preparing its recommendations is to consider the fundamental principles upon which appropriate radiation protection measures can be based while leaving to the various national protection bodies the responsibility of formulating the specific advice, codes of practice or regulations that are best suited to the needs of their individual countries. The Commission maintains its traditional contact with medical radiology and the medical profession generally.
   Status NGO
   Publications Annals of the ICRP (4)
   Protection of the Public in the Event of Major Radiation Accidents. ICRP Pub. 40, 1984.

International Co-operative Alliance (ICA)

11 Upper Grosvenor Street, London W1X 9PA
01–499 5991

Activities Acts as the central body of the world-wide co-operative movement.
Status International NGO
Publications Co-op Consumers (12); ICA News (12); Review of International Co-operation (4)
-NR

International Council Against Bullfighting (ICAB)

c/o World Society for the Protection of Animals, 106 Jermyn Street, London SW1Y 6EE
01–839 3026/3066
-NR

International Council for Bird Preservation (ICBP)

219C Huntingdon Road, Cambridge CB3 0DL
0223 277318
Assistant Director, Network Relations Miss Jane Fenton
Activities Determining the status of bird species and their habitats throughout the world; compiling data on all endangered species; identifying conservation problems and priorities; initiating, promoting and co-ordinating conservation projects and international conventions: campaigning against the indiscriminate slaughter of wild birds for exotic food or sport. British and Irish National Sections; representatives in 100 countries.
Status Charity
Publications Newsletter (4): Bulletin; Annual Report

International Dolphin Watch

Parklands, North Ferriby, Hull, Humberside HU14 3ET

International Energy Conservation Group (IECG)

PO Box 16, Stroud, Glos. GL5 5EB
0453 873568
-NR

International Federation of Organic Agriculture Movements (IFOAM)

c/o Wye College (University of London), Wye, Ashford, Kent TN25 5AH
-NR

International Fund for Animal Welfare (IFAW)

Tubwell House, New Road, Crowborough, E. Sussex TN6 2QH
Activities Campaigns in the field against the killing of seals, whales, polar bears and vicuna; methods include airlifts, surveys, petitions and fund raising. HQ in the USA, offices in Holland and Switzerland.
Publications IFAW Newsletter
-NR – L

International Institute for Environment and Development (IIED)

3 Endsleigh Street, London WC1H 0DD
01–388 2117
Executive Vice-President Richard Sandbrook
Aims To undertake policy studies on environmental and developmental issues of concern to international institutions, national governments and NGOs; to bridge the gap between those who have ideas and those who make decisions.
Activities Environmental planning and management; human settlements; future energy; applied ecology and marine management; Antarctic resources; European environmental policy. Runs an information service [see EARTHSCAN]; operates a Joint Environmental Service of technical advice and assistance with the International Union for the Conservation of Nature and Natural Resources (IUCN). Publications available through Earthscan. Offices in Washington and Buenos Aires.
Status Charity
Publications Earthscan Bulletin (6); Annual Report
Bartlem, Todd. *Policy Framework: the importance of government incentives in renewable energy development.* 1984.
Haigh, Nigel. *EEC Environmental Policy and Britain.* ENDS for IIED. 1984.
Horberry, John. *Environmental Guidelines Survey: an analysis of environmental procedures and guidelines governing development aid.* 1983.

International Law Association (ILA)

3 Paper Buildings, Temple, London EC4Y 7EU
01–353 2904
Activities Interests include environmental protection, etc.
-NR

International League for the Protection of Cetaceans (ILPC)

2 Meryon Court, Rye, E. Sussex TN31 7LY
0797 223649
Executive Director Dr Sidney J. Holt
Aims To protect and conserve dolphins and whales.
Activities Conducting and sponsoring relevant scientific research; informing the general public; acting as a node of an information network of organisations concerned with cetacean biology and protection. Member of the European Environmental Bureau, IUCN, Wildlife Link and the Environment Liaison Centre, Nairobi.
Status Voluntary
Publications Series of Occasional Papers on whales and whaling.

International League for the Protection of Horses (ILPH)
PO Box 166, 67A Camden High Street, London NW1 7JL 01–388 1449

Assistant Secretary Mrs S. Baum

Aims To monitor and take action to obtain reasonable transportation conditions for the hundreds of thousands of horses transported across Europe for ultimate slaughter; to investigate and remedy any form of cruelty to equine animals in Great Britain and Ireland.

Activities Pressing for reforms and national and international legislation for the better treatment of horses; promoted the Exportation of Horses Act 1937 and procured orders to protect horses during transportation; stopped the deplorable traffic in live horses from America and Canada to Europe for slaughter and was instrumental in obtaining many other reforms both in the UK and abroad. The League runs Homes of Rest for horses in Norfolk, Surrey and Dublin.

Status Voluntary

Publications Annual Report

-NR

International Maritime Organization (IMO)
4 Albert Embankment, London SE1 7SR 01–735 7611

Information Officer Roger Kohn

Aims To develop internationally agreed measures for the improvement of safety at sea, for the prevention of marine pollution from ships and for the facilitation of maritime traffic.

Activities Adoption of international conventions, protocols, codes and recommendations relating to the above; provision of technical assistance; arranging seminars, workshops, etc.

Status United Nations agency

Publications IMO News (4)
Proceedings of the IMO/UNDP International Seminar on Reception Facilities for Wastes. 1984.
Supplement to the Regulations for the Prevention of Pollution by Oil. 1984.

International Petroleum Industry Environmental Conservation Association (IPIECA)
1st Floor, 1 College Hill, London EC4R 2RA 01–248 3447/8

Executive Secretary S. Hope

Aims To provide a focal point of contact for the petroleum industry with the United Nations Environment Programme (UNEP) and other bodies on the impact of petroleum industry operations on the environment and its protection.

Activities Has observer status with the UN Economic and Social Council; has an Oil Spills Committee.

Status Association of companies and associations

-NR

International Physicians for the Prevention of Nuclear War (IPPNW)
South Bank House, Black Prince Road, London SE1 7SJ 01–735 8171 ext.146

European Director B. Dembitzer

Aims To develop and disseminate knowledge relevant to the prevention of nuclear war.

Activities As an international federation of physicians' organisations, IPPNW organises meetings and world congresses and provides co-ordination among existing medical groups as well as helping the formation of new ones; co-operates with international organisations and both governmental and non-governmental bodies in their efforts for nuclear disarmament; helps promote medical education curricula for the prevention of nuclear war. 34 affiliated groups worldwide (22 in Europe).

Status Voluntary

Publications IPPNW News Report (4)
Chivian, Eric *et al.*, (eds), *The Last Aid: the medical dimensions of nuclear war*, W.H. Freeman, San Francisco.

International Planned Parenthood Federation (IPPF)
18–20 Lower Regent Street, London SW1Y 4PW 01–839 2911

Activities Concerned with population and development, mainly in the Third World.

Publications People (4)

-NR

International Primate Protection League (IPPL)
Regent Arcade House, 19–25 Argyll Street, London W1V 2DU 01–837 7227

UK Representative C. Rosen

Aims To promote the conservation and welfare of primates.

Activities Education, fund raising and monitoring all trade in primates; support for rehabilitation programmes; placement of unwanted monkeys and apes; involvement in legislative and regulatory matters affecting primates. IPPL has contributed toward achieving primate export bans in many tropical countries. Its Advisory Board is composed of experts in zoology, anthropology, medicine, biology, veterinary medicine and psychology; in countries where primates live, IPPL's Field Representatives work to create and preserve national parks and sanctuaries and for the strict regulation

of primate hunting, trapping and sale.
Represented in 22 countries.
Status Voluntary
Publications International Primate Protection League Newsletter (3)

International Society for the Prevention of Water Pollution

Little Orchard, Bentworth, Alton, Hants.
GU34 5RB 0420 62225/02514 24837
Chairman R.M. Earl
Aims To prevent water pollution worldwide; to raise funds to this effect; to promote research into the causes of water pollution; to disseminate information to organisations concerned with water.
Activities Correspondence worldwide with persons and organisations concerned with water and water pollution; raising funds to provide research and to acquaint those concerned with the results; contact with journalists to provide factual material for the media; maintaining contact with a team of correspondents in various countries; can provide speakers for meetings. 2 branches.
Status Voluntary; charity

International Society for the Protection of Animals (ISPA)

This organisation is now incorporated into the WORLD SOCIETY FOR THE PROTECTION OF ANIMALS

International Solar Energy Society UK Section (UK-ISES)

19 Albemarle Street, London W1X 3HA
01–493 6601
Hon. Secretary F.C. Treble
Aims To advance the utilisation of solar energy.
Activities The Society's interests embrace all aspects of solar energy. It organises a bi-annual Congress and technical 1–day conferences and publishes the proceedings as well as a variety of relevant literature. Branches in the Midlands and North West.
Status Learned society
Publications Journal of Solar Energy (12); Sun at Work in Britain(2)
-NR

International Tanker Owners Pollution Federation Ltd (ITOPF)

Staple Hall, Stonehouse Court, 87–90
Houndsditch, London EC3A 7AX 01–621 1255
Managing Director John Archer
Aims To administer the Tanker Owners Voluntary Agreement concerning Liability for Oil Pollution (TOVALOP), a voluntary compensation plan offered by the world's tanker owners to meet the costs of oil pollution clean-up and damage; to provide

technical advice on oil spills and a consultancy service on contingency planning.
Activities The Federation's major activity is providing emergency advice at the scene of oil spills; its technical staff are at constant readiness to attend the site of major spills anywhere in the world and give advice as to the most appropriate and cost-effective methods of clean-up. ITOPF also maintains a comprehensive information service including a technical library and a computerised databank of oil spills; in addition, the staff organise and carry out training courses on contingency planning and other aspects of oil pollution throughout the world.
Publications International Tanker Owners Pollution Federation Newsletter (2)
Series of 12 Technical Information Papers.

International Tree Crops Institute

2 Convent Lane, Bocking, Braintree,
Essex CM7 6RN
-NR

Interskill

4 Market Place West, Morpeth, Northumberland NE61 1HE 0670 57434
Contact David Brazier
Aims To make the skills developed at Morpeth Centre and Eigenwelt Studies available to organisations on an in-service basis by providing training courses and personal and organisational development consultancy to agencies in the health and welfare services, using humanistic methods.
Activities Has a wide range of client organisations throughout the UK, principally health authorities, social service and probation departments and voluntary agencies in the welfare field.
Status Independent consultancy

Intervention Board for Agricultural Produce

Fountain House, 2 Queen's Walk, Reading,
Berks. RG1 7QW 0734 583626
Aims To implement within the UK the guarantee functions of the Common Agricultural Policy of the EEC. Responsible to the Agriculture Ministers.
Status Statutory

Iridology Research

188 Old Street, London EC1V 9BP 01–251 4429
Director John Morley
Aims To conduct research to contribute to the body of knowledge of iridology and clinically to validate iridic signs and pathology; to educate the public and support practitioners of iridology; to provide a consultation service for the public – photography and iris diagnosis.
Activities Maintaining a directory of practitioners; providing a consultation service;

education and support of practitioners through seminars with eminent iridologists; photography service for practitioners; research into the mechanisms of iridology; public education about iridology.

Status Voluntary research institute
Publications Newsletter (occasional)

Irish Anti-Vivisection Society (IAVS)
Crosshaven, Co. Cork, Ireland 831146
Hon. Secretary Michael O'Donovan *Public Relations Officer* Charles Slatter
Aims To secure the total abolition of all experiments causing suffering or distress of any kind to animals; in the meantime, to sponsor, promote or assist interim measures of partial reform.
Activities Political activity aimed at changing the present law and statutory regulations pertaining to experiments on live animals; encouraging, through awards and grants from the IAVS Humane Research Fund, the discovery of techniques not involving the use of living animals and the wider use of known alternatives.
Status Voluntary
Publications IAVS News Bulletin (3) Annual Report

Irish Campaign for Nuclear Disarmament
16 Lower Liffy Street, Dublin 1, Ireland 0001–73 0877
National Secretary Dermot Nolan
Aims To achieve the abolition of all nuclear weapons; to promote unilateral measures of disarmament as a step toward the complete abolition of nuclear weapons, leading to general and complete disarmament; to promote the abolition of all military alliances and the strengthening of Irish neutrality; to stop any Irish involvement in the production of nuclear weapons through nuclear energy, uranium mining, etc.
Status Voluntary
Publications Disarmament Today (6)
-NR

Irish Council Against Bloodsports
67 Newtown Avenue, Blackrock, Co. Dublin, Ireland 881054
-NR

Irish Futures Society
Shelbourne House, Shelbourne Road, Ballsbridge, Dublin 4, Ireland 0001–68 3311
Hon. Secretary Nóirín Carmody
Aims To act as an information, document-ation and co-ordination centre for futures studies, research and other activities in Ireland; to analyse, promote, undertake and/or disseminate research in long-term social, economic, technological and other forecasting concerning the facts, concepts

and opinions on which the future of society may depend; to channel the findings of studies among its members, to the media, educators, scientists, technologists, industri-alists, community leaders, policy makers and other interested parties; to liaise with other bodies with similar interests.
Activities Organising symposia, seminars and other events; establishing a futures data-base, network and/or directory for the use of members and other interested parties.
Status Registered friendly society
Publications *Unemployment – a Perma-nent Reality.* 1983.

Irish Gas Board
see BGE – IRISH GAS BOARD

Irish National Petroleum Corporation
Harcourt House, Harcourt Street, Dublin 2, Ireland 0001–75 7911
-NR

Irish Organic Farmers' and Growers' Associ-ation (IOFGA)
Black Castle, Navan, Co. Meath, Ireland 046 23363
Aims To share and disseminate infor-mation, ideas and experience of organic production; to research and study improved methods of organic farming and gardening; to aid the marketing and promotion of organic food in Ireland; to provide a means of contact between members.
Activities Farm walks, conferences, work-shops, seminars; publishing articles; producing a booklist and a products list of items that are often otherwise hard to obtain, such as organic fertilisers, safe sprays, etc. Members in every county in Ireland.
Status Voluntary
-NR – L

Irish Small Farmers Association
Carnaree, Ballymote, Co. Sligo, Ireland
-NR

Irish Society for the Prevention of Cruelty to Animals (ISPCA)
1 Grand Canal Quay, Dublin 2, Ireland 0001–77 5922
Executive Secretary Edward Kennedy
Aims To prevent and alleviate animal suffering.
Activities Investigating cases of cruelty; co-ordinating the work of branches throughout the country; educating and advising the public on animal welfare; negotiating with government departments on matters including legislation dealing with transport of animals, dog control, slaughter of animals, conservation of wildlife, etc. Co-operates

with the World Federation for the Protection of Animals. Local branches.
Status Voluntary
Publications Annual Report

Irish Wildbird Conservancy (IWC)
Southview, Church Road, Greystones, Co. Wicklow, Ireland 0001–87 5759
Director Richard Nairn
Aims To promote conservation, education and research in relation to wild birds and their environment in Ireland; generally to promote ornithology in Ireland.
Activities Managing a series of nature reserves which are owned or leased; actively involved in protection of other important wildlife areas through contacts with landowners, local authorities and government departments; carrying out national surveys of birds and their habitats; courses and conferences on bird watching and conservation; publishing books, journal and newsletter. A network of local branches runs programmes of activities for members.
Status Voluntary
Publications Irish Birds (1);
Irish Wildbird Conservancy Newsletter (4);
Annual Report

Irish Wildlife Federation
8 Westland Row, Dublin 2, Ireland 0001–76 1276
-NR

Irish Youth Hostels Association/An Oige
39 Mountjoy Square, Dublin 1, Ireland
-NR

Isles of Scilly Environmental Trust
c/o Town Hall, St Mary's, Isle of Scilly
TR21 0LW 0720 22537
Aims To promote the conservation of wildlife, the landscape and archaeological features, the management of access for visitors and the provision and co-ordination of information and interpretive services.
-NR

IUCN Conservation Monitoring Centre
219C Huntingdon Road, Cambridge CB3 0DL
0223 277314
Senior Technical Assistant Ms L. Wright
Activities Collecting and collating conservation data on a world scale, particularly that relating to threatened species of plants and animals, to protected areas and to the wildlife trade, to produce on an integrated database; this data is used to provide a service to the conservation and development communities. Information is supplied in the form of Red Data Books, Protected Areas Directories and specialist publications; contracts are also undertaken to provide detailed data on request. The information is of use to governments and agencies, development banks, conservation organisations, scientists and the media.
Publications Traffic Bulletin (5)
-NR

J

Jersey Wildlife Preservation Trust (JWPT)

Les Augres Manor, Trinity, Jersey,
Channel Islands 0534 61949

Secretary Simon Hicks

Aims To build up under controlled
conditions breeding colonies of animal
species threatened with extinction in the wild
state; to organise special expeditions to
rescue seriously threatened species; by
studying the biology of those species, to
amass and correlate data which would help
toward protecting those endangered
animals in the wild state; to promote interest
in wildlife conservation throughout the
world.

Activities Species selection according to
conservation criteria; ownership of IUCN-
registered endangered species by country
of origin; distribution of endangered species
by breeding loan; associated field research;
independent funding for each species; residential training courses and scholarships;
breeding unit support in country of origin.
The Trust is an international organisation with
a membership of 13,000; it explains the need
for conservation through its membership, the
media and the Zoological Park in Jersey, for
which there exists an Education Department.
The Trust operates a training centre, runs a
3–week summer school, publishes an annual
scientific journal and special scientific
reports and staff regularly give papers at
conferences throughout the world. 4
Wildlife Preservation Trusts.

Status Charity

Publications The Dodo (1);
The Dodo Dispatch (3) (for junior members);
Jersey Wildlife Preservation Trust News-
letter (2); Annual Report

Joint Advisory Committee on Nutrition Education

c/o Health Education Council, 78 New Oxford
Street, London WC1A 1AH 01–637 1881

Contact Dr J. Brown
-NR

Joint Advisory Committee on Pets in Society (JACOPIS)

4th Floor, Walter House, 418–422 Strand,
London WC2R 0PL 01–836 2843

Hon. Secretary Norman J. Hart

Aims To promote the introduction of a
national dog warden service funded by a
sensible increase in the licence fee; to
provide advice and information to local
government on running a dog warden
service and guidelines on promoting responsible pet ownership.

Activities Producing publications on the
subject of the dog warden service, including
briefing notes and handbook; producing
guidelines for local authorities and public
codes of practice on the subject of pets on
housing estates, parks and beaches, which
have been published in co-operation with the
relevant local authority associations; where
appropriate, JACOPIS attends exhibitions
and runs seminars on topics relating to pets
in society.

Publications *The JACOPIS Response to
the Government's Proposals on Dog
Licensing.* 1985.
JACOPIS – 10 Years On. 1983.

Joint Committee for the Conservation of British Insects (JCCBI)

c/o Institute of Terrestrial Ecology, Furzebrook
Research Station, Wareham, Dorset BH20 5AS
09295 51518

Hon. Secretary Dr Michael G. Morris

Aims To review the status of threatened
insects, recommending and initiating
conservation measures; to support other
national and international conservation
bodies and entomological societies and
provide a forum for discussion of topics on
the conservation of insects.

Activities The JCCBI, through sponsorship, supports and supervises research on
British insects, particularly obtaining data
relevant to their survival; it organises and
runs surveys of particular species, e.g. Heath
Fritllary, Adonis Blue, Chequered Skipper
and other butterflies, and on rare and
endangered dragonflies; it organised the
survey of the Large Blue and, with sponsorship, is carrying out trial reintroductions; it
produced *A Code for Insect Collecting* and
is currently producing a guide to introductions
and reintroductions. It provides a forum for
the exchange of conservation information
relating to insects and acts as a representative for entomologists in Britain on other
conservation bodies.

Status Voluntary

Joint Committee of Amenity Societies

2 Chester Street, London SW1X 7BB
01–235 3081

Aims To discuss new problems arising

from the official recognition of conservation areas in the Civic Amenities Act 1967.
Activities Brings together various conservation bodies concerned with historic buildings.
-NR

Joint Committee on the Medical Aspects of Water Quality
This committee no longer exists

Joint Unit for Research on the Urban Environment (JURUE)
c/o ECOTEC, Priory House, 18 Steelhouse Lane, Birmingham B4 6BJ 021–236 9991
-NR

JONAH (Jews Organised for a Nuclear Arms Halt)
21 Edmunds Walk, London N2 0HU 01–883 7296
General Secretary Vicky Joseph
Activities Speaking to Jewish adult education groups, women's groups, schools, university and college Jewish societies, synagogues, etc.; acting as Jewish witness to demonstrations, non-violent direct action, etc. within the wider peace movement; organising major public meetings with well-known speakers; celebrating Jewish festivals and drawing connections with peace. Branches in Brighton and Leeds.
Status Voluntary
Publications JONAH Newsheet (4)

Jourdain Society
Dairy Cottages, Ranmore Common, Dorking, Surrey RH5 6SP

Hon. Secretary Melvin Grey
Aims To promote study, education and research in ornithology and zoology.
-NR

Journalists Against Nuclear Extermination (JANE)
14 Mornington Grove, London E3 4NS
Secretary Richard Keeble
Aims To campaign amongst journalists for unilateral nuclear disarmament and against the distortion and censorship of the nuclear arms issue in the media; to encourage the setting up of branch groups to stimulate debate and improve links between journalists and nuclear disarmament groups; to work closely with the Campaign for Press and Broadcasting Freedom; to encourage the Trades Union Congress to promote unilateral nuclear disarmament in the labour movement; to strengthen links with journalists in Europe; to highlight the threat to journalists' professionalism posed by the government's plans to control the media in the event of a major international crisis.
Activities Holding public meetings; attending international seminars; developing links with other groups, particularly in the trade union and labour movements; action in support of the above aims.
Status Voluntary
Publications JANE Newsletter (6)

Just Defence
The Rookery, Adderbury, Banbury, Oxon. OX17 3NA 0295 810993
-NR

K

Keep Britain Tidy Group (KBTG)

Bostel House, 37 West Street, Brighton,
E. Sussex BN1 2RE 0273 23585

Director General D.J. Lewis

Aims To protect and enhance the amenities of town and country in the UK, particularly by promoting the prevention and
control of litter and by environmental
improvement schemes. Recognised by
government as the national agency for litter
abatement.

Activities The Group's programmes are
based on independent research and
national and international experience and
expertise. These programmes include: the
systematic litter abatement programme
called The Keep Britain Tidy Community
Environment Programme which includes the
Environmental Education Programme for
schools; the Tidy Team Programme for
Industry; the Programme for Youth Groups;
the Marine Litter Research Programme; and
the Beautiful Britain programme of national
promotions, information and publicity,
including the national Beautiful Britain in
Bloom competition. 7 branches.

Status Voluntary; charity

Publications Beautiful Britain News (1);
Annual Report

Dixon, Trevor R. & Dixon, T.J., *Marine Litter
Research Programme Stage 5: marine litter
surveillance on the North Atlantic ocean
shores of Portugal and the Western Isles of
Scotland.* 1983.

*Our Europe: environmental awareness and
language development through school
exchanges* (teacher's handbook and activity
folder). 1985.

Keep Scotland Tidy Campaign

Old County Chambers, Cathedral Square,
Dunblane, Central FK15 0AQ, Scotland
0786 823202

Activities The Scottish arm of the Keep
Britain Tidy Group; local projects work with
local authorities, schools and community
groups to increase awareness and change
attitudes to the litter problem and to
encourage practical schemes.
-NR

Kent Trust for Nature Conservation (KTNC)

PO Box 29, Maidstone, Kent ME14 1YH
0634 362561

Chief Executive Fred Booth

Aims To record, study and protect places
and objects of natural beauty or scientific
interest; to promote study and research; to
establish and maintain sanctuaries and
reserves; to promote and encourage the
objects of the Trust by publications, lectures,
displays and visits for schools and public.

Activities Managing 37 nature reserves by
means of the Trust's voluntary conservation
corps; providing conservation advice to local
authorities, organisations and the public;
giving advice on planning applications and
to public inquiries where there is any
adverse conservation impact. Lectures,
displays, exhibitions; production of leaflets
aimed at both adults and young people;
organising the Kent Watch Club for
under–18s as part of the national Watch Club.
Local branches.

Status Charity

Publications Kent Trust Bulletin (3); local
group newsletters (3)

Laboratory of the Government Chemist (LGC)
Cornwall House, Stamford Street, London SE1 9NQ 01–928 7900
Librarian P.W. Hammond
Aims To provide a comprehensive service of analysis and advice to the public and private sectors; to function, under various Acts of Parliament, as an impartial official analyst or referee in cases of disputed analyses.
Activities Work on public health and environmental protection is concerned with the chemical analysis, research and development in the fields of food, medicines, agriculture, pesticides, toxic metals, waters and exposure to dust and particulates, including asbestos.
Status Statutory
Publications Report of the Government Chemist (1)

Lair
49 Pratt Street, Camden Town, London NW1 0BJ
Activities Feminist group opposed to all animal oppression and exploitation.
-NR

Lake District Special Planning Board (LDSPB)
National Park Office, Busher Walk, Kendal, Cumbria LA9 4RH 0539 24555
National Park Officer John Toothill
Aims As the National Park and Local Planning Authority for the Lake District National Park, to preserve and enhance the natural beauty of the area and to promote its enjoyment by the public; to have regard to the social and economic wellbeing of the local population.
Activities Town and country planning; countryside planning and management; land management and landscape protection; maintenance of footpaths; providing facilities for visitors, such as information centres, car parks, holiday accommodation, a ranger service and the Brockhole Visitor Exhibition Centre.
Status Statutory
Publications The Lake District Guardian (1); Annual Report; Cumbria and Lake District Joint Structure Plan.

Lancashire Trust for Nature Conservation (LTNC)
The Pavilion, Cuerden Valley Park, Bamber Bridge, Preston, Lancs. PR5 6AX 0772 324129
Hon. Secretary Julian Taylor
Aims To promote and foster nature conservation interests and activities in Lancashire, including Greater Manchester and Merseyside.
Activities Raising funds to acquire, improve and manage local nature reserves; co-operating with statutory bodies to protect habitats and wild-life; surveying and recording sites of scientific and conservation interest; encouraging interest in conservation by providing interpretive literature and running programmes of lectures, meetings and projects for local members' groups which number about 12.
Status Voluntary; charity
Publications Lapwing (3)

Lanchester Wave Energy Group
see SEA ENERGY ASSOCIATES

Land Decade Educational Council
The London Science Centre, 18 Adam Street, London WC2N 6AH 01–930 2903
-NR

Land Resources Development Centre (LRDC)
Tolworth Tower, Ewell Road, Surbiton, Surrey KT6 7DY 01–399 5281
Librarian & Information Officer Philip Reilly
Aims To assist developing countries in mapping, investigation and assessment of land resources. LRDC is one of the scientific units of the Overseas Development Administration.
Activities Resource appraisal in developing countries; recommendations on the use of resources for the development of agriculture, livestock husbandry and forestry; advice on related subjects to overseas governments and organisations; scientific personnel available for appointment abroad; lectures and training courses in the basic techniques of resource appraisal and development.
Status Statutory
Publications Current Awareness Bulletin (12) (inc. Library Accessions List)

Landlife
[formerly Rural Preservation Association]
The Old Police Station, Lark Lane, Liverpool
L17 8UU 051–728 7011
Director Grant Luscombe
Aims To promote and encourage for the benefit of the nation the improvement, protection and preservation of the British countryside and the ecological enrichment of the urban environment; to stimulate and educate the public on these topics.
Activities Operating the Greensight Project which undertakes the treatment, using native species of plants, of some 50 derelict land sites in Liverpool; the project provides a professional consultancy service for survey work, planning, implementation and management; it also develops school nature study and school garden books. An Urban Wildlife Unit consisting of ecologists, educationalists, graphic artists and administrative staff surveys open spaces, produces teacher packs and undertakes guided walks. Landlife owns a 6½-acre wildflower nursery (free catalogue with s.a.e.) and runs an EEC-funded training scheme in wildflower horticulture and landscape ecology for 17–19 year olds. 5 branches.
Status Charity; company limited by guarantee
Publications *Bringing the Countryside into Your School.*
School Garden Book

Landscape Institute
Nash House, Carlton House Terrace,
London SW1Y 01–839 4044
-NR

Landscape Overview Dartmoor
26 Cross Street, Moretonhampstead, Devon
TQ13 8NL 0647 40904
Director R.N. Young
Aims To engender a greater awareness of the relationship between natural resources and their multiple use, the history and present layout of the landscape.
Activities Courses encouraging the enjoyment and understanding of the landscape in all its aspects; running a school of airphoto interpretation of the land and its resources; private consultancy particularly relating to site interpretation and airphoto interpretation.
Status Private sector educational
Publications *Habitat Changes in West Berkshire (as detected by interpretation of 1963 and 1976 1/10,000 scale airphotos).* With maps at 1/25,000 scale. (Nature Conservancy Council contract)

Landscape Research Group Ltd (LRG)
Dale Cottage, The Dale, Eyam, Sheffield,
S. Yorks. S30 1QU 0433 30936
Secretary Mrs Carys Swanwick
Aims To advance education and research, encourage interest and exchange information for the public benefit in landscape and related fields, ranging from wilderness to city.
Activities Organising meetings, symposia, seminars, etc., the purpose of which is to encourage collaboration among a wide range of disciplines whose fields of interest overlap; emphasis is placed on the ecological nature of landscapes.
Status Charity; company limited by guarantee
Publications Landscape Research (3)

Laurieston Hall
Laurieston Hall, Castle Douglas, Dumfries &
Galloway DG7 2NB, Scotland 06445 275
Aims To demonstrate the benefits and problems of communal living, skill sharing, non-hierarchical decision making, self-sufficiency, income sharing and the breaking down of traditional age and sex roles.
Activities Running events on a variety of themes such as gardening, natural therapies, arts and feminism; growing our own produce, generating our own electricity and collecting wood for heating and cooking; working on neighbouring farms and building projects; involvement with the peace movement. Members are all part of a housing co-operative and renovate, convert and construct new accommodation as numbers increase.
Status Commune/co-operative
Publications Laurieston Hall Newsletter (1)
Eno, Sarah & Treanor, Dave, *Collective Housing Handbook,* 150pp.

Lawyers Ecology Group
113 Chancery Lane, London WC2A 1PP
-NR

Lawyers for Nuclear Disarmament (LND)
2 Garden Court, Temple, London EC4Y 9BL
Joint Secretaries Owen Davies, Edward Rees
Aims To advise and support individuals and organisations which object to the existence of nuclear weapons; to research and publicise the legal implications of the possession and use of nuclear weapons; to propose and foster national and international legislation.
Activities Practical legal advice to peace groups and organisations; providing speakers and publications on a wide variety of legal

issues created by nuclear weapons and the disarmament movement. 5 branches.
Status Voluntary
Publications LND Newsletter (4)
The Illegality of Nuclear Warfare.
Non-Violent Direct Action (legal advice pack).
A Tax on Peace: the peace tax movement and the law.

League Against Cruel Sports (LACS)
83–87 Union Street, London SE1 1SG
01–407 0979
Executive Director Richard Course
Aims To seek the abolition of hunting wild animals with dogs.
Activities Campaigning through Parliament and local government for changes in legislation to protect wild animals; talks and film/slide shows to schools, youth clubs, etc.; staging exhibitions by means of an exhibition vehicle which attends shows throughout the year; selling promotional goods.
Status Voluntary
Publications Cruel Sports (3/4)

League for the Introduction of Canine Control (LICC)
PO Box 326, London NW5 3LE
Secretary Mrs J. Martin
Aims To publicise all acts of civil disobedience by irresponsible dog owners and to motivate Parliament to bring in strict canine legislation.
Activities Lobbying MPs on stricter dog controls; increasing public awareness of the diseases passed by canines to human beings; disseminating fact sheets to the public, local authorities and Parliament; increasing the League's membership.
Status Voluntary
Publications Newsletter (4)

Leeds Anti-Nuclear Group
20 Kelso Road, Leeds, W. Yorks. LS2 9PR
0532 446795
-NR

Leicestershire & Rutland Trust for Nature Conservation
1 West Street, Leicester LE1 6UU 0533 553904
-NR

Letcombe Laboratory
Letcombe Regis, Wantage, Oxon. OX12 9JT
02357 3327
Aims To conduct research into the growth of crops in relation to soil conditions and cultivation.
Status Institute of the Agricultural and Food Research Council (AFRC)
-NR

Liberal Ecology Group (LEG)
77 Dresden Road, London N19 3BG
Chairman Robert Hutchison
Aims To encourage understanding of the ecological perspective in the Liberal Party and to bring more of the Party's policy statements and resolutions into accordance with that perspective.
Activities Conferences, meetings and publications at local and national level; briefings for Liberal Party activists.
Status Political pressure group
Publications LEG Newsletter (3)
LEG Manifesto 1985.

Liberals and Social Democrats Against Bloodsports (LASDAB)
116 High Street, Gosport, Hants. PO12 1DU
0705 528017
National Organiser Peter Chegwyn
Aims To campaign within the Liberal/SDP Alliance against all hunting with hounds and against organised hare coursing; to lobby support for Party policies calling for legislation to abolish such bloodsports.
Activities Briefing MPs, councillors, members and supporters; lobbying support for motions and resolutions at constituency, regional and national level; presenting the case against hunting and coursing at every opportunity, especially through the media; seeking manifesto commitments from the Alliance to legislate against hunting and coursing.
Status Voluntary
Publications LASDAB Newsletter
Information for Councillors on the Case Against Hunting.

Life Style Movement
Manor Farm, Little Gidding, Huntingdon, Cambs. PE17 5RJ 08323 383
General Secretary Mrs Margaret Smith
Aims To work for a fairer distribution of the Earth's resources; to encourage others to join in this commitment by voluntarily undertaking to live more simply so that others may simply live.
Activities Members can either accept the Life Style commitment as a personal guideline or join or help to form a Life Style group; groups arrange their own activities; the Movement holds an annual conference and occasional weekend events.
Status Voluntary
Publications Life Style Movement Newsletter (4)
-NR

Lifestyle 2000 Ltd (LS2000)
Tirmorgan, Pontyberem, Dyfed SA15 4HP, Wales 0269 871014
Director David Stephens

Aims To educate people and carry out research toward enabling people to earn their living whilst consuming a minimum of the natural resources of the Earth; to publish the results of such research.
Activities Developing Tirmorgan Farm on permaculture principles as a demonstration project and study centre; operating an index-linked savings scheme providing capital to fund ecologically beneficial projects; acquiring land and buildings for ecologically desirable projects, especially tree planting; operating a local exchange trading system to stimulate ecologically beneficial economic activity. Information about Lifestyle 2000 is published in Practical Alternatives.
Status Company limited by guarantee

Light Rail Transit Association (LRTA)
36 Wimbledon Place, Bradwell Common, Milton Keynes, Bucks. MK18 8DR
Hon. Secretary R.N.H. Jones
Aims To advocate and otherwise support the retention, extension and development of efficient public transport and especially of light rail transit systems and tramways.
Activities Library service (mainly historical material) available by post to members; study tours to Europe and elsewhere; visits within the UK; publishing books and two journals. Regional branches.
Status Voluntary
Publications Tramway Review (historical) (4); Modern Tramway (12)

Lincolnshire & South Humberside Trust for Nature Conservation
The Manor House, Alford, Lincs. LN13 9DL 05212 3468
Administrative Officer Mrs M. Gilleard
Aims To safeguard wildlife and natural beauty; to inform, interest and educate the public about the need to care for the countryside and to encourage people to take an active part in the Trust's work.
Activities Establishing nature reserves to safeguard a representative sample of wild places; managing reserves and other sites to make the best use of land available for conservation; facilitating public enjoyment of the countryside through the use of reserves and nature trails; promoting conservation through publications, lectures, exhibitions and advertising; providing practical advice to local authorities, farmers and land managers; conducting wildlife surveys and research; encouraging the involvement of young people in conservation through schools, colleges and universities. Local branches.
Status Voluntary
Publications Newsletter (2)

Liquefied Petroleum Gas Industry Technical Association
17 Grosvenor Crescent, London SW1X 7ES 01–245 9511
-NR

liu Academy of Traditional Chinese Medicine
13 Gunnersbury Avenue, Ealing Common, London W5 3XD 01–993 2549
Activities Provides teaching to diploma standard in many different areas of traditional Chinese medicine.
-NR

Local Enterprise Development Unit (LEDU)
Lamont House, Purdy's Lane, Newtownbreda, Belfast BT8 4AR 0232 691031
Activities Performs similar functions to the Council for Small Industries in Rural Areas (CoSIRA).
-NR

London Co-operative Enterprise Board (LCEB)
63–67 Newington Causeway, London SE1 6BD 01–403 0300
Activities Provides help with financing worker co-operatives in London.
-NR

London Cycling Campaign (LCC)
Tress House, 3 Stamford Street, London SE1 9NT 01–928 7220
Aims To campaign for more and better cycling facilities in London; to encourage more people to use bicycles.
Activities Lobbying locally and throughout London; consultations with political parties, British Rail and cycling bodies and with borough councils through LCC borough groups; organising events, such as the annual Round London Bike Ride, the Pedals in the Park cycle fair and evening and Sunday rides from April to October. 20 branches.
Status Voluntary
Publications Daily Cyclist (4)
On Your Bike: the guide to cycling in London. North and North West London Cycling Map. South London Route Guide.

London Energy and Employment Network (LEEN)
316A Richmond Road, Twickenham, London TW1 2PD 01–891 0989
Aims To provide technical support to energy-based employment projects in London. LEEN is a federation of organisations active in the energy field.
Activities Project development; new product assessment; advice on marketing

and finance; prototype development; energy audits; training, etc.
-NR

London Green Belt Council
52 Sharp's Lane, Ruislip, London HA4 7JQ
08956 34121
Hon. Secretary L.H. Buckham
Aims To keep the problems and prospects of London's Green Belt as a whole under review, to represent them to appropriate authorities and to advise member organisations on planning and other relevant matters.
Activities Making representations to government and planning authorities and at public inquiries on policy matters affecting the Green Belt; 5 members' meetings per year plus sub-committees as necessary; circulating notes on planning matters affecting the Green Belt. Membership consists of organisations, not individuals.
Status Voluntary
Publications The London Green Belt Council Notes (±8)

London Open Radio
2 Warwick Crescent, London W2 6NE
01–289 7163/4
Activities Campaigning for free access to the airwaves by the community; seeking to set up a co-operative London radio station.
-NR

London Planning Aid Service (LPAS)
c/o TCPA, 17 Carlton House Terrace, London SW1Y 5AS 01–930 8903/4/5
Contact Andy Roscoe
Aims To give advice and support, free of charge, to community groups, tenants' associations and action groups on planning and environmental issues.
Activities Assisting groups with preparation of local plans; advising groups on council and lobbying procedures; supporting and contributing to campaigns on planning, housing and transport; advising the public on their legal rights in planning law; producing community manuals on aspects of planning. 90 volunteers in Greater London.
Status Voluntary
Publications Planning Aid Newsletter (12)
Bailey, Ron, *Abolition of the Metropolitan Counties: a denial of civil liberties*, 1984.
Planning Advice for Women's Groups. 1985.
Preventing Demolition. 1985.

London Wildlife Trust
1 Thorpe Close, London W10 5XL 01–968 5368
Aims To encourage awareness of London's natural history and of its amenity value for Londoners; to identify sites of wildlife interest and devise ways for their conservation and

use and, where necessary, to campaign to save sites under threat.
Activities Campaigning within the Greater London area to save threatened sites and habitats; setting up nature reserves to protect wildlife; carrying out wildlife surveys. Helping community groups create new habitats in deprived areas; providing advice to councils and encouraging them to implement conservation policies; promoting nature education in schools and colleges and attempting to raise people's awareness of the importance of wildlife in their environment. Groups of members in each London borough.
Status Voluntary
Publications Wild London (4)
-NR

Long Ashton Research Station (LARS)
University of Bristol, Long Ashton, Bristol, Avon BS18 9AF 0272 392181
Scientific Liaison Officer R.K. Atkin
Aims To undertake research on weeds, plant growth regulators and strategic aspects of crop protection, relating to arable and fruit crops.
Activities Main research activities cover crop protection interests, including weed, disease and pest control, disease forecasting, spray application and plant-pathogen relations; weed science; plant science, including plant growth regulators, nutrition and environmental physiology; and food science. The Station's multidisciplinary-based research programmes give increasing emphasis to improving the efficiency of production of arable crops and to assessing the effects of changing husbandry practices on the agricultural-environmental interface.
Status Research institute of the Agricultural and Food Research Council
Publications Annual Report
Long Ashton Symposium Series, e.g. 9th Symposium: Brent, K.J. & Atkin, R.K. (eds), *Rational Pesticide Use*, CUP, 1985.

Lord Dowding Fund for Humane Research
51 Harley Street, London W1N 1DD 01–580 4034
Director Dr Robert Sharpe
Aims To promote, by advocacy and the sponsorship of scientific projects, the replacement of living animals in research by alternative techniques.
Activities Sponsorship of specific projects; meetings and symposia; collating material from many countries; pursuing correspondence and personal contacts; fund raising; publishing leaflets and a journal which is distributed in 20 countries. 42 branches.
Status Voluntary
Publications The Bulletin (2)

Lothian Energy Group
Centre for Human Ecology, University of Edinburgh, 15 Buccleuch Place, Edinburgh EH8 9LN 031–667 1011 ext.6799
Joint Co-ordinators/Company Secretaries Angus and Abigail Marland
Aims To encourage the rational use of the Earth's resources, through education, practical demonstration and research.
Activities Particular emphasis on energy conservation, renewable energy and closed-cycle agricultural systems; designed and created the national Living With Energy exhibition in 1982, which is on a UK-wide tour and the text of which is available in booklet form. Present activities include setting up an energy conservation and advice centre in Edinburgh and a rural resources centre outside the city.
Status Charity; limited company

Low Energy Supply Systems (LESS)
82 Colston Street, Bristol, Avon BS1 5BB 0272 272530
Executive Richard St George
Aims To provide, for the Urban Centre for Appropriate Technology (UCAT), a retail outlet and installation service for renewable energy equipment suitable for domestic purposes and other small-scale applications.
Activities Supplying such items as: solar collectors and ancillary equipment such as pumps and temperature controllers; battery-charging windmills and solar cells and related equipment such as battery banks, towers and regulators; air recirculators, low-energy lights and low-voltage appliances. LESS also acts as an agent for a composting toilet and for small-scale workshop equipment particularly suitable for organisations working in developing countries.
Status Commercial
Publications LESS Catalogue (1)

Low Energy Systems
63 Greenlawns, Skerries, Co. Dublin, Ireland 490396
Principal Brian F. Hurley
Activities Research, development and design in wind power technology; site surveying.
Status Commercial

M

Macaulay Institute for Soil Research
Craigiebuckler, Aberdeen, Grampian AB9 2QJ,
Scotland 0224 38611
    Aims To conduct practical studies of the
soils of Scotland with a view to maintaining
and improving their fertility; to undertake
related research in the various branches of
soil science.
    Activities Areas of study include: mineral
soils; peat and forest soils; the nature of soil
organic matter; soil microbes; plant physiology; the productivity of soils; and the ferti-
liser requirements of crops.
    Status State-aided institute of the Agricul-
tural and Food Research Council
    Publications Annual Report
-NR – L

Macclesfield Groundwork Trust
Brook Bank House, Wellington Road,
Bollington, Macclesfield, Cheshire SK10 5JS
0625 72681
    Executive Director W.S. Menzies
    Aims To work in partnership with the
public, private and voluntary sectors to
improve the environment for the benefit of
the community.
    Activities Environmental improvement
projects; environmental education; promotion
of access to the countryside; project management services to the voluntary sector, public
authorities, landowners, etc.; non-profit
development in tourism and recreation, e.g.
cycle hire, visitor centre; publishing local
guide books.
    Status Charity
    Publications Annual Report
Cheshire Peaks and Plains: a cycle guide.
*Cheshire Peaks and Plains by Public
Transport.*

Mammal Society
c/o The Linnean Society, Burlington House,
Piccadilly, London W1V 0LQ 01–434 4479
    Aims To promote the study of mammals.
    Activities Annual conference and annual
symposium; conducting distribution surveys;
arranging youth activities; advice to statutory
bodies; support for research projects;
specialist groups; bringing together
amateurs and professionals with an interest
in mammals. Publications include a journal
and newsletter, the Handbook of British
Mammals, popular accounts of wood mice,
foxes, fallow deer, moles, shrews and mink
and a number of guides: live trapping, bat

identification, otter spraint analysis, identification of remains in owl pellets, scientific
names of British mammals, etc.
    Status Voluntary; charity
    Publications Mammal Review (4); Mammal
Society Newsletter (4); Notes from the
Mammal Society [in the Journal of Zoology]
(2)

Man and the Biosphere Programme (MAB)
see UNESCO (*under* Organisations Not Based
in the UK . . .)

Manx Nature Conservation Trust
Ballacross. Andreas, Isle of Man 062488 434
    Hon. Secretary R.J. Pritchard
    Aims To record and study places of scien-
tific interest and to protect these; to establish
and manage nature reserves and bird sanctuaries; to promote and encourage research
in natural sciences; to spread knowledge and
encourage interest in the above.
    Activities Managing the Trust's reserves;
administering two visitor centres; public
meetings, including field meetings at
reserves and other sites of interest, lectures
and fund raising events; sale of promotional
material from the Royal Society for Nature
Conservation.
    Status Charity; company limited by
guarantee, without share capital
    Publications Manx Nature Conservation
Trust Newsletter; Annual Report
-NR

Marchwood Engineering Laboratories
see CENTRAL ELECTRICITY GENERATING
BOARD

Marine Action Centre
The Bath House, Gwydir Street, Cambridge
CB1 2LW
    -NR

Marine Biological Association of The United Kingdom (MBA)
The Laboratory, Citadel Hill, Plymouth, Devon
PL1 2PB 0752 21761
    Director & Secretary Prof. E.J. Denton
    Aims To promote research contributing to
zoological, botanical, physical, chemical and
physiological science and to increase our
understanding of life in the sea.
    Activities Research in all branches of
marine science and publication of the results.

Accommodation available for British and foreign scientific workers who wish to carry out independent research. The MBA runs the Marine Pollution Information Centre which acts as a national documentation and information centre on marine pollution; it also publishes bibliographies on pollution.
Status Research institute grant-aided by the Natural Environment Research Council
Publications Journal of the Marine Biological Association of the UK (1) (contains the Annual Report)

Marine Biological Laboratory
see CENTRAL ELECTRICITY GENERATING BOARD

Marine Conservation Society (MCS)
4 Gloucester Road, Ross-on-Wye, Herefordshire HR9 5BU 0989 66017
General Secretary Dr Bob Earll
Aims To undertake, for the benefit of the public, the study and conservation of the marine environment; to develop programmes of education, research and publicity designed to further the Society's conservation work.
Activities Running a wide range of marine projects, expeditions and courses to encourage the public to take an interest in the marine environment and to become involved in its conservation; lobbying and involvement with Marine Nature Reserves are also part of the Society's activity programme. Research projects provide innumerable benefits, including the production of reports, identification guides and, for the purposes of publicity and education, photographic slide sets. Events include an annual symposium, workshops and meetings of the Society's nationwide regional groups.
Status Charity
Publications Sea (4)

Marine Information and Advisory Service (MIAS)
see INSTITUTE OF OCEANOGRAPHIC SCIENCES

Marine Pollution Control Unit
see DEPARTMENT OF TRANSPORT, Marine & Ports Directorate

Marine Pollution Information Centre
see MARINE BIOLOGICAL ASSOCIATION OF THE UNITED KINGDOM

Martin Centre for Architecture and Urban Studies
University of Cambridge, 6 Chaucer Road, Cambridge CB2 2EB 0223 69501 ext.286
Librarian J. Owers

Aims To provide a framework within which funded research and postgraduate studies are organised in the University's Department of Architecture in the fields of architectural studies and urban and regional planning.
Activities Current work is concerned with building and environmental design, architectural acoustics, energy conservation, building in earthquake areas, development and management; in addition, a number of studies investigate human factors in building design and use and aspects of the history of architecture and planning.
Status Academic

Marwell Preservation Trust Ltd
Marwell Zoological Park, Colden Common, Winchester, Hants. SO21 1JH 096274 406
General Manager Peter Hickman
Aims To conserve endangered species through captive breeding; to educate people in the need to care for wildlife; to research into the management of wild animals in captivity.
Activities Maintaining large breeding groups of endangered species, particularly hoofed animals such as antelope, deer, zebra and wild horses, as well as carnivores such as snow leopards, Siberian tigers and Asian lions; also various other species. Talks are given at our education centre. Membership helps raise funds.
Status Charity
Publications Marwell Zoo News (4); Annual Report

McCarrison Society
36 Bowness Avenue, Headington, Oxford OX3 0AL 0865 61272
Secretary Mrs Margaret Clark
Aims To study the relationship between nutrition and health, by means of research, dissemination of information and funding of publications.
Activities Annual weekend conference, open to the public; public lectures twice a year; producing a journal. Branch in Scotland.
Status Voluntary
Publications Nutrition and Health (4)

Media Women for Peace
5 Franconia Road, London SW4 9NB 01-720 9851
Co-ordinator Wendy Rose-Neil
Aims To enable women working in all areas of the media to help promote international trust and peace building and to break down barriers of hatred and suspicion through the media and their skills as communicators.
Activities Regular meetings and discussions; creating links with other organisations working for peace and international

understanding; acting as an information and resource centre for other groups seeking help on using the media as a form of communication.
Status Informal network
Publications Newsletter (occasional)

Mediating Network
25B Harecourt Road, London N1 2LW
01–226 5441
London Contact Wendy Freebourne
Aims To create bridges between people and organisations who are working for the development of humanity and the evolution of the planet.
Activities Regular local meetings and national gatherings; attending festivals and gatherings to network those there; organising forums and networking events; celebrations and social activities; publishing the newsletter. Local groups.
Status Informal network
Publications The Mediator (6)

Medical Association for Prevention of War (MAPW)
Tress House, 3 Stamford Street, London
SE1 9NT 01–261 1266
Secretary Dr A. Poteliakhoff (01–435 1872)
Aims To consider the ethical responsibilities of doctors and health workers in relation to war; to urge that resources used for war be diverted to health care and development; to co-operate with health workers in all countries holding similar aims.
Activities Gathering and disseminating information on the causes and effects of war, particularly nuclear war; research, lectures and conferences; taking part in the work of Professions for Disarmament and Development, the World Disarmament Campaign and the UNA Network for Disarmament and Development; affiliated to International Physicians for the Prevention of Nuclear War and to the National Peace Council. Local branches.
Status Voluntary
Publications Medicine and War (3); Newsletter

Medical Campaign Against Nuclear Weapons (MCANW)
7 Tenison Road, Cambridge CB1 2DG
0223 313828
Administrator Ms Bernadette Hayes
Aims To keep under review available information on the health implications of nuclear weapons, nuclear war and related subjects; to act as a reference agency for information on these matters; to provide information to the medical and related professions and to the public; to seek the co-operation of the medical and related

professions in all countries for these aims. As members of the medical profession and persons involved in health care, we are convinced that the prevention of nuclear war offers the only possibility of protecting people from its medical consequences and we advocate nuclear disarmament as the only certain way of preventing such a catastrophe.
Activities The 1985/6 focus of MCANW is on health needs and the cost of Trident. MCANW, in collaboration with the Medical Association for Prevention of War (MAPW), have formed a Joint Parliamentary Committee with contacts in both Houses of Parliament. MCANW provided evidence to the British Medical Association inquiry into the medical effects of nuclear war and is affiliated to International Physicians for the Prevention of Nuclear War. It produces a large amount of resource material, including books, pamphlets, video tapes and slide collections. 48 branches.
Status Voluntary
Publications MCANW Newsletter (3)
The Human Cost of Nuclear War. 1983. 164pp.
The Medical Consequences of Nuclear Weapons. Rep. 1983. 39pp.

Medical Research Council (MRC)
20 Park Crescent, London W1N 4AL
01–636 5422
Press & Information Officer Miss K. Ravey
Aims To advance knowledge that will improve the health of individuals in the community: this includes advances in social, environmental and preventive medicine as well as in the treatment of the sick.
Activities Promoting the balanced development of medical and related biological research in this country; details of research are published annually in the Medical Research Council Handbook. 57 branches. Special Units:
Environmental Epidemiology Unit, Southampton General Hospital, Southampton, Hants. SO9 4XY 0703 777624
Radiobiology Unit, Harwell, Didcot, Oxon. OX11 0RD 0235 834393
Toxicology Unit, Medical Research Council Laboratories, Woodmansterne Road, Carshalton, Surrey SM5 4ES 01–643 8000
Status Research council
Publications MRC News (4); Medical Research Council Handbook (1); Annual Report

Men of the Stones
The Rutland Studio, Tinwell, Stamford, Lincs. PE9 3UD 0780 63372
General Secretary (Alderman) A.S. Ireson, MBE
Aims To stimulate interest in and conser-

vation of good buildings; to encourage greater use of stone and natural and local materials in building; to ensure that new buildings harmonise with others in the same locality; to promote craftsmanship in stone masonry and related skills.

Activities Preparing reports on ancient and historic buildings and sites; collecting and preserving pictorial and literary records; advising on the preservation, repair and use of period buildings and the re-use of good stone; co-operating with local authorities, government departments and societies; publicity, lectures, exhibitions and visits.

Status Voluntary

Publications Annual Report
Clifton-Taylor, Alec & Ireson, A.S., *English Stone Building*, Victor Gollancz, 1983, 288pp.

Men of the Trees (MotT)
Turners Hill Road, Crawley Down, Crawley, W. Sussex RH10 4HL 0342 712536

National Executive Secretary Mrs E. Sandwell

Aims To promote and encourage the planting and protection of trees and education of the necessity of increased world tree cover.

Activities Co-ordinating a programme of meetings, lectures, tree planting and advice centres undertaken throughout the world; managing the Family Tree Scheme for the Tree Council; publishing the journal. 27 branches throughout the world, 18 of which are in the UK.

Status Charity

Publications Trees (2)

Meteorological Office
London Road, Bracknell, Berks. RG12 2SZ 0344 420242

Press Officer/Marketing Services D. Houghton

Activities Observation and research in all aspects of meteorology; also able to advise on aspects of wind, wave and solar energy. 15 regional centres.

Status Statutory

Publications The Meteorological Magazine (12)

Ministry of Agriculture, Fisheries and Food (MAFF)
Whitehall Place, London SW1A 2HH
01–233 3000/5550

Activities Responsible for administering government policy for agriculture, horticulture and fishing in England and for many food matters in the UK; some of the Ministry's responsibilities of animal health extend to Great Britain. In association with the other Agricultural Departments in the UK and the Intervention Board for Agricultural Produce,

it is responsible for the administration of the common agricultural and fisheries policies and for various national support schemes. It administers schemes for the control and eradication of animal and plant diseases and for assistance to capital investment in farm and horticultural businesses and land drainage; it also exercises responsibilities relating to applied research and development. The Agricultural Development and Advisory Service (ADAS) [*see below*] is part of the Ministry. The Ministry sponsors the food and drink manufacturing industries and distributive trades; it is concerned with the supply and quality of food, food compositional standards, food hygiene and the labelling and advertising of food and has certain responsibilities for ensuring public health standards in the manufacture, preparation and distribution of basic foods.

Fisheries Department Great Westminster House, Horseferry Road, London SW1P 2AE
Division 1: Fisheries research and development; marine pollution matters, including interference with fishing activities; disposal of wastes; offshore oil and gas exploration; other mineral workings at sea; oil spill clearance and radioactivity. [*Enquiries:* 01–216 6268]
Division 2: Economic policy for the sea fish industry, marketing and international trade matters; harbours; fisheries statistics. [*Enquiries:* 01–216 7549]
Division 3: EEC Common Fisheries Policy; matters relating to quota allocations, access arrangements, conservation of fish resources and fisheries negotiations with non-member states; law of the sea; fishery limits; conservation of whales.
[*Enquiries:* 01–216 7349]
Division 4: Quota management for UK fleet; planning and control of fishery protection services; salmon and freshwater fisheries, shellfish and fish farming; sea fisheries committees, constitution and appointments. [*Enquiries:* 01–216 7348]
Sea Fisheries Inspectorate: 01–216 6165
Marketing Policy and Potatoes Division Great Westminster House, Horseferry Road, London SW1P 2AE
Developments and improvements in agricultural and horticultural marketing; co-operation and producer groups; legal position and taxation of co-operatives; the Agricultural and Horticultural Co-operation Scheme 1971 and grants to fruit and vegetable groups under EEC Regulation 1035/72; Food From Britain; FEOGA grants under the EEC Marketing and Processing Regulation 355/77; Agricultural Marketing Act 1958; effects on agriculture and fisheries of Restrictive Trade Practices legislation; potatoes. [*Enquiries:* 01–216 6277]

Emergencies, food quality and pest controls Whitehall Place, London SW1A 2HH

Standards Division (food, fertilisers and feedingstuffs), Great Westminster House, Horseferry Road, London SW1P 2AE
Food standards, labelling, composition, safety, additives and contaminants; fertilisers and feedingstuffs standards. [*Enquiries*: 01–216 6421]
Pesticides and Infestation Control Division, Great Westminster House, Horseferry Road, London SW1P 2AE [*Enquiries*: 01–216 6261]

Land Whitehall Place, London SW1A 2HH

Land Improvement Division, Great Westminster House, Horseferry Road, London SW1P 2AE
Aid for capital investments on farms, hill farming, the improvement of farm structure and related matters; EEC Standing Committee on Agricultural Structure; co-ordination of capital grants.
[*Enquiries*: 01–216 6433]
Land Use and Tenure Division: Administration of agricultural holdings legislation; smallholdings policy; land acquisition, management and disposal; policy on use of land for non-agricultural purposes; agricultural implications of planning and countryside legislation and forestry policy.
[*Enquiries*: 01–216 6068]
Land Drainage Division: Land drainage administration and organisation; arterial drainage; sea defence, including Thames tidal defences; farm drainage and water supply. [*Enquiries*: 01–216 6636]
Environment Co-ordination Unit, Great Westminster House, Horseferry Road, London SW1P 2AE
Co-ordination of the Ministry's work on environmental issues, including pollution, conservation and rural affairs.
[*Enquiries*: 01–216 6802]

Horticulture and Agricultural Resources Policy Whitehall Place, London SW1A 2HH

Horticulture Division, Great Westminster House, Horseferry Road, London SW1P 2AE
Policy for commercial production, marketing and distribution of horticultural produce and hops; beekeeping and commercial honey production; international (inc. EEC) horticultural trade matters; financial assistance to the horticulture industry and remanet work on grants for wholesale horticulture markets; grading and standardisation of fresh horticultural produce; liaison with Covent Garden Market Authority, Apple & Pear Development Council and other relevant bodies.
[*Enquiries*: 01–216 7355]
Plant Health Division, Great Westminster House, Horseferry Road, London SW1P 2AE
Policy on plant health matters; administration of EEC Plant Health Regime and of domestic legislation to avoid plant health risk in imports, exports and home-produced crops; licensing of imports of plant material, certain organisms and forestry trees; measures to improve the health of domestic planting material, including the Plant Health Propagation Scheme (PHPS) and the Seed Potato Classification Scheme (SPCS). [*Enquiries*: 01–216 6767]
Agricultural Resources Policy Division, Eagle House, 90–96 Cannon Street, London EC4N 6HT
Agricultural training and wages; credit for agriculture and horticulture; liaison with specialised financial institutions; agricultural rating; taxation of agriculture and horticulture; energy policy matters; supply of fertilisers and other inputs into agriculture; metrication of agriculture and horticulture; liaison with Agriculture EDC.
[*Enquiries*: 01–623 4266 ext.203]
Plant Variety Rights Office and Seeds Division, White House Lane, Huntingdon Road, Cambridge CB3 0LF
Plant breeders' rights; national lists of varieties; seeds commodity and marketing matters; relations with the National Institute of Agricultural Botany and the National Seed Development Organisation Ltd.
[*Enquiries*: 0223 277151 ext.382]

Animal Health Whitehall Place, London SW1A 2HH

Division 1, Government Buildings, Hook Rise South, Tolworth, Surbiton, Surrey KT6 7NF
(a) Notifiable and other diseases; (b) animal health aspects of import and export of animals and animal products, including poultry; (c) general matters concerning the veterinary profession; (d) import and export of captive birds; (e) rabies; (f) pig and poultry health schemes. [*Enquiries*: 01–337 6611 ext.579 or (a) ext.468; (b) ext.402; (c-f) ext.517]
Division 2: (a) Animal welfare on farms; (b) animal welfare in markets and in transit; (c) secretariat of the Farm Animal Welfare Council. [*Enquiries*: 01–337 6611 (a) ext.559; (b) ext.504; (c) ext.370]
Division 3, Tolworth Tower, Surbiton, Surrey KT6 7DX
(a) Eradication of brucellosis and tuberculosis; (b) control of veterinary medicines (Medicines Act 1968); (c) livestock breeding. [*Enquiries*: 01–399 5191 (a) ext.71; (b) ext.85; (c) ext.428]
Meat Hygiene Division, Tolworth Tower, Surbiton, Surrey KT6 7DX
Public health matters concerning inspection and hygiene, import and export of: (a) poultry meat; (b) red meat; (c) meat products; (d) co-ordination of EEC matters generally for Animal Health group.
[*Enquiries*: 01–399 5191]

Agricultural Development and Advisory Service (ADAS) Great Westminster House, Horseferry Road, London SW1P 2AE
Agricultural Development and Advice Division: Administrative matters relating to ADAS, including Experimental Centres. [*Enquiries*: 01–216 7573]
Agriculture, Great Westminster House, Horseferry Road, London SW1P 2AE [*Enquiries*: 01–216 7281]
Agricultural Science, Great Westminster House, Horseferry Road, London SW1P 2AE [*Enquiries*: 01–216 6155] (Chemistry Division 01–216 6103) (Biology Division 01–216 6311)
Land and Water Service, Great Westminster House, Horseferry Road, London SW1P 2AE [*Enquiries*: 01–216 6281]
Veterinary, Government Buildings, Hook Rise South, Tolworth, Surbiton, Surrey KT6 7NF [*Enquiries*: 01–337 6611 ext.562] (Central Veterinary Laboratory, New Haw, Weybridge, Surrey KT15 3NB 0932 41111 ext.267)
Wales: Park Avenue, Aberystwyth, Dyfed SY23 1PQ [*Enquiries*: 0970 615022 ext.230]
Advisory services as agents for the Secretary of State for Wales, covering agriculture, agricultural sciences, land drainage, lands, veterinary (including veterinary investigation).

Mobilisation for Laboratory Animals
51 Harley Street, London W1N 1DD
01–580 4034/01–631 0612
   Chairman Brian Gunn (NAVS)
   Aims To oppose the government's White Paper proposals *Scientific Procedures on Living Animals* (Cmnd.8883) on the grounds that they will not improve existing legislation at all. Mobilisation's member societies are Animal Aid, British Union for the Abolition of Vivisection, National Anti-Vivisection Society and Scottish Anti-Vivisection Society.
   Activities Campaigning throughout the UK to ensure that future legislation is meaningful and for the benefit of the animals rather than those who exploit them. Campaigning takes the form of picketing commercial laboratories performing cruel and unnecessary tests such as those relating to cosmetics, tobacco and alcohol, LD50 toxicity tests, psychological and behavioural research and warfare experiments. Informative postcards produced for the campaign's supporters to send to MPs.
   Status Voluntary alliance

Mocrafts
Old Carpenter's Shop, 6–9 Fountains Row, Market Overton, Oakham, Leics. LE15 7PJ
   Aims To promote the concept of craftwork and small family enterprises being conducted from domestic premises; to interpret the planning laws relating to this; to consider the social and educational implications of cottage industries.
-NR

Montgomery Trust for Nature Conservation (MTNC)
8 Severn Square, Newtown, Powys SY16 2AG, Wales 0686 24751
   Conservation Officer David North
   Aims To conserve, protect and enhance the wildlife communities in the county, with particular attention to those species which are either rare or of national importance.
   Activities Acquisition and management of nature reserves; education through public lectures, discussions, film shows, publications, newsletters, displays, special events and liaison with land-using bodies; publicity through the media and the public advertising of the Trust's activities and achievements; publication of conservation and ecology reports.
   Status Charity
   Publications Montgomery Trust for Nature Conservation Newsletter (4)
   Montgomery Bird Report.

Moredun Institute (Animal Disease Research Association)
408 Gilmerton Road, Edinburgh EH17 7JH
031–664 3262
   Aims To investigate the etiology (causation) of diseases in farm livestock and to formulate methods of prevention; to contribute toward increasing livestock productivity.
   Activities Departments include Biochemistry, Clinical, Parasitology, Pathology, Physiology and Microbiology.
   Status State-aided institute of the Agricultural and Food Research Council

Morpeth Centre for Psychotherapy
4 Market Place West, Morpeth, Northumberland NE61 1HE 0670 57434
   Contact Sheila Ashley
   Aims To provide counselling, groupwork, psychotherapy, psychodrama and opportunities for personal growth and development.
   Activities A number of counsellors and therapists work at the Centre or in association with it. Clients are seen by appointment; ongoing groups also available.

Morpeth Meditation
1 Algernon Terrace, Wylam, Northumberland NE41 8AX 06614 2601
   Contact Barbara Irvine
   Aims To make available to people the yoga of the heart, a spiritual practice outside the

confines of established religious traditions, in which silent meditation plays a central part.

Activities Meetings are held in Morpeth and at other venues in the Tyneside area; retreats are held about once every two months; all these are open to the public and beginners are catered for as well as the more experienced.

Status Independent non-profit organisation

Mother Earth
12 Mason Close, Malvern, Worcs. WR14 2NF
Assistant Director Brian Elliot
Aims To promote the growing of nutritious food by environmentally sympathetic methods.
Activities Organic gardening and appropriate agriculture; community gardening; inner city planting.
Publications Mother Earth

Mothers for Peace
30 Gledhow Wood Grove, Leeds. W. Yorks. LS8 1NZ 0532 667552
National Co-ordinator Pat Dale
Aims To promote peace and friendship between nations, especially across the East-West divide, to break down the fears and suspicions which prevent disarmament; to seek understanding and mutual trust between mothers despite race, creed or ideology.
Activities Exchange visits between mothers from Britain and North America and Europe, particularly from the Eastern bloc and the Soviet Union.
Status Voluntary
Publications Mothers for Peace Newsletter (4)
Mothers for Peace – USA and USSR Visits 1984. 1985.

Mutual Aid Centre
18 Victoria Park Square, London EZ 9PF
01–980 6263
Aims To encourage and promote small-scale co-operation by finding new and practical ways in which people can come together to provide services for themselves and each other.
Activities Efforts are concentrated on projects which are of immediate and direct benefit to the communities they serve but which may be copied elsewhere; these include Britain's first motorists' co-operative, recycling workshops and commuter study clubs.
Status Charity

N

Napier College Wind Energy Group
Colinton Road, Edinburgh EH10 5DT
031–447 7070

Contact W.S. Bannister (Senior Lecturer, Mechanical Engineering)

Aims To investigate the performance and utilisation of small vertical axis wind turbines, including aerodynamic studies, control strategies and methods of electrical power generation.

Activities Theoretical analysis of performance of straight-bladed vertical axis wind turbines for a range of configurations; testing of a small wind turbine in a wind tunnel and on an outdoor site; wind tunnel testing of blades and wind turbine attachments; design and testing of a novel generator and of control instrumentation; participation in the work of the British Wind Energy Association.

Status Academic/research
-NR

National Advisory Committee on Nutrition Education
see JOINT ADVISORY COMMITTEE ON NUTRITION EDUCATION

National Advisory Unit for Community Transport (NAUCT)
Keymer Street, Beswick, Manchester M11 3FY
061–273 6038

Director Trevor Meadows

Aims To provide information and advice to groups which are starting up or running community transport schemes, i.e. for people who do not have private transport and are unable to use public transport.

Activities Advice on constitutions, funding, vehicle specifications, operations, preparation of feasibility studies; visiting groups and projects in most parts of England. Liaison with regional and national networks of community transport operators, with local and central government, with national, regional and local voluntary organisations, with coach builders and vehicle equipment firms and with academic and research establishments. Undertaking specific projects such as research into the mobility of people with disabilities in a given location. Publications, e.g. on the planning of dial-a-ride schemes. 3 branches.

Status Voluntary

Publications *Starting Up* (on how to run a community minibus), 3rd edn.

National Agricultural Centre (NAC)
Stoneleigh, Kenilworth, Warwicks. CV8 2LG
0203 51549/51540

Liaison Officer J.E.Y. Hardcastle, OBE

Activities An out-station of the Agricultural and Food Research Council (AFRC); provides a base for various organisations in agriculture and related fields.
-NR

National Anti-Fluoridation Campaign (NAFC)
36 Station Road, Thames Ditton, Surrey KT7 0NS
01–398 2117

Chairman Patrick Clavell Blount

Aims To prevent public water fluoridation.

Activities Spreading the case against this form of compulsory medication as widely as possible by every means available. No formal branches, but each member acts as a local contact.

Status Voluntary
-NR

National Anti-Vivisection Society Ltd (NAVS)
51 Harley Street, London WIN 1DD 01–580 4034

Aims To awaken the conscience of mankind to the iniquity of painful experiments on animals in all parts of the world and to obtain legislation totally prohibiting all such experiments.

Status Voluntary

Publications Animals' Defender (6); The Campaigner (6)
-NR

National Association for Environmental Education (NAEE)
West Midlands College of Higher Education, Gorway, Walsall, W. Mids. WS1 3BD
0922 31200

Information Officer N.S. Farmer (17 Westbourne Road, Sheffield S10 2QQ)

Aims To promote environmental education (EE) at all levels; to bring together teachers, lecturers and others concerned with education and the environment. (The term 'environmental education' embraces the recognition of values, clarification of concepts and development of skills and attitudes needed to understand the inter-relatedness of Man, his culture and his biophysical surroundings; practice in decision-making; concern for environmental quality; and the adoption of a code of behaviour.)

Activities Lobbying for financial or other facilities for EE in schools; encouraging teacher training in EE; acting as a channel for outside bodies to help teachers of EE with information and materials. The Association has produced a Statement of Aims setting out the objectives of EE at all levels in detail; it also produces a journal, a newsletter, a series of practical teachers' guides and other publications; it holds national conferences, study conferences and courses and has working parties; it is represented on many national bodies, including the Council for Environmental Education and the Field Studies Council.

Status Professional association

Publications Environmental Education (2); NAEE Newsletter (3)

National Association for Outdoor Education
50 High View Avenue, Grays, Essex RM17 6RU

Hon. Secretary Charlie Care

Aims To encourage standards in outdoor education (OE) appropriate to the needs and abilities of young people; to identify, examine and report upon issues concerning OE; to foster an efficient information service; to advance the recognition of OE as an accepted approach to learning and as an integral part of the UK education service.

Activities Maintaining an Advice and Information Centre; liaising with governing bodies, operating authorities and practitioners, training agencies and statutory and voluntary environmental agencies; organising study week-ends, day seminars and workshops; publishing papers. National Advice and Information Centre at DMIHE, High Melton, Doncaster, S. Yorks. DN5 7SZ

Status Voluntary

Publications Adventure Education (6)
Adventure Games: a problem solving approach to Outdoor Education.
Safety Principles in Outdoor Education.

National Association of Development Education Centres
128 Buckingham Palace Road, London SW1W 9SH 01-730 0972

Aims To promote education about the Third World and the interdependence of North and South.

Activities Co-ordinating and supporting the work of over 30 Development Education Centres in the UK and Ireland.
-NR

National Association of Field Studies Officers (NAFSO)
23 Faversham Avenue, Chingford, London E4 6DT 01-524 2844

Secretary Mrs J. Adams

Aims To provide a voice for its members to express their views on problems of field studies and environmental education in general; to provide a medium through which members can remain in touch; and to provide advice to its members.

Activities Annual conference at which members and other interested individuals can review developments and discuss and see aspects of field studies in other parts of the country; weekend conferences throughout the year, dealing with specific aspects of field teaching; providing advice to environmental bodies; producing the journal and newsletter. NAFSO is the only organisation in the British Isles concerned solely with those individals whose professional work is the direct teaching of field/environmental studies; it is a member of the Council for Environmental Education.

Status Voluntary association

Publications NAFSO Newsletter (4); NAFSO Journal (1)
Field Studies Code for the Countryside.

National Association of Inland Waterway Carriers (NAIWC)
Fleet Chambers, 58 Jameson Street, Hull, Humberside HU1 3LS 0482 27281

Secretary R.K. Lang

Aims To protect and organise the inland waterway carrying industry and to represent them at all levels; to act on behalf of members for the purpose of negotiating wages and conditions in the privately owned sector; generally to consult and co-operate on all questions and matters of common interest to members.

Status Trade association

National Association of Loft Insulation Contractors (NALIC)
PO Box 12, Haslemere, Surrey GU27 3AN 0428 54011

Secretary Gillian A. Allder

Aims To promote loft insulation and to uphold standards of practice as carried out by contractors; to liaise with government.

Status Trade association

National Association of Water Power Users
Exchange Chambers, 10B Highgate, Kendal, Cumbria LA9 4SX 0539 20049

Secretary J.M. Hopkinson

Aims To protect and promote the use of water to generate energy.

Activities Maintaining a panel of engineers and consultants expert in water power,

as well as a register of second-hand plant available. Members include users of turbines and water wheels.
-NR

National Board for Science and Technology (Republic of Ireland)
Shelbourne House, Shelbourne Road, Dublin 4, Ireland 0001–68 3311
The Board's work programme is no longer relevant to environmental matters

National Canine Defence League (NCDL)
1–2 Pratt Mews, Camden Town, London NW1 0AD 01–388 0137
Secretary Maj. D.C. Crouch
Aims To promote care and welfare of stray and abandoned dogs; to educate on responsible dog ownership; to help with formulating canine legislation.
Activities Maintaining 14 rescue centres where dogs are rehabilitated when necessary, after which a new home with responsible people is sought; no healthy dog is ever destroyed.
Status Charity
Publications NCDL News (2); Annual Report

National Cavity Insulation Association Ltd (NCIA)
PO Box 12, Haslemere, Surrey GU27 3AN 0428 54011
Secretary Gillian A. Allder
Aims To raise standards within the industry; to advise and protect those who commission cavity wall insulation services.
Status Trade association

National Centre for Alternative Technology
see CENTRE FOR ALTERNATIVE TECHNOLOGY

National Coal Board (NCB)
Hobart House, Grosvenor Place, London SW1X 7AE 01–235 2020
Coal Research Establishment (CRE)
Stoke Orchard, Cheltenham, Glos. GL52 4RZ 0242 673361
Librarian Carol Ann Minter
Activities Research into coal utilisation: combustion, gasification, briquetting, liquefaction, developing coal use and environmental control, e.g. desulphurisation of coals, processes and effluents.
Publications CRE Annual Report
Coal Utilisation Research Laboratories (CURL)
c/o BCURA Ltd, Randalls Road, Leatherhead, Surrey KT22 7RZ 03723 79222
Activities Research includes fluidised bed combustion.

Mining Research and Development Establishment
Ashby Road, Stanhope Bretby, Burton-on-Trent, Staffs. DE15 0QD 0283 216161
Status The NCB is a nationalised industry

National Council for Animals' Welfare
126 Royal College Street, London NW1 0TA
-NR

National Council for the Conservation of Plants and Gardens (NCCPG)
c/o Royal Horticultural Gardens, Wisley, Woking, Surrey GU23 6QB 0483 224234
General Secretary R.A.W. Lowe
Aims To foster and co-ordinate effective action toward the conservation of garden plants and gardens the benefit of which is in danger of being lost to mankind.
Activities Co-ordination of a scheme of designated National Collections – specified plant groups maintained in reference collections by participating gardens; establishing a network of affiliated groups to foster the Council's aims at local level through surveys, propagation, exhibiting, etc.; liaising with other organisations or individuals active in this field. 34 Local groups; 260 National Collections.
Status Voluntary
Publications Newsletter (2)

National Council for Voluntary Organisations (NCVO)
26 Bedford Square, London WC1B 3HU 01–636 4066
Librarian Clive Evers
Aims To extend the involvement of voluntary organisations in responding to social issues; to be a resource centre for voluntary organisations; to protect the interests and independence of voluntary organisations.
Activities Departments and units likely to be of use to environmental organisations include:
Community Schemes Unit – supports agencies involved with Manpower Services Commission programmes;
Employment Unit – supports local community-based employment initiatives;
Information Department & Library – general inquiries relating to voluntary sector activities; maintains files and other literature on a wide variety of subjects and organisations;
Inner Cities Unit – advice and information to voluntary and community organisations concerned with inner city regeneration and community involvement;
Rural Department – information and guidance on rural policy and on voluntary initiatives in rural areas.

Status Voluntary; charity; company limited by guarantee
Publications Rural Viewpoint (6); Annual Report
Davies, Anne. *Government Grants: a guide for voluntary organisations*. 1984.
Voluntary Organisations: an NCVO directory 1985/86 (8th edn). 1985.

National Council on Inland Transport (NCIT)
5 Pembridge Crescent, London W11 3DT
01–727 4689
Hon. Secretary K. Meyer
Aims To promote the development of a national transport policy and the provision of adequate public transport facilities and the proper assessment of the real cost to the community of the various forms of transport.
Activities Acting as an independent forum for the exchange of views between local authorities and other bodies; publishing literature and organising public meetings and conferences; co-operating with other organisations in the furtherance of its aims.
Status Voluntary
-NR

National Energy Efficiency Forum (NEEF)
99 Midland Road, London NW1 2AH
01–387 4393
Aims To enable research, consumer, environmental and professional organisations to exchange information and discuss developments in the field of energy policy, particularly energy conservation.
Activities Acting as an information exchange; has initiated a project to develop 'energy conservation areas' by bringing together representatives of local government, central government, private industry, financial institutions, nationalised industries and others.
Status Voluntary
-NR

National Energy Management Advisory Committee (NEMAC)
c/o Energy Officer, Cornwall Health Authority Works Dept, St Clement Vean, Tregolls Road, Truro, Cornwall TR1 1NR 0872 74242 ext. 7169
Chairman Michael Snedker
Aims To represent energy users' views at national level, having access to the Secretary of State for Energy and his department to comment on proposals or legislation relating to energy efficiency.
Activities Providing a forum for energy management needs, including new technology, education, conferences, liaising with the energy supply industry at home and abroad to promote more efficient use of energy resources. NEMAC draws its representation from the independent Energy Management Groups (EMGs) of the UK, which are based in all the population areas of the UK and hold regular meetings which form the basis for exchange of ideas and act as a catalyst/forum, generating implementation of these ideas and thus creating savings in industry, commerce, private and public sectors, leisure industries, etc. A national conference is organised annually, with an exhibition of equipment; target setting and monitoring are encouraged for all companies participating. NEMAC has central government backing for the EMG movement and there are now over 70 EMGs, with over 5,000 members.
Status Voluntary
Publications Energy Management (12) (through Dept of Energy)

National Engineering Laboratory (NEL)
Birnie Hill, East Kilbride, Glasgow G75 0QU
03552 20222
Activities Provides a wide range of specialist services for the engineering industry, including full-scale testing facilities. Work includes noise control studies and the development of the Oscillating Water Column system of wave power generation; established the National Wind Turbine Test Centre in 1984.
Status Laboratory of the Dept of Trade and Industry
Publications NEL Newsletter; Annual Report
-NR

National Federation of Agricultural Pest Control Societies Ltd
Agriculture House, 25–31 Knightsbridge, London SW1X 7NJ 01–235 8440
Secretary R.V.N. Surtees
Aims To promote organised block control of rabbits and other pests (mammal or bird) in England and Wales; to advise rabbit clearance and pest control societies on legal and administrative matters; to consult with the Ministry of Agriculture on enforcement procedures.
Activities Acting as a pressure group on behalf of pest control societies; acting as a forum for the interchange of ideas and problems among the societies; working for the improvement of pest control in the country.
Status Co-operative Society
-NR

National Federation of City Farms (NFCF)

The Old Vicarage, 66 Fraser Street, Windmill Hill, Bedminster, Bristol, Avon BS3 4LY 0272 660663

General Secretary Mike Primarolo

Aims To promote City Farms and Community Gardens and similar projects like market gardens or farm-type projects attached to institutions, in the interests of social welfare; to encourage their use by the public; to develop awareness, especially in young people, by enabling them to partici-pate in rural activities; to provide facilities which will integrate people with mental and physical disabilities into everyday life.

Activities Co-ordinating the requirements of the national network and providing the means for communication and exchange of ideas, information and skills; liaising and working in partnership with national bodies to pilot new projects and to encourage mutual help and practical results; developing educational materials and arranging training courses. Branches consist of City Farms all over the UK.

Status Voluntary

Publications City Farmer (4)

National Federation of Community Organis-ations (NFCO)

8–9 Upper Street, Islington, London N1 0PQ 01–226 0189

Director Judy Weleminsky

Aims To promote the activities of community associations and organisations in the areas of education, recreation, leisure and social welfare; to represent community organisations at local and national level to government departments and to other national voluntary organisations; to assist in the promotion of new community organisations.

Activities Conferences, seminars and training courses for people involved in working with neighbourhood-based community organisations, whether paid or voluntary; practical assistance and advice to community organisations; promotion of community projects, local federal organis-ations and national activities; publications and information service. Regional offices in Leeds and Bristol.

Status Voluntary

Publications Community (4)

Pinder, Caroline. *Community Start Up: how to start a community group and keep it going*. NFCO/National Extension College, 1984. 212pp.

Twelvetrees, Alan. *Democracy and the Neighbourhood*. NFCO, 1985. 112pp.

National Federation of Housing Co-ops

34 Argylle Mansions, Hammersmith Road, London W14 8QC 01–603 0048
-NR

National Federation of Self-Employed and Small Businesses Ltd (NFSE)

32 St Anne's Road West, Lytham St Anne's, Lancs. FY8 1NY 0253 720911

Head of Administration Jim Dickin

Aims To promote free enterprise and improve the climate for self-employed people and small businesses.

Activities Maintaining pressure on all political parties through our national structure of members supported by specialised staff; major test cases are taken right through to the House of Lords and the Court of Human Rights; providing a unique legal insurance service on items not normally covered by standard employers and public liability insurance, including an in-depth tax investi-gation; members' local problems, e.g. plan-ning applications, are supported where poss-ible by our 250 local branches.

Status Voluntary

Publications First Voice (12)

National Federation of Young Farmers' Clubs (NFYFC)

YFC Centre, National Agricultural Centre, Kenilworth, Warwicks. CV8 2LG 0203 56131

General Secretary F.E. Shields, MBE

Aims To involve young people in rural areas in a wide range of activities designed to increase their awareness of countryside issues and their development as respon-sible and self-reliant members of society.

Activities Practical community and conservation work; craft training; local and international exchange visits; conferences and discussion groups on topical subjects, with visits to clubs by guest speakers; competitions, including crafts, public speaking, safe and efficient use of machinery, conservation, stock judging, farm manage-ment, sports, etc. Over 1,000 local branches.

Status Voluntary; charity

Publications The Young Farmer (7)

National Federation of Zoological Gardens of Great Britain and Ireland

Zoological Gardens, Regent's Park, London NW1 4RY 01–586 0230

Assistant Secretary Miss D.F. Andrews

Aims To act in defence and development of animals through conservation, research into animal management, husbandry, transpor-tation; to provide the public with oppor-tunities for learning about the relationship between Man, the animal kingdom and the natural world; to achieve these objects by setting appropriate standards and encouraging their acceptance, realisation and further development.

Activities Has 2 committees: the Conservation and Animal Management Committee whose purpose is to encourage the breeding and conservation of endangered species and to deal with matters relating to animal management; and the Marketing Committee whose purpose is to help members improve their marketing, interpretation and presentation techniques. Through its meetings and newsletters, the Federation provides a useful forum for discussion of matters of mutual concern to its members and a means of pooling experience and knowledge for common benefit, as well as a means of circulating information on matters of common interest.

Status Charity

Publications Zoo Federation News (3)

National Foundation for Homoeopathic Medicine
[formerly the Homoeopathic Medical Foundation)

1 The Drive, Gosforth, Newcastle upon Tyne NE3 4AH

Aims To spread knowledge of homoeopathy throughout the community.

Activities Raising funds for projects; research and publishing; public talks, first-aid courses, study groups.

Publications The Homoeopathic Alternative (4)

-NR

National Fuel Poverty Forum (NFPF)

26 Bedford Square, London WC1B 3HU
01-636 4066

Activities Concerned with the problems of domestic consumers of fuel and with energy conservation and fuel prices.

-NR

National Gas Consumers' Council

4th Floor, 162 Regent Street, London W1R 5TB
01-439 0012

Aims To consider any matter affecting the interests of consumers of gas generally, including matters relating to the supply of gas; to notify their conclusions to the British Gas Corporation where appropriate; to consider and report to BGC on any matter referred to them by BGC; to consider and report to the Secretary of State for Trade and Industry on any matter referred to them by the Secretary of State. The Council consists of a chairman and up to 30 other members appointed by the Secretary of State; membership includes the chairmen of the Regional Gas Consumers' Councils and such other persons as the Secretary of State may think fit.

Status Statutory
-NR

National Gas Turbine Establishment

Pyestock, Farnborough, Hants. GU14 0LS
0252 44411

Activities Conducts a substantial engine noise research programme; supplied evidence to the Commission on the Third London Airport on air pollution from aircraft gas turbine engines.

Status Research establishment of the Ministry of Defence
-NR

National Heritage Memorial Fund

Church House, Great Smith Street, London SW1P 3BL 01-212 5414

Secretary Brian Lang

Aims To provide financial assistance toward the cost of acquiring, maintaining or preserving land, buildings, works of art and other objects of outstanding interest which are also of importance to the national heritage.

Activities The Fund is a safety net for the national heritage. Assistance is given where the Trustees feel that this is essential in order to save a building from demolition or undesirable alteration or to preserve it in an appropriate manner; to keep an object or collection in this country; or to ensure that heritage land is not spoiled by undesirable development. Any non-profit-making body, one of whose main purposes is the conservation of the national heritage, may apply to the fund; private persons are not eligible.

Status Charity

Publications Annual Report

National Industrial Fuel Efficiency Service (NIFES)

NIFES House, Sinderland Road, Broadheath, Altrincham, Cheshire WA14 5HQ 061-928 5791

Commercial Manager Dr Eric Strecker (021-454 4471)

Aims To provide energy advisory and mechanical and electrical design services to industry, commerce, public authorities and government departments throughout the UK and overseas.

Activities Energy audits and in-depth energy surveys; Combined Heat and Power studies; waste heat recovery; District Heating and refuse incineration projects; design and consultancy services for energy plant; project management of complete installations; monitoring and target setting; electronic energy management system appraisal and specification; fuel conversion; training courses for operational and management staff. 7 branches.

Status Commercial

Publications NIFES Monitor (4);
Comparison of Energy Costs chart (4)
Energy Manager's Handbook. Graham &
Trotman, 1985.
Fuel Efficiency Handbook.

National Industrial Materials Recovery Association (NIMRA)
4 Stanley Park Road, Wallington,
Surrey SM6 0EU 01–669 3153/4
Aims To assist industry to make more
profitable use of waste which occurs in manu-
facture; to conserve essential materials.
Publications Industrial Recovery (12)
-NR

National Institute for Research in Dairying
University of Reading, Shinfield, Reading,
Berks.RG2 9AT 0734 883103
Information Officer J.A. Irvine
Status State-aided institute of the Agricul-
tural and Food Research Council
-NR

National Institute of Agricultural Botany
Huntingdon Road, Cambridge CB3 0LE
0223 276381
-NR

**National Institute of Agricultural Engin-
eering (NIAE)**
Wrest Park, Silsoe, Bedford, MK45 4HS
0525 60000
Head of Information Services Dept Dr
G.F. Forster
Aims To undertake agricultural engineering research and development.
Activities Engineering research and
development into the mechanisation and
control of agricultural and food processes,
including: energy conservation in glass-
houses; handling and utilisation of animal waste;
animal welfare, by improvement of handling
and housing; improvement of the human
environment in and around agricultural
machines.
Status Research institute of the Agricultural
and Food Research Council
Publications General Report (biennial)
Oliver, B. *Heat Recovery to Reduce the
Energy Requirements of Anaerobic Diges-
tion. Part 1: Predictions.* 1984.

**National Institute of Medical Herbalists
(NIMH)**
41 Hatherley Road, Winchester, Hants. SO22
6RR 0962 68776
General Secretary Mrs. J. Hicks
Aims To promote and encourage the study
and practice of medical herbalism.
Activities Dissemination of information;
maintaining the register of practitioners;
publishing the journal. Membership by

examination only, following full training with
the School of Herbal Medicine.
Status Professional association
Publications New Herbal Practitioner (2/3)

National Joint Equine Welfare Committee
Bransby Home of Rest for Horses, Bransby,
Saxilby, Lincs, LN1 2PH 0427 788464
Hon. Secretary P.E. Hunt
Aims To care for rescued horses, ponies
and donkeys; to campaign for equine
welfare.
Activities Attending horse sales all over
the country; providing a sanctuary for
equines in need. Local branches.
Status Charity
Publications Newsletter; Annual Report
-NR

National Maritime Institute
see NMI LTD

National Nuclear Corporation (NNC)
Booths Hall, Chelford Road, Knutsford,
Cheshire WA16 8QN 0565 3800
Contract Information Services Department
Activities The national supplier and
contractor for nuclear power stations in the
UK.
-NR

National Peace Council (NPC)
29 Great James Street, London WC1N 3ES
01–242 3228
Secretary Sheila Oakes
Aims To educate people in the ways of
peace and to increase awareness and
knowledge of the problems of war, peace
and disarmament and their possible
solutions.
Activities As an independent umbrella
organisation within the peace movement,
the NPC facilitates the effectiveness of and
co-operation between over 200 member
organisations and associates by providing
channels of communication, a forum for
debate and information.
Status Voluntary
Publications Annual Report

National Physical Laboratory (NPL)
Queens Road, Teddington, London TW11 0LW
01–977 3222
Head of Information Services Dr K.
Dennis
Aims To provide national measurement
standards and techniques; to maintain a
consistent national system for measurement
and calibration; to conduct research on
materials, information technology and
computing.
Activities Environment-oriented activities
include research on noise measurement and

hearing protection; monitoring ionising radiations; techniques for monitoring atmospheric pollution; development of standards for thermal insulation materials; development of engineering materials; and research on corrosion. Informal advice, consultancy, measurement services and commissioned research can be provided.

Status Station of the Dept of Trade and Industry

Publications NPL News (2); Annual Report; Points of Contact (directory)

National Planning Aid Unit

c/o TCPA, 17 Carlton House Terrace, London SW1Y 5AS 01-930 8903

Contact Brian Anson, Mike Beazley

Aims To provide advice and assistance on all aspects of the planning system, especially to communities suffering a poor environment. -NR

National Pure Water Association

Southern Ash, Gilberts Lane, Whixall, Whitchurch, Shropshire SY13 2PR 094872 642

Secretary N. Brugge

Aims To prevent the pollution of the public water supply, especially by fluoridation.

Activities Dissemination of information; meetings and publicity. Local branches.

Status Voluntary

Publications National Pure Water Association Newsletter

National Radiological Protection Board (NRPB)

Chilton, Didcot, Oxon. OX11 0RQ 0235 831600

Principal Information Officer M.J. Gaines

Aims To advance the acquisition of knowledge on the protection of mankind from radiation hazards; to provide information and advice to persons, including government departments, with responsibilities in the UK relating to the protection from radiation hazards either of the community as a whole or of particular sections of the community. Established under the Radiological Protection Act 1970 to be national point of authoritative reference. The Board consists of a chairman plus 7–12 other members appointed by the Health Ministers after consultation with the UK Atomic Energy Authority and the Medical Research Council.

Activities Concerned with both ionising and non-ionising radiations; research into radiation protection; providing information and advice to government departments, organisations and relevant persons; providing technical services to persons and organisations concerned with radiation hazards; publishing technical reports. Centres at Leeds and Glasgow.

Status Statutory

Publications Radiological Protection Bulletin (6).
Living with Radiation.
The Work of the NRPB 1981–83. (both available from HMSO)

National Remote Sensing Centre (NRSC)

Space Dept, Royal Aircraft Establishment, Farnborough, Hants. GU14 6TD 0252 24461 ext. 2291

Manager M.J. Hammond

Aims To introduce new users to earth resources satellite data and to demonstrate how the data can be used for a variety of applications; to provide facilities, services and products to all users of remote sensing data.

Activities Supplying remote sensing data and imagery; assisting British industry in its remote sensing activities; providing facilities for research into and development of image processing, analysis and interpretive techniques; acting as a focal point for the development of remote sensing techniques and their applications; providing education and training facilities in remote sensing. 2 regional centres.

Status Statutory

Publications NRSC Newsletter (4)

National Right to Fuel Campaign

207 Cutler Heights Lane, Bradford, W. Yorks. BD4 9JB 0274 681022

Secretary Barry Clark

Aims To campaign for: the end of the fuel Boards' right to disconnect for debt; adequate income for everyone's fuel needs; a comprehensive domestic insulation programme; more investment in cheaper renewable energy sources; a warm, well-lit home for everyone.

Activities Local and national campaigning for the above aims. 20 local groups and 200 affiliated bodies.

Status Voluntary

Publications Fuel News (4)
Boardman, Brenda. *The Cost of Warmth.* 1984. 38pp.
Fuel Poverty in Northern Ireland. 1985. 28pp.

National Society Against Factory Farming Ltd (NSAFF)

41 Mercator Road, Lewisham, London SE13 5EH 01-852 1832

Hon. Secretary Mrs L.J. Newman

Aims To relieve the suffering of all factory farmed animals by lobbying Parliament, instituting private prosecutions where justified; to promote a return to free range rearing.

Activities Alerting the press and MPs to deliberate acts of cruelty and keeping them informed of our actions; keeping members informed of the facts about factory farming

and of the Society's activities; telling subscribers where they can buy non-factory farmed produce. 2 branches.
Status Limited company
Publications NSAFF News (3)

National Society for the Abolition of Cruel Sports (NSACS) and Care for the Wild (CFW)
26 North Street, Horsham, W. Sussex RH12 1BN
0403 50557
General Secretary Mrs Thelma How
Aims To stop and prevent the suffering of wild animals of all species; to promote investigation into the value of each species in the web of life and particularly the effect that mankind's actions have on wildlife; to explain the interrelationship of animals in nature and their interdependence and thereby encourage in mankind empathy and a desire to protect them; to persuade the public to cherish wildlife and influence the authorities to protect it.
Status Charity
Publications Newsletter (4)

National Society for Clean Air (NSCA)
136 North Street, Brighton, E. Sussex BN1 1RG
0273 26313
Information Officer & Editor Jane Dunmore
Aims To secure environmental improvement by promoting clean air through the reduction of air pollution, noise and other contaminants, while having due regard for other aspects of the environment; to advance the investigation, consideration and discussion of all forms of pollution in order to achieve its reduction or prevention.
Activities Annual conference, annual training workshops, meetings and exhibitions; the Society has its own press and publishes a journal, proceedings of conferences and workshops, technical papers and reports, books and educational material. The Society's HQ houses an Information Department and Library. 12 branches.
Status Voluntary
Publications Clean Air (4)
NSCA Environmental Glossary. 1985. 96pp.
NSCA Reference Book. 2nd edn, 1985. 306pp.
Dawson, Hylton. *Noise and Society.* 1984. 44pp.

National Society of Master Thatchers
25 Little Lane, Yardley Hastings, Northampton
NN7 1EN 060129 280
-NR

National Society of Non-Smokers
Information and Advice Centre, Latimer House,
40–48 Hanson Street, London W1P 7DE
01–636 9103
Hon. Director & Secretary Tom Hurst

Aims To reduce tobacco smoking in the interests of the nation's health; to secure a smoke-free environment in public places; to persuade young people not to start smoking; and to help smokers give up the habit. Also concerned about the spread of smoking in developing countries.
Activities Providing a daily free advice service for telephone and personal callers; running courses; mailing information; selling a dummy cigarette. The Society does all within its power to act upon the Declaration by the Expert Committee of the UN World Health Organisation that 'Smoking-related diseases are such important causes of disability and premature death in developed countries that the control of cigarette smoking could do more to improve health and prolong life in these countries than any other single action in the whole field of preventive medicine'.
Status Voluntary; charity
Publications Non-Smoker (4)

National Trust for Places of Historic Interest or Natural Beauty
36 Queen Anne's Gate, London SW1H 9AS
01–222 9251
Press & Publicity Secretary Warren Davis
Aims To promote the permanent preservation for the benefit of the nation of land and buildings of beauty or historic interest.
Activities Owns and protects 522,458 acres of our finest countryside, 452 miles of unspoilt coastline (through the Enterprise Neptune campaign) and 276 houses which are open to the public. Its properties include 109 famous gardens, 1,145 farms, 21 wind and water mills, lakes and hills, 103 prehistoric sites, 11 Roman antiquities, including part of Hadrian's Wall, 44 nature reserves and important bird sanctuaries. The Trust has 1,193,946 members who are entitled to free entry to properties for which an admission charge is made to the public. Regional branches.
Status Charity incorporated by Act of Parliament
Publications National Trust (3); List of Properties Open (1)

National Trust for Scotland (NTS)
5 Charlotte Square, Edinburgh EH2 4DU
031–226 5922
Secretary Miss Katherine M. Dawson
Aims To promote the permanent preservation for the benefit of the nation of lands and buildings in Scotland of historic or national interest or natural beauty.
Activities Maintains, staffs and opens to the public many of the finest examples of Scotland's heritage of fine buildings, beautiful landscape and historic sites. Cares for some

100 properties covering 100,000 acres, including castles, gardens, little houses, historic sites, islands, mountains, waterfalls and coastline. Local branches.
Status Voluntary; charity
Publications Heritage Scotland (4); Guide to Properties (1)

National Vegetable Research Station (NVRS)
Wellesbourne, Warwick CV35 9EF 0789 840382
Liaison Officer Dr C.C. Wood
Aims To carry out research on vegetables grown in the open ground, with the object of improving their quality, yield, etc.
Activities Conducting research in the following areas: plant breeding; soil science; biochemistry; plant physiology; entomology; plant pathology; weed science. Members' Days are held three times per year.
Status Grant-aided research institute of the Agricultural and Food Research Council
Publications Annual Report

National Waterways Transport Association (NWTA)
Room 314, Melbury House, Melbury Terrace, London NW1 6JX 01–262 6711 ext. 6315
Hon. Secretary D. Silk
Aims To bring together all those involved in or concerned with large-scale inland waterway freight transport in the UK; to present to government, local authorities, industry, trade unions, commerce and the public the economic and environmental benefits of inland waterway transport.
Activities The Association is controlled by an executive committee of 12 members which meets bi-monthly.
Status Independent association
Publications National Waterways Transport Association Newsletter (3)

National Zoological Association of Great Britain
Stowlangtoft, Bury St Edmunds, Suffolk IP31 3JW
Activities Concerns include conservation, animal health and welfare and wild animal legislation.
Status Trade association
-NR

NATTA (Network for Alternative Technology and Technology Assessment)
c/o Appropriate Technology Group, Faculty of Technology, Open University, Walton Hall, Milton Keynes, Bucks. MK7 6AA 0908 653197
Co-ordinator Dr D.A. Elliott
London NATTA: 14 Peto Place, London NW1 4DT 01–407 4478
Aims To provide a communications channel for information on alternative technology and generally to promote the development of AT in the UK, focusing in particular on renewable energy systems.
Activities Providing a forum for discussion; holding an annual conference which enables members to shape overall policy; running an information exchange for members and an advisory service for careers in alternative technology; publishing a newsletter on current AT developments and producing various publications on different aspects of AT. NATTA can supply speakers, an exhibition and a slide show.
Status Voluntary network
Publications NATTA Newsletter (6)

Natural Energy Association
35 Sydenham Road, Guildford, Surrey GU1 3RX 0483 68552
Activities Acts as a forum for people who want to take an active part in or learn about renewable sources of energy.
Publications Natural Energy and Living (4) -NR

Natural Environment Research Council (NERC)
Polaris House, North Star Avenue, Swindon, Wilts. SN2 1EU 0793 40101
Public Relations Officer Bernard Moran
Aims To encourage, plan and carry out research in the physical and biological sciences relating to the natural environment and its resources, in order to understand Man's impact on his surroundings and their influence on his activities; from this knowledge, sensible policies for the exploitation of resources can be formed. The Council consists of a chairman and up to 19 other members appointed by the Secretary of State for Education and Science, to whom the Council is responsible.
Activities Carrying out fundamental, strategic and applied research through the Council's component and grant-aided institutes and by grants to universities, and in collaboration with national and international organisations. The sciences supported include: geological sciences; physical and biological oceanography; marine and freshwater biology; hydrology; terrestrial ecology; some aspects of atmospherics and meteorology; Antarctic studies; and pollution.
Status Statutory
Publications NERC Newsjournal (4); Annual Report
see also the NERC research institutes: BRITISH GEOLOGICAL SURVEY; FRESHWATER BIOLOGICAL ASSOCIATION; INSTITUTE FOR MARINE ENVIRONMENTAL RESEARCH; INSTITUTE OF HYDROLOGY; INSTITUTE OF MARINE BIOCHEMISTRY; INSTITUTE OF OCEANOGRAPHIC SCIENCES; INSTITUTE OF

TERRESTRIAL ECOLOGY; MARINE BIOLOGICAL ASSOCIATION OF THE UNITED KINGDOM; SCOTTISH MARINE BIOLOGICAL ASSOCIATION; SEA MAMMAL RESEARCH UNIT; UNIT OF COMPARATIVE PLANT ECOLOGY

Natural Health Network
Chardstock House, Chard, Somerset, TA20 2TL 04606 3229
Chairman Maurice Newbound
Aims To promote the use of natural therapies; to support co-operation with similar organisations involved in orthodox or complementary medicine and therapies.
Activities Dealing with enquiries from the public; assisting in setting up new Natural Health Centres; taking part in exhibitions; organising the annual Holistic Health Gathering and Forum at Cirencester. 10 branches and over 50 Centres.
Status Voluntary
Publications Natural Health Network Newsletter (4)

Natural Medicines Group
PO Box 5, Ilkeston, Derbys. DE7 8LX
General Secretary Mrs. P. Viner
Aims To persuade the Minister of Health to appoint a Natural Medicines Committee, equal in status to the current DHSS Review Committees, composed of experts from the four identified systems of licensed natural medicines (herbal, homoeopathic, biochemic, anthroposophic) to adjudicate on all matters within the framework of the Medicines Act appertaining to the licensing of products in these areas.
Activities The main thrust of the Group's work in 1985 has been and will continue to be the achievement of parliamentary support for its aims, and meetings with the DHSS and the Minister to further these aims, in order that freedom of choice in medicine can be retained.
Status Voluntary
Publications Natural Medicines Group Bulletin (4)
Towards Retaining Freedom of Choice in Medicine.

Nature Conservancy Council (NCC)
Northminster House, Northminster Road, Peterborough, Cambs. PE1 1UA 0733 40345
Contact Librarian
Scotland: 12 Hope Terrace, Edinburgh EH9 2AS 031–447 4784
Wales: Plas Penrhos, Penrhos Road, Bangor, Gwynedd LL57 2LQ 0248 355141
Aims Established by Parliament to be responsible for the conservation of flora, fauna, geological and physiographical features throughout Great Britain. The

Council consists of a chairman and 13 other members appointed by the Secretary of State for the Environment; there are separate Advisory Committees for England, Scotland and Wales, appointed by the Council with the approval of the Secretary of State.
Activities Establishing and managing National Nature Reserves (NNRs); advising government and all bodies and individuals whose activities affect Britain's wildlife and wild places; scheduling Sites of Special Scientific Interest (SSSIs) and notifying them to owners and occupiers, local planning authorities and the Secretary of State; commissioning and carrying out relevant research and surveys and making grants available within its sphere of interest. Council's duties are considerably widened under the Wildlife and Countryside Act 1981, particularly in relation to SSSIs, Marine Nature Reserves and Limestone Pavement Orders. Has an Advisory Committee on Birds and an Advisory Committee on Animals Endangered in Trade. 15 regional offices.
Status Statutory
Publications Topical Issues (4); Naturopa (3) (distributed on behalf of Council of Europe); Research Reports Digest; Annual Report
Nature Conservation in Great Britain.
Nature Conservation and River Engineering.

Nature Reserves Committee (NRC) (Northern Island)
Hut 6, Castle Grounds, Stormont, Belfast BT4 3ST 0232 768716
Contact Secretary
Aims To advise the government on nature conservation in Northern Ireland.
Status Statutory
Publications Annual Report
-NR

Neighbourhood Energy Action (NEA)
Energy Projects Office, 2nd Floor, Sunlight Chambers, 2–4 Bigg Market, Newcastle upon Tyne NE1 1UW 0632 615677
Administrator Sara Addington
Aims To assist communities to conserve energy, alleviate fuel poverty and create jobs through the formation of local energy projects throughout the UK.
Activities Providing advice and information to groups on specific aspects of establishing and running projects; running training courses, seminars and conferences for energy projects; general policy work in the field of fuel poverty; publication of information packs, briefing notes, training notes and a bulletin for projects and groups planning projects.
Status Voluntary; charity
Publications Energy Action Bulletin (6)

see also SCOTTISH NEIGHBOURHOOD
ENERGY ACTION

Neighbourhood Use of Buildings and Space (NUBS)

15 Wilkin Street, Kentish Town, London
NW5 3NG 01-267 9421
Director John Knights
Aims To assist voluntary groups who could
not otherwise afford professional advice to
develop their embryonic ideas for using
derelict land and buildings in inner city
areas.
Activities Providing a full architectural
service; the first 40 hours of advice are
supplied free.
Status Charity
-NR

New Era Centre

The Abbey, Sutton Courtenay, Abingdon, Oxon.
OX14 4AF 0235 847401
Director Fred J. Blum
Aims To be a meeting place for people
concerned with a kind of personal development which helps them to realise their true
potentialities and be actively involved in the
human community. We are convinced that
we are at the threshold of a new global
understanding of the future of humanity.
Activities Organising day and weekend
conferences concerned with various
aspects of the development of consciousness
and current social issues; three long-term
projects enable us to explore these issues at
greater depth:
(i) life style and its implications for the
environment; (ii) the building of a society
without unemployment; (iii) the kind of
personal development necessary to bring
about a living awareness of these issues and
open ways for transformation. Residential
programme for people who come for longer
periods of time.
Status Charity
Publications Annual Programme

New Villages Association

c/o Food and Energy Research Centre,
Evesham Road, Cleeve Prior, Evesham,
Worcs. WR11 5JX
Aims To establish a number of new villages
that are stable, largely self-sufficient settlements with populations of less than 2,000
supplying most of their needs from local
resources and having an independent
internal economy, using methods which are
ecologically acceptable and humanly
satisfying.
-NR

Newcastle Photovoltaics Applications Centre (NPAC)

Faculty of Engineering, Newcastle Polytechnic,
Ellison Building, Ellison Place, Newcastle upon
Tyne NE1 8ST 091-232 6002
Manager Dr N.M. Pearsall
Aims To further the development and
deployment of photovoltaics in the UK and
overseas; to increase the awareness of both
industry and the general public of the potential benefits of electricity generation from
solar energy.
Activities Undertakes contract research
on many aspects of photovoltaics, including
the development of high-efficiency solar
cells, measurement and evaluation of cells
and modules, marketing and deployment
strategy and development of new applications; also undertakes studies of the economic and environmental impact of photovoltaic power generation. The Centre runs
training courses on the use of solar energy
for the generation of electricity and acts as a
source of information on all aspects of
photovoltaics.
Status Research institute
Publications
*Register of Activities in Photovoltaics in the
United Kingdom.* 1983.

Newport and Nevern Energy Group (NNEG)

Energy Advice Centre, Long Street, Newport,
Dyfed SA42, Wales 0239 820912
Hon. Secretary Mrs Liz Williams
Aims To promote energy conservation and
the use of natural energy resources for the
benefit of the local community.
Activities Energy conservation advice;
advice on solar panels, wind turbines, etc.;
running energy-saving projects, e.g. bottle
banks, recycling of waste paper, tree
planting, draughtproofing and loft insulation
of local public buildings; bulk purchase of
insulation materials and straw fuel briquettes
for members. Campaigning for energy
conservation to be taken seriously by local
and national government; organising meetings, conferences, energy shows and competitions; encouraging local businesses
involved in energy conservation; job creation
in the energy field.
Status Voluntary
Publications Newport & Nevern Energy
Group Newsletter (2/3)

NIREX (Nuclear Industry Radioactive Waste Executive)

Building 173.6, AERE, Harwell, Didcot, Oxon.
OX11 0RA 0235 24141 ext. 3028
Information Officer Peter Curd
Aims To advise the UK nuclear industry on
how it can best discharge its obligations for
radioactive waste management and disposal;

to develop disposal routes; and then to operate disposal facilities when constructed.
Activities Maintaining an up-to-date inventory of waste arisings in the UK; considering disposal options for each type; planning and developing waste transport and disposal facilities; selecting and providing sites suitable for the development of repositories for low and intermediate level waste; managing the construction and operation of repositories; monitoring research and development progress.
Status Industrial/commercial
Publications Plaintalk (4)

NMI Ltd
[formerly National Maritime Institute]
Hampton Road, Teddington, London TW11 0LW 01–977 0933
Head of Applied Fluid Mechanics Division Dr M.E. Davies
Aims To provide a consultancy service, modelling, testing and field trials in hydrodynamics, aerodynamics and related subjects.
Activities Environment-related studies include: pollution dispersion and hazard analysis; environmental aspects of wind in building complexes; wind protection shelter belts; and wind and wave climate. Has developed a theoretical and experimental capability in wave and wind energy.
Status Non-profit company limited by guarantee
-NR

Noise Abatement Society
PO Box 8, Bromley, Kent BR2 0UH 01–460 3146
Chairman John Connell
Aims To eliminate excessive and unnecessary noise from all sources by taking all possible steps under the existing law to protect from assault by noise; to inform the public of the dangers to health and their legal rights against those who create noise.
Status Voluntary
-NR

Norfolk Naturalists' Trust
72 Cathedral Close, Norwich, Norfolk NR1 4DF 0603 2540
Director Miss Moira Warland
Aims To protect and manage nature reserves and other sites of conservation value; to stimulate interest in the beauty and variety of wild nature; to explain the importance of conservation; to maintain the greatest diversity of plants and animals, particularly endangered ones.
Activities Establishing sanctuaries in different parts of Norfolk, especially by providing the ideal habitat for rarer species; providing facilities for nature study,

research and quiet enjoyment where and when these do not unduly disturb wildlife; involving young people in the work of the Trust. Regional groups.
Status Charity
Publications Norfolk Naturalists' Trust Newsletter; Annual Report

Norfolk Wildlife Park Trust
Norfolk Wildlife Park, Great Witchingham, Norwich, Norfolk NR9 5QS 060544 274
Director Philip Wayre
Aims To promote the conservation of European wildlife and in particular the breeding and conservation work of the Norfolk Wildlife Park; to promote environmental education, particularly for young people, in the field of European wildlife.
Activities Maintaining a large representative collection of European mammals and birds under semi-natural conditions with special emphasis on breeding rare or endangered species with a view to reintroducing young animals to the wild to build up depleted wild populations.
Status Charity
Publications Annual Report
-NR

North East Civic Trust
3 Old Elvet, Durham DH1 3HL 0385 61182/ 0632 329279
Director Neville Whittaker
Aims To preserve, improve and protect the regional environment; to be both a pressure group and an executive agency.
Activities Young people's practical projects (Enterprise Awards); advice and information service; publications; general registry and promotion of voluntary civic and amenity societies; practical improvement schemes for working industry.
Status Charity
Publications Amenity (6); Annual Report

North East River Purification Board
Woodside House, Mugiemoss Road, Persley, Aberdeen, Grampian AB2 2UQ, Scotland.
-NR

North of Scotland Grassland Society
Grassland Division, School of Agriculture, 581 King Street, Aberdeen, Grampian AB9 1UD, Scotland 0224 40291
Hon. Secretary Charles K. Mackie
Aims To advance methods of production and utilisation of grass and forage crops for the promotion of agriculture and the public benefit; to advance education and research into these crops and to publish research results for public benefit.
Activities Organising farm walks to study at first hand new developments and

methods used by successful grassland farmers; arranging meetings and conferences to hear and discuss results of research and development; running competitions to highlight certain topics and indicate the most successful practices.
Status Voluntary
Publications Norgrass (1)
-NR

North of Scotland Hydro-Electric Board (NoSHEB)
16 Rothesay, Edinburgh EH3 7SE 031–225 1361
Activities Responsible for generating, distributing and selling electricity in northern Scotland, including the island groups; operates 1050 MW of conventional hydro-electric plant and 700 MW of pumped storage. Installing large wind turbine systems to reduce fuel costs in isolated areas currently served by diesel generation.
Status Statutory
-NR

North Pennines Protection Group
Unthank Hall, Haltwhistle, Northumberland NE49 0HX 0498 20500
Chairman Richard Sowler
Aims To preserve the North Pennines as an area of unspoilt countryside.
Activities Concerned at present with actively opposing plans to mine coal by opencast methods on a large scale in the area.
Status Voluntary

North Sea Bird Club (NSBC)
c/o Phillips Petroleum Co. E-A, The Adelphi, John Adam Street, London WC2N 6BW 01–389 2759
Secretary Dr. R.A.F. Cox
Aims To provide a recreational pursuit for people employed on offshore installations and to encourage interest in birds and their environment; to collate and analyse recorded observations of birds seen on or around offshore installations.
Activities Records made by offshore observers are held on computer at Aberdeen University; following systematic printout and review of these records, the Club compiles an annual report. The Club's records are available to anyone who wishes to use them for worthwhile research; membership of the Club is open to all oil companies operating in the North Sea.
Status Voluntary
Publications Annual Report

North Wales Naturalists' Trust (NWNT)
High Street, Bangor, Gwynedd LL57, Wales 0248 351541
Administrative Officer Miss E.K. Moyle
Aims To conserve nature by managing

nature reserves and promoting the conservation of wildlife with all concerned with the use and management of the countryside.
Activities Through its local branches the Trust helps people of all ages to enjoy and learn more about wildlife and the countryside by means of field excursions, film shows, talks, nature trails and projects; branches maintain the nature reserves in their area. The Trust provides help and advice to landowners, farmers, local authorities, schools, colleges, government and voluntary bodies and is frequently consulted before planning decisions are made; it also records information about natural history and protects nesting sites.
Status Voluntary
Publications North Wales Naturalists' Trust Newsletter (3); Annual Report

North West Buildings Preservation Trust (NWBPT)
Environmental Institute, Greaves School, Bolton Road, Swinton, Manchester M27 2UX 061–794 9314
Company Secretary Norman Bilsborough
Aims To restore and preserve buildings or structures which are of historic or architectural interest in the north west region as a whole.
Activities Purchasing derelict or vacant buildings, either listed or in conservation or improvement areas, and preparing reports, designs and surveys, thereby identifying a future use for the buildings; with the help of grant aid, restoring and renovating the buildings with a view to selling for suitable future use.
Status Charity
Publications North West Buildings Preservation Trust Newsletter (2)

North West Civic Trust (NWCT)
Environmental Institute, Greaves School, Bolton Road, Swinton, Manchester M27 2UX 061–794 9314
Deputy Director (Administration) & Secretary Mrs Pauline Roscoe
Aims To encourage high quality in architecture and planning; to preserve buildings of architectural distinction or historic interest; to protect the beauty of the countryside; to eliminate dereliction and prevent ugliness, whether from bad design or neglect; to stimulate public interest and inspire a sense of civic pride.
Activities Regional Environmental Resource Centre; Granada Environmental Library, providing books, periodicals, planning documents, educational material, films, slides and audio-visual aids; exhibition material available. Education through talks, lectures, exhibitions and conferences and

through educational courses and publications; providing an out-of-school resource for environmental education and opportunities for voluntary work by young people; undertaking project work, including conservation studies, land reclamation and landscaping; planning aid and advisory service; recreational development; development of interpretive techniques; Regional Information Service on Vacant Buildings (RISVB) through the publication of a digest of vacant buildings of historic or architectural interest which are for sale, with suggested uses. 186 Civic and Amenity Societies in the north west.
Status Charity
Publications Contact (2); North West Civic Trust Bulletin (6); RISVB Digest (4)

North West Water Authority
Dawson House, Liverpool Road, Great Sankey, Warrington, Cheshire WA5 3LW 092572 4321
Activities Maintaining water supply and treatment, sewerage, sewage treatment and disposal, pollution control, rivers management, fisheries, land drainage and certain recreation amenities throughout the north west, an area extending from Crewe to Carlisle and serving around 7 million people. 4 main divisional offices.
Status Statutory
-NR

North Western Naturalists' Union (NWNU)
59 Moss Lane, Bramhall, Stockport, Cheshire SK7 1EQ 061–439 2899
Hon. General Secretary W.E. Addison
Aims To further the study of natural history in the north west; to participate in surveys of various kinds and to encourage the collection of data; to be aware of sites of particular interest and to provide appropriate evidence when conflicts arise.
Activities Encouraging the activities of constituent natural history societies in the region by publishing details of them; publishing a list of speakers; arranging field meetings open to their members on topics such as bryophytes, lichens, fungi and the natural history of the Bollin Valley; providing a corporate insurance scheme for members; publishing articles on natural history, especially with relevance to the north west.
Status Voluntary
Publications North Western Naturalists' Union Newsletter (4); Journal (1)

North York Moors National Park Authority
The Old Vicarage, Bondgate, Helmsley, N. Yorks. YO6 5BP 0439 70657
National Park Officer D.C. Statham
Aims Under the National Parks & Access to the Countryside Act 1949, to conserve and enhance landscape, promote the enjoyment of National Park areas and to have due regard for the socio-economic wellbeing of local communities.
Status Statutory
-NR

Northamptonshire Trust for Nature Conservation Ltd (NTNC)
Lings House, Billing Lings, Northampton NN3 4BE 0604 405285
Development Officer Tim Goodwin
Aims To further nature conservation in Northamptonshire by promoting public interest and understanding; to provide protection for special sites and advice to public and private landowners and managers.
Activities Professional staff and voluntary helpers work in pursuance of the above aims; members are provided with many talks, outings and identification days relating to the county's wildlife. Regional and local groups.
Status Voluntary
Publications Northamptonshire Trust for Nature Conservation Newsletter (3)

Northern Heritage Trust Ltd (NHT)
3 Old Elvet, Durham DH1 3HL 0385 61182
Executive Director Neville Whittaker
Aims To acquire, restore and return to use historic buildings in the five north-eastern counties.
Activities Concerned with a wide variety of historic buildings, from 17th-century thatched cottages in North Yorkshire to stately homes in Northumberland; currently working on six properties, with many more pending.
Status Charity; limited company
Publications Annual Report

Northern Ireland Amenity Council
123 York Street, Belfast BT15 1AB 0232 249286
Executive Secretary John Clarke
Aims To encourage and promote an active interest in the whole environment through close co-operation between central and local government and statutory and voluntary bodies, always with the particular interest of encouraging individual effort.
Activities Conducting annual Best Kept exercises relating to towns, villages and housing estates within Northern Ireland and streets and buildings within Belfast City; publishing reports and holding seminars and conferences relating to environmental matters; awarding street plaques and certificates of merit to individual householders.
Status Voluntary (seeking to become a charitable limited company)
Publications Annual Report

Northern Ireland CND (NI-CND)
10 Stranmillis Park, Belfast BT9 5AU
0232 665368/665161
Co-ordinator Robin Wilson
Activities Organising public protest against nuclear arms; promoting non-violent direct action; supporting the peace camp at RAF Bishopscourt. Local branches.
Status Voluntary
-NR

Northern Ireland Cycling Federation
144 Princes Way, Portadown, Co. Armagh BT63 5EN, N. Ireland
-NR

Northern Ireland Electricity Service (NIES)
Danesfort, 120 Malone Road, Belfast BT9 5HT
0232 661100
Activities Responsible for the generation, transmission and distribution of electricity in Northern Ireland, together with marketing of electrical energy and electrical appliances. Operates 4 power stations and has 6 area offices.
Status Statutory
Publications
A Strategy for the Future: electricity supply in Northern Ireland. 1983.

Northern Ireland Voluntary Trust (NIVT)
Howard House, 1 Brunswick Street, Belfast BT2 7GE 0232 245927
Director Hugh Frazer
Aims To encourage and support the efforts of voluntary and community groups to tackle the worst effects of Northern Ireland's serious social, economic and community problems and to promote community involvement and self-help.
Activities Providing seeding grants to help new projects get started; advice and guidance to people starting new projects; a Priority Estates Programme of advice to tenants on improving the environment on run-down public housing estates; a Rural Initiatives Project to support, advise and stimulate community projects in rural areas; producing reports, information kits and videos for people involved in voluntary initiatives.
Status Voluntary; charity
Publications NIVT News (3); Annual Report

Northern Region Co-operatives Development Association Limited (NRCDA)
Bolbec Hall, Westgate Road, Newcastle upon Tyne NE1 1SE 0632 610140
Senior Development Officer Norman Watson
Aims To promote workers' and community co-operatives.

Activities Providing help with grants, premises, market research, preparing a business plan and cash flow, legal advice and registration; running education and training schemes for people intending to start co-operatives. 4 branches.
Status Voluntary
Publications Co-ops North East (4); Annual Report
Co-operatives and the Local Economy.

Northumberland and Newcastle Society
6 Higham Place, Newcastle upon Tyne NE1 8AF 0632 614384
Secretary Mrs Jill Boyd
Aims To preserve and increase the beauty and amenities of the county and city which now includes that part of Tyne & Wear north of the River Tyne.
Activities Monitoring development in the area; checking planning applications; making representations at public inquiries; offering expert advice to city and district councils. Representatives of local amenity societies and civic societies are included on our committees and we are represented on other bodies; the Society is recognised as the county committee of the Council for the Protection of Rural England (CPRE). Activities for members include educational visits, lectures and symposia.
Status Charity
Publications Northumberland & Newcastle Society Newsletter (3)
-NR

Northumberland National Park & Countryside Committee
Eastburn, South Park, Hexham, Northumberland NE46 1BS 0434 605555
National Park Officer A.A. Macdonald
Aims Under the National Parks & Access to the Countryside Act 1949, to conserve and enhance landscape, promote the enjoyment of National Park areas and to have due regard for the socio-economic wellbeing of local communities. The Committee consists of 27 members, including 9 appointed by the Secretary of State for the Environment, 15 members of Northumberland County Council and 3 district councillors.
Status Statutory
Publications Northumberland National Park Plan (quinquennial)
-NR

Northumberland Wildlife Trust
Hancock Museum, Barras Bridge, Newcastle upon Tyne NE2 4PT 0632 320038
Hon. Secretary T. Tynan
Aims To encourage habitat and species conservation within the old county of Northumberland; to acquire and manage

nature reserves; to promote an awareness in the community of wildlife and the need for its conservation.

Activities Managing 37 nature reserves covering 1,700 hectares; advising statutory and voluntary bodies, landowners and local authorities to further nature conservation in Northumberland; educating children through local Watch groups whose membership totals 300; educating adults (membership 4,500) through local groups, public meetings and publications. 13 branches.

Status Voluntary

Publications Roebuck (3)

Northumbria Seekers

Holpeth House, Corbridge, Northumberland NE45 5BA 043471 2258

Secretary Pamela West

Aims To consider the spiritual nature of Man and the holistic world view.

Activities Organising a programme of lectures and workshops by well-known and reliable speakers, both local and from farther afield, in order to make available to people in the north as much as possible of what is best in New Age thinking.

Status Educational association

Publications Annual Programme

Northumbrian Energy Workshop Ltd (NEW)

Tanners Yard, Gilesgate, Hexham, Northumberland NE46 3NJ 0434 604809

Sales & Marketing Co-ordinator Norman Rogers

Aims To promote the use of renewable sources of energy, particularly wind energy conversion systems; to demonstrate their technical and economic viability for industrial and domestic uses, thereby increasing the availability of high quality equipment.

Activities Design, supply, installation and maintenance of wind, solar and hydro energy conversion systems in the 50 W–300 kW range; systems available for independent power supplies or connection to the mains grid network; supply of associated equipment and services, such as monitoring equipment, batteries, inverters, control equipment, low-voltage appliances, books, site surveys. Specialist design and manufacture of wind energy systems and ancillary equipment for use in the UK and abroad; supply and installation of small hydro systems and of datalogging equipment.

Status Co-operative

Northumbrian Water

Northumbria House, Regent Centre, Gosforth, Newcastle upon Tyne NE3 3PX 091–284 3151

Activities Responsible to the Secretary of State for the Environment for water supply, water conservation, sewerage and sewage

disposal, prevention of river pollution, fisheries, land drainage and the recreational use of water in the north-east of England.

Status Statutory

Northumbrians for Peace (NfP)

Shitlington Cottage, Shitlington Crags, Wark, Northumberland NE48 3QB 0660 30330

Secretary Keith Turnbull

Aims To provide a forum for discussion and to campaign around the issues of: a world free of nuclear weapons and all other weapons of mass destruction; Britain's unilateral abandonment of its nuclear weapons as an initial step toward world disarmament; the establishment of a nuclear-free zone in Europe, to include both Warsaw Pact and NATO countries.

Activities Organising public meetings on relevant specific topics; working party meetings to formulate plans of action; demonstrations, stalls, leafletting and dissemination of information through the media. Local branches.

Status Voluntary

Publications Northumbrians for Peace Bulletin (10)

Nottinghamshire Environment Advisory Council (NEAC)

Link House, 110 Mansfield Road, Nottingham NG1 3HL 0602 503681

Secretary Dr R. Middleton

Aims To work for an improvement of all aspects of Nottinghamshire's physical environment.

Activities Organising local improvement schemes, e.g. in derelict industrial areas; promoting bottle/can banks and improvement of waste disposal facilities; tree planting schemes; seeking to increase the general awareness of the public on problems of environmental pollution.

Status Voluntary

Publications Annual Report

Nottinghamshire Trust for Nature Conservation Ltd (NTNC)

2–12 Warser Gate, Nottingham NG1 1PA 0602 501034

Contact J.M. McMeeking

Aims To conserve wildlife and plants, to establish nature reserves and to advance research in the natural sciences.

Activities Establishing and managing nature reserves in Nottinghamshire; promoting education through interpretation on reserves; co-operating closely with local and other authorities to promote the cause of nature conservation in the county. Local branches.

Status Voluntary

Publications Newsletter (3); Annual Report

Nuclear Energy Board/An Bord Fuinnimh Nuicleigh (NEB) (Republic of Ireland)
20–22 Lower Hatch Sreet, Dublin 2, Ireland
001–76 4375/6223
Contact F.J. Turvey
Aims To protect the public from the potentially harmful effects arising from the peaceful uses of ionising radiation.
Activities Advising government on nuclear energy and associated matters; regulating all activities relating to radioactive substances and irradiating apparatus; drafting safety regulations and codes of practice; monitoring radiation in the environment; providing a personnel dosimetry service; promoting knowledge of and research in nuclear science.
Status Statutory
Publications Nuclear Energy Board News (occasional)

Nuclear Engineering Society
c/o UKAEA, Risley, Warrington, Cheshire
WA3 6AT 0925 31244
Aims To increase members' knowledge and understanding of the science and engineering of all aspects of nuclear power in the UK and abroad.
Activities Meetings at which lectures on various engineering and scientific subjects are given by leading speakers drawn from Risley-based organisations and elsewhere, nationally and internationally; summer visits to works and sites of engineering interest; competitions in the oral presentation of papers, for senior and junior members; annual dinner with a distinguished speaker where present and past members can meet.

Status Voluntary
-NR

Nuclear Industry Radioactive Waste Executive
see NIREX

Nuclear Information Network (NIN)
This network no longer exists

Nuclear Weapons Freeze Advertising Campaign
Fairfield House, Biggleswade, Beds. SG18 0AA
Aims To promote the concept of a freeze on existing levels of nuclear weapons by both superpowers as a first step toward reducing their nuclear arsenals.
-NR

Nucleus
188 Old Street, London EC1V 9BP 01–250 1219
Activities Exploring the potential use of computers in information services provided by alternative technology and New Age groups.
-NR

Nutrition Society
Chandos House, 2 Queen Anne Sreet, London W1M 9LE 1–580 5753
-NR

Nutritional Reform Society
16 West Parade, Norwich, Norfolk NR2 3DW
0603 22820
-NR

O

Offa's Dyke Association (ODA)
West Street, Knighton, Powys LD7 1EW, Wales
0547 528753
Correspondence Secretary Mrs Glenys
Beech
Aims To link walkers, historians, conservationists and those who live and work locally
in promoting the conservation, improvement
and better knowledge of the Welsh Border
in general and the Offa's Dyke Path and 8th-
century Earthwork in particular.
Activities Acting as a pressure group on
relevant official bodies; providing information
to members, walkers and other visitors by
means of maps, guides and other publications, by operating an information office
which deals with 8,000 visitors and 3,000
correspondents per year, and by being
associated with a Heritage Centre at
Knighton; carrying out practical work on path
inspection and maintenance.
Status Voluntary; charity
Publications Offa's Dyke Association
Newsletter (3)
Kay, K. & E. (eds), *Walks Along Offa's Dyke.*
Noble, Frank (ed. Dr. M. Gelling), *Offa's
Dyke Reviewed.*

Office of Population Censuses and Surveys (OPCS)
St Catherine's House, 10 Kingsway, London
WC2B 6JP 01–242 0262
Activities Responsible for the regulation of
civil marriages, the registration of births,
marriages and deaths in England and Wales
and control of the registration services; the
analysis of vital health and demographic statistics and publication of reports thereon; the
periodic census of the population; and
research into the attitudes and circumstances of the general public or of particular
groups of individuals.
Status Statutory (government department)
Publications Population Trends (4)
General Household Survey. (Series GHS, no.
12) 1984. [Covers population, housing,
employment, education and health]
Population Projections 1981–2021. (Series
PP2, no.12) 1984.
Martin, Jean & Roberts, Ceridwen, *Women
and Employment: a lifetime perspective,*
1984.

Offshore Energy Technology Board
Dept of Energy, Thames House South, Millbank,
London SW1P 4QJ 01–211 3000
Aims To advise and assist the Secretary of
State for Energy on how best to evaluate,
promote and secure technological developments leading to improvements in: the
efficient and economic exploitation of the oil
and gas resources on the UK Continental
Shelf; the standards laid down by the Department in pursuance of its statutory responsibilities for safety; and the competitiveness of
British industry in the field of offshore oil
and gas. The Board, which is constituted for
the whole of the UK, consists of a chairman
and 13 other members appointed by the
Secretary of State.
Status Statutory
-NR

Oil Companies International Marine Forum (OCIMF)
6th Floor, Portland House, Stag Place, London
SW1E 5BH 01–828 7696
Director I. B. Blackwood
Aims To promote safety and prevent
pollution from tankers and at terminals.
Activities Co-ordinating and presenting oil
industry views to the International Maritime
Organization (IMO) and to governmental and
inter-governmental bodies; reviewing technical documents and referring matters of
concern to OCIMF committees and member
companies; advising member companies on
national legislation and regulations affecting
the oil industry regarding safety and pollution
of the sea; sponsoring industry research
projects; co-operating with other international industry organisations having an
interest in marine pollution and safety. Any
oil company in the world may apply to
become a member of OCIMF.
Status Voluntary association
Publications Annual Report
*International Safety Guide for Oil Tankers
and Terminals.* 2nd edn, 1984.

Oldham & Rochdale Groundwork Trust
Bank House, 8 Chapel Street, Shaw, Oldham,
Lancs. OL2 8AJ 0706 842212
Director Robin Henshaw
Aims To co-ordinate a community-based
campaign to enhance the environment of
the boroughs of Oldham and Rochdale, with
particular reference to the countryside of
the urban fringe.
Activities Working with community
groups, volunteers, the unemployed, local
authorities, private landowners and local

businesses to enhance derelict and under-used land; schemes are concerned with scenic amenity, nature conservation, improved farming, enhanced recreational opportunities and community involvement. The Trust also runs environmental education courses and a ranger service.
Status Voluntary; charity

Omnibus Society
6 Ardentinny, Grosvenor Road, St Albans, Herts. AL1 3BZ 0727 57078
Activities The study of passenger road transport and discussion of problems of traffic, engineering and methods of operating buses, coaches, trolley-buses and tramcars.
Publications The Omnibus Magazine

Open Centre
188 Old Street, London EC1V 9BP
01–278 6783 ext.3
Contact Answering Service Secretary
Aims To provide under one roof a unique variety of personal growth, educational and therapeutic groups and introductory events with a humanistic orientation (all approaches used are active, client-centred and emphasise responsible self-develop-ment); to foster a more creative use of free time and contribute to a less stressful and more fulfilling human environment.
Activities Group and individual sessions offered in the following modalities: Gestalt, Bioenergetics, Transactional Analysis, Encounter and Self-Discovery, Postural Inte-gration, Primal Integration, Pulsing, Felden-krais Method, Energetic Rolearena and Gentle Dance.
Status Voluntary collective
Publications The Open Centre brochure (3).

Open Spaces Society (OSS) _Nicola Hodgson, Kate Ashbrook 01491 573535_
[formally the Commons, Open Spaces & Foot-paths Preservation Society]
25A Bell Street, Henley-on-Thames, Oxon.
RG9 2BA 0491 573535 _HQ@oss.org.uk,_
General Secretary Kate Ashbrook
Aims To protect common land, town and village greens, open spaces and public paths and defend the rights of the public there; to advise authorities, commons committees, voluntary bodies and the public on their statutory rights and how to exercise and safeguard them.
Activities Campaigning for stronger laws to protect common land, open spaces and rights of way and to secure legal access to all open country; the Society is consulted on applications to develop common land and it services and is represented on the Common Land Forum which seeks to weld alternative views into a basis for commons legislation;

the Society manages and preserves open spaces given to or bought by it and publishes handbooks and guidance notes on the law of commons and paths.
Status Voluntary
Publications Open Space (3)
Clayden, P., _Our Common Land: the law and history of commons and village greens_, 1985.
Clayden, P. & Trevelyan, J., _Rights of Way: a guide to law and practice_, Open Spaces Society/Ramblers Association, 1983.

Open University Energy Research Group (OUERG)
Open University, Walton Hall, Milton Keynes, Bucks. MK7 6AA 0908 653335
Departmental Secretary Mrs Jenny Brown
Aims To study energy demand reduction and supply provision, based on conversion principles; to undertake modelling of energy systems to guide policy decisions.
Activities Studies include: alternative sources of energy supply (solar, wind, biomass, etc.); resource system and ecosys-tem modelling; novel conversion routes; energy policy issues; building and transport demand.
Status Academic
Publications Annual Report

Opencast Mining Intelligence Group (OMIG)
Croft House, Calverley Road, Oulton, Leeds, W. Yorks. LS26 8JQ 0532 822252
Secretary Malcolm Brocklesby
Aims To promote the adoption and implementation of a responsible policy for opencast coalmining based on a factual assessment of the UK's need for opencast coal and the environmental impact on the rural landscape, agricultural land and adjacent communities.
Activities Collecting information relating to the UK energy market, with particular refer-ence to the supply, demand and reserves of coal, the potential for conservation and the visual and agricultural limitations in the rehabilitation of opencast sites; assessing the realistic demand for coal, as opposed to the inflated forecasts from government and supply industries seeking greater capital allocations; presenting such information to those responsible for making decisions on opencast mining at local and national level.
Status Voluntary
-NR

Operation Groundwork
see GROUNDWORK TRUST

Organic Farmers and Growers Co-operative
9 Station Yard, Needham Market, Ipswich, Suffolk IP6 8AT
-NR

Organic Growers Association (OGA)
Aeron Park, Llangeitho, Tregaron,
Dyfed SY25 6TT, Wales 097423 272
Secretary Charles Wacher
Aims To represent the interests of organic
fruit and vegetable growers; to provide a
forum for discussion and mutual support; to
educate the public about the benefits of
organic agriculture.
Activities Conferences, workshops, farm
walks; special packaging for organic
growers.
Status Voluntary; charity
Publications New Farmer & Grower (4)

Organic Living Association (OLA)
St Mary's Villa, Hanley Swan, Worcs. WR8 0EA
Director & Secretary Dennis C. Nightin-
gale-Smith
Aims To integrate the production and
consumption of organically grown vegetables,
fruit, cereals and dairy produce; to promote
health in humans, farm animals and food
crops; to promote the establishment of
ecological, self-sufficient villages; to
educate the public and pressurise the authorities to these ends.
Activities Organising festivals, assemblies,
lectures, conferences, meetings, visits and
demonstrations; providing advice on organic
growing, nutrition and appropriate medical
treatment.
Status Voluntary
Publications Organic Living Association
Newsletter (6)

Orkney Heritage Society (OHS)
20 Main Street, Kirkwall, Orkney KW15 1BU
0856 3619
Hon. Secretary Mrs Marjorie Linklater
Aims To stimulate public interest in, and
care for, the beauty, history and character
of Orkney; to safeguard and record the rich
archaeological monuments (by employing a
full-time Resident Field Archaeologist); to
examine planning matters in conservation
areas.
Activities Organising talks to the public on
conservation matters; making representations
to the Orkney Islands Council on matters
concerned with preservation of ancient
monuments and development of tourist
attractions which are enhanced by these
and historic buildings; seeking ways to
protect sunken ships from World War 1 in
Scapa Flow from being looted; three
members' outings each year to places of
interest on various islands. The archaeologist
works closely with the Council and the
Tourist Board.
Status Voluntary
Publications OHS Newsletter (1); Orkney
Heritage (biennial)

Osteopathic and Naturopathic Guild Ltd
Villa Merlynn, 18 Elgin Road, Talbot Woods,
Bournemouth, Dorset BH4 9NL 0202 769297
Secretary James Hewlett-Parsons
Activities Providing student training in
naturopathy and osteopathy through the
Naturopathic and Osteopathic Training
Centre to the qualifying standard of full
membership of the Guild as an Incorporated
Osteopath and/or Consultant Naturopath.
Status Professional association; company
limited by guarantee
Publications Newsletter; Prospectus

Osteopathic Association of Great Britain
26 Monmouth Street, Bath, Avon BA1 2AP
Hon. Secretary Ian L. Cameron
Aims To support and advance research
into the principles, theory and practice of
osteopathy.
Status Professional association
Publications British Osteopathic Journal
-NR

Otter Haven Project
5 Mornish Road, Branksome Park, Poole, Dorset
BH13 7BY
-NR

Otter Trust
Earsham, Bungay, Suffolk NR35 2AF 0986 3470
Hon. Administrator Mrs Jeanne Wayre
Aims To promote the conservation of
otters throughout the world, with especial
emphasis on the European (British) Otter
Lutra l. lutra.
Activities Breeding otters, especially
Lutra l. lutra, in captivity so that young animals
bred at Earsham can be reintroduced to the
wild to build up depleted wild populations;
providing factual information to the public on
all aspects of the natural history of otters
and their conservation. Local branches.
Status Charity
Publications Otter Trust Newsletter (2);
Annual Report
-NR

Overseas Development Administration
(ODA)
Eland House, Stag Place, London SW1E 5DH
01–213 3000
Scotland: Abercrombie House, Eaglesham
Road, East Kilbride, Glasgow G75 8EA 03552
41199
Activities Deals with British development
assistance to overseas countries, including
capital aid on concessional terms and technical co-operation (mainly in the form of
specialist staff abroad and training facilities
in Britain), provided directly to developing
countries or through multilateral aid organis-

ations, including the UN and its specialised agencies.

Status Statutory (government department)

Oxford Forestry Institute (OFI)
[formerly Commonwealth Forestry Institute]

Dept of Plant Sciences, University of Oxford, South Parks Road, Oxford OX1 3RB
0865 511431

Director Dr J. Burley

Aims To provide education, training, research, information and advice on the biology, technology and socio-economics of tropical and temperate forestry, land use and environments.

Activities Research and education in the following: forest and land use policy and economics; tropical natural forest inventory; ecology and management; exploration, evaluation, conservation and genetic improvement of trees for industrial plantations and for rural development; plantation silviculture management and appropriate technology of wood use; anatomical, chemical and energy properties of wood; pathology and entomology of forests and trees; social and community forestry and agroforestry systems.

Status Research institute

Publications Tropical Forestry Papers (occasional)

Oxford University Future Studies Group (OUFSG)

Walden, 2 Shirelake Close, Oxford OX1 1SN
0865 250274

Contact Piers Cherryl

Aims To encourage 'Future Studies' in and beyond the University. [Future Studies: the study of emerging ideas; defining them more clearly, exploring their consequences and communicating them to to others, with especial emphasis on the development of structures for a long-term sustainable society.]

Activities Arranging talks, workshops, discussions and visits for students in the University on relevant topics (e.g. new economics, thinking skills, Gaia, United Nations); networking with various national organisations with similar interests; providing feedback on the work of independent researchers and research institutes concerned with Future Studies; maintaining a library of FS materials; compiling a Future Studies A-Z in order to keep track, clarify and explain to others about the ideas the group has discovered.

Status Student society

Publications Oxford University Future Studies Group Bulletin (4)
Future Studies A-Z.

P

Pagan Parenting Network
Blaenberem, Mynyddcerrig, Llanelli,
Dyfed SA15 5BL, Wales
Co-ordinator Nicola Miles
Aims To provide a forum for discussion and exchange of ideas and experiences for parents seeking to bring up their children to live in harmony with nature and to become caring and responsible future guardians of Earth and her creatures, aware of the spiritual interconnectedness of all life.
Activities Planning small gatherings; publishing the newsletter.
Status Informal network
Publications Pagan Parenting Network Newsletter (4)

Pagans Against Nukes (PAN)
Blaenberem, Mynyddcerrig, Llanelli,
Dyfed SA15 5BL, Wales
Contact P.V. Cozens, Nicola Miles
Aims To promote the banishment of nuclear technology from our Mother Earth and the re-establishment of a culture that lives in harmony with Her, that the Earth be greened anew.
Activities Co-ordinating activities by pagans (i.e. those whose primary spiritual orientation is to the Earth Mother, reverencing Her and all life upon Her) in a variety of traditions toward the above aims; participating in the wider Green movement and further developing its spiritual dimension; working on spiritual and magical levels toward the above aims; publishing the magazine. Local branches.
Status Voluntary (open membership)
Publications *The Pipes of PAN* (4)
Remembering: myths of creation.

PAN International (Pesticides Action Network)
c/o Oxfam Public Affairs Unit, 274 Banbury Road, Oxford OX2 7DZ 0865 56777
Contact Dave Bull, Dorothy Myers
-NR

PANDORA (Powys Against Nuclear Dumping on Rural Areas)
This organisation no longer exists

Parents Against Lead
17 Holland Park Gardens, London W14 8DZ
01–603 5778
-NR

PARLIGAES (Parliamentary Liaison Group for Alternative Energy Strategies)
19 Albemarle Street, London W1X 3HA
01–493 0604
Aims To be a forum and information service for parliamentarians, presenting them with information on current and future energy strategies, with particular emphasis on the social and environmental implications of different options.
Activities Arranging a series of lectures at Westminster with distinguished speakers from a wide range of energy disciplines; conducting personal briefings and correspondence with MPs and Lords interested in alternative energy and alternative strategies; producing a bulletin for parliamentarians.
Status Informal all-party group
Publications PARLIGAES Bulletin (not for general distribution)

PARTIZANS (People Against Rio Tinto-Zinc And Subsidiaries)
218 Liverpool Road, London N1 1LE
01–609 1852
Co-ordinator Roger Moody
Aims To research the activities of British mining companies, particularly Rio Tinto-Zinc, and through publications, shareholder actions, publicity and specific campaigns to focus on their negative impacts (e.g. Third World uranium mining).
Activities Acting as a shareholders' pressure group within RTZ; publishing research documents; co-ordinating overseas actions; direct actions at company offices; students' activities, particularly against recruitment; anti-nuclear actions.
Status Voluntary
Publications Parting Company (6)
RTZ Uncovered. 1985.

Pax Christi (Peace Education Centre)
St Francis of Assisi Centre, Pottery Lane,
London W11 4NQ 01–727 4609
Aims To work for peace through justice and non-violence, especially in raising the consciousness of the Catholic community on issues of international peace.
Activities Campaigning against the arms trade and nuclear weapons; project for prisoners of conscience; peace education through films and talks in schools, churches, etc.; summer projects for young people; summer hostels for visitors to England;

publishing fact sheets and other material for groups, teachers, etc.
Publications Justpeace (10)
-NR – L

Peace Advertising Campaign (PAC)
PO Box 24, Oxford OX1 3JZ 0865 723011
Administrator Mark Levene
Aims To use all available forms of media to keep peace and disarmament issues in the public consciousness; to work closely with peace groups, nuclear-free zones and other peace-oriented associations for this purpose.
Activities Design, production and marketing of 5– and 10–foot high bill-boards advertising peace; production of a range of linked materials, including stickers, badges, small posters and postcards; contract work for nuclear-free zones, peace groups and similar organisations; acting as a billboard booking agency for groups and organisations involved in peace, environmental and Third World issues.
Status Non-profit company
Publications PAC Catalogue

Peace Education Network (PEN)
33 Churchill Avenue, Kenton, London HA3 0AX
01–907 9803
Secretary Mary Hale
Aims To provide for communication amongst teachers and others wishing to make education a force for peace; to provide practical support for such individuals and local groups; to promote peace education among the public at large; to promote links with those similarly involved in other countries; to promote research and development in the field of peace education.
Activities Acting as a communication channel between those with specific needs and those able to help; encouraging peace education workers and attracting newcomers by publicising action in peace education; publicising resource centres and available teaching materials through regional workshops and journal articles; supporting PEN's local groups.
Status Voluntary
Publications PEN Newsletter (4)

Peace Makers' Relief Society
6 Endsleigh Street, London WC1H 0DX
Aims To collect funds to assist people who encounter financial difficulties because of their witness for peace.
-NR

Peace Network
197 Piccadilly, London W1V 9LF 01–734 5244
-NR

Peace News (PN)
8 Elm Avenue, Nottingham NG3 4GF
0602 503587
Aims To promote non-violent revolution; to construct non-violent alternatives in all areas of our lives.
Status Collective
Publications Peace News (26)
-NR

Peace Pledge Union (PPU)
Dick Sheppard House, 6 Endsleigh Street, London WC1H 0DX 01–387 5501
Contact Jan Melichar
Aims To give voice and strength to the politics of non-violence and war resistance; to search for and practise non-violent approaches to the problems facing all individuals and citizens who want a world without war. The PPU is non-sectarian and is not associated with any political party.
Activities Members sign the pledge: 'I renounce war and will never support or sanction another.' The PPU puts particular emphasis on exhibitions illustrating pacifist thought, education in schools and colleges and communication with the public. Issues of active concern include conscientious objection to military service; militarism and military recruiting; Northern Ireland; nuclear power; official secrets; racialism; and the arms trade.
Status Voluntary
Publications The Pacifist (12); Studies in Nonviolence (triennial)
-NR – L

Peace Tax Campaign
13 Goodwin Street, London N4 3HQ 01–263 2246
National Co-ordinator Dave Ford
Aims To secure legislation enabling those who have conscientious convictions against paying for war preparations to have an appropriate proportion of their income tax payments diverted from defence to peacebuilding
Activities Educating public opinion; lobbying MPs, Churches, trade unions, political parties, etc.; studying the requirements of true peace in the world and how it can be achieved and maintained. Local branches.
Status Voluntary
Publications Peace Tax Campaign Newsletter (5)

Peak and Northern Footpaths Society
15 Parkfield Drive, Tyldesley, Manchester M29 8NR 061–790 4383
Hon. General Secretary Derek Taylor
Aims To preserve, maintain and defend the rights of the public to the use and enjoyment of the public highways, footpaths,

bridleways and byways and to the right of recreation over commons in the Northern and Midland counties, particularly in the Peak District.
Activities Inspecting public rights of way; erecting and maintaining direction posts and footbridges. The Society has 40 voluntary inspectors.
Status Voluntary
Publications Annual Report

Peak National Park Centre
Losehill Hall, Castleton, Derbys. S30 2WB
0433 20373
Principal Peter Townsend
Aims To create a deeper understanding and love for the countryside in order to conserve it; to enable the public to increase their knowledge and enjoyment of the countryside; to highlight the problems and issues in the countryside today.
Activities General public courses in natural history, archaeology, landscape photography, crafts and customs, walking, cycling and landscape painting; field courses for schools and further education students; courses for teachers in environmental science and geography for the young school leaver; in-service training for countryside staff, including ranger training, countryside interpretation, working with volunteers, nature conservation and landscape conservation; national and international conferences on environmental issues; publication of conference reports.
Status Educational (run by Peak National Park)
Publications Annual Programme
Land Management for Conservation in European Heritage Landscapes. 1984.
Towards Conservation. 1983

Peak Park Joint Planning Board
National Park Office, Aldern House, Baslow Road, Bakewell, Derbys. DE4 1AE 062981 4321
Contact National Park Officer or Head of Information Services
Aims To conserve landscape, control development and provide facilities for visitors to the 542 sq.m. National Park; to combine support for the local economy with conservation and provision for recreation.
Activities In addition to its role as planning authority, the Board provides architectural and forestry advice. Its facilities for visitors include: 8 information centres and points; the Peak National Park Centre [*see separate entry*]; 7 hostels, caravan and camp sites; camping barns; cycle hire centres; guided discovery trails; evening slide shows; publications; ranger service (76 sq.m. of access land); public transport information and

special tickets; Tissington, High Peak and Monsal trails; youth and schools service.
Status Statutory
Publications Peakland Post (1) (free)
A Tale of Two Villages. [Integrated rural development]
Moorland Erosion Study, Phase 1 & 2 Reports.

Peat Development Authority (Republic of Ireland)
76 Lower Baggot Street, Dublin 2, Ireland
0001–68 8555
-NR

Pedestrians Association
[formerly Pedestrians Association for Road Safety (PARS)]
1 Wandsworth Road, London SW8 2LJ
01–735 3270
General Secretary Mrs Felicity Rea
Aims To protect and preserve the rights and mobility of those on foot; to campaign for more and better pedestrian crossings, creation of pedestrian precincts and safe streets, removal of obstructions and parked cars from the footway and strict observance and enforcement of speed limits and other road traffic laws.
Activities Lobbying central government and local authorities; publicising the cause of 'the walking majority'; educating and disseminating information; giving advice to public and members; occasional lectures and talks. 10 branches.
Status Voluntary; charity
Publications Walk (3)

Pembrokeshire Coast National Park Committee
County Offices, Haverfordwest, Dyfed SA61 1QZ, Wales 0437 4591
National Park Officer N.J. Wheeler
Aims Under the National Parks & Access to the Countryside Act 1949, to conserve and enhance landscape, promote the enjoyment of National Park areas and to have due regard for the socio-economic wellbeing of local communities. Constituted as a separate committee of Dyfed County Council, the Committee consists of 18 members, including 6 appointed by the Secretary of State for Wales.
Status Statutory
-NR

Pennine Way Council
236 Lidgett Lane, Leeds, W. Yorks. LS17 6QH
0532 691751
Treasurer Reginald Smith
Aims To secure the protection of the Pennine Way, to provide information about the Way to the public and to educate users

of the Way and its environs in a proper respect for the countryside.

Activities Meetings three times a year in Leeds at which a wide variety of matters concerning the Pennine Way is raised, discussed and pursued through the various channels available; council officers continuously deal with correspondence requesting information regarding the walking of the Way.

Status Charity

Publications Pennine Way Council Newsletter (2); Accommodation & Camping Guide (biennial)

Pensioners for Peace

7 Sandfield, Bromsberrow Heath, Ledbury, Herefordshire HR8 1NX 053181 485
-NR

People For A Non-Nuclear World

3 The Close B, Heath Lane, Blackheath, London SE3 0UR
-NR

People's Dispensary For Sick Animals (PDSA)

PDSA House, South Street, Dorking, Surrey RH4 2LB 0306 888291

Press & Public Relations Officer Marilyn Marchant

Aims To provide free professional veterinary treatment for sick and injured animals whose owners cannot afford private fees; to promote responsible pet ownership.

Activities Maintaining 57 Animal Treatment Centres and an additional 36 Auxiliary Service Areas; in 1984 the PDSA provided more than 1¼ million treatments.

Status Charity

Publications Busy Bees News (6) (for 5–11 year olds)

People's Trust For Endangered Species (PTES)

Hamble House, Meadrow, Godalming, Surrey GU7 3JX 04868 24848

Director W.J. Jordan

Aims To conserve the environment through the protection of animals, plants and wild places.

Activities Fund raising by means of direct appeal letters: the funds are used to make the public more aware of the need for conservation and to support anti-poaching campaigns, scientific research and other projects relating to the survival of many endangered species.

Status Charity

Publications People's Trust for Endangered Species News (2/4)

Performing and Captive Animals Defence League (PADL)

2 Southcombe Street, London W14 0RA
01–603 0712
-NR

Permaculture Association (Britain)

PO Box 500, 8 Elm Avenue, Nottingham NG3 4GF

Co-ordinator Helen Woodley

Aims To encourage the design and creation of productive landscapes for food, shelter, raw materials and wildlife protection, such that, once established, the landscape sustains itself like a natural ecology and needs a minimum of human intervention.

Activities Running courses and working weekends; information exchange; planning a garden display for the Stoke-on-Trent National Garden Festival 1986; displays at fairs and festivals; advising on garden/farm design; publishing a newsletter and other literature on sustainable land use.

Status Charity

Publications Permaculture News (2/3)

Pesticides Action Network

see PAN INTERNATIONAL

Pet Registry

PO Box 206, Harrow, London HA1 3UY
01–936 9115

Director H.M. Cohen

Aims To protect household pets from straying, getting lost or being stolen for the purposes of vivisection, the fur trade, breeding, export or fighting.

Activities Each animal is given a unique registration number by means of a simple, painless tattoo (usually on the inside of the leg or on the ear); the number is stored on the Registry's central computer with the owner's name and address, thus enabling an animal to be instantly identified. 120 branches.

Pheasant Trust

Great Witchingham, Norwich, Norfolk NR9 5QS
060544 274

Hon. Director Philip Wayre

Aims To conserve rare pheasants and other forms of wildlife.
-NR

Phenolic Foam Manufacturers' Association

24 Ormond Street, Richmond, Surrey TW10 6TH 01–948 4153

Status Trade association
-NR

Philosophers For Peace

108 Ledbury Road, London W11 2AH
01–229 0174

Contact   Thomas Clough Daffern
Aims   To help facilitate the effective sharing of ideas, perspectives and research among those interested in exploring the philosophical issues involved in peace in the widest sense; to promote the growth of wisdom and insight and explore deeper metaphysical implications of the nuclear threat.
Activities   UK branch of International Philosophers for the Prevention of Nuclear Omnicide, participating in their activities, attending conferences, contributing papers, convening gatherings, etc.; currently in the process of launching the Co-operative Peace Research Network which is designed to promote more co-operation and mutual sharing of insights between different disciplines and groups; regular meetings and participatory workshops.
Status   Informal network

Planning Aid For Londoners (PAFL)
26 Portland Place, London W1N 4BE
01–580 7277
Contact   Co-ordinator
Aims   To offer free, quick, independent, professional advice on town planning problems, particularly for those unable to engage a planning consultant; to provide an additional and complementary service to the information and advice already given by local authorities.
Activities   PAFL is the town planning professional response in London to the principles embodied in the legal aid system. Help can be offered with planning-related issues about which a planning department would be unlikely to offer assistance, for instance marshalling arguments to oppose or support a planning application (particularly when submitted by the local authority itself); supporting groups or individuals through the public inquiry process; or preparing alternative schemes to those proposed in a local plan. By offering help in these ways, planning aid helps people gain confidence to pursue their own issues themselves.
Status   Voluntary (under the auspices of the Royal Town Planning Institute)
Publications   Annual Report

Plant Breeding Institute
Maris Lane, Trumpington, Cambridge CB2 2LQ
0223 840411
Aims   To produce new and improved varieties of agricultural crop plants; to undertake research in those scientific disciplines that provide the information necessary for the conduct of breeding programmes; and to advance plant breeding technology.
Activities   Conducting breeding programmes with wheat, barley, oats, potatoes, sugar-beet, oil-seed rape, field beans and certain herbage legumes; there is also work with novel crops such as *Triticale* and macaroni wheat; attention is paid not only to production characteristics and agronomic performance, but also to quality and processing needs.
Status   State-aided institute of the Agricultural and Food Research Council
Publications   Annual Report
-NR – L

Plymouth Urban Wildlife Group
c/o Natural History Section, City Museum, Drake Circus, Plymouth, Devon PL4 8AJ
0752 668000 ext. 4376
Chairman   David Curry
Aims   To protect Plymouth's wildlife and semi-natural habitats and to increase the understanding and enjoyment of it by all who live and work within the city.
Activities   Identifying sites of wildlife value and the rare species within the city in order to protect them and provide management advice where necessary; advising the local authority on the practical problems of urban wildlife conservation and the creation of new habitats; raising the level of awareness of Plymouth's wildlife among adults and children and encouraging local groups in their efforts to study and conserve it; acting as an umbrella group for all organisations involved in conserving Plymouth's wildlife and representing their views to the local authority. 9 organisatons are represented on the Group
Status   Voluntary

Political Ecology Research Group Ltd (PERG)
34 Cowley Road, Oxford OX4 1HZ 0865 725354
Director   Peter Taylor
Aims   To further the understanding of the relationships between ecological problems and industrial, economic and political structures.
Activities   Undertaking commissioned research on environmental problems such as pollution, accident hazards and the impact of technology, especially energy-related developments. Research has included nuclear power hazards, mining and resource issues, toxic waste, agricultural strategy, energy policy and alternative sources, arms control and nuclear proliferation and wildlife issues; clients have included local and national government, environmental groups and trade unions. Sister organisation in USA.
Status   Limited company
Publications   Semi-annual Report
*Alternative.Energy Strategies in the EEC.
The Effects of a Severe Reactor Accident at the Proposed Sizewell B Station upon Agri-*

culture and Fisheries in the United Kingdom and Neighbouring Countries. Research Report 11, 1984. 51pp.
Emergency Planning for a PWR Reactor at Sizewell.
The Environmental Impact of a Projected Uranium Development in County Donegal, Ireland. Research Report 9, 1983. 180pp.

Population Concern
231 Tottenham Court Road, London W1P 0HX
01–631 1546/01–637 9582
Director Eric McGraw
Aims To promote planned parenthood as a basic human right and to establish a balance between the world's population and its resources; to raise awareness about world population growth and its effects on social and economic development and the environment.
Activities Raising funds in the UK for population and development programmes around the world; providing an information and education service for schools, organisations and interested individuals on world population and related issues.
Status Voluntary
Publications World Population Data Sheet (1); Donors' Report (1)
Population Misconceptions. 1984.

Positive Health Network
Orchard Cottage, Church Side, Epsom, Surrey KT18 7SX
-NR

Practical Alternatives (PA)
Tirmorgan, Pontyberem, Dyfed SA15 4HP, Wales 0269 871014
Proprietor David Stephens
Aims To reduce pollution and the destruction of the natural environment by enabling people to avoid waste in their everyday lives; to make progress toward a conserver economy creating meaningful jobs and finding new ways of living for the future.
Activities Developing and marketing resource-saving products; advising on reducing energy consumption and condensation in housing; designing solar heated houses; publishing a journal.
Status Sole trader/consultancy
Publications Practical Alternatives (irregular)

Primate Society of Great Britain
Membership Secretary Dr H.0. Box, Dept of Psychology, University of Reading, Whiteknights, Reading, Berks. RG6 2AL
-NR

Prince of Wales' Committee
6th Floor, Empire House, Mount Stuart Square, Cardiff CF1 6DN 0222 495737/495875
Director David Cox, LVO, MBE
Aims To encourage projects, particularly by young people and voluntary groups, to improve the environment throughout Wales; to provide a forum for the discussion of problems particular to Wales and to promote environmental education.
Activities Managing a grant scheme for selected projects; advice to voluntary bodies on how to plan and carry out improvement schemes; organisation and sponsorship of seminars; representation on bodies concerned with the environment in Wales; organisation of the annual Prince of Wales' Award Scheme for environmental projects in Wales. Sub-offices in Swansea and Mold.
Status Charity

Professional Institutions Council for Conservation (PICC)
12 Great George Street, Parliament Square, London SW1P 3AD 01–222 7000
Secretariat:
61 Brown Street, Manchester M2 2JK
Aims To encourage greater liaison and co-operation between the professions concerned with the planning, management and development of natural resources; to develop an awareness within the professions and elsewhere of the need for a wider knowledge of conservation and of the optimum use of natural resources; to encourage the inclusion of various aspects of conservation in appropriate professional and academic qualifying courses; and to bring environmental problems and their possible solutions to the attention of government, local authorities and public and private organisations.
Activities Discussion meetings, dissemination of information; production of reports on environmental issues.
Status Voluntary
Publications PICC Newsletter (4)
-NR

Professions for World Disarmament and Development
12 Kelmore Grove, East Dulwich, London SE22 9BH 01–693 3860
Contact Alan Race

Progressive League
Albion Cottage,Fortis Green, London N2 9EP
01–452 8358
Editor of Journal Mrs F. Cockerell
Aims To be a forum for discussion and debate over a wide range of public issues in order to find a synthesis of tomorrow's thinking; to explore the fullest development

of human potential and the unity of intellectual, aesthetic and physical aspects of life.
Activities Lectures, discussions, conferences, social activities.
Status Voluntary
Publications Plan (12)

Project Icarus
Raglan House, 4 Clarence Parade, Southsea, Hants. PO5 3NU 0705 827460
   Manager Louise Carne
   Aims To combat harmful addictions and educate the public by production of audiovisual and written material in the health education field, with particular reference to addictions.
   Activities Promotion and distribution of films, videos, audio tapes, posters and books on drug addiction, alcoholism, smoking, venereal disease, family planning, spinal paralysis, burns and scalds.
   Status Voluntary
   Publications Hurley, Graham, *Lucky Break?*

Protection and Conservation of Animals and Plant Life
29 Broughton Drive, Grassendale, Liverpool L19 0PB 051–494 0470
   -NR

Psychologists for Peace
114 Middleton Road, London E8 4LP
   Secretary Ann Malkin
   -NR

Psychotherapy Centre
67 Upper Berkeley Street, London W1H 7DH 01–262 8852
   Contact Secretary
   Aims To help people resolve their emotional problems, relationship difficulties, neurotic behaviour patterns and psychogenic conditions by proven psychological methods, without theory, drugs or religion; to achieve this through a network of trained psychotherapists and by training, treatment, referral and publishing.
   Activities Training begins with the intending practitioner being a patient himself, enabling him to learn through self-discovery and release of potential; this is followed by lectures and practical work, including giving therapy under supervision and giving talks; the course can be taken, days or evenings, in London over 4 years. Treatment by psychotherapists on the register is for the whole personality, not for symptoms, a process of release rather than

suppression. For referral, prospective patients should write to the Centre, stating problem and age and enclosing £1; they are then sent a pamphlet answering the usual questions and providing details on nearest registered therapists. Talks, articles, broadcasts arranged. Local branches.
   Status Voluntary
   Publications You (4)
Therapy Not Theory Handbook. 1984.
Brian, R.K., *Why Be Psycho-analysed Before Becoming a Psychotherapist, Hypnotherapist or Counsellor?* 1984.

Pugwash Conferences on Science and World Affairs
Flat A, Museum Mansions, 63A Great Russell Street, London WC1B 3BJ 01–405 6661
   Contact Prof. J. Rotblat
   Aims To be a focus for an international group of scientists committed to the prevention of nuclear war.
   Activities Organising conferences at which distinguished speakers provide scientific evidence on the effects of nuclear weapons. National Pugwash Groups in many countries.
   Status Voluntary
   Publications Pugwash Newsletter (4); Proceedings of Pugwash Conference (1)
The Arms Race at a Time of Decision (Annals of Pugwash 1983). Macmillan, 1984. *Nuclear Strategy and World Security* (Annals of Pugwash 1984). Macmillan. 1985 *see also Executive Office address under* Organisations Not Based in Britain. . .

Pure Rivers Society
74 Dagenham Avenue, Dagenham, Essex RM9 6LH
   Aims To act as a central and advisory body for the purposes of maintaining pure rivers; to uphold the legal rights of riparian owners.
   -NR

Pure Water Preservation Society
Lane End, Highlands Lane, Westfield, Woking, Surrey GU22 9PU 04862 60385
   Chairman Pearl Coleman
   Aims To oppose the use of public water supplies for mass medication, particularly fluoridation.

Pye Research Institute
c/o Soil Association, Walnut Tree Manor, Haughley, Stowmarket, Suffolk IP14 3RS 044970 235
   -NR

Q

Quaker Peace and Service (QPS)

Friends House, Euston Road, London NW1 2BJ
01-387 3601   071 - 387 - 3601

General Secretary   Andrew Clark

Aims   To support and promote the concerns of Quakers in Britain which stem from their historic testimony against all war.

Activities   Through committees and their staff, initiating and supporting projects and programmes in the following fields of work: disarmament, reconciliation, Third World poverty, international relations, peace education and development education. The geographical spread of the work includes Britain, Eastern and Western Europe, the Middle East, Africa, Asia and Latin America. Local branches consist of the 450 Quaker Meetings in Britain.

Status   Charity (central dept of the Religious Society of Friends)

Publications   (QPS Reporter (4)
Bridging the East-West Divide.
Northern Ireland – a Problem to Every Solution.

Quaker Social Responsibility and Education

Friends House, Euston Road, London NW1 2BJ
01-387 3601

Aims   To express the Quaker sense of social responsibility and to further the concerns arising from it; this includes the sense of responsibility for the environment.

Activities   Conferences; support to local Quakers; publications.

Status   Religious society

Publications   Quaker Social Responsibility & Education Journal (3)
Nuclear Energy: can we live with it – or without it?

R

Radiation Hazards Campaign
This campaign has now ceased to function

Radioactive Waste Management Advisory Committee (RWMAC)
Dept of the Environment, Romney House, 43 Marsham Street, London SW1P 3PY 01-212 6685
Secretary P.J. Towey
Aims To advise the Secretaries of State for the Environment, Wales and Scotland on major issues relating to the development and implementation of an overall policy for the management of civil radioactive waste, including the waste management implications of nuclear policy, of the design of nuclear systems and of research and development and the environmental aspects of the handling and treatment of wastes. Under an independent chairman (Prof. P.T. Matthews), the Committee currently consists of 9 independent members, 4 members from the nuclear and electricity generating industries and 4 from the trade unions with members in those industries.
Status Statutory
Publications Annual Report

Radiochemical Inspectorate
see DEPARTMENT OF THE ENVIRONMENT

Railway Development Society (RDS)
BM-RDS, London WC1N 3XX 01-405 0463
Contact General Secretary
Aims To promote the retention and development of rail transport in the UK.
Activities Lobbying Parliament; publishing literature; organising public meetings; establishing branches throughout the UK; liaising with British Rail officials at all levels; assisting the formation of user groups on threatened lines; co-ordinating the rail user group movement. 10 local branches.
Status Voluntary
Publications Railwatch (4)
Guide for Rail Users Groups.
How to Fight a Rail Cut.

Railway Path Project
35 King Street, Bristol, Avon BS1 4DZ 0272 28893
Engineer John Grimshaw
Aims To create, construct and maintain routes for pedestrians and cyclists that are safe from conflict with motor traffic.
Activities Sponsoring and managing survey and construction projects throughout Britain; advice and assistance to groups and local authorities interested in path construction projects; assessing the potential of newly redundant railway lines for conversion to railway paths and cycle routes. Local branches.
Status Voluntary
Publications *Report of Scottish Railway Path & Cycle Route Project 1985.*

Ramblers' Association
1-5 Wandsworth Road, London SW8 2LJ 01-582 6878
Aims To protect footpaths and other rights of way and increase access to open country; to defend outstanding landscapes; to encourage people to walk in the countryside.
Activities Carrying out these aims at a national level through the employment of staff to run national campaigns, lobby MPs, etc.; and at local level through the activities of the voluntary workers in its Areas and Groups who tackle problems on paths, both by reporting them to highway authorities and by carrying out practical work such as stile building and waymarking. The 44 Areas and 240 local groups also have programmes of rambles and other events.
Status Voluntary; charity
Publications Rucksack (4); Footpath Worker (4)
Trevelyan, John & Clayden, Paul, *Rights of Way: a guide to law and practice,* Ramblers' Association/Open Spaces Society, 1983

Raptor Trust
Boulsdon House, Newent, Glos. GL18 1JJ 0531 820286
Director Jemima Parry-Jones
Aims To research into all aspects of raptor biology; to disseminate information relating to birds of prey and their environment.
Activities Running an educational zoo and captive breeding programme.
Status Charitable research institute (est. 1985)

Rare Breeds Survival Trust Limited
4th Street, National Agricultural Centre, Stoneleigh Park, Kenilworth, Warwicks. CV8 2LG 0203 51141
Secretary John H. Wood Roberts
Aims To re-establish endangered breeds

of domestic farm animals and retain essential genes.

Activities Endeavouring, by research, specific studies, husbandry and by displays and events, to re-establish and retain at least a nucleus of breeds that have reached a critical level of population, so that their genetic pool is not lost forever, either through accident, disease, changing econ-omics or fashion. Organising shows and sales; producing publications and breeding records. At present 42 breeds are on the Trust's lists.

Status Charity

Publications The Ark (12)

Rational Technology Co-operative
This organisation no longer exists

Real Food Campaign
This campaign has now ceased to function

Reclamation Association
16 High Street, Brampton, Huntingdon, Cambs. PE18 8TU 0480 55249

Secretary Mrs J.G. Tilley

Aims To promote reclamation and recyc-ling of materials.

Status Trade association

Red Deer Commission
Knowsley, 82 Fairfield Road, Inverness, High-land IV3 5LH, Scotland 0463 231751

Secretary N.H. McCulloch

Aims To further the conservation and control in Scotland of red deer, sika deer or such other deer as may be specified from time to time by the Secretary of State; to keep under review all matters relating to such deer.

Activities Carrying out census work on the basis of which advice may be given to any owner of land on questions relating to the carrying of stocks of deer on that land; assessing damage to woodlands by deer; and other deer management studies. The Commission has a statutory duty with powers to prevent damage to agriculture and forestry by deer; a staff of skilled stalkers is available for direct action where necessary anywhere in Scotland.

Status Statutory

Publications Annual Report

Regenerative Technology
22 Greywethers Avenue, Swindon, Wilts. SN3 1QF 0793 20544 (evenings)

Consultant John A. Farrar

Aims To provide methods and equipment which are cheap enough to be accessible to everyone and suitable for small-scale manufacture so that people generally can meet their real needs.

Activities Providing an information service about the alternatives which meet the needs of people; publishing literature on tech-nology; healing by means of Bach flower remedies.

Status Commercial
-NR

Regional Studies Association
29 Great James Street, London WC1N 3ES 01-242 0363

Executive Secretary Gloria Frankel

Aims To provide a forum for the exchange of ideas and information on regional problems; to publish the results of regional research; to stimulate studies and research in regional planning and related fields.

Activities Conferences, meetings, seminars. 12 branches.

Status Charity

Publications Regional Studies (6); Regional Studies Association Newsletter (6)
Report of an Inquiry into Regional Problems in the United Kingdom, Geo Books, 1983.

Register of Traditional Chinese Medicine (RTCM)
7A Thorndean Street, London SW18 4HE 01-947 1879

Registrar & Secretary to the Council Carol Daglish

Aims To promote the practice of acupunc-ture according to the theories of traditional Chinese medicine; to inform the public about acupuncture as an integrated and compre-hensive system of medicine; to promote high standards of training, qualification and prac-tice among its members.

Activities Liaising with government bodies; representing and protecting the interests of members; seminars for members; liaising and promoting connections with acupuncture bodies in the People's Republic of China; informing the public about acupuncture and the work of the Register and its practitioner members. Membership is gained by those who have completed a recognised course of training in traditional Chinese medicine or who pass an examin-ation of theoretical and clinical competence set by the Register; knowledge of Western anatomy, physiology, pathology and medi-cine is also a prerequisite of membership.

Status Voluntary

Relaxation for Living
29 Burwood Park Road, Walton-on-Thames, Surrey KT12 5LH 0932 227826

Hon. Secretary Mrs Amber Lloyd

Aims To promote the teaching of physical relaxation to combat the stress, strain, anxiety and tension of modern life; to ease pain,

reduce fatigue, improve sleep and lessen phobias.
Activities Small group relaxation classes; teacher training; study days; publication of self-help leaflets, tapes, correspondence course and newsletter. (Large s.a.e. with inquiries.)
Status Charity
Publications Relaxation for Living Newsletter (4)

Remote Sensing Society (RSS)
c/o Dept of Geography, University of Reading, 2 Earley Gate, Reading, Berks. RG6 2AU 0734 665633
Hon. General Secretary Dr P.M. Mather
Aims To promote the study and use of remote sensing techniques in measuring and managing the Earth's resources.
Activities Organising a programme of workshops and lectures at various centres in the UK; annual conference.
Status Voluntary
Publications International Journal of Remote Sensing (12); News & Letters (4); Proceedings of Annual Conference (1)

Remote Sensing Unit
University of Aston, Gosta Green, Birmingham B4 7ET
-NR

Research Council for Complementary Medicine (RCCM)
Suite 1, 19A Cavendish Square, London W1M 9AD 01–493 6930
Secretary H.D. Wicks
Aims To encourage the incorporation of what is best in Complementary Medicine into the mainstream of modern medical practice (examples of such therapeutic techniques are longstanding and well-structured therapies such as acupuncture, homoeopathy, medical herbalism, chiropractic and osteopathy).
Activities Sponsoring and initiating research to the highest scientific standards; providing access to existing and historical literature and data; building bridges between orthodox and complementary organisations and practitioners; publishing as relevant.
Status Charity
Publications RCCM Newsletter (3/4); Journal & Proceedings (1)

Research Society for Natural Therapeutics (RSNT)
PO Box 509, London SW6 1QN 01–381 9799
Hon. Secretary Brian Lamb
Aims To inaugurate original research into new or neglected therapeutic and diagnostic techniques.
Activities Outings to establishments

demonstrating research into matters concerning health; meetings to discuss the effectiveness of various therapeutic measures.
Status Research society

Resource Economy Ltd
see PRACTICAL ALTERNATIVES

Resource Research
Meadow Farm, Greenham, Wellington, Somerset TA21 0JW 0823 672134
Architect John Shore
Activities Non-profit research and development relating to the independent servicing of people and dwellings. Work includes solar conservatories and highly insulated self-build housing, solar space and water heating, small-scale wind power, water conservation and recycling toilet systems. Information distributed to the public through published reports, lectures, workshops, demonstrations and by correspondence (s.a.e. for details; £1 for specific advice).
Status Self-funding, non-profit

Resource Use Institute Ltd (RUI)
14 Lower Oakfield, Pitlochry, Tayside PH16 5DS, Scotland 0796 3211/2569
Secretary & Manager Dr E.C. Kirby
Aims To help develop resource-based industries, especially but not exclusively in Scotland; to teach the principles of raw material development; and to conduct any work which it is thought can help toward these ends.
Activities Collection and assessment of information on resources; technological advice; studies in resource accounting, carrying capacity, financial reform and the application of mathematical methods to chemistry.
Status Company limited by guarantee
Publications Carrying Capacity Assessment: a resource accounting methodology for assessing the sustainability of national economies in the context of population, resources, environment and development. Report of a pilot study in Kenya, including a Generic Computer Model. UNESCO/FAO, 1984.

Resources Centre (Republic of Ireland)
168 Rathgar Road, Dublin 6, Ireland
Contact Co-ordinator
Aims To be a source of information, documentation, contact and stimulus.
-NR

Right Livelihood Foundation
Viking House, Wybourn Drive, Onchan, Isle of Man
London branch: 01–935 2989

Executive Trustee Jakob von Uexkull
Aims To honour, support and publicise those working on practical solutions to the real problems in the world today, so that their projects will be copied, providing working realities in various fields when the breakdown of the old world order intensifies.
Activities Presents an annual $50,000 prize, the Right Livelihood Award (the Alternative Nobel Prize), in Stockholm on 9 December, the day before the Nobel presentations; nominations for the Award are submitted to an international selection board. The purpose is to support those working to create sustainable and just solutions in both the Third World and the industrialised countries; the Award honours healing and holistic, instead of divisive and reductionist, science and recognises the value of traditional knowledge; information about the Award winners is published. Branches in London and Stockholm.
Status Charity

Road Haulage Association (RHA)
104 New King's Road, London SW6 4LN
01–736 1183
-NR

Rossendale Groundwork Trust Ltd
New Hall Hey Farm, New Hall Hey Road, Rawtenstall, Rossendale, Lancs. BB4 6HR
0706 211421
Executive Director Peter Wilmers
Aims To conserve and improve the landscape and environment of Rossendale and to promote the understanding and enjoyment of its countryside and heritage.
Activities Working in partnership with individuals, societies, schools, private firms, farmers, public bodies, local and central government to carry out an ambitious programme of projects throughout Rossendale, ranging from mending dry stone walls, waymarking footpaths, farm open days, tree planting and training in countryside skills to school nature projects, publications, trails, footpath and bridleway guides, conservation of natural features or old buildings, development of farm tourism, countryside management schemes and major derelict land reclamation schemes; in addition, the Trust is converting a derelict farm into a permanent visitor/volunteer centre and hostel, to provide a base for voluntary conservation work. Has two supporting organisations, The Rossendale Groundworkers and Access Rossendale.
Status Voluntary
Publications Annual Report

Rothamsted Experimental Station
see COMMONWEALTH BUREAU OF SOILS; SOIL SURVEY OF ENGLAND AND WALES

Rowett Research Institute
Greenburn Road, Bucksburn, Aberdeen, Grampian AB2 9SB, Scotland 0224 712751
Director Prof. W.P.T. James
Activities Investigating the way microbial action in anaerobic digesters can help to control pollution caused by agricultural and domestic wastes and can be a source of energy for farm or other use; carrying out experiments on a pilot plant and, with the North of Scotland College of Agriculture, on large-scale plant. The main work of the Institute relates to the nutrition of farm livestock, including the applied aspects of feeding and management of animals.
Status State-aided research institute of the Agricultural and Food Research Council
Publications Annual Report
-NR

Royal Agricultural Society of England (RASE)
National Agricultural Centre, Stoneleigh, Kenilworth, Warwicks. CV8 2LZ 0203 555100
Public Relations Officer Andrew Singleton
London Office: 35 Belgrave Square, London SW1X 8QN 01–235 5323
Aims To encourage good husbandry, agricultural craftsmanship and forestry; to confer and co-operate with other societies and governments at home and abroad; to exchange views and information and generally to encourage the dissemination of knowledge.
Activities Organising the Royal Show, a 4–day trade fair that is the most comprehensive agricultural show in the world; in addition, the Society organises a number of technical farming demonstrations each year, both at the NAC and at locations throughout the country. Other activities include: presenting an annual conference programme aimed at keeping farmers and everyone else involved in the industry up-to-date with latest trends and developments; extending communication to the non-farming community; interpreting farming to schools and the general public through events and open days.
Status Charity (founded by Royal Charter in 1840)
Publications NAC News (4); RASE Journal (1)
Fream's Agriculture.
Reference Book & Buyers' Guide.

Royal Aircraft Establishment (RAE)
Farnborough, Hants. GU14 6TD 0252 24461 ext. 2685

Activities The Solar Cell Section of the Space Department has expertise in the following areas of photovoltaics for alternative energy systems: calibration of solar cells for use as primary performance standards (EEC-approved agency); performance measurement and environmental testing of solar cells and arrays; solar cell and array technology; design and installation of experimental units.

Status Statutory (Ministry of Defence Establishment)
-NR

Royal Botanic Gardens, Kew (RBG Kew)
Kew Green, Kew, Richmond, Surrey TW9 3AB
01-940 1171
Contact Enquiries Unit
Aims To conduct investigations on plants; to provide advice and publications, especially on taxonomy, distribution, conservation and utilisation of tropical plants; to care for national reference collections of living plants, herbarium specimens, a seed bank, a museum of economic botany and a library and archives; under the National Heritage Act 1983, to provide for admission of the public to the Gardens for education and enjoyment.
Activities Maintaining the Gardens and opening them to the public; guided tours by arrangement; public lectures; open days; enquiries and identification service; research facilities for *bona fide* investigators; conducting investigations in taxonomy, biochemistry, anatomy and genetics; preparation of flora, especially of tropical areas; distribution of plant material for research and conservation; 3-year horticultural diploma course; List of publications available on request; RBG Kew is closely associated with IUCN and World Wildlife Fund botanical publications. Branch at Haywards Heath, W. Sussex.
Status Statutory research institute
Publications Kew Magazine (4); Kew Record of Taxonomic Literature (1) (HMSO) Hepper. F.N. (ed.), *The Royal Botanic Gardens, Kew: gardens for science and pleasure.* HMSO, 1983.

Royal Botanical and Horticultural Society
55 Brown Street, Manchester M2 5DS
-NR

Royal Commission on the Ancient and Historical Monuments of Scotland
54 Melville Street, Edinburgh EH3 7HF
031-225 5994
Activities Responsible for compiling an inventory of ancient and historical monuments in Scotland and specifying those most worthy of preservation; for emergency

survey of listed buildings; for the supply of archaeological information to the Ordnance Survey for mapping purposes and for the National Monuments Record of Scotland.
Status Statutory

Royal Commission on Ancient and Historical Monuments in Wales
Edleston House, Queen's Road, Aberystwyth, Dyfed SY23 2HP, Wales 0970 4381
Activities Responsible for compiling an inventory of ancient and historical monuments in Wales and specifying those most worthy of preservation; for emergency surveys of listed buildings; and for the National Monuments Record for Wales.
Status Statutory

Royal Commission on Environmental Pollution (RCEP)
Church House, Great Smith Street, London SW1P 3BL 01-212 8620
Secretary T.E. Radice
Aims To advise on matters, both national and international, concerning the pollution of the environment; on the adequacy of research in this field; and the future possibilities of danger to the environment. To inquire into and report independently on any matters within its terms of reference (but with no executive function). Constituted for Great Britain and Northern Ireland.
Activities Topics reported on to date include: industrial pollution; pollution in British estuaries and coastal waters; pollution control progress and problems; air pollution control; nuclear power and the environment; agriculture and pollution; and a new study on pollution by wastes.
Status Statutory
Publications *Pollution by Wastes,* HMSO, 1985.

Royal Entomological Society (RES)
41 Queen's Gate, London SW7 5HU 01-584 8361
Registrar G.G. Bentley
Aims To promote the improvement and diffusion of entomological science.
Activities Convening meetings on all aspects of entomology; publishing the results of entomological research; maintaining a large entomological library. More informally, generating discourse between entomologists, particularly at the Society's Rooms. Publications include identification handbooks, three scientific journals, volumes of symposia and a bulletin.
Status Learned society established by Royal Charter; charity
Publications Royal Entomological Society Bulletin

Royal Environmental Health Institute of Scotland

Virginia House, Virginia Street,
Glasgow G1 1TX
-NR

Royal Forestry Society of England, Wales & Northern Ireland

102 High Street, Tring, Herts. HP23 4AH
044282 2028
Contact Director
Aims To advance the knowledge and practice of forestry and arboriculture.
Activities Providing an information service for members and others; offering careers advice; arranging visits on a local or national basis to estates and other places of interest at home and abroad; co-operating with other similar bodies. Local branches.
Status Charity
Publications Quarterly Journal of Forestry (4)

Royal Geographical Society (RGS)

1 Kensington Gore, London SW7 2AR
01–589 5466
Publications Geographical Journal (3)
-NR

Royal Horticultural Society (RHS)

PO Box 313, 80 Vincent Square, London
SW1P 2PE 01–834 4333
Secretary J.R. Cowell
Aims To collect and disseminate information concerning the cultivation of all plants and trees and to encourage every branch of horticulture.
Activities Maintains a garden at Wisley, Surrey, which is open to memebers of the Society and to the general public; members can send plants and fruits to the laboratory at Wisley for identification. Flower shows are held frequently at the Society's Halls in London.
Status Charity
Publications The Garden (12); The Plantsman (4)
Wisley Handbooks (series of 40 titles)

Royal Horticultural Society of Ireland (RHSI)

Thomas Prior House, Merrion Road, Dublin 4,
Ireland 0001–68 4358 (mornings)
Secretary Mrs Monica Nolan
Aims To encourage and improve horticulture, both ornamental and useful, in the home and community.
Activities Arranging lectures, demonstrations, gardening courses, garden visits, garden tours at home and abroad, shows and plant sales.
Status Voluntary

Royal Institute of British Architects (RIBA)

66 Portland Place, London W1N 4AD
01–580 5533
Aims To promote the general advancement of civil architecture; to extend the body of knowledge upon which the practice of architecture is based.
Activities Through the Code of Professional Conduct, standards of admission, conditions of engagement and its extensive publications, the Institute seeks to assure the public of the standards of integrity and competence of members and to see that in meeting clients' requirements, architects have regard to the broader use and environmental implications of their work.
Status Learned society
Publications RIBA Journal (12); RIBA Directory of Members (1); RIBA Directory of Practices (1)
-NR

Royal Institute of Public Health and Hygiene (RIPHH)

28 Portland Place, London W1N 4DE
01–580 2731
Secretary W.A. Waddell
Aims To promote the advancement of public health and hygiene in all its branches, especially personal, domestic and industrial hygiene; to aid, encourage and provide means for the study of public health, preventive medicine and hygiene; to recognise and assist work done toward raising the standard of the environment and conditions in which the community lives and works.
Activities Conducting courses and examinations, including: courses for registered medical practitioners in environmental health and related subjects; independent examinations in Food Hygiene, Health and Welfare, Hairdressing, Anatomical Pathology Technology, Anatomical Technology, Hospital and General Hygiene, Bakery Hygiene, Meat and Poultry Hygiene, Canning Hygiene and Dairy Hygiene.
Status Charity
Publications Health and Hygiene (4)

Royal Institution of Chartered Surveyors (RICS)

12 Great George Street, Parliament Square,
London SW1P 3AD 01–222 7000
Public Relations Officer Margaret Cox
Aims To advance the profession of surveying by securing the optimal use of land to meet social and economic needs; to survey the structure of buildings and advise on their maintenance and conservation; and to manage and develop mineral resources.
Activities Sponsoring the national RICS/The Times Conservation Awards Scheme to encourage the conservation and

improvement of buildings and the environment; members' activities include the conservation of land and buildings, advice on energy saving, minerals exploitation and the restoration of worked land. The Institution offers evidence to government and other public bodies on all matters affecting conservation and the development of land and the countryside; represented on the council of the Farming and Wildlife Advisory Group. 31 local branches.
Status Professional institution
Publications Chartered Surveyor Weekly (52); Chartered Land Surveyor/Chartered Mineral Surveyor (4)
-NR

Royal Meteorological Society
James Glaisher House, Grenville Place, Bracknell, Berks. RG12 1BX 0344 22957
Executive Secretary D.R. Grant
Aims To advance meteorological science by publishing results of new research and spreading well-founded knowledge.
Activities Holding discussion meetings in London and other centres; publishing journals. Local branches.
Status Voluntary; learned society
Publications Weather (12); Journal of Climatology (6); Quarterly Journal of the Royal Meteorological Society (4)

Royal Scottish Forestry Society
1 Rothesay Terrace, Edinburgh EH3 7UP
031–225 1300/031–226 3157
Secretary W.B.C. Walker
Aims To keep members fully informed of all developments and current issues relating to forestry at home and abroad.
Activities Maintaining an employment register for qualified foresters; running award schemes for students; organising an annual excursion to various parts of Scotland, with a forestry theme. The Society's regions have their own activities and excursions throughout the year. Local branches.
Status Voluntary
Publications Scottish Forestry (4)

Royal Society
6 Carlton House Terrace, London SW1Y 5AG
01–839 5561
Executive Secretary Dr P.T. Warren
Aims To promote the natural sciences, including mathematics, technology and medicine.
Activities Providing grants and fellowships for research and awards for outstanding work; publishing scientific papers; holding scientific meetings; acting as non-governmental UK member of international scientific unions; arranging scientific exchange

agreements with overseas academies. Recently directed a study into acid rain.
Status Learned society
Publications Philosophical Transactions of the Royal Society (irreg.); Proceedings of the Royal Society (irreg.)

Royal Society for Nature Conservation (RSNC)
The Green, Nettleham, Lincoln LN2 2NR
0522 752326
General Secretary Dr F.H. Perring
Aims To promote the conservation of nature for the purposes of study and research and to educate the public in understanding and appreciation of nature and the need for its conservation.
Activities Incorporated by Royal Charter as the national association of 46 Nature Conservation Trusts with similar objectives. Functions include: acquisition and management of nature reserves; influencing land users to accept wildlife conservation principles; education of youth and the general public to understand and care for wildlife; advising and assisting the Trusts and representing their interests at national level; organising conferences and seminars for officers and members of Trusts; promoting interpretive projects; publishing pamphlets and books on nature conservation topics; producing a magazine. In association with the Sunday Times, the RSNC co-sponsors the Watch Club which is a national club for those up to the age of 18 and is the junior wing of the Nature Conservation Trusts.
Status Voluntary; charity
Publications Natural World (3); Annual Report

Royal Society for the Prevention of Accidents (RoSPA)
Cannon House, The Priory, Queensway, Birmingham B4 6BS 021–233 2461
Aims To prevent, by educational means, accidents on the roads, in the home, in leisure pursuits, in commerce, industry and agriculture.
Activities Stimulating interest in accident prevention through local and national organisations and through training courses, conferences and national publicity campaigns; liaising with local road safety, home safety and agricultural safety committees and industrial safety groups; running training courses for home safety officers, road safety officers and all levels of staff in industry. The Society acts as the principal agent of the government for the co-ordination of road safety activities throughout the UK. Industrial training centre in Birmingham.
Status Charity
-NR – L

Royal Society for the Prevention of Cruelty to Animals (RSPCA)
The Causeway, Horsham, W. Sussex RH12 1HG 0403 64181
Director of Press & Public Relations Mike Smithson
Aims To prevent cruelty and promote kindness toward all animals.
Activities Maintaining a force of 250 uniformed Inspectors assigned to areas in England and Wales, which acts as a law enforcement agency; undertaking practical animal welfare through its nation-wide homes, clinics and hospitals; lobbying Parliament for legislative reform after careful research by its specialist staff; instructing children and students in the proper care and regard for animals. Local branches.
Status Charity
Publications Animal Ways (5); Animal World (5); Today; Annual Report

Royal Society for the Protection of Birds (RSPB) 0176768055l 2767680551
The Lodge, Sandy, Beds. SG19 2DL 0767 80551
Director General Ian Prestt
Scotland: 17 Regent Terrace, Edinburgh EH7 5BN 031–556 5624/ 9042
Director (Scotland) Frank Hamilton
Wales: Frolic Street, Newtown, Powys SY16 1AP 0686 26678
Wales Officer Roger Lovegrove
N. Ireland: Belvoir Park Forest, Belfast BT8 4QT 0232 692547
Northern Ireland Officer Dinah Browne
Aims To conserve and protect wild birds; to promote interest, research and enjoyment of birds; to acquire and manage land for birds and other wildlife; to discourage the wanton destruction of any bird not killed for the purpose of food (but to take no part in the question of killing game birds); to work with other bodies having similar objectives.
Activities Acquisition and management of nature reserves; research and surveys; monitoring and responding to development proposals, land use practices and pollution; protection of rare and endangered species; investigation of offences under the Wildlife and Countryside Act. Education in schools and colleges; children's Young Ornithologists' Club; publications, publicity campaigns, exhibitions; production of films on birds; fund raising. Regional branches in England.
Status Voluntary; charity
Publications Birds (4); Bird Life (YOC) (6); Annual Report

Royal Society of Arts (RSA)
6–8 John Adam Street, Adelphi, London WC2N 6EZ 01–930 5115

Assistant Secretary (Environment) Timothy Cantell
Aims The RSA's Committee for the Environment seeks to identify and anticipate major environmental problems and provide a forum for their discussion.
Activities Conferences and seminars are organised several times a year, usually with published proceedings, and have covered topics such as urban wasteland, forestry, renewable sources of energy, acid rain and the Irish Sea. The Society also co-sponsors (and provides the secretariat for) the annual Pollution Abatement Technology Award which seeks to recognise and publicise innovations in technology which reduce or avoid pollution of the environment. List of publications and details of the above Award available on request.
Status Voluntary; charity
Publications RSA Journal (12)

Royal Society of Health
13 Grosvenor Place, London SW1X 7EN 01–235 9961
Activities Interests include the prevention of environmental pollution, including that of air, water and land; health in society; food and nutrition.
-NR

Royal Town Planning Institute (RTPI)
26 Portland Place, London W1N 4BE 01–636 9107
Secretary-General David Fryer
Aims To advance the science and art of town planning in all aspects, including local, regional and national planning, for the benefit of the public.
Activities Acts as a watchdog on standards of professional practice and conduct; conducts examinations; organises meetings and conferences; develops policy statements through working parties of members and represents the interests of planning through the media and to government. Provides a bibliographic, information and library service and publishes a journal and other publications. 14 local branches.
Status Professional institute
Publications The Planner (12)

Royal Zoological Society of Scotland (RZSS)
Scottish National Zoological Park, Murrayfield, Edinburgh EH12 6TS 031–334 9171
Director R.J. Wheater
Aims To promote, facilitate and encourage the study of zoology and kindred subjects and to foster and develop public interest in and knowledge of animal life.
Activities Maintaining and developing the Scottish National Zoological Park (Edinburgh Zoo); conserving species by main-

taining viable breeding groups of animals; participating in breeding schemes through involvement with the Anthropoid Ape Advisory Panel, the Common Management of Species Group and a number of international organisations (this is reflected by the number of animals on loan in and out of the collection); operating a major conservation education programme involving over 47,000 children. The collection is used by several universities in Scotland for research projects, provided that such research is not in any way stressful to the animals concerned. The collection is visited by 500,000 people each year. Membership of the Society, including Associates, is 9,000; the volunteer programme has 120 participants.

Status Charity

Publications Species News (4); Annual Report; Guidebook (updated every 18 months)

RURAL (Society for the Responsible Use of Resources in Agriculture and on the Land)

Bore Place, Chiddingstone, Edenbridge, Kent TN8 7AR 073277 255/708

Aims To encourage the responsible use of resources in the management of land, animals and other factors in the production of food and other products; to promote ecological factors in land use, reduced dependence on support energy in agriculture, reduced wastage and profitable rural employment.

Activities Workshops and practical demonstrations on farms; discussion meetings on land use and agricultural policy; study groups; maintaining a register of practitioners; issuing a series of RURAL Reports.

Status Voluntary; charity -NR

Rural Preservation Association

see LANDLIFE

Rural Resettlement Group (RRG)

27A Sydney Street, Brightlingsea, Essex CO7 0BG 0206 304315

Co-ordinator Dick Kitto

Aims To support the movement of people back to the countryside.

Status Voluntary

Publications *Rural Resettlement Handbook.* 3rd edn. Prism-Alpha/Lighthouse, 1984. 300pp.

Rural Voice

26 Bedford Square, London WC1B 3HU 01–636 4066

Secretary David M. Clark

Aims To provide a forum for discussion of rural socio-economic issues; information exchange; campaigning on current legislation; developing self-help in the countryside.

Activities Co-ordinating an alliance of nine national voluntary rural organisations; annual conference; regular committee meetings; organising the Village Ventures competition through member bodies.

Status Voluntary alliance

S

Sacred Trees Trust (STT)
31 Kings Avenue, Leeds, W. Yorks. LS6 1QP
0532 459219
Press Officer Simon Musk
Aims To foster the spiritual and metaphysical appreciation of indigenous broad leaved trees, their folk use, healing properties and legend/lore; to reinstate Ancient Groves and establish new groves; to locate and classify legendary and important Great Trees and to nurture, repair and replant the Great Trees.
Activities Compiling the Gazetteer of Sacred Trees and the Book of Sacred Trees; the former will demark the extent of legendarily important or spectacular trees throughout the UK and also the position of the Ancient Groves used by early man – this is needed to protect and nurture them. The Book of Sacred Trees is a monumental work involving the legends, history, folk usage, healing powers, cultivation requirements and ecological benefits of all trees. The STT is open to all people but will have a special significance to New Agers. Since its inauguration in 1983 it has achieved charitable status and the opening of the first new grove in Britain for over 1,000 years; another new grove is being negotiated at present and a network of groves throughout the UK is planned; the emphasis is on nurturing wildwood rather than imposing paths and tidiness and each grove will greatly benefit wildlife and flora. 14 area groups.
Status Voluntary; charity
Publications Roots (6)
The Earth's Children.
The Healing Trees.

Safe Routes to Schools Project
35 King Street, Bristol, Avon BS1 4DZ 0272 28893
Surveyor Dave Sharpington
Aims To identify and create safe routes to schools by investigating the opportunities for improvement within the physical environment.
Activities Studies for local authorities to determine the geography of school journeys, incidence of accidents, etc.; undertaking school pupil questionnaire surveys and compilation of returns; proposals for traffic management to make child pedestrian and cycle trips safer, based on school travel patterns.
Status Voluntary
Publications

Safe Routes to Schools: a study for the Greater London Council.

Salford and Trafford Groundwork Trust (SATGT)
6 Kansas Avenue, Weaste, Salford, Manchester M5 2GL 061-848 0334
Projects Manager Graeme McLearie
Aims To achieve conservation through co-operation; to promote the improvement of the urban fringe; to develop more understanding of the differing needs of town and country and bring the countryside to people's doorsteps.
Activities Landscaping; planting in derelict land; consultancy and advisory work; talks and displays.
Status Charity

Sand and Gravel Association (SAGA)
48 Park Street, London W1Y 4HE 01–499 8967
Aims To promote the idea that precious land which has already made at least two contributions (usually farming and then sand or gravel extraction) should be restored for a further service, to the community.
Activities Annual restoration awards to member companies; dissemination of information.
-NR

Save and Recycle (Textiles) Ltd
31A Hill Avenue, Amersham, Bucks. HP6 5BX
02403 4105
-NR

SAVE Britain's Heritage
68 Battersea High Street, London SW11 3HX
01–228 3336
Chairman Sophie Andreae
Aims To campaign for the retention and rehabilitation of historic buildings and areas.
Activities Publicising threats to historic buildings of all types through press releases, reports and exhibitions; occasionally preparing its own schemes for alternative use of threatened buildings; also active on broader issues of preservation policy. Welcomes details of threatened buildings, with photographs if possible, from correspondents.
Status Charity
Publications *The Best Buildings in Britain.* Martin, Kit & Binney, Marcus. *The Country House: to be or not to be.*

Save Our Stags
1 Guernsey Avenue, Broomhill, Bristol,
Avon BS4 4SH
-NR

School of Peace Studies
University of Bradford, Bradford, W. Yorks.
BD7 1DP 0274 733466
Professor of Peace Studies James
O'Connell
Aims To study peace; to research into
teaching on factors that condition the main-
tenance and repair of peace.
Activities Undergraduate and post-
graduate teaching; research into issues of
peace and war. Resource centre for those
concerned with the issues of peace;
producing publications.
Status University department
-NR

Schools Against The Bomb
11 Goodwin Street, London N4 3HQ 01–263 0977
Contact Andrew McIntyre
-NR

Schumacher Society
Ford House, Hartland, Bideford, Devon
EX39 6EE 02374 293
Aims To promote a decentralised,
ecological society as explained by the late
Dr E.F. Schumacher.
Activities Organising annual lectures;
operating a mail-order book service;
publishing the journal.
Status Voluntary
Publications Resurgence (6)
Kumar, Satish (ed.), *Schumacher Lectures
vol.2.*

Science and Engineering Research Council
(SERC)
Polaris House, North Star Avenue, Swindon,
Wilts. SN2 1ET 0793 26222
London Annexe: Garrick House, 3–5 Charing
Cross Road, London WC2H 0HW
Secretary to the Council Dr J.A. Catterall
Aims To support and encourage scientific
research and education in universities and
similar institutions, in its own establishments
and in collaboration with international
organisations.
Activities SERC's Divisions include:
Astronomy, Space and Radio; Nuclear
Physics; Science; and Engineering. Its estab-
lishments include: Daresbury Laboratory;
Rutherford Appleton Laboratory; Royal
Greenwich Observatory; and the Royal
Observatory in Edinburgh.
Status Statutory
Publications Annual Report
-NR

Scientific and Medical Network (SMN)
Lake House, Ockley, Dorking, Surrey RH5 5NS
0306 711268
Hon. Secretary George Blaker
Aims To broaden the contemporary framework of thought, especially in science and
medicine, to include phenomena that occur,
but for which there is no adequate expla-
nation along orthodox materialistic lines.
Activities Holding large public conferences (the May Lectures) and small seminars
either by invitation of self-selection; cassette
recordings of talks; circulation of research
papers; week-long residential gatherings to
discover wider horizons for the young;
education; publication of articles.
Status Voluntary
Publications Network Newsletter

Scientists Against Nuclear Arms (SANA)
London Production Centre, Broomhill Road,
Wandsworth, London SW18 4JQ
01–871 3360/3369
Administrative Officer Rebecca Miles
Aims To promote and co-ordinate the
activities of scientists wishing to assist those
working to halt and reverse the nuclear arms
race.
Activities Providing reliable factual information and well-informed speakers;
producing publications, contributions to the
media and scientific journals; promoting
awareness amongst members of the scientific
community of their special responsibility
toward achieving nuclear disarmament.
SANA is active nationally and locally in
providing information to the various peace
and disarmament organisations and to MPs,
Churches, trade unions, county and borough
councillors and other individuals with influence on public policy; and also in informing
the general public. Local branches.
Status Voluntary
Publications SANA Newsletter (4)
Briefing Packs on Nuclear Issues (nos 1, 2 &
3)
*Nuclear Winter: a new dimension for the
nuclear debate.*
*The Problems and Prospects of
Disarmament.*

Scottish Anti-Vivisection Society (SAVS)
121 West Regent Street, Glasgow G2 2SD
041–221 2300
Organising Secretary John F. Robins
Aims To promote the total suppression of
vivisection and other scientific procedures on
animals, children and unconsenting adults;
and to promote kindness to and protection
of animals.
Activities Raising public awareness of the
issue through demonstrations, distribution of
literature, education and public speaking;

encouragement of non-animal research techniques; political lobbying to attain legislation restricting current scientific practices involving animals and phasing out all animal research.
Status Voluntary
Publications SAVS Newsletter (4); Annual Report
-NR

Scottish Beekeepers' Association (SBA)
44 Dalhousie Road, Kilbarchan, Strathclyde PA10 2AT, Scotland 05057 2680
Publicity Convenor David Blair
Aims To encourage an expansion of the ancient craft of beekeeping, within Scotland and beyond.
Activities Publicising the art through shows, films and slides (the two major honey shows in Scotland being at Ingleston, in conjunction with the Royal Highland Show, and the Scottish National Honey Show at Ayr; local affiliated associations also run their own shows); encouraging new beekeepers through education and use of the Association library; publishing the magazine. 40 affiliated associations.
Status Voluntary
Publications The Scottish Beekeeper (12)
An Introduction to Bees and Beekeeping.

Scottish Business in the Community
Eagle Star House, 25 St Andrew Square, Edinburgh EH2 1AF 031–556 9761/2
Director Graham Ross
Aims To help industry, commerce and the professions to contribute to the health of the community, with emphasis on local action in places where individual firms produce or sell their goods and services.
Status Voluntary
[*see also* BUSINESS IN THE COMMUNITY]

Scottish Campaign for Nuclear Disarmament (SCND)
420 Sauchiehall Street, Glasgow G2 3JD 041–331 2878
General Secretary Margaret Morton
Aims To promote nuclear disarmament for Britain with the overall objective of stopping and then reducing the nuclear arms race between the superpowers.
Activities Currently concentrating on opposition to the Trident nuclear missile submarine programme and nuclear expansion in the North Atlantic, as well as the Nuclear-Free Scotland campaign and the Scottish Nuclear Freeze campaign (which shares the above address); maintaining a liaison role between the other main organisations in the Scottish peace movement; providing an educational service linked to the above campaigns. Specialist sections

concentrate on Churches, trade unions, youth, students and political parties. Activities involve public demonstrations, production of literature, lobbying of local and national government bodies and the media and generally raising awareness. 120 local branches and 80 affiliated organisations.
Status Voluntary
Publications Scottish CND News (6)

Scottish Civic Trust
24 George Square, Glasgow G2 1EF 041–221 1466
Administrative Director Mrs Sadie Douglas
Aims To stimulate interest in and action for the conservation and improvement of the environment in town and country; to foster high standards in planning, design, restoration and new building.
Activities Has been given the responsibility, by the Scottish Development Department, of commenting on proposals to demolish or alter listed buildings; comments are also sought on future plans. 140 registered civic societies.
Status Charity
Publications New Grapevine (4); The Scottish Review; Annual Report
Historic Buildings at Work: a guide to the historic buildings of Scotland used by central government.

Scottish Conservation Projects Trust (SCP)
70 Main Street, Doune, Central FK16 6BW, Scotland 0786 841479
Director Nicholas Cooke
Aims To promote and support practical environmental conservation by volunteers to improve the wildlife, landscape and amenity value of rural and urban Scotland.
Activities Organising residential work-camps; running training courses in relevant skills; practical help to a network of affiliated local groups; managing special schemes to involve schools, community groups and the unemployed in practical conservation work. The Trust is the Scottish sister-body of the British Trust for Conservation Volunteers (BTCV) and has local offices in Glasgow and Edinburgh; it markets BTCV publications in Scotland, including technical publications on footpaths, hedging, drystone dyking, coast lands, woodlands, waterways and wetlands. 4 branches.
Status Voluntary
Publications Curam (4)

Scottish Co-operatives Development Committee (SCDC)
c/o Co-operative Union, 100 Morrison Street, Glasgow G5 8LP 041–429 2556

Aims   To foster the growth of workers' co-operatives in Scotland.
-NR

Scottish Countryside Rangers Association (SCRA)

Pentland Hills Ranger Centre, Hillend Park, Biggar Road, Edinburgh EH10 7DU
031–445 3383
Secretary   Susan Manson
Aims   To promote and encourage high standards of professionalism amongst countryside rangers in Scotland in all the varied aspects of their work; to assist in the development of communications and exchange of ideas amongst members and between the Association and other agencies.
Activities   Carrying out work on conservation education, safety and wildlife recording; organising training conferences, meetings, field meetings, conferences and displays on Scottish Ranger Services; representation on and regular meetings with other interested organisations; publicising Ranger Services nationally and circulating information on vacancies. Sub-committees on training, education and the journal. Membership open to countryside rangers, to others as non-voting associate members. All the many Ranger Services throughout Scotland are regarded as branches.
Status   Voluntary
Publications   SCRAmble (4)

Scottish Crop Research Institute

Mylnefield, Invergowrie, Dundee, Tayside DD2 5DA, Scotland 08267 731
Contact   Information Officer
Aims   To improve the productivity, quality and health of crops by studying their breeding, culture and protection from diseases and pests; to conduct fundamental research which contributes to the establishment of scientific principles.
Activities   Breeding cultivars of improved quality and yield potential and enhanced pest and disease resistance; barley (especially for malting), swede, rape and kale for forage, potato, raspberry and black currant are major crops in the programme. Improving crop production techniques and providing information benefitting plant breeding by investigating the physiological basis of crop growth (especially potato, raspberry and field bean); weed science is also studied. Improving crop health by devising control measures for fungal, bacterial and viral diseases, for nematode and insect pests which damage crops directly by feeding or indirectly by transmitting or providing pathways for disease infection.

Status   State-aided research institute of the Agricultural and Food Research Council
Publications   Annual Report

Scottish Development Agency (SDA)

120 Bothwell Street, Glasgow G2 7JP
041–248 2700
Activities   The Agency's Small Business Division performs similar functions to the Council for Small Industries in Rural Areas (CoSIRA).
Status   Statutory
-NR

Scottish Development Department

New St Andrew's House, St James Centre, Edinburgh EH1 3SZ 031–556 8400
London Office: Dover House, Whitehall, London SW1A 2AU 01–233 3000
Activities   Responsibilities cover policy and functions affecting the physical development of Scotland, including town and country planning, housing, urban renewal, roads and transport, water supplies and sewerage, control of air and river pollution, building control and conservation of historic buildings and ancient monuments.
Planning   Division 1: Development planning in Grampian, Highland, Borders and Dumfries & Galloway Regions; Orkney, Shetland and Western Isles; Offshore Petroleum Development (Scotland) Act 1975; National Scenic Areas; Countryside (Scotland) Act 1967; liaison with Countryside Commission for Scotland, Nature Conservancy Council and Forestry Commission.
[*Enquiries:* 031–556 8400 ext.5386]
Division 2: Development planning in Strathclyde, Tayside, Fife, Central and Lothian Regions; general planning questions; legislation and land compensation. [*Enquiries:* 031–556 8400 ext.5486]
Housing   Division 1: Local authority housing plans and capital allocation; housing support grant; tenants' rights, including sale of council houses; grants to voluntary bodies.
[*Enquiries:* 031–556 8501 ext.2960]
Division 2: Rehabilitation policy; improvement and repairs grants; home insulation grants; housing action areas; slum clearance; Housing Corporation in Scotland; Housing Associations; Rent Acts; private sector housing. [*Enquiries:* 031–556 8501 ext.2975]
Division 3: Urban renewal policy; urban programme; travelling people; Scottish Special Housing Association.
[*Enquiries:* 031–556 8501 ext.3113]
Estates Services   Advice on all estate development and management problems; operation of Historic Buildings Bureau.
[*Enquiries:* 031–556 8400 ext.4843]
Roads and Transport   Division 1: Motorway and trunk road policy, programming and

financial planning; implementation of trunk road programme; land acquisition and disposal; motorway service areas; crofter counties and township road programmes; grants for road improvements; procedural work on compulsory purchase orders for local authority roads; roads legislation and road traffic legislation; road safety; road noise insulation; Scottish Road Safety Advisory Unit. [*Enquiries:* 031–556 8400 ext.5056]

Division 2: Scottish Transport Group; assistance to ferry services, piers and harbours; orders empowering harbours authorities to improve harbour facilities and control harbour management; Highland transport; rail and air services; bus policy; airports, including assistance to CAA aerodromes; assistance to certain Highlands & Islands air services; grants for provision of rail freight facilities; policy on tolls on Erskine, Forth and Tay Road Bridges; EEC transport matters; road haulage; inland waterways; local roads and public transport policy; transport policies and programmes; Strathclyde Passenger Transport Executive.
[*Enquiries:* 031–556 8400 ext.5158]

Ancient Monuments and Historic Buildings Ancient Monuments Division, 3–11 Melville Street, Edinburgh EH3 7QD: Scheduling; scheduled monument consent; grants toward repair; preservation and presentation of monuments in government care; archaeological investigation of threatened sites; royal parks and palaces.
[*Enquiries:* 031–226 2570 ext.225]

Historic Buildings Division, 25 Drumsheugh Gardens, Edinburgh EH3 7RN: Listing of buildings of architectural and historic importance; listed building consent; conservation areas; grants for monuments, listed buildings and conservation areas. [*Enquiries:* 031–226 3611 ext.265]

Civil Engineering and Water Services Pentland House, 47 Robb's Loan, Edinburgh EH14 1TY Division 1: Structural advice and design; pollution control (aquatic environment); research; water resources and statistics; water bylaws. [*Enquiries:* 031–443 8681 ext.543]

Division 2: Water, sewerage, coast protection and flood prevention schemes; water and sewerage administration, including appeals, water orders, water bylaws, compulsory purchase orders; solid waste disposal; arterial drainage. [*Enquiries:* 031–443 8681 ext.541]

Division 3: Water sewerage, coast protection and flood prevention schemes; PES; estimates and grants; water finance; marine works; fluoridation. [*Enquiries:* 031–443 8681 ext.447]

Pollution Control: Water supply, water pollution, sewerage; radioactive waste management; oil pollution; clean air; noise; statutory nuisances; refuse collection and disposal; litter. [*Enquiries:* 031–443 8681 ext.222]

HM Industrial Pollution Inspectorate for Scotland Pentland House, 47 Robb's Loan, Edinburgh EH14 1TY: Pollution control services, regulatory and advisory; hazardous wastes; air pollution control, radioactive waste management and control of radioactive substances; offensive trades. [*Enquiries:* 031–443 8681 ext.325]

Scottish Education and Action for Development (SEAD)
29 Nicolson Square, Edinburgh EH8 9BX
031–667 0120/0129
Resource Centre: 031–667 8550
Supervisor D. Palmer (Resource Centre)
Aims To promote Scottish/Third World links with a view to a fairer distribution of the world's resources; to educate the Scottish public on Third World problems; to identify and campaign against the causes of economic and social deprivation in Scotland and the Third World.
Activities Providing support and information to interested groups and individuals; maintaining a library and resource centre; research to challenge the role of multinational companies in societies; campaigning for better media coverage and the organisation of courses and conferences relating to key development issues; publishing books and reports on Scottish and Third World development.
Status Charity
Publications SEAD Network (6)
Electronics and Development: Scotland and Malaysia in the international electronics industry. 1985.
Multinationals and Changes in Technology: Scotland and the Third World.
SEAD/Lauder Tech. Coll., 1984.

Scottish Environmental Education Council (SEEC)
c/o Dept of Biology, Paisley College, High Street, Paisley, Strathclyde PA1 2BE, Scotland
041–887 1241
Hon. Secretary Dr D.J. Curtis
Aims To promote environmental education in all sectors of education in Scotland; to provide a forum for the exchange of ideas and information between all the individuals and groups concerned; to act as a national centre for information and advice in this field.
Activities Promoting environmental education through meetings, conferences and occasional publications; providing a computerised information service in collab-

oration with the Council for Environmental Education (CEE); sharing also in the CEE publications; supporting local environmental education projects and initiatives.

Status Voluntary

Publications REED (Review of Environmental Education Developments) (3) (with CEE); CEE Newsheet (10) (with CEE); Annual Report
Learning for Living: environmental education in Scotland. 1985.

Scottish Field Studies Association (SFSA)

Elie Estate Office, Elie, Leven, Fife KY9, Scotland 0333 330133
Kindrogan Field Centre: Enochdhu, Blairgowrie, Tayside PH10 7PG 025081 286

Executive Secretary Alex S. McLeod

Aims To promote the development of field studies in Scotland and to create among all age groups a greater awareness and understanding of the Scottish countryside. [The term 'field studies' embraces a variety of specialist and general subjects, including archaeology, botany, ecology, geography, geology, painting and photography.]

Activities Providing facilities for field studies; courses; consultation and co-operation with statutory and voluntary bodies; maintaining a well-equipped residential field centre at Kindrogan.

Status Voluntary

Publications Annual Report

Scottish Fuel Poverty Action Group (SFPAG)

3–5 Chapel Lane, Falkirk, Central FK1 5BB, Scotland
-NR

Scottish Georgian Society

see ARCHITECTURAL HERITAGE SOCIETY OF SCOTLAND

Scottish Health Education Group (SHEG)

Wood Burn House, 9 Canaan Lane, Edinburgh EH10 4SG 031–447 8044

Media & Publicity Officer John W. Dennison

Aims To improve the lifestyle of the population in relation to health; to help each person to make the best possible choice for optimum health and wellbeing ('Be all you can be').

Activities Applying a vigorous health education policy across Scotland; the programme includes alcohol, smoking, immunisation, dental health, mental health and the elderly.

Status Statutory (Division of the Common Services Agency of the Scottish Health Service)

Scottish Inland Waterways Association (SIWA)

11 Arden Street, Edinburgh EH9 1BR
031–229 7149

Secretary Nancy M. Philp

Aims To promote the use of the Scottish inland waterways for all commercial and recreational purposes.

Activities Co-ordinating the activities of the various local canal societies; promoting the interests of all waterway users to local and national government; developing public knowledge of the inland waterways.

Status Voluntary

Scottish Institute of Agricultural Engineering (SIAE)

Bush Estate, Penicuik, Lothian EH26 0PH, Scotland 031–445 2147

Director Dr D.P. Blight

Aims To conduct research and development in agricultural engineering, with particular reference to the engineering properties of soils, especially the effects of compaction, the mechanisation of potato growing and handling, the conservation of forage, the behaviour of tractors and machinery on slopes and other aspects of engineering of particular importance to agriculture in Scotland.

Activities Design of equipment to measure soil compaction *in situ;* investigations into the soil compaction produced by tractors and machinery; reduced cultivations for cereals.

Status Research institute (in association with the British Society for Research in Agricultural Engineering)

Scottish Landowners' Federation (SLF)

18 Abercromby Place, Edinburgh EH3 6TY
031–556 4466

Director David J. Hughes Hallett

Aims To represent the interests of rural landowners in Scotland.

Activities Lobbying government and statutory organisations; providing advice on technical matters to members. Local branches.

Status Voluntary

Publications Landowning in Scotland (4)
-NR

Scottish Marine Biological Association (SMBA)

Dunstaffnage Marine Research Laboratory, PO Box 3, Oban, Argyll, Strathclyde PA34 4AD, Scotland 0631 62244

Director Prof. R.I. Currie

Activities All aspects of marine research, including environmental studies in the UK and overseas; much of the work of the Laboratory is concerned with waters off the west coast of Scotland, with studies being undertaken

on current movement, sediment processes, biology and in aquaculture. Work is undertaken for both government and private sector.
Status Company limited by guarantee
Publications Annual Report
-NR

Scottish Neighbourhood Energy Action (SNEA)
Unit 1/1, 8 Elliot Place, Finnieston, Glasgow G3 8EP 041–226 3064
Field Officer Tony Nec
Aims To promote and support local insulation and energy advice projects; to assist in providing training opportunities for these projects; to help local projects find funding; to represent the interests of Scottish neighbourhood energy groups to local and national government; to work with similar bodies in England.
Status Voluntary
Publications Heating Action (4)
-NR – L

Scottish Ornithologists' Club (SOC)
21 Regent Terrace, Edinburgh EH7 5BT
031–556 6042
Secretary & Treasurer John C. Davies
Aims To encourage the study of Scottish ornithology and co-ordinate the activities of Scottish ornithologists; to encourage ornithological work in Scotland and conservation of Scottish birds.
Activities Organising two conferences a year; arranging field trips throughout the year; lecture programme for branches during the winter; running the Bird Bookshop, the best ornithological bookshop in the world, the profits from which benefit Scottish ornithology. 13 branches.
Status Voluntary
Publications Scottish Birds (2); SOC News (4)
Thom, Valerie M. *Birds in Scotland.*

Scottish Pure Water Association
3 Moray Drive, Clarkston, Glasgow G76 8NW
041–644 3822
Secretary Mrs Rosemary Morrison
Aims To prevent the addition to the public water supply of fluorides or any other substances intended to affect the human system or likely to cause pollution.
Activities Maintaining a long-standing attempt to have proven scientific findings regarding the dangers of fluoride compounds accepted by political and health authorities in this country; alerting the general public in order to prevent the fluoridation of water supplies in all areas.
Status Voluntary

Scottish Rights of Way Society Ltd
28 Rutland Square, Edinburgh EH1 2BW
031–447 9242
Hon. Secretary R.A. Dickson
Aims To preserve, defend and acquire public rights of way in Scotland; to preserve or restore such rights of way as may be in danger of being lost.
Activities Acting to ensure the erection, restoration and repair of bridges, guideposts, notice or direction boards and plates, fences, stiles, gates and resting places in connection with public rights of way; and also the repairing of the roads or pathways themselves. Defence and prosecution, directly or indirectly, of suits or actions for the preservation or recovery of such rights of way.
Status Voluntary
Publications Annual Report

Scottish River Purification Boards Association (SRPBA)
City Chambers, Glasgow G2 1DU 041–221 9600
Aims To facilitate the exchange of information on river pollution problems.
-NR

Scottish Society for Prevention of Cruelty to Animals (SSPCA)
19 Melville Street, Edinburgh EH3 7PL
031–225 6418/6419
Chief Executive Sir Cameron Rusby, KCB, LVO
Aims To prevent cruelty to animals and to encourage kindness and humanity in their treatment.
Activities The Society's 27 uniformed Inspectors, based from Shetland to Galloway, patrol Edinburgh, Dundee and 25 counties, carrying out the Society's policy of preventing cruelty by education, advice and warning; in serious cases evidence is lodged with Procurators-Fiscal. The Society maintains an animal care centre in Dundee, a rest farm for horses and dog boarding kennels near Edinburgh and has an ambulance for large animals. In special circumstances the Society may meet the cost of veterinary treatment. 47 local branches help by propagating the aims of the Society and raising funds.
Status Charity
Publications Annual Report

Scottish Society for the Prevention of Vivisection (SSPV)
10 Queensferry Street, Edinburgh EH2 4PG
031–225 6039
Director Clive Hollands
Aims To protect animals from cruelty; to prevent the infliction of suffering; to abolish vivisection.
Activities Primarily concerned with influ-

encing the public, particularly Parliamentary opinion, on the way in which animals are used in laboratories in Britain and throughout the world, as well as other aspects of Man's exploitation of the animal kingdom. The Society's Annual Pictorial Review provides a yearbook on animal experimentation and the campaign to oppose all such practices.

Status Voluntary

Publications Annual Pictorial Review (April) (free)

Scottish Solar Energy Group (SSEG)

Dept of Physics, Heriot-Watt University, Riccarton, Edinburgh EH14 4AS 031–449 5111

Secretary Dr J.I.B. Wilson

Aims To promote research, development and application of solar energy in Scotland.

Activities Organising meetings, conferences, seminars and visits; promoting publicity and campaigns for solar energy; disseminating information on solar energy; dealing with general queries on solar energy from the public.

Status Voluntary

Publications Scottish Solar Energy Group Newsletter (3/4)

North Sun 84: proceedings of international conference, Edinburgh 1984.

Scottish Tree Trust

30 Edgemont Street, Shawlands, Glasgow G41 3EL 041–649 2462

President Greer Hart

Aims To set up small reserves in remote areas for the purpose of creating suitable woodlands of native trees; to inspire people all over Scotland to do the same, thus setting up a national network; to enable ordinary people to have more say in the countryside.

Activities Building bothies for later use as work/study centres; planting trees. The Trust has two reserves near Lochgilphead in Argyll, totalling 30 acres of young Scots pine and oak, and an education centre; tree stocks come from two small nurseries and also from city tenement window ledges – the Trust was founded by city-dwellers with a concern for the planet and the destructive forces at work on it. Active support is given to any group campaigning for conservation, with the emphasis on youth. The Trust's funds come from its membership.

Status Charity

Publications Scottish Tree Trust Newsletter

Scottish Wild Land Group (SWLG)

93 Queen Street, Alva, Stirling, Central FK12 5AH, Scotland 0259 60102

Co-ordinator Mrs Terry Smith

Aims To promote the conservation of Scotland's wild land, fauna and flora by increasing public awareness of problems, helping to co-ordinate the efforts of groups and individuals to create a strong voice for conservation and by pressing for the recognition of conservation as an integral part of the national economy.

Activities Maintaining a close watch on relevant developments in Scotland; liaising with other conservation bodies; participating in consultative processes regarding relevant developments; hosting discussions and meetings and giving talks and slide shows on relevant topics; lobbying MPs and government bodies; establishing a network of local contacts throughout Scotland.

Status Voluntary

Publications Wild Land News (2)

Scottish Wildlife Trust (SWT)

25 Johnston Terrace, Edinburgh EH1 2NH 031–226 4602

Chief Executive Bernard Gilchrist

Aims To conserve all forms of wildlife and their habitats in Scotland by establishing reserves, providing interpretative facilities, carrying out surveys and advising landowners and planning authorities.

Activities Volunteers are active through 10 local branches in reserve management, countryside planning, fund raising and promotion. There is a full programme of local activities, including field visits and lectures.

Status Voluntary; charity

Publications Scottish Wildlife (3)

Scottish Youth Hostels Association (SYHA)

7 Glebe Crescent, Stirling, Central FK8 2JA, Scotland 0786 72821

General Secretary James Martin

Aims To help all, but especially young people of limited means living and working in industrial and other areas, to know, use and appreciate the Scottish countryside and places of historic and cultural interest in Scotland; and to promote their health, recreation and education, particularly by providing simple hostel accommodation for them on their travels.

Activities Maintaining 80 youth hostels; providing activity holidays involving pony trekking, sailing, canoeing, hillwalking, wind surfing and cycling. 5 district offices.

Status Voluntary

Publications Scottish Hosteller (2); Handbook (1)

SCRAM (Scottish Campaign to Resist the Atomic Menace)

11 Forth Street, Edinburgh EH1 3LE 031–557 4283/4284

Editor Steve Martin

Aims To inform the public about the hazards of the nuclear fuel chain; to oppose by non-violent means all further nuclear developments in Scotland and elsewhere; and to press for a long-term energy strategy based on energy conservation and the use of renewable energy sources.

Activities Having developed from opposition to the planned reactor at Torness, SCRAM works with groups throughout Britain opposing every aspect of the nuclear chain, from uranium mining to nuclear weapons. The group publishes a journal for the anti-nuclear, safe energy and disarmament movements, runs an extensive information service and library and a mail order service; it has published many pamphlets and a book. Local branches.

Status Voluntary
Publications SCRAM Journal (6)

SCREAM (South Coast Radiation Elimination Action Movement)
This organisation has been disbanded

SDP Greens
69 Cambridge Road, Oakington, Cambridge CB4 5BG 022023 3200
Director Mike Bell
Aims To provide a network for like-minded people within the Social Democratic Party; to promote the ideas and information from the wider Green movement within the SDP; to attract the Green vote to the SDP/Liberal Alliance.
Activities Making submissions to national policy committees; running an information stall and fringe meetings at the Council for Social Democracy and Assembly; producing a newsletter containing news of progress, forthcoming events and reproduced articles from other organisations and magazines.
Status Voluntary
Publications Green View (4)

Sea Energy Associates (Lanchester Polytechnic Wave Energy Group)
Coventry (Lanchester) Polytechnic, Priory Street, Coventry, W. Mids. CV1 5FB 0203 24166 ext.7655
Project Director Dr N.W. Bellamy
Aims To develop a system for extracting energy from ocean waves, particularly for application to island and isolated communities.
Activities Research and development, particularly of the Sea Clam system, using outdoor floating models and mechanical test rigs; mathematical modelling of components and complete system; design studies. Funded by government and industry.
Status Research unit
-NR

Sea Mammal Research Unit
c/o British Antarctic Survey, Madingley Road, Cambridge CB3 0ET 0223 311354
Status Research institute of the Natural Environment Research Council
-NR

Sea Shepherd Fund
see SOCIETY AGAINST VIOLATION OF THE ENVIRONMENT

Seabird Group
c/o Royal Society for the Protection of Birds, The Lodge, Sandy, Beds. SG19 2DL 0767 80551
Assistant Secretary Ms L. Underwood
Aims To circulate news of work in progress on seabirds and to promote co-operative research on them.
Activities Main activities include surveys at breeding colonies of seabirds, annual monitoring of populations, observations of seabirds at sea, winter surveys of beached birds and collection of corpses for scientific examination. Annual grants to members to carry out aspects of this work.
Status Voluntary
Publications Seabird Group Newsletter (3); Seabird (1)

Seal Preservation Action Group
The Green, Scarton, Longhope, Stromness, Orkney KW16 3PG
Activities Campaigning against the killing of seals in British and international waters.
-NR

Seal Sands Conservation Group
Lyndhurst, 111 Roman Road, Linthorpe, Middlesbrough, Cleveland TS5 5QB 0642 819559
Contact Dr Bill Hall
Aims To protect the area of Seal Sands, a Site of Special Scientific Interest in the Tees estuary, from reclamation and development by the Tees & Hartlepool Port Authority.
-NR

Seed Bank and Exchange
Cowcombe Farm, Gipsy Lane, Chalford, Stroud, Glos. GL6 8HP
Co-ordinator Caroline Barnett
Aims To encourage interest in our native wild plants and other vanishing foreign wild species, with a view to developing active concern, especially among farming and forestry interests.
Activities Supplying British wild flower seeds and other unusual medicinal plants from abroad; over 400 varieties available, probably the widest range in the country. All seeds available free to members of the Seed Exchange and also through the mail order catalogue. Publications include a guide, an

information booklet and a newsletter. (Send two 2nd class stamps for details.)
Status Voluntary
Publications Seed Bank & Exchange Newsletter (1)
The Wild Seed Grower's Guide.

Seminarium into the Psyche, Architecture and Rural Knowledge (Centre for Esoteric Studies) (The S*P*A*R*K)

Well Close, Rothbury, Northumberland NE65 7NZ 0669 20430
Director of Studies Derrick Wilbie-Chalk
Aims To be a 'bridge resource' linking intellectual and professional knowledge and expertise with spiritual and psychic sensitivity to meet the increasingly urgent desire of individuals to heighten both their personal and group consciousness in their search for truth, beauty and greater understanding.
Activities Strategically sited in rural Northumberland, the Seminarium caters for small groups of students researching into the region's early Christian past and the earth configurations and energies of its more sacred areas. Study of the psyche and alternative therapies, including music, colour and dance, will lead to courses in the appreciation of art and architecture, with particular reference to nature and the local early culture; students wishing to carry out private research along similar lines may use it as a base. Facilities include a library, research room/drawing office, music room and garden; field trips are organised to archaeological sites, old buildings and landscape-temples; visiting lecturers; personal counselling. Maintains links with bodies in the north-east with similar interests.
Status Research centre
Publications The S*P*A*R*K (occasional)

SERA (Socialist Environment and Resources Association)

9 Poland Street, London W1V 3DG 01-439 3749
Co-ordinator Andy Roberts
Aims To formulate socialist policies toward the environment and enlist the support of the labour movement; to demonstrate the relevance of such policies to other environmental organisations and the general public.
Activities Organising within the trade unions, the Labour Party and generally on the left, to introduce an ecological perspective into socialist thinking; persuading local councillors, MPs and journalists to take environmental issues seriously; holding public meetings and conferences to link people together and discuss the issues; writing and publishing to provide information which will be useful to people working for democratic control of the economy and of technology. Local branches.

Status Voluntary
Publications New Ground (4)
-NR

Severn Barrage Group

University of Bristol, Senate House, Bristol, Avon BS8 1TH 0272 24161
-NR

Severn-Trent Water Authority

Abelson House, 2297 Coventry Road, Sheldon, Birmingham B26 3PU 021-743 4222
Regional Manager, Information Services Bob Mozley
Aims To manage the complete water cycle within the Trent and Severn Basins, including water supply, water reclamation, land drainage, pollution control, fisheries, conservation and recreation.
Activities Providing services concerned with water supply and distribution, sources management, purification and the creation and maintenance of the distribution system; movement of waste water from the consumer to water reclamation works and provision of suitable treatment to ensure the return of suitably pure water to the river system; creation and maintenance of land drainage and flood prevention works; monitoring and control of pollution; control of fisheries; provision of recreational facilities.
Status Statutory
Publications Stream (12)

Shareholders Question Investment in the Arms Race (SQIAR)

Pump Close, Shilton, Burford, Oxon. OX8 4AB 0993842 480
Co-ordinator Margot Miller
Aims To collect together a group of people interested in investing small amounts in shares in the major nuclear weapons manufacturing companies in the UK, to raise the debate about the design, manufacture and deployment of these weapons amongst shareholders and directors.
Activities Purchasing minimal amounts of shares; following company reports and the financial press; raising questions to boards of directors, attending company AGMs, EGMs, etc.
Status Voluntary

Sheffield Centre for Environmental Research (SCER)

356 Glossop Road, Sheffield, S. Yorks. S10 2HW 0742 731650
Director & Secretary P.A. Booth
Aims To promote research in, and to advance knowledge of and education in, the planning and design of the physical and social environment.
Activities Undertaking research contracts

with local and national organisations;
research seminars; continuing professional
development courses.
Status Charity

Shell Better Britain Campaign (SBBC)
c/o Nature Conservancy Council, Northminster
House, Northminster Road, Peterborough,
Cambs. PE1 1UA 0733 40345
Administrator Mrs V. Pollard
Aims To help voluntary community groups
protect or improve their environment for the
benefit of the community through practical
action schemes.
Activities Providing information through
the Campaign Information Pack; advice from
representatives of the partners (British Trust
for Conservation Volunteers, Civic Trust,
Nature Conservancy Council, Shell UK Ltd).
Small grants available to help groups get
things done; campaign workshops where
participants can share problems; travel
grants for training courses and visits to other
environmental projects; achievement
awards in recognition of outstanding work
carried out by groups.
Publications Better Times (2)
Campaign Information Pack.

Shell UK Oil
PO Box 148, Shell-Mex House, Strand,
London WC2R 0DX 01–438 3000
-NR

Shropshire Trust for Nature Conservation (STNC)
Agriculture House, Barker Street, Shrewsbury,
Shropshire SY1 1QP 0743 241691
Conservation Officer John J. Tucker
Aims To promote nature conservation in
Shropshire.
Activities Acquiring and managing nature
reserves; providing advice on conservation
management; conservation education. 12
branches.
Status Voluntary
Publications Shropshire Wildlife (3)
Ecological Flora of the Shropshire Region.
1985. 368pp.

Skills Exchange Network for a Stable Economy (SENSE)
1 Merstow Cottages, Merstow Place, Evesham,
Worcs. WR11 4AY
Co-ordinator John Porter
Aims To facilitate contact between people
wishing to learn and exchange practical
skills.
Activities Contacting and providing lists of
people nation-wide who are willing to teach
a variety of skills; publishing a newsletter
listing courses and other information about
opportunities for learning skills more formally

(SENSE does not originate courses itself).
The network depends entirely on people
volunteering their help (s.a.e. for details).
Status Voluntary
Publications SENSE Newsletter (2)

Slowboat Travel
39 Botley Road, Oxford OX2 0PT 0865 247675
Aims To contribute to the redevelopment
of canal transport, not only through fare-
paying passengers but also by moving
freight.
Activities Offers canal holidays on a
70–foot narrowboat travelling between
Camden Lock and Runcorn, April-October;
passengers can board or leave the boat at
will, like using a train.

Small Communities Research Union (SCRU)
13 The Rose Walk, Newhaven, E. Sussex
BN9 9NH 07912 4980
Aims To build up a body of knowledge
which will help communities to form; to help
people form groups and find land and
finance.
Publications SCRUtiny
-NR

Small Industries Group (Somerset)
Dunwear Bungalow, River Lane, Dunwear,
Bridgwater, Somerset TA7 0AA 0278 424456
Development Officer Fred Wedlake, MBE
Aims To tackle unemployment by helping
new businesses to start; to help existing businesses to expand, encouraging and stimulating local trade and providing new job
opportunities for young people.
Activities Developing derelict sites for
starter or permanent premises; counselling
and advice on problems; help with planning
and other applications to local, district and
county councils; producing a trades directory; mounting exhibitions. All services are
free and confidential. (Similar SIGs have
been set up in Dorset and Devon.)
Status Voluntary
Publications Directory of Members,
Trades & Services
-NR

Smallfarmers' Association (SFA)
PO Box 71, Beaufort House, 15 St Botolph Street,
London EC3A 7HR 01–247 4187
Hon. Secretary Mrs Ruth Weiss
Aims To promote the family farm; to make
farming more accessible to new entrants; to
prevent the decline of rural communities.
Activities Making Parliamentary
submissions, e.g. to the Select Committee
on Agriculture; making representations to
committees of inquiry; publicising objectives through publications and the media;
liaising with MPs; holding seminars and

conferences and producing conference reports. The Association works at a national level, but local groups are based on constituencies in order to relate more effectively to local MPs.
Status Voluntary
Publications The Smallfarmer (6); Annual Report

Smallholders' Association
Tollywood Farm, Bishop's Lydeard, Taunton, Somerset TA4 3BT 0823 432279
Aims To represent smallholders and those who pursue some form of self-sufficiency.
-NR

Smiling Sun
11 Forth Street, Edinburgh EH1 3LE 031-557 4283/4284
Aims To inform and educate people on issues related to energy, particularly nuclear power and nuclear weapons.
Activities Running a shop and information centre and a mail order service; stalls at local events and festivals.
Status Voluntary
-NR

Snowdonia National Park Authority
National Park Office, Penrhyndeudraeth, Gwynedd LL48 6LS, Wales 0766 770274
Information Officer Miss Marian Rees
Aims To preserve the natural beauty of the Snowdonia area and to promote access for recreational activities compatible with that area whilst having due regard for the economic welfare of its inhabitants.
Activities Environmental advice on agriculture and forestry, planning, information, wardening and estate work.
Status Statutory (Dept of Gwynedd County Council)

Social Democratic Green Group
see SDP GREENS

Social Science Research Council
see ECONOMIC AND SOCIAL RESEARCH COUNCIL

Socialist Countryside Group (SCG)
9 Poland street, London W1V 3DG 01-439 3749
Aims To bring rural social and ecological issues to the attention of the labour movement and to campaign for socialist policies within rural areas.
Activities Publishing discussion papers on heritage, the rural economy, agricultural subsidies, pollution, etc.; consequent campaigning, often in conjunction with other organisations, with emphasis on local campaigns and activities. Local branches.
Status Voluntary

Publications Socialist Countryside Group Newsletter
-NR

Socialist Environmental Scientists Group
c/o Dept of Oceanography, University of Liverpool, Bedford Street North, Liverpool L69 3BX
-NR

Society Against Violation of the Environment (SAVE)
[formerly Sea Shepherd Fund]
40 Kelvingrove Street, Glasgow G3 7RZ 041-332 4903
Director David McColl
Aims To campaign on issues of ecological concern, particularly in connection with wildlife and environmental pollution.
Activities Ongoing campaigns include: a 3-year whale and dolphin investigation project to ensure compliance with the International Whaling Commission's moratorium and to highlight the massive slaughters of dolphins and porpoises around the world; actions against seal hunts around the world (Canada, South Africa, Uruguay, Norway, etc.); investigating the indiscriminate slaughter of seabirds in the North Atlantic; and lobbying against the continued irresponsible dumping of nuclear, toxic and industrial wastes.
Status Voluntary
Publications SAVE Report (4)
Pirate Whaling: a history of the subversion of international regulations. 1985.

Society for Environmental Improvement Ltd (SEI)
Crickhowell, Powys NP8 1TA, Wales
Activities Operating the Centre for Alternative Technology, Machynlleth. [see separate entry]
Status Charity

Society for Environmental Therapy (SET)
31 Sarah Street, Darwen, Blackburn, Lancs. BB3 3ET
Secretary Andy Beckingham
Aims To research into the environmental causes of disease; to promote low-technology medicine; to communicate the findings of both lay and professional members.
Activities Examining illness caused by food, air or water and listening open-mindedly to reports of safe treatments, avoiding the trap of labelling ideas as 'unorthodox'; holding scientific conferences; analysing support and treatment for sufferers; carrying out research and producing a newsletter containing lay and scientific reports and features on members' work and ideas. The

Society shares the science journal *Nutrition and Health* with the McCarrison Society and has published an anthology of papers. Local branches.
Status Charity
Publications SET Newsletter
-NR

Society for the Interpretation of Britain's Heritage (SIBH)
10 Priory Crescent, Lewes, E. Sussex BN7 1HP
0273 472970 (H) 0273 475400 ext.722 (B)
Secretary Bill Lanning
Aims To encourage a high standard of interpretation to heighten public awareness and appreciation of Britain's heritage; to provide a forum for discussion and exch-ange of ideas; to disseminate knowledge of interpretive philosophy, principles and techniques; to promote the value and role of interpretation.
Activities Holding one or two national weekend conferences a year to study inter-pretive techniques in various parts of the UK, plus an additional annual national meeting/seminar to look in detail at a theor-etical or practical aspect of interpretive technique; series of regional meetings, work-shops or seminars reflecting the needs and interests of the membership; publishing conference proceedings and advisory leaflets on specific aspects of practice; running a national award scheme (the Carnegie Interpret Britain Award) reco-gnising good interpretive practice; making representations on national issues which affect the main aims and objectives of the Society.
Status Voluntary
Publications Heritage Interpretation (3)
Feehally, Maya, *Helping the Stones to Speak*, 1984.

Society for the Preservation of Beers from the Wood
Ye Olde Watling, Bow Lane, London
EC4M 9AY 01-855 1040
-NR

Society for the Protection of Ancient Build-ings (SPAB)
37 Spital Square, London E1 6DY 01-377 1644
Secretary Philip Venning
Aims To educate public opinion in the proper treatment of ancient buildings and to prevent ill-considered and conjectural restoration.
Activities Giving the benefit of the Society's long experience in the repair and reconditioning or adaptation of ancient build-ings to all who are concerned with such work; running courses and scholarships, seminars and lectures; working to secure

the protection of old buildings, large or small, as an integral part of the historical and archi-tectural heritage of the nation. Branches in Avon, Norfolk and Yorkshire.
Status Charity
Publications SPAB Journal (4)

Society for Radiological Protection (SRP)
c/o NRPB, Chilton, Didcot, Oxon. OX11 0RQ
0235 831600
Hon. Secretary G.C. Roberts (ext.348)
Aims To aid in the development of the scientific, technological, medical and legal aspects of radiological protection, including nuclear safety, and allied subjects in the manner of a learned society; and to promote and improve radiological protection as a profession.
Activities Meetings, conferences and lectures, with emphasis on those subjects which contribute to the knowledge and prac-tice of radiological protection; recognition of individual achievement by the award of medals and bursaries; has established a certificate of competence in applied health physics for suitably qualified and experi-enced persons.
Status Voluntary; learned society
Publications Journal of the Society for Radiological Protection (4)

Society of Chemical Industry
14–15 Belgrave Square, London SW1X 8PS
01–235 3681
Activities Interests include air and water pollution.
-NR

Society for Clean Air (0273)26313

Society of Environmental Engineers (SEE)
Owles Hall, Owles Lane, Buntingford, Herts.
SG9 9PL 0763 71209
Activities Concerned with engineering and technical aspects of the environment, including contamination control.
-NR

Society of Homoeopaths
101 Sebastian Avenue, Shenfield, Essex
CM15 8PP
Hon. Secretary S.A. Tibbs
Aims To provide support for professional homoeopaths and those training to become such; to develop and maintain high standards for the practice of homoeopathy; to provide facilities by which members can exercise, develop and disseminate their knowledge, skill and experience.
Activities Organising public and private seminars, professional conferences and Society meetings; maintaining a register of professional practitioners who meet the standards of the Society and comply with its

code of ethics and rules of practice.
Regional groups.
Status Professional association; company
limited by guarantee
Publications The Homoeopath (4)
-NR

Society of Irish Foresters/Cumann Forao-iseoiri Na Eireann
c/o Royal Dublin Society, Ballsbridge, Dublin 4,
Ireland 0001–86 7751
Hon. Secretary Eugene Griffin
Aims To advance and spread in Ireland
the knowledge of forestry in all its aspects.
Activities Holding indoor and outdoor
meetings on topics relating to forestry;
annual study tour and guided forest walks;
publishing a scientific journal.
Status Voluntary
Publications Irish Forestry (2)
O'Carroll, Niall (ed.), *The Forests of Ireland*,
2nd edn, Turol/Marion Boyars, 1984.

Society of Occupational Medicine
c/o Royal College of Physicians, 11 St Andrews
Place, London NW1 4LE 01–486 2641
Activities Concerns include the medical
aspects of noise and other pollutants in the
working environment.
Publications Journal of the Society of Occupational Medicine (4)
-NR

Society of Osteopaths
12 College Road, Eastbourne, E. Sussex
BN21 4HZ 0323 638606
-NR

Society of Sussex Downsmen
93 Church Road, Hove, E. Sussex BN3 2BA
0273 771906
General Secretary Philip Palmer
Aims To protect the Sussex Downs and to
encourage their use in ways that will not
spoil their beauty and traditional character.
Activities Opposing unsuitable development; encouraging improvement projects;
consulting with local planning authorities and
liaising with other bodies; making grants
available to suitable projects; weekend walks
and other activities.
Status Voluntary; charity
Publications News Sheet; Annual Report

Society of Teachers of the Alexander Tech-nique (STAT)
10 London House, 266 Fulham Road, London
SW10 9EL 01–351 0828
Executive Secretary Mrs S. Langley
Aims To make the Alexander Technique
more widely known and to maintain
professional standards; to facilitate contact
between members; to encourage research;

to prevent abuse or exploitation by untrained
members.
Activities Providing information on the
Alexander Technique and lists of teachers
throughout the world.
Status Professional association
Publications Newsletter (2); Journal
(occasional)

Soil and Water Management Association (SaWMA)
22 Edgerton Grove Road, Huddersfield,
W. Yorks. HD1 5QX 0484 29417
Technical Secretary Geoff Baldwin
Aims To promote knowledge of methods
and theories on treatment, cultivation,
drainage and irrigation of soils.
Activities Training courses and workshops
combining conferences and demonstration
sessions; visits to farms, estates and research
stations; technical exhibits at major agricultural shows and demonstrations; publishing a
journal and booklets.
Status Voluntary; charity
Publications Soil and Water (4)

Soil Association
Walnut Tree Manor, Haughley, Stowmarket,
Suffolk IP14 3RS 044970 235
Contact General Secretary
Aims To promote organic farming and
discourage the indiscriminate use of
persistent pesticides and artificial fertilisers.
Activities Advising farmers who wish to
know more about organic husbandry;
conducting courses in the principles and
practice of organic husbandry; demonstrating the advantages of organic methods
through conferences, lectures and exhibitions; sponsoring the marketing of organic
produce; promoting research and arranging
field trials; co-operating with other organisations in the ecological movement; issuing a
magazine and running a bookshop. Local
groups.
Status Charity
Publications Soil Association Journal (12)
-NR – L

Soil Survey of England and Wales (SSEW)
Rothamsted Experimental Station, Harpenden,
Herts. AL5 2JQ 05827 63133
Head of Survey Dr P. Bullock
Aims To evaluate the soil resources of
England and Wales and contribute to their
efficient use; specifically, to collect and
organise information about the soil types of
the country in the form of classifications,
maps and explanatory texts that can be used
in transferring results of research and experience in land use from one area to another
and in planning further research.
Activities Production of soil maps at

various scales, including consultancy work
for the private sector; interpreting maps and
soil experience, thus providing objective
information invaluable to farmers, foresters,
educationalists, environmentalists, planners,
civil engineers and water authorities; developing a soil information system for evaluating soil properties and predicting the suitability of land for potential uses – this system
will output data in the form of reports, tabu-
lations, statistical summaries and graphics,
including derivative maps. 6 regional
centres, 11 sub-centres.
Status State-aided institute of the Agricultural and Food Research Council
Publications Annual Report
Regional Bulletins (Soils and their use in individual regions)

Solar Energy Laboratory
Dept of Mechanical Engineering, University of
Birmingham, Birmingham B15 2TT
021–472 1301
-NR

Solar Energy Ltd
8–16 South Wharf Road, London W2 1PE
01–258 0443
-NR

Solar Energy Unit (SEU)
Dept of Mechanical Engineering & Energy
Studies, University College, Newport Road,
Cardiff CF2 1TA 0222 44211
Director Prof. B.J. Brinkworth
Aims To conduct research, development
and testing of equipment for the applications
of solar energy.
Activities Research on systems and
components for solar energy thermal and
electrical energy conversion; computer
modelling and simulation; testing and certification of equipment; monitoring of meteorological data and live system performance;
participation in international collaboration
through the European Community and the
International Energy Agency; contributing to
the framing of British and International Standards. Staff of the Unit issue about 50 technical reports and 20 publications per year.
Status Research institute
Publications Helios (3); Directory of
Suppliers & Services in Renewable Energy
(1)

Solar Trade Association (STA)
19 Albemarle Street, London W1X 3HA
01–629 7459
Aims To raise standards within the solar
industry and to provide a greater understanding among the public, government and
media of the advantages of solar energy use;

to support the industry in its export
endeavours.
Activities Working for changes in the law
to facilitate more widespread application of
solar technology; keeping members
informed about standards, legislation, regulations and advances in technology; concili-
ation and arbitration services deal with
problems arising between members and
customers.
Status Trade association; company limited
by guarantee
Publications Solar Trade Association
Newsletter (12)

Solid Fuel Advisory Service (SFAS)
Hobart House, Grosvenor Place, London
SW1X 7AE 01–235 2020
Aims To provide a full technical and
advisory service on all matters relating to solid
fuel and solid fuel heating.
Activities Providing advice through 8
regional offices and 60 local offices.
-NR

Solid Smokeless Fuels Federation
Devonshire House, Church Street, Sutton-in-
Ashfield, Notts. NG17 1AE 0623 550411
General Manager I. MacKay
Aims To promote the development and
efficient use of solid smokeless fuels for
domestic use, combining the resources of the
whole solid fuel industry in co-operation
with local authorities and government
departments.
Activities Providing a comprehensive
range of services to local authorities and
private householders through mobile and
static exhibitions and literature giving guidance and advice on the correct use of solid
smokeless fuels and appliances, house
improvements, clean air and general house
heating.
Status Non-profit organisation

Solway Marine Investigations
Grove Cottage, Birkby, Maryport, Cumbria
CA15 0RG 0900 813159
Contact Dr E.J. Perkins
Activities Research and consultancy in
marine pollution, sediment transport, effects
of drilling and dredging, etc.
Status Consultancy
-NR

Solway River Purification Board
Rivers House, Irongray Road, Dumfries,
Dumfries & Galloway DG2 0JE 0387 720502
Director C.P. James
Aims To prevent pollution of the rivers of
south-west Scotland.
Activities Administration of pollution
prevention legislation, including inspecting

and sampling of discharges to rivers, and the rivers and tidal waters themselves; issuing consents to discharges; maintaining a hydrological network of river gauging and rainfall measurement stations. Divisional office at Newton Stewart.
Status Statutory
Publications Annual Report

Somerset Trust for Nature Conservation (STNC)

Fyne Court, Broomfield, Bridgwater, Somerset TA5 2EQ 082345 587
Chairman Dr C.E.D. Smith
Aims To safeguard the wildlife of Somerset.
Activities Acquiring and managing nature reserves; running nature trails and guided walks; lobbying for wildlife preservation. Local branches.
Status Voluntary
Publications Somerset Trust for Nature Conservation Newsletter (3)

Sons of Neptune Group

1 Cromwell Parade, Scarborough, N. Yorks. YO11 2DP 0723 360828
Contact Freddie Drabble (founder member)
Aims To oppose the building of sewage works on Scarborough's Marine Drive and generally to oppose pollution of the heritage coast in the Scarborough area.
Activities Regular meetings to discuss progress of current projects; letters to the press; contact with other groups in the cause of conservation work; involvement in other areas of conservation activity with special reference to the coastline; occasional charity events.
Status Voluntary

South London Consortium (SLC)

125 Camberwell Road, London SE5 0HB 01–701 0326
Deputy Director Miss Mary E. Ince
Aims To carry out research and development in all technical aspects of housing and in energy-related matters.
Activities Development of procedures for: energy efficiency in local authority buildings; dealing with condensation; transferring technical/research information to officers of member authorities.
Status Joint committee of local authorities (London Boroughs of Lambeth, Lewisham and Southwark)

South of Scotland Electricity Board (SSEB)

Cathcart House, Spean Street, Glasgow G44 4BE 041–637 7177
Aims To initiate and undertake the development of all means of generation of electricity in the South of Scotland district; to plan and carry out an efficient and economical distribution of supplies of electricity to persons in that district. The Board consists of a chairman and 4–8 other members appointed by the Secretary of State for Scotland.
Status Statutory
Publications Annual Report & Accounts -NR

South West Water Authority

3–5 Barnfield Road, Exeter, Devon EX1 1RE 0392 50861
Activities Responsible for water supply, water conservation, sewerage and sewage disposal, prevention of river pollution, fisheries, land drainage and the recreational use of waters in the south-west of England.
Status Statutory -NR

South West Way Association

1 Orchard Drive, Kingskerswell, Newton Abbot, Devon TQ12 5DG 08047 3061
Membership Secretary Mrs Mary Macleod
Aims To make the path a continuous walk, without gaps, and indeed to get it finished; to see that this, a coastal path, is wherever possible really on the coast and is a true footpath, not on roads nor merely running alongside them; to improve standards of waymarking and maintenance.
Activities Providing a body of informed opinion to promote the interests of users of the South West Way; some of the membership have considerable experience of long distance path walking and can offer practical advice of the kind usually needed by walkers. The Association publishes a newsletter, a guide and two footpath descriptions a year.
Status Charity
Publications South West Way Association Newsletter (2); Annual Guide

Southern Water Authority

Guildbourne House, Worthing, W. Sussex BN11 1LD 0903 205252
Activities Responsible for water supply, water conservation, sewerage and sewage disposal, prevention of river pollution, fisheries, land drainage and the recreational use of waters in the southern counties catchment area.
Status Statutory -NR

St Andrew Animal Fund

10 Queensferry Street, Edinburgh EH2 4PG 031–225 2116
Secretary Clive Hollands
Aims To promote humane attitudes toward

animal life and the development of a proper understanding and appreciation of all living things.
Activities Providing financial and other support for projects designed for the welfare and protection of animals, including grants for the development of humane, non-animal methods of research; no task too great nor too small.
Status Voluntary; charity

Staffordshire Nature Conservation Trust (SNCT)
Coutts House, Sandon, Stafford ST18 0DN 08897 534
Hon. Secretary H. Haseley
Aims To protect the countryside, the habitats found there and the plants, birds and animals that live there; to encourage people of all ages, particularly the young, to take a pride and interest in the richly varied countryside of Staffordshire and to respect its wildlife wherever it may occur.
Activities Establishing nature reserves, with a variety of habitats, for the protection of species of plants and animals found in the county; 1,000 acres of reserves are controlled and managed by the Trust for the benefit and promotion of wildlife; providing advice for local authorities, farmers, landowners and others to encourage them to practise conservation in all activities involving the use of their land; providing information for members of the Trust about its activities; educating members and the public through talks, lectures and visits. 8 local groups.
Status Voluntary
Publications SNCT Newsletter (2)

Standing Committee of Analysts to Review Methods for Quality Control of the Water Cycle (SCA)
see DEPARTMENT OF THE ENVIRONMENT, Water Directorate

Standing Joint Committee on Natural Stones
Admin House, Market Square (North Side), Leighton Buzzard, Beds. LU7 0525 375252
Aims To represent trade and professional organisations concerned with the use of natural stone for structural purposes and with its preservation.
-NR

Stoke Lacy Herb Farm
Bromyard, Herefordshire HR7 4HJ 043278 232
Activities Runs occasional half-day herb schools in the summer, including instruction on growing, propagating, harvesting and after-preparation of herbs.
-NR

Stone Federation
Admin House, Market Square (North Side), Leighton Buzzard, Beds. LU7 0525 375252
Aims To represent the interests of the natural stone industries for structural purposes, including cleaning and restoration.
Status Trade association
-NR

Stop Sizewell B Association (SSBA)
PO Box 9, Leiston, Suffolk IP16
Membership Secretary Gillian Bargh
Aims To oppose the building of a Pressurised Water Reactor at Sizewell in Suffolk.
Status Voluntary
Publications Newsletter (occasional)

Streetwork
c/o Notting Dale Urban Studies Centre, 189 Freston Road, London W10 6TH 01-968 5440
Contact Diana Shockness, Debbie McMullen
Aims To promote urban environmental education, helping people of all ages to understand, analyse and finally improve their own surroundings.
Activities Undertaking research; promoting urban studies centres; providing an advisory service; workshops and seminars for teachers, planners, community groups, etc.; publishing a bulletin.
Status Voluntary; charity
Publications BEE (Bulletin of Environmental Education) (12)

Stroud Green Forum
23 Lower Street, Stroud, Glos. GL5 3LE 04536 70962
Co-ordinator John Marjoram
Aims To strengthen links between those working for the environment, peace, alternatives, social justice and spiritual development; to find new ways to resolve conflicts by working together with groups and sharing viewpoints.
Activities Organising talks, debates, dayschools, exhibitions, displays and a local Spring Festival.
Status Voluntary
Publications Green Forum Journal (4)

Structural Insulation Association (SIA)
45 Sheen Lane, London SW14 8AB 01-876 4415
Secretary John Fairley
Aims To press for higher standards of thermal insulation for all types of buildings; to urge the regulatory authorities to introduce a mandatory thermal insulation standard for ground floors in new housing; to urge government to provide improved financial incentives toward the cost of insulating existing buildings and to increase its publicity about the advantages of thermal insulation; to press

for more realistic sound insulation requirements for separating walls and floors in
housing; to monitor Building Research
Establishment and other government publications concerned with fire protection
topics; to urge the case through the media
for greater and more efficient use of
insulation.
Activities Maintaining close contact with
relevant government departments; representing members' interests, especially on
British Standards Institution committees;
producing publications; action in furtherance
of above aims.
Status Trade association
Publications *Thermal Insulation of
Buildings.*

Student Ecology Movement
see STUDENT GREEN NETWORK

Student Green Network (SGN)
13 King Street, Cross Heath, Newcastle-under-
Lyme, Staffs. ST5 9HQ
Contact Robin Wiles
Aims To promote Green philosophies
amongst students.
Activities SGN is a network of Green
groups in colleges in the UK; the groups are
entirely autonomous and share no one ideo-
logical line, being free to affiliate to any
other body. SGN conferences are hosted by
different Green groups in turn, providing a
chance for groups to share experiences and
for the host group to stimulate interest on
campus. A newsletter is produced, usually
by a different Green group each time. More
than 30 such groups are now part of the
network.
Status Informal network
Publications Student Green Network
Newsletter
-NR – L

Students Against Nuclear Energy (SANE)
9 Poland Street, London W1V 3DG
-NR

Students Against Nuclear Energy (Scotland) (SANE Scotland)
11 Forth Street, Edinburgh EH1 3LE
031–557 4283/4284
Aims To inform students about the dangers
of nuclear power and nuclear weapons and
the links between them; to campaign for an
end to nuclear/military research and recruitment in colleges; to promote the potential for
jobs conversion to socially useful work.
Activities Campaigning to stop companies
involved in the military/nuclear industrial
complex recruiting amongst college students
on campus and to end their funding of
courses, etc.; informing students about the

links between nuclear power and weapons
and campaigning against both; calling for the
removal of resources from military and
nuclear bodies and their transference to non-
military sources and uses. Membership
open to all, including non-students. Company
profiles and broadsheets produced.
Status Voluntary
Publications SANE Scotland Newsletter
-NR

Suffolk Countryside Campaign
Greenacre, Beyton, Bury St Edmunds, Suffolk
IP30 9AB 0359 70491
Organiser John Matthissen
Aims To preserve the Suffolk countryside
while it is still a heritage and before it
becomes a memory; to help environmentally-
aware farmers faced with competition from
agribusiness.
Activities Petitioning for the withdrawal of
grants which aid landscape destruction; initiating Parish Landscape Surveys which docu-
ment the erosion of traditional landscape;
publicising good practice in conservation;
lobbying councillors and MPs.
Status Voluntary
-NR

Suffolk Preservation Society (SPS)
Little Hall, Market Place, Lavenham, Sudbury,
Suffolk CO10 9QZ 0787 247179
Director John Popham
Aims To promote the protection, preservation and improvement of the countryside,
towns and villages of the County of Suffolk.
Activities Campaigning for a better
environment for Suffolk; monitoring planning
applications and landscape change with
district committees and parish representatives; restoration of buildings; free advisory
service on planning, landscape and architectural matters; publication of architectural
trails; members' events. Local branches.
Status Voluntary
Publications Preservation News (3)

Suffolk Trust for Nature Conservation (STNC)
Park Cottage, Peasenhall, Saxmundham, Suffolk
IP17 1DQ 0728 3765
Director D.R. Moore
Aims To conserve in Suffolk our natural
heritage of wildlife for the benefit of this and
future generations.
Activities Owns or manages 40 nature
reserves; educates the public, especially
young people, about wildlife; advises landowners and others about conservation of the
countryside. 8,000 members. 12 local
branches.
Status Voluntary; charity

Publications Suffolk Trust for Nature Conservation Newsletter (3)

Support Community Building Design Ltd (SUPPORT)
1 Ferdinand Place, London NW1 8EE
01–482 0595
Aims To develop and design new buildings or conversions to meet the needs and budgets of tenants' associations, women's organisations, ethnic minorities and other community groups; to support their control over the development of the projects and the design of the buildings they use.
Activities Offers a complete range of architectural services as well as feasibility and costing advice to groups London-wide; works collectively with representatives of the project, explaining fully the technical and design aspects and thus enabling real participation in design by client groups. The main types of projects are community centres, tenants' halls, workplaces and community resources, women's projects, nurseries and play projects, youth facilities, ethnic minority projects, projects for the disabled, open space projects and housing.
Status Co-operative

Surrey Trust for Nature Conservation (STNC)
Hatchlands, East Clandon, Guildford, Surrey GU4 7RT 0483 223526
Hon. Administrative Secretary Miss G.E. Dougherty
Aims To acquire, maintain and manage nature reserves for the conservation of wild species living naturally within them; to record, study and protect sites of ecological interest.
Activities Promoting, organising and encouraging study and research for the wider education in and appreciation of our countryside; arranging field meetings, recording groups and open days at reserves; carrying out practical conservation work, using the Trust's volunteer conservation corps; giving information and advice to local authorities to help in the preparation of structure plans; investigating and advising on threats to the environment. Was the first county Trust to organise an Educational Nature Trail and subsequently develop a permanent educational facility at one of its reserves. Local branches.
Status Voluntary
Publications Surrey Trust for Nature Conservation Newsletter (3)
-NR

Survival International
29 Craven Street, London WC2N 5NT
01–839 3267
Projects Officer Marcus Colchester

Aims To defend the rights of threatened tribal peoples to survival, self-determination and the use and ownership of their traditional lands.
Activities Supporting projects with tribal peoples in the fields of health, education and land rights; speaking out on tribal people's rights; publishing on the problems faced by tribal peoples and the solutions they themselves propose; representing tribal peoples at human rights fora; educating the public through speakers, films, slide shows and exhibitions. 4 branches.
Status Voluntary
Publications Survival International News (4); Survival International Review (1); SI Urgent Action Bulletin (12)
Is God an American?
Witness to Genocide.

Sussex Alliance for Nuclear Disarmament (SAND)
187 Eastern Road, Brighton, E. Sussex BN2 5BB
0273 681181
Secretary Ms Eileen Daffern
Aims To enable peace and disarmament groups in Sussex to exchange ideas and information, provide mutual support and plan activities in common.
Activities All groups campaign against the escalation of the nuclear weapons race represented by cruise, Pershing and Trident missiles; they study non-nuclear defence options and deplore money spent on preparation for war rather than on alleviating poverty at home and world-wide.
Status Voluntary alliance
Publications SAND Newsletter (12)

Sussex Trust for Nature Conservation
Woods Mill, Shoreham Road, Henfield, W. Sussex BN5 9SD 0273 492630
Administrative Officer Miss Catherine Eldridge
Aims To establish and maintain nature reserves; to promote public interest in wildlife and the countryside.
Activities Maintaining 40 nature reserves through the Trust's volunteer conservation corps; promoting interest in natural history and conservation through educational work with children and adults, including organising school parties three days a week and day courses for adults once a month. 12 regional groups, each with its own programme of events; several Watch groups for children.
Status Charity
Publications Sussex Trust for Nature Conservation Newsletter (3)

Swan Rescue Service
Shotesham St Mary, Norwich, Norfolk NR15 1XX
050842 248
Contact   Rina, Sheila or Len
Aims   To rescue, treat and care for swans
in Britain injured by human leisure activities,
power cables, etc.; to alleviate unnecessary
suffering inflicted by man.
Activities   Rescue, treatment, fund raising,
producing artwork for merchandise sales.

Status   Voluntary; charity
Publications   Swan Rescue Service News-
letter (2)
Townsend, Pamela, *White Spirit, Fly Free,*
Sidgwick & Jackson/Corgi.

Swansea Energy Group
This group no longer exists

T

TACIN (Town and Country Information Network)
Upper Butts, Orcop, Herefordshire HR2 8SF
0981 540263
Prestel Mailbox: 981540263
Telecom Gold: 83:ELO002
Co-ordinator Barry Cooper
Aims To help organisations and individuals find out how to get things done locally, by providing information about relevant organisations and publications.
Activities A computerised database (TACINdex), available through electronic mail (Telecom Gold), provides lists of organisations and publications; the TACINdex is updated as new information is received and aims to cover every aspect of local life, including local workshops, co-operatives, community-based schools, holistic medical centres, locally organised transport, help and care for the elderly and handicapped, community newspapers, etc. Selections from the database are published quarterly for those without access to electronic mail. The TACIN network has over 300 nodes.
Status Private company
Publications TACINdex printout (4)

Tandem Club
7 Westwood Road, Maidstone, Kent ME15 6BB
0622 44468
Publicity Officer Paul Goodrick
Aims To promote and encourage tandem cycling.
Activities Providing a spares and advice service relevant to tandems; publishing a handbook and magazine in which members can provide details in advance of runs in their area. Local branches.
Status Voluntary
Publications Tandem Club Magazine (6); Handbook (1)

Tay River Purification Board (TAY RPB)
3 South Street, Perth, Tayside PH2 8NJ, Scotland
0738 27989
Director & River Inspector J.A. Rangeley
Aims To promote the cleanliness of the rivers, other inland waters and tidal waters in the Board's area; to conserve the water resources of the area.
Activities The Board is the water pollution prevention authority for an area of 8,710 sq.km. comprising the catchment areas of the Rivers Earn, Eden, Lunan, Dighty Water, North and South Esk, Tay and all other streams within the watershed; the Board is also the hydrometric authority for this area and operates 29 river gauging stations and a network of rain gauges.
Status Statutory
Publications Annual Report

Teachers for Animal Rights (TFAR)
29 Lynwood Road, London SW17 8SB
Contact Wanda Dejlidko
-NR

Teachers for Peace (TfP)
11 Goodwin Street, London N4 3HQ 01–485 1670
Co-ordinator Hilary Lipkin
Aims To oppose nuclear weapons and to draw attention to the role that education can play in working for a peaceful world; to introduce controversial issues into the classroom (without recruiting for any organisation) so that young people can come to an informed opinion of their own.
Activities Acting as a resource for teachers and peace groups on what is available for teaching peace studies, with special reference to the nuclear threat; giving talks to groups of teachers and peace groups who hold events on peace studies in the community; conferences on peace studies for parents and teachers interested in peace, disarmament and development issues. 55 branches.
Status Voluntary
Publications Teachers for Peace Newsletter(3)

Teilhard Centre
23 Kensington Square, London W8 5HN
01–937 5372
General Secretary John Woodcock
Aims To study and experience more consciously the cosmic process of which we are a part, so that we may participate more effectively in its development; to promote, develop and apply the creative evolutionary ideas of Teilhard de Chardin and others.
Activities Publishing an international journal; maintaining an office, library and archive for research and general reading (open 11–4, Mon.-Fri.); books and cassettes sold by mail order; trans-disciplinary conferences, lectures and seminars; annual Teilhard Lecture; regular small group 'I-Thou' meetings. Membership open to all.
Status Educational charity

Publications   The Teilhard Review &
Journal of Creative Evolution (3)

Television Trust for the Environment (TVE)
46 Charlotte Street, London W1P 1LX
01–637 4602

Director   Robert Lamb

Aims   To encourage international film-
makers and other organisations to produce
programmes on a wide range of environmental issues, as well as to promote public
awareness of the threat to our environment;
to function as a link between programme
makers and environmental groups, with the
ultimate aim of producing environmental
programmes of the highest quality and
creative standards.

Activities   Currently overseeing two major
film series on encroaching deserts and
development in Amazonia, seeking the
involvement of a number of film-makers and
environmental organisations in both series.
Projects in the pipeline include a possible
film on the plight of the homeless, on the
pesticides problem, a catalogue of
recommended blue-chip films on the human
environment and establishing a clearing-
house for films. The Trust produces an information pack, updated every 6 months.

Status   Non-profit Trust

Thames Water Authority
New River Head, Rosebery Avenue, London
EC1R 4TP 01–837 3300

Rivers Division   Nugent House, Vastern
Road, Reading, Berks. RG1 8DB 0734 593333

Activities   Rivers Division is responsible
for land drainage, flood alleviation, river
operations, navigation, health and safety,
emergency planning, pollution control,
fisheries, recreation and amenity and conservation throughout the whole 5,000 sq.miles
of the Thames Water Authority's area.

Status   Statutory

The Other Economic Summit (TOES)
42 Warriner Gardens, London SW11 4DU
01–627 4760

Director   Paul Ekins

Aims   To develop and promote a New
Economics based on personal development,
social justice, satisfaction of the whole range
of human needs, sustainable use of
resources and conservation of the environment; more specifically, to elaborate a
coherent new economic theory, to derive
from it consistent and practicable new economic policies, to encourage and draw attention to examples of the new theory in practice and to achieve the adoption of such new
approaches through campaigning at all
levels.

Activities   TOES' main event, normally a
public rally and conference each year, is
focused on the annual Economic Summit
meetings of the heads of government of the
7 richest industrial nations; it also initiates
research, organises seminars and co-ordinates panels of experts on various aspects of
economics. Its work is communicated
through publication of its Conference Papers
and of a Report and Summary of its Conference each year; a major book based on the
papers commissioned for the 1984 and 1985
Conferences is to be published by
Routledge & Kegan Paul in 1986.

Status   Voluntary

Publications   Report & Summary of Annual
Conference (1)

Theosophical Society
50 Gloucester Place, London W1H 3HJ
01–935 9261

Aims   To encourage the development of
Man's spiritual potential through recognition
of the basic unity of all life.

-NR

Thermal Insulation Contractors' Association
Kensway House, 388 High Road, Ilford, Essex
IG1 1TL 01–514 2120

Status   Trade association

-NR

Third World First
232 Cowley Road, Oxford OX4 1UH 0865 245678

Secretary   Hilary Scannell

Aims   To build an understanding of the politics and economics of world poverty and
underdevelopment and possible options for
change.

Publications   Links (biennial)

-NR

Thornby Hall Foundation
The Hall, Thornby, Northampton NN6 8SW

Aims   To promote a holistic approach to life
and health.

-NR

Threshold Survey of Complementary Medicine
3 Woodlands Park, Girton, Cambridge
CB3 0QB 0223 276500

Contact   Dr Robin Monro

Activities   Operating a computerised information bank on alternative medicine organisations, people and research; conducting
long-term research into the effectiveness of
alternative medicine and its relationship to
conventional medicine.

-NR

Tidal Energy Engineering Group
University of Salford, Salford, Manchester
M5 4WT 061–736 5843

Contact Prof. Eric Wilson
-NR

Timber Growers United Kingdom (TGUK)

Agriculture House, Knightsbridge, London
SW1X 7NJ 01–235 2925

Secretary Ms A.B. Sayers

Aims To represent the interests of private
woodland owners in England, Scotland and
Wales.

Activities Lobbying on behalf of private
forestry; negotiating on taxation and grants;
disseminating timber market information; co-
ordinating training facilities for forestry;
monitoring forestry legislation; public
relations concerning forestry with agriculture and the environment. Office in Scotland
and 12 regional branches.

Status Voluntary (accredited by government and Forestry Commission)

Publications Timber Grower (4)

Timber Research and Development Association (TRADA)

Stocking Lane, Hughenden Valley, High
Wycombe, Bucks. HP14 4ND 024024 3091

Director J.G. Sunley

Aims To represent the interests of the
timber trade and professions.

Activities Carrying out research and
development work with the object of ensuring
that timber is used correctly and economically; because the construction and packaging industries are the largest users of
timber, TRADA's work is mainly concentrated in these areas. TRADA disseminates
information to all those who specify, manufacture and use timber; it also has expertise
in the use of wood residues from biomass
as fuel for process heating and energy use.
Publications include Wood Information
sheets. 9 local advisory offices.

Status Independent research association

Publications TRADA News (3)

Tools for Self-Reliance (TFSR)

Netley Marsh Workshops, Netley Marsh,
Southampton, Hants. SO4 2GY 0703 869697

Co-ordinator Glyn Roberts

Aims To put tools into the hands of those
who will use them, both in this country and
abroad; to help people understand better the
potential and value of tools, the quality of
craftsmanship, the value of employment and
the need for equitable global development.

Activities Collecting unwanted hand tools
through voluntary groups (church,
educational and others), refurbishing them
and providing them cost-free to co-
operative/communal development workers
in the Third World. The main tools sought
are for woodwork, metalwork, sewing,
building, plumbing, blacksmithing and

leatherwork; groups also prepare complete
tool kits; TFSR sends steel to smiths in East
Africa for tool production. Information is
collected on the use, need for and
production of tools in the Third World and
the wider problems of promoting equitable
development at home and overseas. Local
branches, plus the assistance of other
groups.

Status Charity; company limited by
guarantee

Publications TFSR Newsletter (6); TFSR
Special Report (1)

Tories Against Cruise and Trident (TACT)

43 Wilton Grove, London SW19 3QU
01–543 0362

Hon. Secretary Mrs Joanna Bazley

Aims To campaign for the cancellation of
the projected deployment of cruise missiles
and Trident submarines by Britain, as a first
step on the road to nuclear disarmament.

Activities Providing a focus for all people
who vote Conservative but who disagree
with the party's policy of relying on the deter-
rent effect of nuclear armaments for
defence; trying to redress the imbalance in
the political image of the anti-nuclear
weapons movement.

Status Informal group within the Conservative Party

Publications TACT Newsletter

Total Oil (Great Britain) Ltd

33 Cavendish Square, London W1M 0JE
01–499 6393
-NR

Town and Country Information Network

see TACIN

Town and Country Planning Association (TCPA)

17 Carlton House Terrace, London SW1Y 5AS
01–930 8903/4/5

Director David Hall

Aims To promote a better environment by
means of campaigning for effective planning
and more local decision making.

Activities Making representations to
public authorities on planning policies, both
in response to initiatives made by government and to propose its own ideas and
solutions; providing evidence to government
commissions and public inquiries on
subjects of national importance; providing a
full-time planning aid service free of charge
to individuals and community groups. The
TCPA has recently urged the government
to rethink its attitude toward the green belt,
opposed the use of special procedures to
bypass the planning system, pleaded for
proper consultation over the issue of nuclear

waste disposal and was a principal protagonist, representing 14 local authority objectors, at the public inquiry into the proposed Sizewell B Pressurised Water Reactor. It promotes lectures and discussion groups and holds national and regional conferences on various topics several times a year; it is active at international level through the Habitat International Council and is a member of the European Environmental Bureau. It produces a wide range of publications and runs its own bookshop. Local branches.

Status Voluntary; charity
Publications Town & Country Planning (12); Planning Bulletin (50); Annual Report

Town Teacher Limited

All Saints Church, Newcastle upon Tyne NE1 2DS 0632 616993
Project Director/Company Secretary
H. Thompson
Aims To advance environmental education of the public, particularly by the provision of Urban Studies Centres for the benefit of all ages and sections of the community.
Activities Over 20 town trails form the core of Town Teacher resources; they are geared mainly to junior/secondary school pupils but can be modified to most abilities and ages and can be adapted for use elsewhere; most trails have accompanying teachers' notes. Town Teacher also undertakes a whole range of urban studies and heritage activities of varying complexity, both in-school and out-of-school and with the public at large; it has a number of other resources, such as slides, photographs, books, maps and periodicals which can be examined on the premises and in certain cases made available for loan.
Status Charity; company limited by guarantee
Publications Annual Report

Traditional Acupuncture Society

Tao House, Queensway, Leamington Spa, Warwicks. CV31 3LZ 0926 22121
-NR

Transport 2000 Ltd (T2000)

Walkden House, 10 Melton Street, Euston, London NW1 2EJ 01-388 8386
Executive Director Susan Hoyle
Aims To work for the improvement and greater use of bus and rail transport in the interests of accident prevention, social justice, the protection of the environment and the conservation of land and energy. Specifically: to press for co-ordination of rail and bus services; to press for better provision for the needs of pedestrians, cyclists and public transport users; to seek

the maximum use of rail and water for bulk and long distance freight transport.
Activities Lobbying of central and local government; producing researched reports and commissioning in-depth research; providing practical aid to other local and national organisations; setting up and servicing local branches; disseminating information through the media and the newslette and through other publications. 40 branches.
Status Voluntary
Publications Transport Retort (12)
No Time to Weight: the objector's guide to trunk road inquiries.
Paying Heed: financing public transport.

Transport and Road Research Laboratory (TRRL)

Old Wokingham Road, Crowthorne, Berks. RG11 6AU 0344 773131
Director G. Margason
Activities Providing technical and scientific advice and information to contribute to formulating, developing and implementing government policies relating to roads and transport, including their interaction with urban and regional planning; carrying out research and related activities in highway engineering, traffic engineering and safety and in more general transport subjects; concerns include noise and air pollution from traffic. Publications include reports, Overseas Bulletins, leaflets and reprints of published articles.
Highways and Structures Dept: Pavement design and maintenance; materials and construction; ground engineering; bridges.
Safety and Transportation Dept: Human and social factors; road safety; transport planning; special research branch.
Special Research Branch: Policy-orientated studies on transport and land use.
Traffic Engineering and Control Dept: Highway traffic; traffic systems; urban networks.
Vehicle and Systems Assessment Dept: Vehicle engineering; assessment; vehicle safety.
Overseas Unit: Research on transport planning and highway engineering in developing countries on behalf of the Overseas Development Administration.
Status Statutory (Laboratory of the Department of Transport)
Publications Annual Report

Transport For An Improved City (TRAFIC)

377 City Road, London EC1V 1NA 01-837 0731
Aims To campaign against urban motorways in London.
-NR

Transport on Water Association
Northside, Royal Albert Dock, London E16 2RA
01–476 2424
Hon. Director L.E. Faram
Aims To publicise and promote the economic, social and environmental advantages of waterborne transport; to encourage the training and retention of old skills and their application and adaptation to improved methods and technology.
Activities Fund raising by means of barge driving races and other events; liaising with MPs, local government and industries and individuals allied to waterborne industries.
Status Voluntary
Publications Transport on Water Association Newsletter (1)
-NR

Tree Council O 171 828 9928
Agriculture House, Knightsbridge, London
SW1X 7NJ 01-235 8854
Secretary Peter Gerosa
Aims To promote for the public benefit the improvement of the environment through the planting, nurture and cultivation of trees in town and country.
Activities Organising an annual National Tree Week to focus public attention on the need for more trees and better care of trees; discussions by Council members (mainly national organisations having an interest in trees) on problems affecting trees; providing financial assistance to selected tree projects; generally providing advice and information.
Status Charity
Publications Tree News (3)

Tree Foundation
This is the funding charity of the Tree Council, c/o the Tree Council

Trees for People
71 Verulam Road, St Albans, Herts. AL3 4DJ
0727 67196
Aims To encourage young people to plant, propagate and care for trees and shrubs as a group activity.
Activities Providing seedlings, seed, tools and educational materials free of charge to schools wishing to establish a nursery project on a long-term basis.
Status Voluntary; charity
-NR

Tropical Products Institute (TPI)
56–62 Gray's Inn Road, London WC1X 8LU
01–242 5412
Activities Interests include biofuels.
Status Statutory (institute of the Overseas Development Administration)
-NR

TUCRIC (Trade Union & Community Resource & Information Centre)
1st Floor, Market Buildings, Vicar Lane, Leeds, W. Yorks. LS2 7JF 0532 439633
Aims To provide information, research and resources for community, women's and trade union groups and individuals.
Activities Running an inquiry service and reference library which includes information on health, safety, pollution, energy and jobs, mainly from the industrial and legislative angle. Project work and publications, e.g. on sexual harassment at work, women and new technology, hazards of VDUs, etc. Provision of user facilities, e.g. photocopier.
Status Voluntary
Publications Leeds TUCRIC Bulletin (4)
Hazards of VDUs.
Women's Health Bibliography.

Turning Point
The Old Bakehouse, Ilges Lane, Cholsey, Wallingford, Oxon. OX10 9NU 0491 652346
Contact Alison Pritchard
Aims To be the focus for an international network of people who share a common feeling that mankind is at a turning point, that old values, old lifestyles and an old system of society are breaking down and that new ones must be helped to break through.
Activities Members' concerns include environment, sex equality, Third World, peace and disarmament, community politics, appropriate technology and alternatives in economics, health, education, agriculture, religion, etc. Turning Point does not demand adherence to doctrines, manifestos or resolutions; it enables us, as volunteers, to help and to seek help from one another.
Occasional meetings and publications.
Status Voluntary network
Publications Turning Point Newsletter (2)

Tweed River Purification Board (TRPB)
Burnbrae, Mossilee Road, Galashiels, Borders TD1 1NF, Scotland 0896 2425
Clerk J.D. Bell
Aims To carry out the statutory duties and responsibilities imposed on RPBs, namely to promote the cleanliness of the rivers, other inland waters and tidal waters in the Board's area and to conserve the water resources of the area.
Activities Pollution prevention, hydrometric observations, etc.
Status Statutory
Publications Annual Report

Tyne & Wear Building Preservation Trust Ltd (BUTTRESS)
Sandyford House, Archbold Terrace, Newcastle upon Tyne NE2 1ED 091–281 6144

Technical Adviser   Brian Jobling
Aims   To preserve the architectural heritage of the area.
Activities   The principal method of operation is to acquire buildings in need of restoration and, with the assistance of grants, loans and donations, to return them to usable condition; the buildings are then sold and any profit is used to finance further projects.
Status   Charity
Publications   BUTTRESS Newsletter (2)

Tyne & Wear Energy Advice Programme (TWEA)

Energy Projects Office, 2nd Floor, Sunlight Chambers, 2–4 Bigg Market, Newcastle upon Tyne NE1 1UW 0632 615677

Information Officer   Wendy Innes
Aims   To promote the provision of energy advice to the consumer; to provide practical aid to low income consumers through local community insulation projects.
Activities   Educational work with schools, pensioners' groups, local authority staff, advice centre staff and exhibitions; campaigning for a more effective and longer-term energy policy; publishing leaflets, consumer guides to domestic energy use, etc.
Status   Voluntary

Tyne Wear Energy Forum (TWEF)

7 Grange Crescent, Stockton Road, Sunderland, Tyne & Wear SR2 7BN 0783 655277

Secretary   John McGowan
Aims   To enable local voluntary and community organisations who have an interest in energy issues to meet regularly to exchange information and contribute to the energy debate.
Activities   Operating a free postal information exchange service; providing resources for joint campaigns; acting as a focus for combined statements on energy policy by the local community.
Status   Voluntary association

Tyneside Anti-Nuclear Campaign (TANC)

1 Charlotte Square, Newcastle upon Tyne NE1 4XF 0632 616143

Aims   To stop nuclear power and nuclear weapons; to reduce wasted energy and develop alternative energy programmes; and to guarantee employment during the changeover.
Activities   Campaigning against all aspects of the nuclear power programme, from uranium mining to waste dumping; work is mostly carried out by small informal groups tackling specific issues, e.g. the proposal to build a nuclear power station at Druridge Bay.
Status   Voluntary
-NR

U

UK ...
see also UNITED KINGDOM ...

UK Conservation and Development Programme
see CENTRE FOR ECONOMIC AND ENVIRONMENTAL DEVELOPMENT; ENVIRONMENTAL CONSERVATION AND DEVELOPMENT GROUP

UK Offshore Operators Association (UKOOA)
5th Floor, 192 Sloane Street, London SW1X 9OX
01–589 4588
Secretary, Clean Seas & Environmental Committee Ms J. Stephens
-NR

Ulster Architectural Heritage Society
181A Stranmillis Road, Belfast BT9 5DU
0232 660809
Secretary Mrs Elizabeth Cavanagh
Aims To promote the appreciation and enjoyment of good architecture of all periods, from the prehistoric to the contemporary, in the nine counties of Ulster; to encourage the preservation and restoration of buildings of merit or importance; and to increase public awareness of the beauty, history and character of local neighbourhoods.
Activities Outings, lectures, publications.
Status Voluntary
Publications Heritage Newsletter (1)

Ulster Countryside Committee (UCC)
Hut 6, Castle Grounds, Stormont, Belfast
BT4 3SS 0232 768716
Secretary W.L. Reavie
Aims To advise the Department of the Environment for Northern Ireland on matters on which the Department is required to consult it and on any other matters referred to it; and to inquire into and report on matters affecting the natural beauty or amenity of any area or place in Northern Ireland.
Status Statutory
Publications Annual Report

Ulster Society for the Preservation of the Countryside
West Winds, Carney Hill, Holywood, Co. Down
BT18 0JR, N. Ireland 02317 2300/0232 661222
Hon. Secretary Wilfrid M. Capper
Aims To safeguard the amenities of Northern Ireland and do all that is possible to preserve and enhance its beauty for our own and future generations; to arouse and educate public opinion in order to further the promotion of these objectives; to act either directly or through members of affiliated bodies as a centre for giving or obtaining advice and information upon such matters.
Activities Consulting with government departments about new legislation; educating on care for the countryside and conservation generally; promoting long distance footpaths; consulting with local authorities on a wide range of subjects, including rights of way and access; co-operating with the Ordnance Survey on new maps; promoting a series of lectures each year in conjunction with Queen's University, Belfast. Local branches.
Status Voluntary
Publications The Countryside Recorder (2)
-NR

Ulster Society for Prevention of Cruelty to Animals (USPCA)
11 Drumview Road, Lisburn, Co. Antrim
BT27 6YF, N. Ireland 0232 813126
Appeals Organiser Mrs V. Grainger
Aims To obtain justice for animals; to endeavour by every means to put an end to cruelty to animals; and to encourage kindness and humanity in their treatment.
Activities Collecting and caring for unwanted and stray animals; caring for injured animals; dealing with inquiries; visiting schools, libraries, youth clubs, church groups and civic organisations for informative talks and fund raising; investigating complaints about cruelty to animals; visiting abbatoirs and markets and any places where animals are congregated. 15 branches.
Status Charity
Publications Annual Report

Ulster Trust for Nature Conservation (UTNC)
Barnett's Cottage, Barnett Demesne, Malone
Road, Belfast BT9 5PB 0232 612235
Development Officer Dr Susan Christie
Aims To record and study places and objects of natural history interest; to control nature reserves by acquisition or management agreement and to encourage their use for educational activities; to conserve fauna and flora throughout Northern Ireland; to promote lectures and meetings on topics of natural history interest.

Activities Acquiring reserves or negotiating ecological management agreements
with landowners; opposing governmental or
private proposals for drainage, planning or
other issues which may be ecologically detri-
mental; representing the broad conservation view on public issues; educational
work in schools, field clubs, voluntary organisations, etc. Local branches.
Status Voluntary
Publications The Irish Hare (3)

Unit for the Development of Alternative Products (UDAP)

Dept of Combined Engineering, Coventry
(Lanchester) Polytechnic, Priory Street,
Coventry, W. Mids. CV1 5FB 0203 24166
ext. 508
Co-ordinator Brian Lowe
Aims To explore the design, development
and production of socially useful products
for peaceful purposes, with a view to
reducing potential redundancy and creating
new jobs.
Activities Working with individuals and
groups in a technical support role to assist
with the solution of problems and the
commercial evaluation of products. Projects
undergo a development process to take them
through to the point of production. Help is
given to unemployed people to develop
products which will form the basis of new
and satisfying employment. The work is
greatly assisted by students and staff of the
Polytechnic through project activities.
Publications UDAP Newsletter (4)

Unit of Comparative Plant Ecology

Dept of Botany, University of Sheffield, Sheffield, S. Yorks. S10 2TN 0742 78555 ext.4315
-NR

Unit of Marine Invertebrate Biology

Marine Science Laboratories, Menai Bridge,
Gwynedd LL59 5EH, Wales 0248 712641
-NR

United Kingdom Atomic Energy Authority (UKAEA)

11 Charles II Street, London SW1Y 4QP
01-930 5454
Librarian Mrs H.V. Surtees
Aims To carry out research and development on the application of nuclear energy for
civil purposes in the UK; to undertake other
functions agreed with the government,
consistent with the Atomic Energy Authority
Act 1954 and other relevant legislation.
Activities Providing a wide range of
research and development for the British
nuclear industry and regulatory bodies;
undertaking R&D programmes on safety,
environmental aspects of nuclear power,

nuclear fusion and the Fast Breeder
Reactor; using skills derived from this work,
the Authority carries out non-nuclear R&D
on a repayment basis. An Environmental
Safety Group operates services and undertakes research and consultancy on waste
management, land reclamation, hazardous
materials and their safe disposal.
The Authority is responsible for operating
the following establishments:
**Atomic Energy Research Establishment
(AERE)**, Harwell, Oxfordshire: The Authority's largest research laboratory, about half
its effort is concerned with reactor development and nuclear power generally, particularly materials research; there is a related
programme of underlying research; the rest
of the laboratory's effort is divided about
equally between work done for industry and
the public sector in nuclear and non-nuclear
areas.
Culham Laboratory, Abingdon, Oxfordshire: The Authority's centre for research in
nuclear fusion, plasma physics and associated technology; also contract research in
industrial electrotechnology, laser applications and electrostatics.
**Dounreay Nuclear Power Development
Establishment,** Caithness, Scotland: The
principal centre for fast reactor development; concerned with reactor operation,
testing and post-irradiation examination of
fuel elements, reprocessing and development work on components operating in
sodium; site of the Prototype Fast Reactor
(PFR), designed to feed 250 MW of electricity into the national grid; fast reactor
irradiation services for overseas customers;
materials testing reactor fuels fabricated for
UK and overseas customers.
**Risley Nuclear Power Development Estab-
lishment,** Warrington, Cheshire: Incorporates Northern Division HQ, Engineering
Directorate, Technical Services and Planning Directorate, Process Technology and
Safety Directorate and Risley Nuclear
Power Development Laboratories.
Safety and Reliability Directorate,
Culcheth, Warrington, Cheshire:
Concerned with all aspects of safety and
reliability associated with the Authority's
nuclear programme.
**Springfields Nuclear Power Development
Laboratories,** Preston, Lancashire:
Concerned with fuel and plant development
in support of the fuel cycle, including
improving fuel fabrication techniques,
assessing in-reactor behaviour and devel-
oping plant units and processes for fuel
dismantling, reprocessing and waste
treatment.
**Windscale Nuclear Power Development
Laboratories,** Windscale, Cumbria: Princi-

pally concerned with fuel development for both thermal and fast reactor systems; shielded facilities for post-irradiation examination of fuel from gas-cooled and water-cooled reactors; theoretical and experimental work on heat transfer, fluid flow and vibration problems; environmental studies, including iodine trapping and waste handling, particularly the disposal of radioactive sludges; responsible for R&D on plutonium-bearing fuel for fast reactors, active handling technology and the decommissioning of the Windscale Advanced Gas-cooled Reactor.

Winfrith Atomic Energy Establishment, Winfrith, Dorset: Primarily concerned with reactor physics, nuclear data, radiation shielding, criticality, heat transfer and fluid dynamics, reactor safety and control engineering, electronics and nucleonic instrumentation for both thermal and fast reactor systems; also post-irradiation examination of fuel, waste disposal, flask technology and the fabrication of fuels and components for experimental reactors; site of the 100 MW(e) Steam Generating Heavy Water Reactor.
Status Statutory
Publications Atom (12); Annual Report

United Kingdom Federation Against Aircraft Noise
9 Dover Park Drive, London SW15 5BT
01–788 4931
Activities Enabling its member societies to adopt a common approach in their efforts to reduce aircraft noise, air pollution and hazards to safety; particular importance is attached to the siting of airports as a means of attaining these ends.
-NR

United Kingdom Petroleum Industry Association Ltd (UKPIA)
9 Kingsway, London WC2B 6XH 01–240 0289
Activities Comprises private sector oil companies involved in the supply, refining and distribution of oil in the UK. The Environment, Health and Safety (EHS) activities of UKPIA are directed by the EHS Steering Committee chaired by the Environmental Co-ordinator and include a working group on marine pollution, a working group on aqueous effluents and 10 Regional Oil Spill Co-ordinators who are the main contact points with the local oil spill response officials around the country.
-NR

United Kingdom Reclamation Council (UKRC)
16 High Street, Brampton, Huntingdon, Cambs. PE18 8TU 0480 55249
Secretary Mrs Paddy Tilley
Aims To stimulate industrial, commercial, governmental and general public interest in the need for optimising economic reclamation and recycling; to promote or foster, by research and interchange of information, improvements in the processing and marketing of the materials and products of reclamation and encourage the use of reclaimed materials wherever possible. The Council consists of representatives of the majority of the organisations in the UK connected with reclamation and recycling; it replaced the British Reclamation Industries Council in 1984.

United World Education and Research Trust (UWT)
29 Great James Street, London WC1N 3ES
01–242 3228
General Secretary Sheila Oakes
Aims To produce educational material on international relations and related issues and to promote these topics.
Activities Producing publications; sponsoring seminars, conferences and workshops. Associated with the National Peace Council.
Status Voluntary; charity

Universities Federation for Animal Welfare (UFAW)
8 Hamilton Close, South Mimms, Potters Bar, Herts. EN6 3QD 0707 58202
Secretary Lt-Col. T.J. Reynolds
Aims To educate by teaching correct methods for care and management of animals in laboratories, zoos, in the wild, in schools and in the home.
Activities Producing comprehensive textbooks and leaflets and the UFAW Handbook on the Care and Management of Laboratory Animals; giving practical demonstrations and lectures to university societies, biology teachers and environmental health officials; holding an annual symposium with published Proceedings. Full members must be graduates or professionally qualified in some way acceptable to the Council.
Status Charity
Publications UFAW News-sheet; Symposium Proceedings; Annual Report

Uranium Institute
12th Floor, Bowater House, 68 Knightsbridge, London SW1X 7LT 01–225 0303
Secretary-General B. Terence Price
Aims To further the peaceful uses of atomic energy; to provide a forum for the producers and consumers of uranium.
Activities Research into uranium, including supply and demand situation, international trade and public acceptance of nuclear power; annual International Symposium; 4–5 reports issued annually.
Status Research institute

Publications Uranium and Nuclear Energy: Proceedings of the Annual Symposium
An Introduction to Uranium Mill Tailings Isolation and Containment.
Uranium Supply and Demand: perspectives to 1995.

Urban Centre for Appropriate Technology (UCAT)

82 Colston Street, Bristol, Avon BS1 5BB
0272 25850
Co-ordinator Hugh Barton
Aims To demonstrate in an urban context the principles of appropriate technology: conservation of non-renewable resources; avoidance of pollution and waste; self-help and community co-operation; and a fulfilling quality of life and work.
Activities Running a demonstration house, showing a range of energy-saving and recycling techniques, use of solar and wind power and an organic urban garden; an Energy Information Centre gives advice on anything from draught-stripping to heat pumps; an education service is available for local schools and the community. The office houses the independently-run Greenleaf Bookshop and a wholefood cafe. UCAT sponsors two energy action teams and runs a community energy workshop offering courses in energy-saving techniques and appropriate technology. 2 branches.
Status Charity
Publications UCAT Newsletter (2)

Urban Spaces Scheme (USS)

Dept of Food & Biological Sciences, Polytechnic of North London, Holloway Road, London N7 8DB 01–607 2789 ext.2118
Project Manager Monica Hale
Aims To increase the awareness and use of the urban environment for ecological field teaching in schools in North London; to interpret and communicate to teachers of all student age groups the advantages and potential of local field-based studies; and to provide information and ideas for teachers to use.
Activities Providing ecological surveys and data for each site; habitat creation and management advice for schools and community groups; working directly with schools, assisting teachers in devising work programmes on specific topics and providing on-site back-up; establishing an Urban Ecology Resource Centre at a school in Hackney, providing field and classroom facilities for schools pursuing locally-based fieldwork; organising teachers' courses (in conjunction with North London Science Centre and City University); producing concept-based teachers' resources and field teaching materials on a range of topics;

publishing booklets and fact sheets on habitat creation. Branch in Waltham Cross.
Status MSC-funded project
Publications Open Space (6)
Ecological Fieldwork: handbook of sites in North London.
Ecology in the City.
School Nature Project.

Urban Wildlife Group (UWG)

11 Albert Street, Birmingham B4 7UA
021–236 3626
Chairman Peter Shirley
Aims To promote the conservation of sites with natural history interest in the West Midlands; to promote the education of the public, particularly young people, in the understanding, enjoyment and conservation of natural flora and fauna, especially in urban areas.
Activities The Ecology Unit promotes and organises study and research into urban nature conservation and publishes results; the Landscape Unit prepares detailed proposals for community nature parks and other sites and is concerned with practical implementation of site improvement projects; the Planning Unit liaises with local and statutory authorities in formulating planning policies more sympathetic to nature conservation and prepares information packs and reports for local authority planners, explaining the need for urban nature conservation, monitors development proposals and comments on their environmental implications.
Status Charity
Publications Urban Wildlife Group Newsletter (6)
Gardening for Wildlife: how to transform your garden into a wildlife haven.
Planning with Nature: a guide for all who help shape the environment of our towns.

URBED (Urban and Economic Development Group)

99 Southwark Street, London SE1 0JF
01–928 9515
Director Nicholas Falk
Aims To find practical solutions to the problems of regenerating run-down areas and creating new work.
Activities Consultants to local authorities and community groups on re-using redundant industrial buildings and drawing up development strategies for waterside sites; fund raising and promotion, particularly for environmental trusts. Branch in the southwest.
Status Company limited by guarantee
Publications URBED Review (1)
Development Agencies for Wasteland. 1983. 100pp.

Urenco Ltd
18 Oxford Road, Marlow, Bucks. SL7 2NL
06284 6941
   Activities   Uranium enrichment services.
   -NR

United Nations Association,
(01926) 332393
   Environment/Rio : 2
c/o UNA.   0171 839 1784
         Felix Dodds

V

Vegan Society Ltd
33–35 George Street, Oxford OX1 2AY
0865 722166
General Secretary Barry Kew
Aims To further knowledge of and interest in sound nutrition and in veganism and the vegan method of agriculture as a means of increasing the potential of the Earth, to the physical, moral and economic advantage of mankind.
Activities Producing vegan recipe books and reports on vegan health and nutrition; a wide range of leaflets gives the case for veganism on grounds of compassion, health, ecology and economy; talks, film shows, cookery demonstrations, festival stalls; sponsoring relevant research projects, e.g. a bio-fuels project at the Centre for Alternative Technology. 50 branches plus local contacts.
Status Charity
Publications The Vegan (4)

Vegetable Protein Association
LIPC, 76 Shoe Lane, London EC4A 3JP
01–353 0186
Aims To disseminate information on vegetable proteins for human consumption.
-NR

Vegetarian Society of the United Kingdom Ltd
Parkdale, Dunham Road, Altrincham, Cheshire WA14 4QG 061–928 0793
General Secretary Ms Sandra Allen
Aims To improve knowledge of the benefits that a vegetarian diet has to offer in terms of ethics, health, economics, ecology and a reduction of famine in the Third World.
Activities Supplying free literature; sponsoring and assisting research; running regular residential and evening cookery courses; holding courses for speakers and other activists and providing speakers; organising symposia, lectures and courses and participating in exhibitions; operating a mail order book service; publishing books, leaflets, a handbook and journal; encouraging branches to involve themselves in local activities.
Status Charity
Publications The Vegetarian (6); International Vegetarian Handbook (biennial)

Venture Technology Ltd
18 Nuffield Way, Abingdon, Oxon. OX14 1TG
0235 20502
Activities Design and supply of solar photovoltaic power systems, including solar panels, regulators, batteries, support structures and ancillary equipment.
Status Commercial
-NR

Veterinary Information Group on Nuclear Weapons and Pollution (VIGONWP)
11 High Street, Kinver, Stourbridge, W. Mids. DY7 6HG 0384 877158
General Secretary P.M. Penhale
Aims To stimulate interest in and arouse awareness, within the veterinary and allied professions, of the veterinary and agricultural consequences of nuclear war and pollution.
Activities The Group consists of veterinarians and members of related professions and its activities include: keeping under review all available information on the veterinary consequences of nuclear war and pollution; acting as a reference agency on these matters; providing information, by lectures, publications and other means, to the veterinary and related professions and to the public; seeking the co-operation of these professions in all countries for these aims.
Status Voluntary
Publications Newsletter

Victorian Society
1 Priory Gardens, Bedford Park, London W4 1TT 01–994 1019
Secretary Mrs Jennifer M. Freeman
Aims To encourage appreciation of Victorian art and architecture; to preserve 19th and early 20th-century buildings and industrial monuments.
Activities Consulting with local authorities on applications to demolish listed buildings; bringing important threatened buildings to the notice of national and local government; co-operating with the Department of the Environment in compiling the statutory list of buildings of architectural and/or historical interest; making representations at public inquiries; commissioning reports and initiating campaigns to save major buildings; organising weekend conferences, walks and visits and running a summer school jointly with the Victorian Society of America; providing advice and information on the conservation of Victorian buildings and on other topics of importance to the period. Membership of over 3,000. 12 regional groups.

Status Charity
Publications The Victorian Society News-letter (3); Annual

Vigilance
3 West Street, South Petherton, Somerset
TA13 5DQ 0460 40652
Co-organiser Jane Buxton
Aims To campaign against nuclear power and nuclear weapons and for more open government.
Activities Providing access to extensive files of information dating back to 1974; initiating specific projects from time to time; publishing and disseminating leaflets.
Status Voluntary

Vincent Wildlife Trust
Baltic Exchange Buildings, 21 Bury Street, London EC3A 5AV 01–283 1266
Activities Concerns include the conservation of otters.
-NR

Vocational Creativity Group (VOC)
[formerly the Association for Occupational Self-Help]
79 Sutton Avenue, Eastern Green, Coventry, W. Mids. CV5 7ER 0203 463062
Co-ordinator Keith Hudson
Aims To study human creativity within a society which is becoming more 'experiential', 'post-industrial' and 'post-consumerist'; to encourage the formation of new professions concerned with quality of human life and satisfactions in a sustainable socio-economic context.
Activities The formation and encouragement of learning and creativity groups; development and evaluation of learning and creativity techniques; study of the ecological, economic and ethological constraints in a sustainable planet; occasional newsletters and papers.
Status Voluntary
-NR

W

War on Want (WOW)
1 London Bridge Road, London SE1 9SG
01–403 2266
General Secretary George Galloway
Aims To support groups attempting to find
alternative means for organising their own
lives through social and economic changes
which will enable people to have a say in
decisions which affect them and to enjoy the
benefits of their own labour; to educate and
inform the British public about the nature and
causes of poverty and the role of aid and
development in the Third World.
Activities Supporting development
projects throughout the world, including
Britain; funding development education in
the UK; publishing literature on development issues. Non-charitable campaigning
activities are carried out through WOW
Campaigns Ltd. Local branches.
Status Charity
Publications War on Want Newsletter (6)
-NR–L

War Resisters International (WRI)
55 Dawes Street, London SE17 1EL 01–703 7189
Secretary Howard Clark
Aims To strive for the removal of all causes
of war and to work for non-violent alternatives
in the West, the East and the Third World.
Activities Supporting and encouraging
individual war resisters and conscientious
objectors; non-violent demonstrations, direct
action and day-to-day work against militarism, racism, economic exploitation and
other causes of war; non-violent intervention
in situations of crisis and conflict; support for
non-violent struggles against oppression
and injustice; working through national
governments and transnational bodies such
as the United Nations to get laws and political
structures changed; linking individuals and
organisations locally, regionally, nationally
and internationally. Autonomous sections in
18 countries.
Status Voluntary
Publications War Resisters International
Newsletter (6)

WARMER Campaign (WARMth and Energy from Rubbish)
83 Mount Ephraim, Tunbridge Wells, Kent
TN4 8BS 0892 24626
Information Officer Mrs Maggie
Thurgood
Aims To promote the production of energy
from waste, with particular emphasis on
municipal solid waste.
Activities Operating a computerised data-
base and mailing list; exhibitions; study tours;
producing a bulletin.
Status Charity
Publications WARMER Bulletin (4)

Warren Spring Laboratory (WSL)
Gunnels Wood Road, Stevenage, Herts.
SG1 2BX 0438 313388
Aims To undertake applied research and
to provide research services, advice, consultancy and facilities for chemical industry,
minerals industry, materials, recovery from
industrial, commercial and domestic wastes,
air and oil pollution measurements and
abatement processes for industry, government and local authorities.
Activities Environmental technology
includes the following areas: air pollution –
gaseous and particulate pollution, measurement and abatement processes, mathematical and wind tunnel modelling, offensive
odours control and abatement; oil pollution
– studies of the fate of oil at sea, dispersant
testing, dispersant application to oil on the
beach and at sea by boats and aerial
spraying, remote sensing by aircraft of oil
slicks for surveillance of shipping, assessment of recovery equipment for oil spills;
biotechnology – mixed culture fermentation,
downstream separation. Reports are
published.
Status Statutory (laboratory of the Dept of
Trade and Industry)
Publications Annual Report

Warwickshire Nature Conservation Trust (WARNACT)
1 Northgate Street, Warwick CV34 4SP 0926
496848/401111
Development Officer Sara Stewart
Aims To rescue wild plants and animals
and the areas in which they live from obliter-
ation by modern development; to stimulate
enjoyment and awareness of wildlife and
the Warwickshire countryside.
Activities Managing owned and leased
nature reserves where plants and animals can
live and grow in safety; surveying and monitoring natural wildlife habitats; offering
advice and practical help to farmers and
landowners; developing links with planning
authorities; visiting schools and clubs and
arranging exhibitions and community activi-

ties that give special opportunities for involvement in practical conservation projects; organising fund raising events; producing literature on all Trust nature reserves and local nature trails. 8 local branches.
Status Charity
Publications WARNACT News (4)

Wasteland Forum
This forum has been discontinued

Watch Trust for Environmental Education Ltd (WATCH)
22 The Green, Nettleham, Lincoln LN2 2NR
0522 752326
Education Officer Simon Perry
Aims To enable young people (up to the age of 18) to increase their knowledge of wildlife and the natural and man-made environment and to take an active part in conservation. WATCH is both a national club and the junior branch of all 46 county Nature Conservation Trusts.
Activities Major projects have included: assessing pollution levels in the air and in streams; an investigation into acid rain; carrying out a national butterfly census; a conservation project on wildlife in towns; a phone-in project to record the breeding sites of frogs, toads and newts; a project on house martins; and a tree planting scheme. There are national events at, for example, London Zoo, and local study days, excursions and competitions. Over 500 local WATCH Clubs and 450 affiliated school groups throughout the UK.
Status Voluntary; charity (associated with RSNC)
Publications WATCHword (3); local WATCH Newsletters

Water Authorities' Association
1 Queen Anne's Gate, London SW1H 9BT
01–222 8111
-NR

Water Companies' Association
14 Great College Street, London SW1P 3RX
01–222 0644
Director & Secretary M.A. Swallow
Aims To represent at national level the interests of the 28 statutory water companies in England and Wales who between them supply water to 25% of the population.
Status Employers' association
Publications Reflections (4) (in-house)

Water Research Centre (WRc)
John L. van der Post Building, Henley Road, Medmenham, PO Box 16, Marlow, Bucks.
SL7 2HD 0491 571531
Public Relations Officer R.I. Odell

Aims To provide technical leadership, primarily in support of the United Kingdom water undertakings.
Activities Work covers all aspects of water research technology and innovation and is made available to members or through advisory and consulting services; there are three principal facets to the research programme, covering environmental protection, water and waste-water treatment processes and engineering research and development on sewers and water mains; information on toxicity and biodegradability is available to industry, local authorities and river authorities through INSTAB. The Centre operates from 3 Laboratories and a Scottish office:
WRc Environment (above address) *Librarian* Mrs M. Blake. Protection of the aquatic environment; water quality and health; sewage and solid waste disposal.
WRc Engineering, PO Box 85, Frankland Road, Blagrove, Swindon, Wilts. SN5 8YR 0793 488301 *Librarian* Mrs K. Lenik. Sewers and water mains; application of information technology to water industry operations.
WRc Processes, Elder Way, Stevenage, Herts SG1 1TH 0438 312444 *Librarian* Mrs G.M. Cox. Treatment of water, sewage and sewage sludge.
WRc Scottish Office, 1 Snowdon Place, Stirling, Central FK8 1NH 0786 71580 *Contact* R. Fellows
Status Research institute
Publications Aqualine Abstracts (26); Research Programme (1); Annual Report

WaterAid
1 Queens Anne's Gate, London SW1H 9BT
01–222 8111
Director David Collett
Aims In general, to increase understanding and practical action concerning the water and sanitation needs of the world's poorest countries; in particular, to mobilise such interest within the British water industry.
Activities Development education within and beyond the British water industry; attaching people of appropriate skills and experience from within that industry, on a low cost basis, to realistic water or sanitation programmes in the Third World; providing funding assistance to self-help projects in the Third World, particularly where such projects appear to be setting a pattern which others could follow.
Status Voluntary; charity
Publications WaterAid News (3)

Water Recovery Group
39 Westminster Crescent, Burn Bridge, Harrogate, N. Yorks. HG3 1LX

Chairman Alan Jervis
Activities Acting as a co-ordinating group for assisting local groups active in the voluntary restoration of waterways, in association with the Inland Waterways Association. Over 30 local groups around the country.
Status Voluntary
-NR

Watt Committee on Energy Ltd
The London Science Centre, 18 Adam Street, London WC2N 6AH 01–930 7637
Company Secretary J.G. Mordue
Aims To promote and assist research and development and other scientific or technological work concerning all aspects of energy; to disseminate knowledge generally concerning energy for the benefit of the public at large.
Activities Studying specific energy-related topics, including the industrial, commercial and domestic aspects of energy; educational activities; meetings and reports on these and other topics; providing speakers and exhibition material; representing British professional institutions.
Status Charity
-NR

Wave Energy Research Group
Dept of Mechanical Engineering, University of Edinburgh, King's Buildings, Mayfield Road, Edinburgh EH9 3JL 031–667 1081 ext.3276
Contact S.H. Salter (Reader in Mechanical Engineering)
Aims To conduct general research into renewable energy.
Activities Model testing of wave power devices (pioneered and developed the 'nodding duck' system); design and construction of full-size power conversion mechanisms for wind and wave energy, using high-pressure oil hydraulics; flywheel storage; transmissions for road vehicles.
Status University research unit

Weed Research Organization
Begbroke Hill, Yarnton, Oxford OX5 1PF 08675 3761
Activities The main official centre in Great Britain for research and information on weed problems and chemical and other methods of weed control. The Weed Control Department has Research Groups on annual crops, grass and fodder crops and perennial crops; the Weed Science Department has Research Groups on herbicide, environmental studies, microbiology and weed biology; other Groups study development botany, aquatic weeds and uncropped land, and tropical weeds.
Status Institute of the Agricultural and Food Research Council (AFRC)

Publications Biennial Report
-NR

Well Hall Country College
Well Alford, Lincs. LN13 0ET 05212 6521
Activities College of agriculture and horticulture run entirely on organic principles. Offers full-time courses (elementary, intermediate and advanced), summer schools and short courses.
-NR

Welsh Anti-Nucliar Alliance/Cynghrair Wrth Niwclear Cymru (WANA/CWNC)
14 Stryd Newydd, Aberystwyth, Dyfed SY23 2AT, Wales 0970 615735
Organiser Nic Lampkin
Aims To assist and inform all organisations in Wales concerned about the danger of nuclear power and nuclear weapons and the prospect of nuclear waste disposal in mid-Wales; to promote a conservation and renewable energy strategy for Wales that will stimulate employment; to liaise with international anti-nuclear organisations.
Activities Providing information files, newsletters, resources and contacts; fund raising and financing of anti-nuclear projects for affiliated groups; gave evidence as an official objector at the Sizewell B Inquiry; campaigning with CND against cruise, Pershing and Trident missiles; campaigning for a Nuclear-Free Wales; trading in campaign materials.
Status Voluntary alliance
Publications WANA News (6)

Welsh Beekeepers' Association (WBKA)
Derwen Fach, Llandygwydd, Cardigan, Dyfed SA43 2QU, Wales 023987 553
Hon. Secretary E.G. Verge
Aims To develop co-operation among all beekeepers throughout Wales for the advancement of the craft; to conduct national examinations and honey shows; to co-operate with other national beekeeping associations.
Activities The Council meets four times a year and sends representatives to sit on the Welsh National Honey Show Committee which is held concurrently with the Royal Welsh Show each year; the Association actively supports the Welsh Beekeeping Centre at Coleg Howell Harris in Brecon, which it was instrumental in setting up in 1983. 16 affiliated associations.
Status Voluntary
Publications The Bulletin (4)

Welsh Development Agency (WDA)
Treforest Industrial Estate, Pontypridd, Mid-Glam. CF37 5UT, Wales 044385 2666

Director (Land Reclamation) Gwyn Griffiths
Aims To regenerate the economy and improve the environment in Wales.
Activities Gives 100% grants to cover costs incurred by local authorities in carrying out approved projects to reclaim derelict land in Wales; also supports other worthwhile schemes to improve the environment, such as projects sponsored by the Prince of Wales' Committee; provides factories and investment funds to attract new industrial development in Wales. 8 Area Offices.
Status Statutory
Publications Wales Ahead (4); Annual Report

Welsh Office/Y Swyddfa Gymreig

Crown Buildings, Cathays Park, Cardiff CF1 3NQ 0222 825111
London office: Gwydyr House, Whitehall, London SW1A 2ER 01–233 3000
Activities Has responsibility in Wales for ministerial functions relating to: health and personal social services; education (except for terms and conditions of service, student awards and the university); the Welsh language and culture; local government; housing; water and sewerage; environmental protection; sport; agriculture and fisheries; forestry; land use, including town and country planning; countryside and nature conservation; new towns; ancient monuments and historic buildings; roads; tourism; the urban programme in Wales; and the operation of the European Regional Development Fund in Wales and other EEC matters. It has oversight responsibilities for economic affairs and regional planning in Wales.
CADW: Welsh Historic Monuments, Brunel House, 2 Fitzalan Road, Cardiff CF1 1UY: Conservation of historic monuments and buildings; management, marketing and presentation of monuments in State care; rescue archaeology. [*Enquiries:* 0222 465511]
Agriculture Department Cathays Park, Cardiff CF1 3NQ 0222 825111
Division 1 (Commodities and Marketing): Coordination of agricultural policy briefing; annual review; Common Agricultural Policy; EEC Marketing and Processing Scheme; marketing policy; Agricultural and Horticultural Co-operation Scheme; Agricultural Advisory Panel; commodities, including support schemes for milk, beef, sheep, pigs, poultry, arable and horticulture. [*Enquiries:* 0222 824424/823832]
Division 2 (Animal Health, Land Drainage and Fisheries): Animal health; animal welfare; livestock improvement; meat hygiene, including hygiene standards and slaughterhouses; matters relating to the veterinary profession and veterinary medi-

cines; land drainage grants; sea fisheries, including conservation and management of stocks and aid to the fishing industry, harbour grants; inland fisheries, including diseases of fish; pesticides; emergencies. [*Enquiries:* 0222 823831/824423]
Division 3 (Grants, Subsidies and Lands), PO Box 17, Plas Crug, Aberystwyth, Dyfed SY23 1NG: Land matters and forestry; smallholdings; labour questions, including training, wages and tied cottages; plant health and plant variety rights and seeds; Agricultural Land Tribunal; Farm and Horticulture Development Scheme; Farm Capital Grant Scheme; Horticulture Capital Grant Scheme; Farm Structure and Payment to Outgoers Scheme; Agriculture and Horticulture Grant Scheme; Agriculture and Horticulture Development Scheme; Milk Pasteurisation Equipment Grant Scheme; less favoured areas; non-marketing of milk schemes; hill livestock compensatory allowances; suckler cow premium scheme; Hill Farming Advisory Sub-committee for Wales; Sheep Annual Premium Scheme; Research and Development Divisional Offices; liaison with Health and Safety Executive; conservation; heather and grass burning regulations; injurious weeds. [*Enquiries:* 0970 3162 ext.267]
Agricultural Development and Advisory Service (ADAS), Park Avenue, Aberystwyth, Dyfed SY23 1PQ: Advisory services as agents for the Secretary of State, covering agriculture, agricultural sciences, land drainage, lands, veterinary (including investigation). [*Enquiries:* 0970 615022 ext.230]
Economic and Regional Policy Group Cathays Park, Cardiff, CF1 3NQ
Division 2, Branch B: Steel; energy policy, including liaison with the coal, gas, electricity and oil (other than petrochemicals) industries; Severn Barrage; consumer affairs and appointments to the nationalised industry Consultative Councils and the Welsh Consumer Council. [*Enquiries:* 0222 824060]
Division 3, Branch A: Urban programme, Enterprise Trusts, Urban Development Grant. [*Enquiries:* 0222 823636/825486]
Division 3, Branch C: Countryside and nature conservation; national parks; commons; camping and caravanning; co-ordination of rural policies. [*Enquiries:* 0222 823169]
Transport, Highways and Planning Group Planning Division, Cathays Park, Cardiff CF1 3NQ: Planning policy; planning appeals and other planning cases, including development by other government departments; control of advertisements; new towns; gypsies. [*Enquiries:* 0222 823869/823892]
Planning Services Division, Cathays Park, Cardiff CF1 3NQ: Structure and local plans; policy, procedures and processing; housing

and industrial land availability; professional advice on statutory and general land use planning matters; economic, social and demographic analysis; cartographic services. [*Enquiries:* 0222 823721]

Estates Division, Cathays Park, Cardiff CF1 3NQ: Advice on estates policy and management issues. [*Enquiries:* 0222 823864]

Transport Policy Division, Government Buildings, Ty-Glas Road, Llanishen, Cardiff CF4 5PL: Transport and highways policy: local authority transport and highways grants; research; road safety. [*Enquiries:* 0222 753271 ext.3694]

Roads Administration Division, Government Buildings, Ty-Glas Road, Llanishen, Cardiff CF4 5PL: Motorway and trunk road new construction and improvement schemes; contracts and agreements; land acquisition and management; noise insulation and compensation claims; traffic signs and orders. [*Enquiries:* 0222 753271 ext.3621]

Roads Engineering Division, Government Buildings, Ty-Glas Road, Llanishen, Cardiff CF4 5PL: Investigating the need for, and designing and constructing improvements to, the motorway and trunk road network; setting of standards; signing; road safety; maintenance; traffic studies; traffic statistics; control of development affecting trunk roads; engineering advice on road and bridge matters. [*Enquiries:* 0222 753271 ext.3737]

Industry Department Industry Policy and Liaison Division, Cathays Park, Cardiff CF1 3NQ: Responsibilities include energy conservation. [*Enquiries:* 0222 825111]

Health and Social Work
Department Cathays Park, Cardiff CF1 3NQ
Health Policy Division: Policy on hospital and DHA provided health services; environmental health; health education. [*Enquiries:* 0222 824491]

Housing, Water and Environmental Protection Divisions Cathays Park, Cardiff CF1 3NQ
Housing Division: Includes responsibility for Land Authority for Wales. [*Enquiries:* 0222 823380]

Water and Environmental Protection Division: Water; sewerage and sewage disposal; environmental protection matters; miscellaneous local government matters; sport and recreation. [*Enquiries:* 0222 824141]

Welsh Plant Breeding Station
Plas Gogerddan, Aberystwyth, Dyfed SY23 3EB, Wales 0970 828255
Activities Research includes grass breeding, clover breeding, arable crop breeding, grassland agronomy, seed production, plant biochemistry, chemistry, cytology, developmental genetics and plant pathology.
Status State-aided institute of the Agricultural and Food Research Council
-NR

Welsh Water Authority/Awdurdod Dwr Cymru
Cambrian Way, Brecon, Powys LD3 7HP, Wales 0874 3181
Activities Responsible for water supply, water conservation, sewerage and sewage disposal, prevention of river pollution, fisheries, land drainage and the recreational use of waters in Wales.
Status Statutory
-NR

Wessex Water Authority (WWA)
Wessex House, Passage Street, Bristol, Avon BS2 0JQ 0272 290611
Senior Administration Officer N.G. Wooller
Aims To secure an adequate supply of water of appropriate quality to meet the demands of the community; to ensure that the community's waterborne waste is disposed of harmlessly; to provide for the maintenance of water quality in rivers and other inland waters; to enhance the amenity and recreational potential of waters under the Authority's control, including designated beaches; to maintain, improve and develop fisheries, to provide facilities for effective land drainage and to reduce the incidence of river and sea flooding.
Status Statutory
Publications Annual Report; Annual Plan

West Midlands Think Green Network
3 Tower Street, Birmingham B19 3RL 021–359 3973
Co-ordinator Carol Bickley
Aims To make the West Midlands a more green and pleasant place to live; to provide a focus for liaison and discussion between the member bodies.
Activities Establishing a resource centre to assist action by member groups; initiating a collaborative programme of education, information, practical schemes and other projects; liaising with other national and regional groups. The Network, which was established in 1984, is comprised of organisations within the county who accept that industrial development is necessary to the future of the area but who wish to ensure that there are plenty of green places left.
Status Voluntary
Publications West Midlands Think Green Network Newsletter (4)

West Wales Trust for Nature Conservation (WWTNC) [formerly West Wales Naturalists' Trust]

7 Market Street, Haverfordwest, Dyfed
SA61 1NF, Wales 0437 5462
Director David Saunders
Aims To protect and conserve wildlife in Dyfed; to establish and manage nature reserves; to stimulate interest in the countryside in order to encourage a greater respect for wildlife.
Activities Reserve management; promotional work; field meetings and lectures; biological survey work. 8 local branches.
Status Voluntary; charity
Publications West Wales Trust for Nature Conservation Bulletin (3); Friends of Skomer and Skokholm Reports (2); Pembrokeshire, Carmarthenshire, Ceredigion Bird Reports (1)

Wey & Arun Canal Trust Ltd (Wey-South Project)

24 Griffiths Avenue, Lancing, W. Sussex
BN15 0HW 0903 753099
Hon. Secretary John Wood
Aims To attempt the restoration of the derelict Wey & Arun canal in Surrey and West Sussex.
Activities Working parties every Sunday at various sites along the route of the canal; newcomers welcomed.
Status Voluntary
Publications Wey-South (4)
-NR

Wigan Groundwork Trust

Alder House, Alder Street, Atherton, Manchester M29 9DT 0942 891116
-NR

Wild Animal Protection Society (WAPS)

c/o The Lee Centre, 1 Aislibie Road,
Lee Green, London SE12 8QH
Secretary David White
Aims To save the lives of hunted animals in the Kent, Surrey and Sussex areas by the use of non-violent direct action.
Activities Sabotaging fox, hare and mink hunts. Active on most Saturdays from October to April (fox and hare hunting season) and some Saturdays during the summer months (mink hunting); meeting every Tuesday at 9.30pm.
Status Voluntary

Wild Flower Society (WFS)

68 Outwoods Road, Loughborough, Leics.
LE11 3LY 0509 215598
Aims To promote a greater knowledge of field botany among the general public and in particular among young people; to advance education in matters relating to the conservation of wild flowers and of the countryside; to promote the conservation of the British flora.
Activities Botanical recording, by means of competitions based on a wild flower diary, reports in a periodical magazine and field meetings.
Status Voluntary
Publications Wild Flower Magazine (3)

Wildfowl Trust

Gatehouse, Slimbridge, Glos. GL2 7BT
045389 333 ext.210
Administrative Officer J.H. Longland
Aims To promote the study and conservation of wildfowl and wetland habitat; to provide education and educative recreation for the public by all available means.
Activities The scientific study of wildfowl in the wild state and in captivity and related investigations; conservation of wildfowl by the provision of refuges, manipulation of habitat, protective measures and captive breeding; provision of facilities for educative recreation for people young and old, fit and disabled. 7 centres around the country.
Status Charity
Publications Wildfowl World (2); Wildfowl (1)

Wildlife and Countryside Services

122 Derwent Road, Thatcham, Newbury, Berks.
RG13 4UP 0635 60478
Contact Sue Everett, Paul Goriup
Aims To offer a professional consultancy service to a wide range of land managers and countryside pressure groups, including local authorities, nature conservation trusts, government bodies and private landowners.
Activities Providing professional advice, at home and abroad, on ornithological matters, wildlife and countryside management; specialising in nature conservation plans and reserve management plans, vegetation surveys, collation/presentation/analysis of ecological data, production of nature reserve and countryside interpretive leaflets, environmental impact assessment and site evaluations; some voluntary work undertaken for charitable bodies.
Status Professional consultancy

Wildlife Traffic Monitoring Unit

see IUCN CONSERVATION MONITORING CENTRE

Wiltshire Trust for Nature Conservation

19 High Street, Devizes, Wilts. SN10 1AT
0380 5670
Administrative Officer Mrs Elizabeth M. Gale
Aims To safeguard and manage important

wildlife sites; to increase public awareness and appreciation of the countryside and wildlife; to advise landowners, planning and water authorities on conservation.
Status Charity
Publications Wiltshire Trust for Nature Conservation Newsletter (3); Annual Report

Wind Energy Group (WEG)
345 Ruislip Road, Southall, London UB1 2QX
01–578 2366
Development Manager Richard Lord
Aims To use the resources of the major British companies who form the Group to exploit the use of wind energy.
Activities Manufacture of wind turbines for power generation, for use both in wind farms supplying major distribution grids and in isolated communities for small distribution grids; wind turbine sizes range from 200kW to 3,000kW. Also provides consultancy services in the field of wind engineering, ranging from site selection through wind regime measurement and grid connection to wind turbine stress analysis and performance monitoring. WEG can use the world-wide facilities of its joint venture parent companies; its activities are recorded in the Taylor Woodrow Energy Magazine, published about three times a year; in addition, papers have been published on many aspects of wind engineering, generally for presentation at major conferences.
Status Industrial consortium (Taylor Woodrow Construction, British Aerospace, GEC Energy Systems)

WISE (World Information Service on Energy)
52 Acre Lane, London SW2 5SP ~~01–737 4144~~
UK Relay Person Jan McHarry
Aims To provide an international information service on a wide range of anti-nuclear and safe energy topics; to be a forum for international communication amongst people actively working against nuclear power and promoting appropriate energy sources.
Activities Preparation and publication of detailed news coverage and informed comment on international nuclear and safe energy issues; providing an information service answering specific requests as well as general enquiries; putting people in touch with appropriate contacts and groups relevant to their needs. There are similar WISE offices in many countries.
Status Voluntary
Publications News Communique (26) International Address List 1984.
The Nuclear Fix: a guide to nuclear activities in the Third World.

Women for Life on Earth (WFLOE)
2 Bramshill Gardens, London NW5 1JH
01–272 3449
Network Co-ordinator Veronica Bennett
Aims To promote the links between peace, feminism and ecology by means of non-violent direct action, public education and information exchange.
Activities Putting women in touch with each other locally, nationally and internationally through networking activities; providing speakers, videos and resources for rallies, conferences and local meetings; publishing a magazine of eco-feminist news, ideas and creative expression. Local groups.
Status Voluntary network
Publications Women for Life on Earth (4) Caldecott, Leonie & Leland, Stephanie, *Reclaim the Earth: women speak out for life on Earth.*

Women for World Disarmament
Long's House, North Curry, Taunton, Somerset TA3 6HL 0823490 207
Founder President Kathleen Tacchi-Morris
Aims To promote general and complete disarmament through the machinery of the United Nations, with adequate safeguards which are within its jurisdiction.
Activities Enabling women to express their concern at the long delay in implementing world disarmament; assisting in alerting the public mind to the urgent need for this. Twinned with Weimer (GDR). Local branches.
Status Voluntary

Women's Design Service
1 Ferdinand Place, London NW1 8EE
01–482 5799
Aims To encourage women to become more involved in the design process and the control of the quality of their environment; to provide technical support for women's groups in the Greater London area.
-NR

Women's Farm and Garden Association (WFGA)
175 Gloucester Street, Cirencester, Glos. GL7 2DP
Secretary Mrs. G. Ward
Aims To create interest in and to promote the study and practice of agriculture and horticulture among women throughout the UK and overseas; to give careers advice to young women wishing to enter these professions.
Activities Careers advice; conference weekends; representation on relevant national and international committees.
Status Voluntary; charity

Publications The Women's Farm and Garden Association Newsletter (6); Annual Report & Accounts
Gasson, Dr Ruth, *The Role of Women in British Agriculture.*

Women's Health Information Centre (WHIC)
52 Featherstone Street, London EC1Y 8RT
01-251 6580
Aims To make information on women's health more widely available to women; to support self-help groups; to work for improvements in the health services for women; to publicise and campaign on women's health issues.
Activities Providing a national information and resource centre for women's health issues; working with and acting as a resource for women in health groups, self-help groups, community groups, trade unions and other women's groups, as well as for individual women; no clinical advice, counselling or referral to doctors and clinics. The Centre has a library and issues publications; women are welcome to use the facilities and/or make enquiries by post or phone.
Status Voluntary
Publications WHIC Newsletter (3); Bulletin & Fact Sheet (3); Annual Report
Whose Choice? what women have to say about contraception.

Women's International League for Peace and Freedom (WILPF)
17 Victoria Park Square, London E2 9PB
01-980 1030
Hon. Secretary Alison Britton
Aims To promote peace and freedom with justice, the removal of discrimination on grounds of sex, race or creed and total and universal disarmament.
Activities Working toward disarmament and international understanding, human rights and the status of women; has consultative status with the United Nations. Annual Council, seminars, regular meetings. Local branches.
Status Voluntary
Publications Current Affairs (12); Peace and Freedom (4)

Women's Peace Alliance (WPA)
PO Box 240, Peace News, 8 Elm Avenue, Nottingham NG3 4GF
Secretary Sue Scott
Aims To be a network to link the various women's peace groups; to provide or point the way to resources for groups of varying political perspectives and ways of working.
Activities Keeping isolated women in rural areas in touch with the peace movement; providing news of activities and plans of the various women's peace groups; making

contact with peace women overseas; producing a newsletter, leaflets, booklists, speakers list, suggestions for starting a group, groups list and video list.
Status Voluntary alliance
Publications Women's Peace Alliance List of Events & Newsletter (8/9)
Herstory of the Women's Peace Movement. 1984. 12pp. [Accompanies the exhibition of the same name, available for hire.]

Wood & Solid Fuel Association of Retailers and Manufacturers (WARM)
PO Box 35, Stoke-on-Trent, Staffs. ST4 7NU
0782 44311
-NR

Woodcraft Folk
13 Ritherdon Road, London SW17 8QE
01-672 6031/01-767 2457
National Secretary Douglas Bourn
Aims To unite children, young people and all who are young in spirit and to educate its members in those principles of universal tolerance and equality and brotherhood so necessary to the creation of a world where all may live in peace and co-operation.
Activities Weekly group meetings for both sexes for children from 6 to 16; activities include games, singing, music making and drama, craftwork, discussions, local projects, folk dancing, etc. In addition, groups also have regular outdoor activities, notably hiking, youth hostelling and camping. There are three age groups: 6–9, 10–12 and 13–15; group leaders, all voluntary, are usually parents and others sympathetic to the organisation's aims. 530 local groups.
Status Voluntary
Publications Focus (4); Newsletter (12); Annual Report

Woodland Trust
Autumn Park, Dysart Road, Grantham, Lincs. NG31 6LL 0476 74297
Director J.D. James
Aims To conserve trees and woodland in the UK.
Activities Acquisition of woodland through purchase and as gifts; planting of trees as future woods.
Status Voluntary; charity
Publications Woodland Trust Newsletter

Worcestershire Nature Conservation Trust (WNCT)
Hanbury Road, Droitwich, Worcs. WR9 7DU
0905 773031
Administrator J. Poole
Aims To conserve the flora, fauna and natural countryside of Worcestershire.
Activities Managing over 50 nature reserves throughout the county, totalling

about 1,100 acres; many of these are owned by the Trust, whilst some are the subject of long-term management agreements with landowners; an Education Committee designs nature trails, provides lectures, publishes handbooks and reserve guides, runs the WATCH group (the junior branch of the Trust) and liaises with schools; there is a continuous programme of liaison with statutory authorities and of advice to farmers and landowners.
Status Charity
Publications Worcestershire Nature Conservation Trust Newsletter (3)

Working Group on Chemical and Biological Weapons
Trecarrell Cottage, Trebullett, Launceston, Cornwall PL15 9QE 056682 522
Contact Elizabeth Sigmund
-NR

Working Panel of Local Authority Ecologists
Bradwell Abbey Field Centre, Bradwell, Milton Keynes, Bucks. MK13 9AP
-NR

World Development Movement
Bedford Chambers, Covent Garden, London WC2E 3HA 01–836 3672
Activities Lobbying for fundamental changes to be brought about in rich and poor countries to bring justice to the world's poor and more equitable sharing of resources and opportunities.
-NR

World Disarmament Campaign (WDC)
238 Camden Road, London NW1 9HE 01–485 1067
Campaign Organiser Andrew Dilworth
Aims To campaign for: the abolition of nuclear weapons and all weapons of mass destruction; the abolition, by agreed stages, of conventional arms, leading to general and complete disarmament; transference of military expenditure to end world poverty.
Activities Producing materials and organising projects, meetings and other events to further the aims of the Campaign; launched the World Peace Action Programme, a set of positive proposals for disarmament supported by over 90 peace organisations around the world, in November 1985. Local branches.
Status Voluntary
Publications World Disarmament Campaign Network (4); Letternews

World Energy Conference
34 St James', London SW1A 1HD 01–930 3966
Activities The Central Office at the above address services the International Executive Council which is the governing body of the World Energy Conference; also assists the host National Committees in the organisation of international congresses on all sources of energy; organises Study Committees on energy subjects and supervises publication of reports.
-NR

World Federation for the Protection of Animals
see WORLD SOCIETY FOR THE PROTECTION OF ANIMALS

World Food Assembly (WFA)
UK/Europe Secretariat: 15 Devonshire Terrace, London W2 3DW 01–723 0147
Secretary Robin Sharp
Aims To influence policy on such issues as food aid, International Monetary Fund austerity measures and control of biotechnologies.
Status International coalition of NGOs
Publications *That All May Eat.* (1984 manifesto)
-NR

World Forest Action
6 Glebe Street, Oxford OX4 1DQ
-NR

World Pheasant Association
PO Box 5, Lower Basildon, Goring, Reading, Berks. RG8 9PF 049162 271
Membership Secretary Miss Elaine Ballinger
Aims To develop, promote and support the conservation of all species of the order Galliformes which includes pheasants, grouse, quail, partridge, francolins, currasows and related birds.
Activities Ensuring survival of stocks of gallinaceous birds in natural conditions throughout the world, conserving their habitat and understanding their requirements; ensuring sound and improved methods of aviculture; establishing a databank for the Galliformes and acting as an advisory body to members of the Association and to outside organisations; promoting constructive research; educating the public to a better appreciation of Galliformes and nature in general; establishing reserve collections and buffer stocks of threatened or endangered species; encouraging the conservation of habitats.
Status Voluntary
-NR

World Society for the Protection of Animals (WSPA)
106 Jermyn Street, London SW1Y 6EE 01–839 3026/3066

Director-General Trevor H. Scott
Aims To promote effective means for the protection of animals and for the prevention of cruelty; to undertake and promote the conservation and protection of animals in any part of the world. WSPA was formed as the result of a merger in 1981 between the International Society for the Protection of Animals (ISPA) and the World Federation for the Protection of Animals (WFPA).
Activities Negotiating with government and local authorities; animal protection and wildlife rescue projects and relevant investigative activities world-wide; trained animal protection staff operate out of Regional and Section offices in London, Boston, Basle, Toronto, San Jose, Bogota and Bombay. 360 member societies.
Status Charity
Publications Animals International (4)

World Tree Trust (WTT)
La Capucine, 15 The Drive, Adel, Leeds, W. Yorks. LS16 6BG 0532 673304
Co-ordinators Badi and Colette Lenz-Inebnit
Aims To promote the protection of trees and the increase of tree cover everywhere.
Activities Mobilising a global constituency in support of the United Nations as the most effective avenue to prevent the planet's destruction; participated in the UN's desertification conference at Nairobi and at both the UN Special Sessions for Disarmament at New York; supports the World Conservation Strategy and education efforts by conservation organisations in Britain; maintains a base in Switzerland.
Status Voluntary

World Wildlife Fund (WWF)
Panda House, 11–13 Ockford Road, Godalming, Surrey GU7 1QU 04868 20551
Aims To raise money for the conservation of endangered wild animals, wild plants and wild places and to promote the wise use of the world's natural resources.
Activities WWF is an international organisation with headquarters in Switzerland and national organisations in 27 countries. In Britain, one third of the money raised is spent on projects in this country, often through other bodies such as the county Trusts for Nature Conservation; the remaining funds are spent on international projects or where they are most urgently needed; regional offices carry out fund raising throughout the UK through voluntary supporters' groups; there is an adult and youth membership department and an education branch.
Status Charity

Publications World Wildlife News (4); Worldwise (4) (youth supplement)

Wrekin Trust
Marbury House, St Owen Street, Hereford HR1 2PR 0432 266551
Aims To help people find the spiritual disciplines most suited to them.
Activities Concerned with the spiritual nature of Man and the universe; holds conferences, seminars and workshops, some in series of several weekends to enable in-depth study, on such topics as: the Kabbalah; the Inner Spectrum; astrology and psychology; and meditation training. Holds a major annual conference, 'Mystics and Scientists', which aims to help dissolve the barriers between the sciences and spiritual disciplines. The lecturing panel includes speakers of international repute. Courses are mainly held over weekends, residential and non-residential, as well as 5–day summer schools. The Trust is not affiliated to any particular doctrine or dogma nor does it claim to offer any one way to 'the truth'.
Status Charity
Publications Wrekin Trust Newsletter (3/4)

WWOOF (Working Weekends on Organic Farms)
19 Bradford Road, Lewes, E. Sussex BN7 1RB
Secretary Maureen Pynches
Aims To enable first-hand experience of organic farming and gardening; to encourage members into the countryside; to help the organic movement with additional labour; to facilitate contact with other people in the organic movement.
Activities In return for work on the organic farms, gardens and smallholdings, members receive meals, basic temporary accommodation and transport to and from the local station; details of places in the UK needing help each weekend are listed in the newsletter which also gives details of events, developments and job opportunities in the organic movement (s.a.e. for details). WWOOF also operates a training scheme [Contact Chris Mager, 17 Bourn Bridge Road, Little Abington, Cambridge CB1 6BJ 0223 891223]; experience gained is recorded in the Working Organic Reference Manual & Sourcebook.
Status Voluntary
Publications WWOOF News (6)

WWOOF (Working Weekends On Organic Farms) (Republic of Ireland)
Carrigleigh, Shanballymore, Mallow, Co. Cork, Ireland
Organiser Gilly Wenlock
Aims To help people get first-hand experience of organic farming and gardening,

thereby helping the organic movement which is labour-intensive and does not rely on artificial fertilisers or persistent poisons for pest control.

Activities Upon membership (£2 for Ireland, £3 sterling overseas) you will receive a list of holdings ranging from 1–70 acres where you may stay and work full-time, receiving meals and a place to sleep; length of stay can be a weekend, a week or longer by mutual agreement between host and Wwoofer.

Status Voluntary
Publications WWOOF (Ireland) Newsletter (1)

WWOOF Scotland (Working Weekends On Organic Farms)

Coneyhatch, Netherly by Stonehaven, Grampian AB3 2QE, Scotland 0569 62509
Contact Shona Matheson
-NR

Y

Yarner Trust
Beacon Farm, Dartington, Totnes,
Devon TQ9 6DX 0803 863736
Director & Secretary Eric Clarke
Aims To explore, demonstrate and teach
practical solutions to small-scale, low-input
food production and self-reliant living.
Activities Running both short and residential courses, covering various aspects of
smallholdings such as stock-handling,
compost-making, choice and care of tools,
food production and preparation, soil tilths
and crops, tractor maintenance and fencing;
1–2 day courses cover such activities as
sandal-making, hedging, lambing, cheese-
making and organic gardening; serious
students may also apply for an extended
stay of one year in order to experience the
annual cycle of tasks. In addition to Beacon
Farm, the Trust runs a farm at Welcombe
Barton in north Devon.
Status Charity

Yoga Biomedical Trust (YBT)
3 Woodlands Park, Girton, Cambridge
CB3 0QB 0223 276500
Director Dr Robin Monro
Aims To promote and advance for public
benefit the study and practice of and research
into the therapeutical effects of yoga as a
means of improving the mental, physical
and spiritual health of the community and to
publish results of such research.
Activities Conducting an epidemiological
study of the health of several thousand
persons in the UK who practise yoga; this
study is a long-term project in which
preventive and health promoting effects of
yoga will be explored, as well as management and cure of particular disorders. Information exchange groups are being formed
for doctors, therapists and patients
concerned with particular disorders; clinical
and laboratory studies will also be
undertaken.
Status Charity
Publications Yoga Biomedical Bulletin (4)
-NR

Yoga for Health Foundation
Ickwell Bury, Northill, Biggleswade,
Beds. SG18 9EF 076727 271
Director Howard Kent
Aims To promote the concept of yoga,
especially relating health to the concept of
internal peace and happiness; to work and

research into the whole field of mental
control.
Activities Running a residential centre for
short and long stays for the widest range of
people, from the fit to the seriously disabled;
research work into yoga and training activities for those working in this field, including
specific remedial work. Functions both from
the centre and through a network of local
activities in Britain and some other
countries.
Status Charity
Publications Yoga and Life
-NR

Yorkshire Dales National Park Authority
Yorbridge House, Bainbridge, Leyburn, Richmond, N. Yorks. DL8 3BP 0969 50456
National Park Officer R.J. Harvey
Aims Under the National Parks & Access
to the Countryside Act 1949, to conserve and
enhance landscape, promote the enjoyment
of National Park areas and to have due
regard for the socio-economic wellbeing of
local communities. The Committee consists
of 24 members, including 8 members nominated by the Secretary of State for the
Environment, 12 appointed by the North
Yorkshire County Council and 1 each
appointed by the Cumbria County Council
and by the District Councils of Craven, Rich-
mondshire and South Lakeland.
Status Statutory
Publications Dales Park News (4)
-NR

Yorkshire Naturalists' Trust
see YORKSHIRE WILDLIFE TRUST

Yorkshire Water
West Riding House, 67 Albion Street, Leeds,
W. Yorks. LS1 1AA 0532 448201
Regional Administration Manager M.H.
Bennett
Aims To maintain and improve the present
level of service to the community in relation
to water services; to deal with the inherited
legacy of pollution; to remove, as far as is
practicable, all major constraints relating to
inadequacy of water services facilities on
proposals for real development.
Activities Water supply; sewerage,
sewage treatment and disposal; fisheries;
land drainage; recreation and amenity. Local
divisional offices.
Status Statutory

Publications Annual Report
-NR

Yorkshire Wildlife Trust (YWT)
10 Toft Green, York YO1 1JT 0904 59570
Executive Officer M.E. Goss
Aims To protect places and objects of
natural beauty or ornithological, botanical,
geological, zoological or scientific interest
from injury, ill-treatment or destruction; to
establish, form, own and maintain sanctuaries
or reserves for the preservation of birds or
other animals and to establish form and maintain reserves for wild plants.
Activities Managing 49 nature reserves
and some 40 other sites for private owners;
encouraging other private and public owners
of land to care for wildlife; promoting a
better understanding of the needs of wildlife;
campaigning for better legislation and more
resources.
Status Voluntary
Publications Yorkshire Wildlife Trust
Newsletter (3); Annual Report

Young People's Trust for Endangered Species (YPTES)
19 Quarry Street, Guildford, Surrey GU1 3EH
0483 39600
Director Cyril Littlewood, MBE
Aims To educate young people in matters
relating to the conservation of the world's
natural resources and wild places.
Activities Lecture and film show service;
schools field course and summer school
activities; educational materials for schools,
youth organisations and individual young-
sters; organising fund raising projects for
schools and youth organisations.
Status Charity
Publications Conservation Education;
Whale-Tail News

Youth Environmental Action (YEA)
Archway Development Centre, 173 Archway
Road, London N6 5BL 01–348 3030
Aims To assist, promote and co-ordinate
environmental action and education
amongst young people.
Activities Providing advice and infor-
mation and visiting speakers; co-ordinating
joint activities; producing fact sheets on
environmental issues.
Status Voluntary
Publications YEA Newsletter
-NR – L

Youth for Animal Rights (YFAR)
Hillview, Chaffcombe, Chard, Somerset
TA20 4AH 04606 5090

National Organiser Penny Goater
Aims To encourage young people to
consider the ways animals are treated in
factory farms, vivisection laboratories,
circuses, etc. and to provide help with
campaign ideas so that they can take an
active part.
Activities Campaigning for animal rights.
Status Voluntary (youth branch of Animal
Aid & Compassion in World Farming)
Publications Animals Now (3); Youth for
Animal Rights Newsletter (3)

Youth Hostel Association of Northern Ireland (YHANI)
56 Bradbury Place, Belfast BT7 1RU 0232 224733
Development Secretary John Douglas
Aims To encourage a greater knowledge,
love and use of the countryside; to provide
hostels or other accommodation for its
members on their travels; to take any action
possible to preserve the beauties of the
countryside and to obtain or maintain access
across rights of way.
Activities Has 10 hostels situated in scenic
areas of the Northen Ireland countryside,
providing simple, clean, low-cost accommodation for travellers of limited means,
regardless of age, sex, creed, religion or
nationality.
Status Voluntary
Publications Youth Hostel Magazine (4);
Handbook (1)

Youth Hostels Association (England & Wales) (YHA)
Trevelyan House, 8 St Stephen's Hill, St Albans,
Herts. AL1 2DY 0727 55215
Countryside & Education Officer Rob
Wightman
Aims To help all, especially young people
of limited means, to a greater knowledge,
love and care of the countryside, particularly
by providing hostels and other simple
accommodation for them in their travels and
thus to promote their health, rest and
education.
Activities Managing 260 youth hostels in
England and Wales; promoting educational
facilities such as field studies; advocating
conservation and environmental protection.
Membership of over 250,000 who may also
use 5,000 hostels operated by similar associations in over 45 countries. Local branches.
Status Voluntary; charity
Publications Learning, Living & Leisure
(3); Countryside Bulletin (3); YHA Guide (1)

Z

Zoo Check
Tempo House, 15 Falcon Road, London
SW11 2PH 01–350 1735
> **Aims** To respond to public complaints
> about conditions in zoos, to inform the press
> and to protest to local councils.
> **Activities** Carrying out surveys and
> research; running educational projects on
> alternatives to zoos; challenging zoo estab-
> lishments over keeping wild animals in
> captivity.
> -NR

Zoological Society of London
Regent's Park, London NW1 4RY 01–722 3333
> **Press Officer** Miss Joan Crammond
> **Aims** To advance zoology and animal
> physiology and to introduce the subjects of
> the animal kingdom to the public, through
> maintaining two world-famous zoos and
> through educational and scientific work.
> **Activities** Running London Zoo and Whip-
> snade Park; carrying out extensive scientific
> research in its Institute of Zoology. Work
> includes: scientific meetings and symposia;
> a formal educational programme from
> primary school to university level; scientific
> publications, including the International Zoo
> Yearbook (the world's major zoo reference
> book); and maintenance of a zoological
> library of international repute. The Society
> holds a leading position in conservation
> activities in the British zoo world.
> **Status** Charity
> **Publications** Journal of Zoology (12); Trans-
> actions; International Zoo Yearbook (1);
> Zoological Record (1) (in conjunction with
> BIOSIS)

ORGANISATIONS
not based in the UK or Ireland

These organisations have been included on the grounds that their functions involve or affect British or Irish interests

CONCAWE (Conservation of Clean Air and Water in Western Europe)
Babylon kantoren A, Koningen Julianaplein 30–9, 2595 AA The Hague, Netherlands
Activities CONCAWE is a European consortium of oil companies working for environmental and health protection.

Earthwatch
see UNITED NATIONS ENVIRONMENT PROGRAMME

ECHO (European Commission Host Organisation
177 Route d'Esch, L–1471 Luxembourg
010 352 48 8041
Manager (Education & Training) Ms Bernice Sweeney
Aims To contribute actively to, and to encourage and support the use of, online information in Europe; to offer free access to a range of unique databases online.
Activities Providing access to databases and databanks, including ENREP, an online directory of environmental research projects in the member states of the European Community, and ENDOC, an online directory of over 500 Environmental Information and Documentation Centres in these states and the services they provide; the databases offered by ECHO are mainly of a European nature and range from information on research projects, reports, business and a multilingual terminology databank to user guidance files.
Status Non-commercial
Publications ECHO News (6)

Environment Liaison Centre (ELC)
PO Box 72461, Nairobi, Kenya
010 254 2 24770/340849
Programme Officer Simon Muchiru
Aims To strengthen NGOs working in the fields of environment, sustainable development and connected issues, particularly in the Third World, through the provision of information, financial assistance and training; to build links between environmental NGOs around the world and between them and other NGOs; to facilitate, through two-way communication links, NGO input into and support for the United Nations Environment Programme [*see separate entry*], the UN Centre for Human Settlements and, where appropriate, other intergovernmental organisations.
Activities Operating the Environmental Data System; disseminating information through publications and in response to special requests; advising Third World NGOs on project design and implementation, administration, fund raising and media relations; administering the Small Grants Fund for practical field project initiatives which pay particular attention to the environmental dimensions of development work; building links among NGOs and providing support for issue-oriented and regional networks; organising meetings and international conferences. ELC is focusing particularly on four thematic issues during the period 1985–88: Deforestation/Afforestation; Water Management; Energy; and Sustainable Agriculture. It has drawn up an integrated programme of action for 3 years, entitled 'Working Together for Sustainable Development: building NGO networks and capacities'. 231 member NGOs.
Status International Non-Governmental Organisation
Publications Ecoforum (6); News Alert (6)
Conservation of Species and Genetic Resources.
Safe Use of Pesticides Now and in the Future.

EURATOM (European Atomic Energy Community)
c/o Commission of the European Communities, 200 Rue de la Roi, B–1049 Brussels, Belgium
Aims To assist the growth of nuclear industries in the European Community.
Activities Research; providing access to information; involvement in building nuclear reactors; establishing common laws and procedures for nuclear industries.
-NR

European Atomic Energy Society
c/o Studsvik Energiteknik AB, Fack, S–61182 Nykoping, Sweden
Aims To promote co-operation in nuclear energy research.
-NR

European Environmental Bureau (EEB)
29 rue Vautier, 1040 Brussels, Belgium
010 322 647 0199
Secretary General Ernst R. Klatte

Aims   To co-ordinate environmental NGOs in relation to activities of the European Communities.
Activities   Lobbying; publishing submissions, topical papers and regular bulletins; holding seminars and information meetings.

European Information Centre for Nature Conservation
c/o Council of Europe, BP431 R6, F–67006 Strasbourg, France
Publications   Naturopa (3) (distributed in the UK by the Nature Conservancy Council which is the UK national agency of the Centre)
-NR

European Nuclear Society (ENS)
PO Box 2613, CH–3001 Berne, Switzerland 010 41 31 220382
Secretary General   Dr Peter Feuz
Aims   To promote scientific and technical knowledge and co-operation in the peaceful uses of nuclear energy, bringing together the national nuclear societies of Europe into a federation.
Activities   Fostering contacts between national member societies in Europe; liaising with nuclear societies overseas; sponsoring and co-sponsoring conferences; compiling and issuing policy statements on major topics, e.g. radioactive waste; publishing a journal.
Status   Voluntary
Publications   Nuclear Europe (12)

Food and Agriculture Organisation (FAO)
Viale delle Terme di Caracalla, Rome, Italy
Director-General   Dr Edouard Saouma (Lebanon)
Status   United Nations organisation
-NR

Friends of the Earth International Secretariat
PO Box 17170, 1001 JD Amsterdam, Netherlands 010 31 20 340252

INFOTERRA
see UNITED NATIONS ENVIRONMENT PROGRAMME

Institute for European Environmental Policy (IEEP)
Aloys-Schulte-Strasse 6, BRD–5300 Bonn 1, Federal Republic of Germany 010 49 228 213810
Director   Ernst von Weizsacker
[see description under British branch]
Publications   The Environment in Europe (5)

International Atomic Energy Agency (IAEA)
Vienna International Centre, PO Box 100, A–1400 Vienna, Austria 010 43 222 2360
Director General   Dr Hans Blix
Aims   Under the aegis of the UN, to accelerate and enlarge the contribution of atomic energy to peace, health and prosperity throughout the world; to apply safeguards over nuclear materials to ensure that they are used only for their intended peaceful purposes.
Activities   Organising conferences, symposia and other meetings; publishing proceedings of conferences, etc.; elaborating standards in areas such as nuclear safety; applying safeguards over nuclear materials; conducting research into the peaceful applications of atomic energy in food, agriculture, medicine, industry, etc. The UK is a member state of the IAEA.
Publications   IAEA Bulletin (4); Atomic Energy Review

International Energy Agency (IEA)
2 rue Andre-Pascal, F–75775 Paris Cedex 16, France 010 331 524 9873
Special Advisor for Public Information Lionel Walsh
Aims   To facilitate international co-operation between the 21 participating countries in order to reduce their dependence on oil and to mould a better world energy and demand structure.
Activities   Long-term programme to promote efficient use of energy and increased production and use of alternative sources of energy; operating the Oil Market Information System, with a view to obtaining a better idea of probable future developments in the oil market, and the Emergency Oil Sharing System, to be activated in the case of a loss of 7% or more of the normal oil supply; co-operation in research and development projects in the field of alternative energies and energy conservation. The UK is a member of the IEA.
Publications   Annual Review; Annual Report of Energy Research, Development and Demonstration; Technology Review on the Clean Use of Coal

International Nuclear Law Association (INLA)
Square de Meeûs 29, B–1040 Brussels, Belgium 010 322 513 6845
General Secretary   F. Lacroix
Aims   To promote and undertake research into and provide information on legal problems relating to the peaceful uses of nuclear power, with particular regard to the protection of human beings and the environment.

International Radiation Protection Association (IRPA)
BP no 33, 92260 Fontenay aux Roses, France
010 331 654 7271
Executive Officer G. Bresson
Aims To encourage co-operation amongst those engaged in radiation protection work and to promote the establishment of radiation protection societies throughout the world.

International Research Center on Environment and Development (CIRED)
54 Boulevard Raspail (Room 311), 75270 Paris Cedex 06, France 010 331 544 3849 ext.219
Director Ignacy Sachs
Publications Ecodevelopment News (4)
-NR

International Union for Conservation of Nature and Natural Resources (IUCN)
Avenue du Mont-Blanc, CH–1196 Gland, Switzerland 010 4122 64 7181
Director General Dr Kenton R. Miller
Aims To promote action directed toward sustainable use and conservation of natural resources.
Activities Ensuring that development is sustainable, so that the potential of renewable natural resources is maintained; ensuring that areas of land or sea without special protection (the vast majority) are managed so that natural resources are conserved and that varieties of plants and animals can persist in adequate numbers; protecting areas of land and fresh and sea waters which contain representative or exceptional communities of plants and animals; devising special measures to ensure that species of fauna and flora do not become endangered or extinct. IUCN's Conservation Monitoring Centre is based at Cambridge and Kew and its Environmental Law Centre at Bonn, West Germany. IUCN publications include the World Conservation Strategy, the Red Data Books on endangered species, the UN List of National Parks & Protected Areas and books on conservation-related topics as well as environmental policy and law papers (catalogue available on request). The UK is a state member of IUCN; 3 government agencies and 22 NGOs from the UK are also members. IUCN administers CITES (Convention on International Trade in Endangered Species).
Publications IUCN Bulletin (4)
National Conservation Strategies: a framework for sustainable development.
IUCN, 1984. 52pp.
McNeely, J.A. & Miller, K.R. *National Parks, Conservation and Development: the role of protected areas in sustaining society.*
IUCN/Smithsonian Inst., 1984. 900pp.

Salm, R.V. & Clark, J.R. *Marine Parks and Protected Areas: a sourcebook for planning and managing special areas of the seas and coasts.* IUCN, 1984. 400pp.

OECD (Organisation for European Co-operation and Development)
2 rue Andre-Pascal, 75775 Paris Cedex 16, France
-NR

OECD Nuclear Energy Agency (NEA)
38 Boulevard Suchet, 75016 Paris, France
010 331 524 8200
Aims To promote co-operation between the OECD member countries on the production and uses of nuclear energy.
-NR

Pugwash Conferences on Science and World Affairs
Executive Office: 11A Avenue de la Paix, 1202 Geneva, Switzerland 010 4122 33 1180
Secretary-General Dr M.M. Kaplan
[*see description under British branch*]

SATIS (Socially Appropriate Technology Information Service)
c/o Mauritskade 61A, 1092 AD Amsterdam, Netherlands
General Secretary Paul Osborn
-NR

SIPRI (Stockholm International Peace Research Institute)
Bergshamra, S–171 73 Solna, Sweden
010 468 559700
Activities Conducting research, as an independent institute, into problems of peace and conflict, especially those of disarmament and arms regulation. The staff, the Governing Board and the Scientific Council are international.
-NR

UNESCO (United Nations Educational, Scientific & Cultural Organization)
UNESCO House, 7 Place de Fontenoy, 75700 Paris, France 010 331 568 1000
Chief, Public Liaison Division J.B. de Weck
Environment Mme J. Damlamian
Aims To stimulate progress in education, science, culture, social sciences and communication; to encourage international co-operation in these fields by bringing experts together, by co-ordinating regional and international programmes of action and by providing intellectual and technical assistance to member states.
Activities Environmental concerns include sponsoring and co-ordinating several big international scientific programmes: Man and

the Biosphere (MAB), the Intergovernmental Oceanographic Commission (IOC),
the International Geological Correlation
Programme (IGCP) and the International
Hydrological Programme (IHP); in addition,
it undertakes studies on the implications of
development, researches into the sociological aspects of human settlements and
cultural environment, carries out studies on
population and youth and promotes human
rights and peace; it launches international
campaigns to save monuments in peril and
maintains the World Heritage List; and it is
involved in many educational and communication initiatives.

UNESCO has 160 member states and operates through 22 regional offices, an International Bureau of Education and an International Institute for Educational Planning.
Status United Nations specialised agency
Publications UNESCO Courier (11)

United Nations Environment Programme (UNEP)

PO Box 30552, Nairobi, Kenya 010 2542 333930
Chief, Information Service Spencer
Smith-White
Industry & Environment Office: 17 rue Marguer-
itte, 75017 Paris, France
Aims To monitor and assess change in the
physical state of the Earth's environment, both
natural and human; to inform on destructive
events or trends; and to co-ordinate or cata-
lyse preventive or remedial action by the
international community.
Activities Assessment, in the form of 3
programmes: the Global Environment Monitoring Service (GEMS/EARTHWATCH); the
International Register of Potentially Toxic
Chemicals (IRPTC); and the International
Referral System for Sources of Environmental Information (INFOTERRA). Management, in the fields of environmental law and
protection and in economic and social development. Sectoral activities: environmental
aspects of human health and settlements;
industry; energy; desertification; protection
of soils, water ecosystems and genetic
resources; information, education, training
and technical assistance. UNEP co-operates
closely with the UK Department of the
Environment.

Status United Nations specialised agency
Publications UNEP News (6); State of the
Environment Report (1)
The World Environment 1972–1982.
UNEP/Tycooly (Dublin), 1982. 637pp.
Third World and the Environment.
UNEP/Tycooly (Dublin), 1983. 256pp.

World Commission on Environment and Development

Palais Wilson, 52 rue des Pagnis, CH–1001
Geneva, Switzerland
Director Jim MacNeill
-NR

World Health Organisation (WHO)

1211 Geneva 27, Switzerland 010 4122 91 2111
Director, Division of Environmental Health
Dr B.H. Dieterich
Aims To protect and promote human
health through the prevention and control of
conditions and factors in the environment that
adversely affect health.
Activities Fostering national and international action for the improvement of
drinking water supply and sanitation toward
the global goal of safe water and adequate
excreta disposal, as set forth for the International Drinking Water Supply and Sanitation Decade; development of methodology
for environmental impact assessment in
relation to rural and urban development and
housing; promotion and co-operation in
establishing national policies and
programmes for the health protection of
people against environmental hazards;
assessment of possible adverse health
effects of chemicals in air, water and food
that are of international significance;
promotion and co-operation in the establishment of national strategies and technologies
to ensure the safety of food with a view to
reducing food-borne mortality. WHO has
regional offices in several countries; it co-
operates with the UK in research, exchange
of information and the development of
guiding principles.
Publications World Health (12); WHO
Chronicle (12); Bulletin of the World Health
Organisation (irregular)

USEFUL ADDRESSES

British Medical Association (BMA)
BMA House, Tavistock Square, London WC1H
9JP 01–387 4499

British Standards Institution (BSI)
2 Park Street, London W1A 2BS 01–629 9000

Campaign for Freedom of Information
2 Northdown Street, London N1 9BG
01–278 9686

Central Office of Information (COI)
Hercules Road, London SE1 7DU 01–928 2345

Charities Aid Foundation (CAF)
48 Pembury Road, Tonbridge, Kent TN9 2JD
0732 356323

Charity Commission
14 Ryder Street, London SW1Y 6AH
01–214 6000
Central Register of Charities St Alban's
House, 57–60 Haymarket, London SW1Y 4QX
01–214 6000/8773

Commission for Racial Equality (CRE)
Elliot House, 10–12 Allington Street, London
SW1E 5EH 01–828 7022

**Commission of the European Communities
(UK Office)**
8 Storey's Gate, London SW1P 3AT 01–222 8122
[*N.B. The EEC Commissioner for the Environment is* Stanley Clinton Davis, EEC, 200 Rue
de la Roi, 1049 Brussels, Belgium]

Conservative Party
32 Smith Square, London SW1P 3HH
01–222 9000

Consumers' Association
14 Buckingham Street, London WC2N 6DS
01–839 1222

Directory of Social Change
9 Mansfield Place, London NW3 1HS

Equal Opportunities Commission (EOC)
Overseas House, Quay Street, Manchester
M3 3HN 061–833 9244
London office: 1 Bedford Street, London
WC2E 9HD 01–379 7989

European Parliament Information Office
2 Queen Anne's Gate, London SW1H 9AA
01–222 0411

Housing Corporation
Maple House, 149 Tottenham Court Road,
London W1P 0BN 01–387 9466

Labour Party
150 Walworth Road, London SE17 1JT
01–703 0833

Liberal Party
1 Whitehall Place, London SW1A 2HE
01–839 4092

Manpower Services Commission (MSC)
HQ & Employment Service Division: Moorfoot,
Sheffield, S. Yorks. S1 4PQ 0742 753275
Press & Information Office: Selkirk House, 166
High Holborn, London WC1V 6PF 01–836 1213

**National Association of Community
Relations Councils**
8 Coronet Street, London N1 6HD 01–739 6658

National Consumer Council
18 Queen Anne's Gate, London SW1H 9AA
01–222 9501

National Council for Civil Liberties (NCCL)
21 Tabard Street, London SE1 4LA 01–403 3888

**Northern Ireland Council of Social Services
(NICSS)**
2 Annadale Road, Belfast BT7 3JH 0232 640011

Plaid Cymru
51 Cathedral Road, Cardiff CF1 9HD 0222 31944

Scottish Council for Civil Liberties (SCCL)
146 Holland Street, Glasgow G2 4NG
041–332 5960

**Scottish Council for Community and Volun-
tary Organisations (SCCVO)
[formerly Scottish Council of Social Service]**
18–19 Claremont Crescent, Edinburgh
EH7 4QD 031–556 3882

Scottish National Party (SNP)
6 North Charlotte Street, Edinburgh EH2 4JH
031–226 3661

Social Democratic Party (SDP)
4 Cowley Street, London SW1P 3NB
01–222 4141

Trades Union Congress (TUC)
Congress House, Great Russell Street, London
WC1B 3LS 01–636 4030

Voluntary Services Unit (VSU)
Home Office, 50 Queen Anne's Gate, London
SW1H 9AT 01–213 7079

**Wales Council for Voluntary Action/Cyngor
Gweithredu Gwirfoddol Cymru (WCVA)**
Llys Ifor, Crescent Road, Caerphilly, Mid-Glam.
CF8 1XL 0222 869224

Women's National Commission
Government Offices, Great George Street,
London SW1P 3AQ 01–233 4208

JOURNALS

Further details of some of these journals can be obtained from the **Directory of Environmental Journals & Media Contacts (Council for Environmental Conservation, 1985)** which lists 200 journals and newsletters, with publishing and editorial details, subscription rates, circulation figures and brief summaries of content, together with key contacts in the media.

N.B. Many of these journals are available only through membership of the publishing organisation.

Title	No. of issues per year	Organisation/publisher
ACA Review	1	Anglers' Co-operative Association
ACOPS Newsletter	2	Advisory Committee on Pollution of the Sea
Action for Development	12	Centre for World Development Education
ADIU Report	6	Armament & Disarmament Information Unit
ADL Newsletter	3	Association of Designer-Leather workers
Adventure Education	6	National Association for Outdoor Education
Ag		Compassion in World Farming
Agricultural History Review	2	British Agricultural History Society
Airfields Environment Trust N/1	2	Airfields Environment Trust
Alexander Journal, The		Society of Teachers of the Alexander Technique
Alternative Communities Magazine		Alternative Communities Movement
Alternative Medicine Digest, The	12	Chartsearch Ltd [11 Blomfield St., London EC2M 7AY]
Alternative News	4	Dr Hadwen Trust for Humane Research
Amenity	6	North East Civic Trust
Ancient Monuments Society Newsletter	2	Ancient Monuments Society
Ancient Monuments Society Transactions	1	Ancient Monuments Society
Animal Ways	5	Royal Society for the Prevention of Cruelty to Animals
Animal Welfare Trust Bulletin	2	Animal Welfare Trust
Animal World	5	Royal Society for the Prevention of Cruelty to Animals
Animals' Defender	6	National Anti-Vivisection Society
Animals International	4	World Society for the Protection of Animals
Animals Now	3	Youth for Animal Rights
Annals of the ICRP	4	International Commission on Radiological Protection
Annual Pictorial Review	1	Scottish Society for the Prevention of Vivisection
Apicultural Abstracts	4	International Bee Research Assoc.
Applied Energy	12	Cranfield Institute of Technology
Appropriate Technology	4	Intermediate Technology Development Group
Appropriate Technology for Health		World Health Organisation
Aqualine Abstracts	26	Water Research Centre

Arboricultural Journal	4	Arboricultural Association
Architect's Journal, The	49/50	Architectural Press [9 Queen Anne's Gate, London SW1H 9BY]
Architects for Peace Newsletter	4	Architects for Peace
Architectural Heritage Society of Scotland Journal		Architectural Heritage Society of Scotland
Architectural Review, The	12	Architectural Press [9 Queen Anne's Gate, London SW1H 9BY]
Ark, The	12	Rare Breeds Survival Trust
Arms Control and Disarmament	4	Arms Control & Disarmament Research Unit
ASH Information Bulletin	24	ASH (Action on Smoking & Health)
ASH Supporters' News	4	ASH (Action on Smoking & Health)
Association of Agriculture Journal	1	Association of Agriculture
Association of Professional Foresters Newsletter	4	Assoc. of Professional Foresters
ATindex	4	ATindex
ATLA	4	FRAME (Fund for the Replacement of Animals in Medical Experiments)
Atom	12	UK Atomic Energy Authority
Avon Wildlife	3	Avon Wildlife Trust
Bach Remedy Newsletter, The	3	Bach Flower Remedies Ltd
Back Chat	2	Chiropractic Advancement Assoc.
Badger Protection Society Newsletter	4	Badger Protection Society
BAND Newsletter	6	Book Action for Nuclear Disarmament
Basic	12	British Assoc. of Settlements & Social Action Centres
Basketmakers' Association Newsletter	4	Basketmakers' Association
Bat News	4	Fauna & Flora Preservation Society
Battery Vehicles Review		Battery Vehicle Society
BBC Wildlife	12	BBC Pubs [Broadcasting House, Whiteladies Rd, Bristol BS8]
BBKA News	4	British Beekeepers Association
BBONT Bulletin		Berks, Bucks & Oxon Naturalists' Trust
Beautiful Britain News	1	Keep Britain Tidy Group
BecoN Newsletter	4	Buddhist Ecology Network
BEE (Bull. of Environmental Ed).	12	Streetwork
Bee Breeder, The	1	British Isles Bee Breeders' Assoc.
Bee Craft	12	British Beekeepers Association
Bee Farmers Association Newsletter	8	Bee Farmers Association
Bee World	4	International Bee Research Assoc.
Better Times	2	Shell Better Britain Campaign
Bicycles Bulletin		Friends of the Earth
Bio-Dynamic Agricultural Association Members' Bulletin		Bio-Dynamic Agricultural Assoc.
Biological Conservation	12	Elsevier Applied Science Pubs [Ripple Rd, Barking, Essex]
Bird Life	6	Young Ornithologists' Club (RSPB)
Bird Study	3	British Trust for Ornithology
Birds	4	Royal Society for the Protection of Birds
Black Beast (animal rights)	4	[PO Box 1, Earth 'n Wear, 15 Cowley Rd, Oxford OX4 1HP]
Blue Cross Illustrated	2	The Blue Cross

BNF Nutrition Bulletin	3	British Nutrition Foundation
British Arachnological Society Bull.		British Arachnological Society
British Arachnological Society N/1	3	British Arachnological Society
British Archaeological Abstracts	2	Council for British Archaeology
British Assoc. of Manipulative Medicine Newsletter		British Assoc. of Manipulative Medicine
British Birds	12	British Birds Ltd [Fountains, Park Lane, Blunham, Bedford MK44 3NJ]
British Butterfly Conservation Soc. News Bulletin	2	British Butterfly Conservation Soc.
British Goat Society Journal	12	British Goat Society
British Hedgehog Preservation Soc. N/1		British Hedgehog Preservation Soc.
British Herbalists Union Newsletter		British Herbalists Union
British Herpetological Society Bull.	4	British Herpetological Society
British Homoeopathic Journal	4	Faculty of Homoeopathy
British Hypnotherapy Assoc. Journal		British Hypnotherapy Association
British Journal of Acupuncture		British Acupuncture Assoc. & Reg.
British Journal of Herpetology	2	British Herpetological Society
British Journal of Holistic Medicine	2	British Holistic Medical Assoc.
British Nuclear Forum Bulletin	12	British Nuclear Forum
British Osteopathic Journal		Osteopathic Association of GB
British Peace Assembly Newsletter	6	British Peace Assembly
British Touch for Health Assoc. N/1	4	British Touch for Health Assoc.
BSBI News	3	Botanical Society of the Brit. Isles
BSRAE Association News		British Soc. for Research in Agricultural Engineering
BTO News	6	British Trust for Ornithology
Built Environment	4	Kogan Page [120 Pentonville Rd, London N1 9JB]
Bulletin, The	2	Lord Dowding Fund for Humane Research
Bulletin, The	4	Welsh Beekeepers' Association
Bulletin of the Amateur Entomologists' Society	4	Amateur Entomologists' Society
Bulletin of the British Ornithologists' Club	4	British Ornithologists' Club
Business in the Community Newsletter	4	Business in the Community
BUTTRESS Newsletter	2	Tyne & Wear Building Preservation Trust
Byway and Bridleway	9	Byway and Bridleways Trust
CAITS Quarterly	4	CAITS (Centre for Alternative Industrial & Technological Systems)
CALIP Newsletter	4	Campaign Against Lead in Petrol
CAMBIENT News	3	Cambs & Isle of Ely Naturalists' Trust
Campaign!	12	Campaign for Nuclear Disarmament
Campaign Against Arms Trade N/1	6	Campaign Against Arms Trade
Campaigner, The	6	National Anti-Vivisection Society
Canaan, The	4	Centre for Advice on Natural Alternatives
Captive Animals Protection Soc. N/1		Captive Animals Protection Society
Cartwheel News		Cartwheel
Cat, The	6	Cats Protection League
CAW Bulletin	6	Co-ordinating Animal Welfare
CBA Churches Bulletin	2	Council for British Archaeology
CBA Newsletter	9	Council for British Archaeology
CBA Schools Bulletin	2	Council for British Archaeology

CDA News		Co-operative Development Agency
CEE Newsheet	10	Council for Environmental Education/Scottish Env. Ed. Council
CEED Bulletin	6	Centre for Economic & Environmental Development
CEGB Digest		Central Electricity Generating Board
CEGB Newsletter		Central Electricity Generating Board
CES Newsletter	2	Centre for Energy Studies
Chartered Land Surveyor/Chartered Mineral Surveyor	4	Royal Institution of Chartered Surveyors
Chartered Surveyor Weekly	52	Royal Institution of Chartered Surveyors
CHEC Journal		Commonwealth Human Ecology Council
CHEC Points		Commonwealth Human Ecology Council
Chickens' Lib Newsletter	3	Chickens' Lib
Chiltern News		Chiltern Society
Christian Ecology Group News	4	Christian Ecology Group
Chronicle	12	Dag Hammarskjold Information Centre
City Farmer	4	National Federation of City Farms
Clean Air	4	National Society for Clean Air
CLEAR Newspaper	4	CLEAR (Campaign for Lead-free Air)
Combined Heat and Power	4	Combined Heat & Power Association
Common Futures	4	Future Studies Centre
Commonwealth Forestry Review	4	Commonwealth Forestry Association
Community	4	National Federation of Community Organisations
Community Action	6	[27 Clerkenwell Close, London EC1R 0AT]
Community Currents		Community Projects Foundation
Community Development Journal	3	OUP [Walton St, Oxford OX2 6DP]
Community Health Foundation Programme Newsletter	4	Community Health Foundation
Compassion	2	Beauty Without Cruelty International
Conservation Education		Young People's Trust for Endangered Species
Conservation Matters	3	Cleveland Nature Conservation Trust
Conservation News	3	Conservation Society
Conservation Review	1	Conservation Foundation
Conservation Trust Newsletter	3	Conservation Trust
Conserver, The	4	British Trust for Conservation Volunteers
Conserving Lakeland	2	Friends of the Lake District
Consumer Campaign Newsletter		Consumer Campaign
CONSYDER Newsletter	4	Conservation Society of the Yorkshire Derwent
Contact	3	British Chiropractors Association
Contact	2	North West Civic Trust
Context	4	Assoc. of Conservation Officers
Co-op Consumers	12	International Co-operative Alliance
Co-ops North East	4	Northern Region Co-operatives Development Association
Cornwall Trust for Nature Conservation Newsletter	2	Cornwall Trust for Nature Conservation
Council for Urban Studies Centres Jnl	11	Council for Urban Studies Centres
Country Landowner	12	Country Landowners' Association
Country-Side	3	British Naturalists' Association
Countryside Bulletin	3	Youth Hostels Association
Countryside Campaigner	3	Council for the Protection of Rural England

Countryside Commission News	6	Countryside Commission
Countryside Recorder, The	2	Ulster Society for the Preservation of the Countryside
County Councils Gazette	12	Association of County Councils
Crafts Magazine	6	Crafts Council
Cruel Sports	3/4	League Against Cruel Sports
Cumbria Trust for Nature Conservation Newsletter	3	Cumbria Trust for Nature Conservation
Cumbrian Campaigner		Cumbrians for Peace
Curam	4	Scottish Conservation Projects Trust
Current Affairs	12	Women's International Leage for Peace and Freedom
Cyclebag News	4	Cyclebag
Cycletouring	6	Cyclists' Touring Club
Daily Cyclist	4	London Cycling Campaign
Dales Park News	4	Yorkshire Dales National Park Auth.
Dartington Voice	12	Dartington Hall Trust
Day by Day	12	Fellowship Party
DCR (District Councils Review)	6	Association of District Councils
Deer	3	British Deer Society
Digest, The		BABA
Disarm!	6	Irish Campaign for Nuclear Disarmament
Disarmament Today	6	Irish Campaign for Nuclear Disarmament
Ditchley Newsletter, The	3	Ditchley Foundation
DNT Newsletter		Dorset Naturalists' Trust
Dodo, The	1	Jersey Wildlife Preservation Trust
Dodo Dispatch, The	3	Jersey Wildlife Preservation Trust
Dry Stone Walling Assoc. Newsletter	3	Dry Stone Walling Association
Durham County Conservation Trust Bull.	3	Durham County Conservation Trust
Earthlife News	4	Earthlife Foundation
Earthscan Bulletin	6	Earthscan/International Institute for Environment & Development
Earthwise Magazine	4	Environmental Information Centre
East-West Peace People Newsletter	3/4	East-West Peace People
EBSA Bulletin	3	Estuarine & Brackish-water Sciences Association
ECHO News	6	ECHO (European Commission Host Organisation)
Ecologist, The	6	Ecosystems Ltd [Worthyvale Manor Farm, Camelford, Cornwall PL32 9TT]
Econews	4	Ecology Party
Ecoropa Newsletter	2	Ecoropa
Ecos	4	British Assoc. of Nature Conservationists
Electric Truck & Vehicle World	3	Electric Vehicle Assoc. of GB
Electric Vehicle Developments		Electric Vehicle Development Group
Electricity Newsletter	4	Electricity Consumers' Council
Electronics for Peace Newsletter	6	Electronics for Peace
END Churches Register	4	European Nuclear Disarmament
END Journal	6	European Nuclear Disarmament
ENDS Report	12	Environmental Data Services
Energy Action Bulletin	6	Neighbourhood Energy Action

Energy in Buildings	6	R. J. Dodd Pubs [Fairway House, Dartmouth Rd, Forest Hill, London SE23]
Energy Management	12	Dept of Energy/National Energy Management Advisory Committee
Energy Manager	12	MCM Pub. [Century House, Tanner St., London SE1 3PJ]
Energy News	2	Energy Research Group
Energy Trends (statistics)	12	Dept of Energy
Energy World	12	Institute of Energy
EngND Newsletter	4	Engineers for Nuclear Disarmament
Enterprising London	4	Greater London Enterprise Board
Entomologist's Monthly Magazine	12	Gem Pub. [Brightwood, Brightwell, Wallingford, Oxon. OX1 0QD]
Environment in Europe, The	5	Institute for European Environmental Policy
Environmental Communicators' Org. N/1		Environmental Communicators' Org.
Environmental Education	2	National Association for Environmental Education
Environmental Education & Information		Institution of Environmental Sciences/U. of Salford
Environmental Forum Magazine		Environmental Forum
Environmental Health	12	Institution of Environmental Health Officers
Environmental Impact Assessment Worldletter	6	Centre for Environmental Management and Planning
Environmental Interpretation	6	Centre for Environmental Interpretation
Environmental Pollution: ecological & biological	12	Elsevier Applied Science Pubs [Ripple Rd, Barking, Essex]
Environmental Pollution: chemical & physical	8	Elsevier Applied Science Pubs [Ripple Rd, Barking, Essex]
ESRC Newsletter	3	Economic & Social Research Council
Estuarine, Coastal & Shelf Science	12	Estuarine & Brackish-water Sciences Association
Exhaust Gas Air Pollution Abstracts	24	Associated Octel Co.
Farm and Food Society Newsletter	3	Farm and Food Society
Farm Animal Campaigner	4	Campaign Against Farm Animal Abuse
Farmers Weekly	52	Agricultural Press [Surrey House, 1 Throwley Way, Sutton, Surrey SM1 4QQ]
Farming Business	4	Food From Britain
Fellowship News	4	Fellowship of Cycling Old-Timers
Field Studies	1	Field Studies Council
Fifth Fuel, The	4	Association for the Conservation of Energy
FIOH Newsletter	4	Future In Our Hands
First Voice	12	National Federation of Self-Employed & Small Businesses
FOAL Newsletter	3	Friends of Animals League
Focus	4	Woodcraft Folk
FoE Newspaper	3	Friends of the Earth
FoE (Scotland) Newsletter	3	Friends of the Earth (Scotland)
Food From Britain News		Food From Britain
Footloose (countryside issues)	12	Footloose Ltd [26 Commercial Blgs, Dunston, Tyne & Wear NE11 9AA]
Footpath Worker	4	Ramblers' Association
Forest Products Abstracts	12	Commonwealth Forestry Bureau
Forestry	2	Institute of Chartered Foresters

Forestry Abstracts	12	Commonwealth Forestry Bureau
Fourth World Review	6	Fourth World Movement
FRAME News	4	FRAME (Fund for the Replacement of Animals in Medical Experiments)
Freight	12	Freight Transport Association
Freeze Update	12	British Nuclear Weapons Freeze Council
Friends of the Lake District Report & Newsletter	2	Friends of the Lake District
Fuel and Energy Abstracts	6	Institute of Energy
Fuel News	4	National Right to Fuel Campaign
Fuel Poverty News		Scottish Fuel Poverty Action Group
Futures Network Newsletter	4	Futures Network
Gandhi Foundation Newsletter	4	Gandhi Foundation
Garden, The	12	Royal Horticultural Society
Garden History		Garden History Society
GEE-UP Newsletter	2	Glasgow Environmental Education Urban Projects
General Council & Register of Consultant Herbalists Newsletter	4	General Council & Register of Consultant Herbalists
Geographical Journal	3	Royal Geographical Society
Georgian Group News, The		Georgian Group
Geothermal Energy Project Newsletter		Geothermal Energy Project
Glass and Glazing News	6	Glass and Glazing Federation
Glass Gazette		Glass Manufacturers Federation
Glass Recycling Bulletin		Glass Manufacturers Federation
Gloucestershire Trust for Nature Conservation Newsletter	3	Gloucestershire TNC
GNAT		Glamorgan Nature Conservation Trust
Good Earth	4	Conservation Society (Bromsgrove)
Good Gardeners' Association N/l	6	Good Gardeners' Association
Grapevine	6	Christian Movement for Peace
Grass and Forage Science	4	British Grassland Society
Grass Farmer		British Grassland Society
Great Outdoors, The	12	Holmes McDougall, Ravenseft House, 302 St Vincent St., Glasgow G2 5NL]
Grebe, The	2	Cheshire Conservation Trust
Green Alliance Parliamentary N/l		Green Alliance
Green CND Newsletter		Green CND
Green Collective Mailing	6	Green Collective
Green Deserts	4	Green Deserts
Green Drum	4	Conservation Society (Birmingham)
Green Forum Journal	4	Stroud Green Forum
Green Line	12	[34 Cowley Rd, Oxford OX4 1HZ]
Green View	4	SDP Greens
Greenpeace News	4	Greenpeace
Groundwork Newsletter		Groundwork Foundation
Gwent Trust for Nature Conservation N/l		Gwent Trust for Nature Conservation
Habitat	12	Council for Environmental Conservation
Hampshire & I.0.W. Naturalists' Trust Newsletter	3	Hampshire & IoW Naturalists' Trust
HANG Newsletter		Highland Anti-Nuclear Group

HAPPA Newsletter	3	Horses & Ponies Protection Assoc.
Harwell Information Bulletin	52	Atomic Energy Research Est. (UKAEA)
Hawk Trust News		Hawk Trust
HDRA Newsletter	4	Henry Doubleday Research Association
HEB News	4	Health Education Bureau (RI)
Health and Hygiene	4	Royal Inst. of Public Health & Hygiene
Health and Safety Commission N/1	6	Health and Safety Commission
Health Education Journal	4	Health Education Council
Health Education News	6	Health Education Council
Health Information Centre Newsletter	12	Health Information Centre
Heating Action	4	Scottish Neighbourhood Energy Action
Heating and Ventilating Review	12	[111 St James' Rd, Croydon, Surrey CR9 2TH]
Helios	3	Solar Energy Unit
Herbal Review	4	Herb Society
Herefordshire & Radnorshire Nature Trust Newsletter	2	Herefordshire & Radnorshire Nature Trust
Heritage Education News	2	Heritage Education Group
Heritage Interpretation	3	Society for the Interpretation of Britain's Heritage
Heritage Newsletter	1	Ulster Architectural Heritage Society
Heritage Outlook	6	Civic Trust
Heritage Scotland	4	National Trust for Scotland
Heron	4	Beds & Hunts Naturalists' Trust
Hertfordshire & Middlesex Trust for Nature Conservation Newsletter	3	Herts & Middx TNC
Hertfordshire Society Newsletter	2	Hertfordshire Society
Holistic Medicine	4	British Holistic Medical Association
Homoeopath, The	4	Society of Homoeopaths
Homoeopathic Alternative, The	4	National Foundation for Homoeopathic Medicine
Homoeopathy	6	British Homoeopathic Association
HOPE Newsletter	6	HOPE (Help Organise Peaceful Energy)
Horticultural Abstracts	12	Commonwealth Bureau of Horticulture & Plantation Crops
Howl	3	Hunt Saboteurs Association
HRC News	2	Huntingdon Research Centre
Human Potential Resources	4	LSG plc [PO Box 10, Lincoln LN5 7JA]
Humane Education Journal	3	Humane Education Council
Humane Research Trust Journal	3	Humane Research Trust
Humanist News		British Humanist Association
Hydrological Sciences Journal	4	International Association of Hydrological Sciences
IAVS News Bulletin	3	Irish Anti-Vivisection Society
IAWPRC Newsletter	4	International Association on Water Pollution Research & Control
Ibis	4	British Ornithologists' Union
ICA News	12	International Co-operative Alliance
ICOF Newsletter	1	ICOF (Industrial Common Ownership Finance)
IDS Bulletin	4	Institute of Development Studies
IFAW Newsletter		International Fund for Animal Welfare
IMO News	4	International Maritime Organization
Impact of Science on Society	4	UNESCO

In The Making	1	In The Making
INCPEN	4	Industry Committee for Packaging and the Environment
Industrial Recovery	12	National Industrial Materials Recovery Association
Insect Conservation News	3/4	Amateur Entomologists' Society
Institute for Complementary Medicine Journal	1	Institute for Complementary Medicine
Institute for Complementary Medicine Newsletter	4	Institute for Complementary Medicine
Institute of Horticulture News	4	Institue of Horticulture
Institution of Environmental Sciences Journal		Institution of Environmental Sciences
Intermediate Technology News	2	Intermediate Technology Development Group
International Animal Action		International Association Against Painful Experiments on Animals
International Council for Bird Preservation Bulletin		International Council for Bird Preservation
International Council for Bird Preservation Newsletter	4	International Council for Bird Preservation
International Journal of Environmental Studies	8	[41–42 William IV St, London WC2N 4DE]
International Journal of Remote Sensing	12	Remote Sensing Society
International Primate Protection League Newsletter	3	Internat. Primate Protection League
International Tanker Owners Pollution Federation Newsletter	2	International Tanker Owners Pollution Federation
IOE Library Bulletin	12	Institute of Offshore Engineering
IOE Newsletter		Institute of Offshore Engineering
IPHE Newsletter	12	Institution of Public Health Engineers
IPPNW News Report	4	International Physicians for the Prevention of Nuclear War
Irish Birds	1	Irish Wildbird Conservancy
Irish Forestry	2	Society of Irish Foresters
Irish Hare, The	3	Ulster Trust for Nature Conservation
Irish Wildbird Conservancy Newsletter	4	Irish Wildbird Conservancy
IUCN Bulletin	4	International Union for Conservation of Nature & Natural Resources
IWA Waterways	3	Inland Waterways Association
Jane Newsletter	6	Journalists Against Nuclear Extermination
Jersey Wildlife Preservation Trust N/1	2	Jersey Wildlife Preservation Trust
JONAH Newsheet	4	JONAH (Jews Organised for a Nuclear Arms Halt)
Journal of Animal Ecology	3	British Ecological Society
Journal of Apicultural Research	4	International Bee Research Assoc.
Journal of Applied Ecology	3	British Ecological Society
Journal of the Association of Public Analysts	4	Association of Public Analysts
Journal of Climatology	6	Royal Meteorological Society
Journal of Dairy Research	4	Hannah Research Institute
Journal of Ecology	3	British Ecological Society
Journal of Environmental Education and Information	4	Environmental Institute
Journal of Environmental Management	6	Academic Press [24–28 Oval Rd, London NW1 7DX]

Journal of Fish Biology	12	Fisheries Society of the British Isles/Academic Press
Journal of the Geological Society	6	Geological Society
Journal of the Institute of Energy	4	Institute of Energy
Journal of the Institution of Water Engineers and Scientists	6	Institution of Water Engineers and Scientists
Journal of the Marine Biological Association of the United Kingdom	1	Marine Biological Assoc. of the UK
Journal of Planning and Environment Law	12	Sweet & Maxwell [11 New Fetter Lane, London EC4P 4EE]
Journal of the Society for Radiological Protection	4	Society for Radiological Protection
Journal of the Society of Occupational Medicine	4	Society of Occupational Medicine
Journal of Solar Energy	12	International Solar Energy Society
Journal of Zoology	12	Zoological Society of London
Justpeace	10	Pax Christi
Kent Trust Bulletin	3	Kent Trust for Nature Conservation
Kew Magazine	4	Royal Botanic Gardens/Collingridge
Kew Record of Taxonomic Literature	1	Royal Botanic Gardens/HMSO
Lake District Guardian, The	1	Lake District Special Planning Board
Landowning in Scotland	4	Scottish Landowners' Federation
Landscape Research	3	Landscape Research Group
Lapwing	3	Lancs Trust for Nature Conservation
LASDAB Newsletter		Liberals & Social Democrats Against Bloodsports
Laurieston Hall Newsletter	1	Laurieston Hall
Learning, Living & Leisure	3	Youth Hostels Association
Leeds TUCRIC Bulletin	4	TUCRIC (Trade Union & Community Resource & Information Centre)
LEG Newsletter	3	Liberal Ecology Group
Leicester Wildlife News	4	City Wildlife Project
Letternews	4	World Disarmament Campaign
Liberator	6	British Union for the Abolition of Vivisection
Lichenologist, The	3	British Lichen Society
Life Style Movement Newsletter	4	Life Style Movement
Lincolnshire & South Humberside Trust for Nature Conservation Newsletter	2	Lincs & S. Humberside TNC
Links	biennial	Third World First
LND Newsletter	4	Lawyers for Nuclear Disarmament
London Conserver	4	British Trust for Conservation Volunteers
Mammal Review	4	Mammal Society
Mammal Society Newsletter	4	Mammal Society
Manx Nature Conservation Trust N/1		Manx Nature Conservation Trust
Marwell Zoo News	4	Marwell Preservation Trust
Materials Reclamation Weekly	52	British Waste Paper Association
MCANW Newsletter	3	Medical Campaign Against Nuclear Weapons
Media Women for Peace Newsletter		Media Women for Peace
Mediator, The	6	Mediating Network
Medical Association for Prevention of War Newsletter		Medical Assoc. For Prevention of War

Medicine and War	3	Medical Assoc. For Prevention of War
Meteorological Magazine, The	12	Meteorological Office
MIAS News Bulletin		Institute of Oceanographic Sciences
Modern Tramway	12	Light Rail Transit Association
Montgomery Trust for Nature Conservation Newsletter	4	Montgomery TNC
Mother Earth		Mother Earth
Mothers for Peace Newsletter	4	Mothers for Peace
MRC News	4	Medical Research Council
Municipal Review & AMA News	10	Assoc. of Metropolitan Authorities
NAC News	4	Royal Agricultural Soc. of England
NAEE Newsletter	3	National Association for Environmental Education
NAFSO Journal	1	National Association of Field Studies Officers
NAFSO Newsletter	4	National Association of Field Studies Officers
National Council for the Conservation of Plants & Gardens Newsletter	2	National Council for the Conservation of Plants & Gardens
National Pure Water Association N/1		National Pure Water Association
National Trust	3	National Trust
National Waterways Transport Association Newsletter	3	National Waterways Transport Assoc.
NATTA Newsletter	6	NATTA (Network for Alternative Technology. . .)/Appropriate Tech. Group
Natural Energy and Living	4	Natural Energy Association
Natural Health Network Newsletter	4	Natural Health Network
Natural Medicines Group Bulletin	4	Natural Medicines Group
Natural World	3	Royal Soc. for Nature Conservation
Naturalist	4	Yorks. Naturalists' Union [Doncaster Museum, Chequer Rd, Doncaster, S. Yorks]
Nature	51	Macmillan Jnls [4 Little Essex St., London WC2R 3LF]
Nature and Resources	4	UNESCO
Naturopa	3	Council of Europe (via Nature Conservancy Council)
NCDL News	2	National Canine Defence League
NEL Newsletter		National Engineering Laboratory
NERC Newsjournal	4	Natural Environment Research Council
Network	6	Communes Network
Network	12	Town & Country Planning Association
Network Newsletter		Scientific & Medical Network
New Co-operator, The	4	ICOM (Industrial Common Ownership Movement)
New Farmer and Grower, The	4	British Organic Farmers
New Farmer and Grower	4	Organic Growers Association
New Grapevine	4	Scottish Civic Trust
New Ground	4	SERA (Socialist Environment & Resources Association)
New Herbal Practitioner	2/3	National Inst. of Medical Herbalists
New Internationalist	12	[42 Hythe Bridge St., Oxford OX1 2EP]
New Scientist	52	IPC [Commonwealth Hse, 1–19 New Oxford St., London WC1A 1NG]
New Travel Bulletin	4	Connections
Newport & Nevern Energy Group N/1	2/3	Newport & Nevern Energy Group

Radiological Protection Bulletin	6	National Radiological Protection Board
Railwatch	4	Railway Development Society
RASE Journal	1	Royal Agricultural Soc. of England
RCCM Newsletter	3/4	Research Council for Complementary Medicine
RE News		Energy Technology Support Unit
REED (Review of Environmental Education Developments)	3	Council for Environmental Education/Scottish Environmental Ed. Council
Regional Studies	6	Regional Studies Association
Regional Studies Association N/1	6	Regional Studies Association
Relaxation for Living Newsletter	4	Relaxation for Living
Remote Sensing Society's News & Letters (rep. from Int. Jnl of Remote Sensing)	4	Remote Sensing Society
Research Reports Digest		Nature Conservancy Council
Restoration News		North West Buildings Preservation Trust
Resurgence	6	Schumacher Society
Review of International Co-operation	4	International Co-operative Alliance
RIBA Journal	12	Royal Institute of British Architects
Ring Ouzel	3	Derbyshire Naturalists' Trust
RISVB Digest	4	North West Civic Trust
Roebuck	3	Northumberland Wildlife Trust
Roots	6	Sacred Trees Trust
Routing Out	6	ALARM (Alert Londoners Against Radioactive Materials)
Royal Entomogical Society Bulletin		Royal Entomological Society
RSA Journal	12	Royal Society of Arts
Rucksack	4	Ramblers' Association
Rural Development Abstracts	4	Commonwealth Bureau of Agricultural Economics
Rural Focus	6	Development Commission
Rural Viewpoint	6	National Council for Voluntary Orgs
Rural Wales	3	Council for the Protection of Rural Wales
Ruris	3	Centre for the Study of Rural Society
SAGA Bulletin	3	Sand and Gravel Association
SANA Newsletter	4	Scientists Against Nuclear Arms
SAND Newsletter	12	Sussex Alliance for Nuclear Disarmament
SANE (Scotland) Newsletter		Students Against Nuclear Energy (Scot.)
Sanity	4	Campaign for Nuclear Disarmament
SAVE Report	4	Society Against Violation of the Environment
SAVS Newsletter	4	Scottish Anti-Vivisection Society
Science for People	4	British Society for Social Responsibility in Science
Scientific Horticulture	1	Institute of Horticulture
Scottish Beekeeper, The	12	Scottish Beekeepers' Association
Scottish Birds	2	Scottish Ornithologists' Club
Scottish CND News	6	Scottish CND
Scottish Forestry	4	Royal Scottish Forestry Society
Scottish Health Education Group Bull.	4	Scottish Health Education Group
Scottish Hosteller	2	Scottish Youth Hostels Association
Scottish Review, The		Scottish Civic Trust
Scottish Solar Energy Group N/1	3/4	Scottish Solar Energy Group
Scottish Tree Trust Newsletter		Scottish Tree Trust

Scottish Wildlife	3	Scottish Wildlife Trust
SCRAM Journal	6	SCRAM (Scottish Campaign to Resist the Atomic Menace)
SCRAmble	4	Scottish Countryside Rangers Assoc.
SCRUtiny		Small Communities Research Union
Sea	4	Marine Conservation Society
Seabird	1	Seabird Group
Seabird Group Newsletter	3	Seabird Group
SEAD Network	6	Scottish Education and Action for Development
Seadumping News		Campaign Against Sea Dumping
Seed Bank & Exchange Newsletter	1	Seed Bank & Exchange
Self-Health	4	College of Health
SENSE Newsletter	2	Skills Exchange Network for a Stable Economy
SET Newsletter		Society for Environmental Therapy
Shooting and Conservation	4	British Association for Shooting and Conservation
Shropshire Wildlife	3	Shropshire Trust for Nature Conservation
Sizewell Reactions		East Anglian Alliance Against Nuclear Power
Smallfarmer, The	6	Smallfarmers' Association
SNCT Newsletter	2	Staffs Nature Conservation Trust
SOC News	4	Scottish Ornithologists' Club
Socialist Countryside Group Newsletter		Socialist Countryside Group
Society of Sussex Downsmen News Sheet		Society of Sussex Downsmen
Soil and Water	4	Soil and Water Management Association
Soil Association Quarterly	4	Soil Association
Solar Trade Association Newsletter	12	Solar Trade Association
Solid Fuel	12	Harper Trade Jnls [Harling House, 47 Gt. Suffolk St., London SE1 0BS]
Solid Wastes	12	Institute of Waste Management
Somerset Trust for Nature Conservation Newsletter	3	Somerset TNC
South West Way Association Newsletter	2	South West Way Association
SPAB Journal	4	Society for the Protection of Ancient Buildings
S*P*A*R*K, The		Seminarium into the Psyche, Architecture and Rural Knowledge
Species News	4	Royal Zoological Society of Scotland
Star and Furrow	2	Bio-Dynamic Agricultural Association
STAT Newsletter	2	Society of Teachers of the Alexander Technique
Stream	12	Severn-Trent Water Authority
Student Green Network Newsletter		Student Green Network
Suffolk Trust for Nature Conservation Newsletter	3	Suffolk Trust for Nature Conservation
Sun at Work in Britain	2	International Solar Energy Society
Surrey Trust for Nature Conservation Newsletter	3	Surrey Trust for Nature Conservation
Survival International News	4	Survival International
Survival International Review	1	Survival International
Sussex Trust for Nature Conservation Newsletter	3	Sussex Trust for Nature Conservation
Swan Rescue Service Newsletter	2	Swan Rescue Service
TACINdex	4	TACIN (Town & County Information Network)

TACT Newsletter		Tories Against Cruise and Trident
Tandem Club Magazine	6	Tandem Club
Tarn and Tor	2	Council for National Parks
Teachers for Peace Newsletter	3	Teachers for Peace
Technology and the Environment		Dept of Trade & Industry
Teilhard Review & Journal of Creative Evolution, The	3	Teilhard Centre
TFSR Newsletter	6	Tools for Self-Reliance
Threads	6	Interhelp
Threatened Plants Newsletter	2/3	IUCN Conservation Monitoring Centre [The Herbarium, Royal Botanic Gardens, Kew, Richmond, Surrey TW9 3AB]
Timber Grower	4	Timber Growers United Kingdom
Today		Royal Society for the Prevention of Cruelty to Animals
Topical Issues	4	Nature Conservancy Council
Town & Country Planning	11	Town & Country Planning Association
TRADA News	3	Timber Research & Development Assoc.
Traffic Bulletin	5	IUCN Conservation Monitoring Centre
Transactions of the Ancient Monuments Society	1	Ancient Monuments Society
Transactions of the Assoc. for Studies in the Conservation of Historic Bldgs	1	Assoc. for Studies in the Conservation of Historic Buildings
Transport	6	Chartered Institute of Transport
Transport Management	4	Institute of Transport Administration
Transport on Water Association N/1	1	Transport on Water Association
Transport Retort	12	Transport 2000
Tree News	3	Tree Council
Tree of Life		Assoc. for New Approaches to Cancer
Trees	2	Men of the Trees
Turning Point Newsletter	2	Turning Point
UACTA (United Against Cruelty to Animals)		Animals' Vigilantes
UCAT Newsletter	2	Urban Centre for Appropriate Technology
UDAP Newsletter	4	Unit for the Development of Alternative Products
UFAW News-sheet		Universities Federation for Animal Welfare
UNESCO Courier, The	11	UNESCO
Urban Design Quarterly	4	Urban Design Group [39 Charing Cross Road, London WC2H 0AW]
Urban Wildlife Group Newsletter	6	Urban Wildlife Group
Urban Wildlife News	4	Nature Conservancy Council
URBED Review	1	URBED (Urban & Economic Development Group)
Vegan, The	4	Vegan Society
Vegetarian, The	6	Vegetarian Society of the UK
Veterinary Bulletin	12	Commonwealth Bureau of Animal Health
Victorian Society Newsletter, The	3	Victorian Society
Wales Ahead	4	Welsh Development Agency
Walk	3	Pedestrians Association
WANA News	6	Welsh Anti-Nuclear Alliance
War on Want Newsletter	6	War on Want

BIBLIOGRAPHY
1983–5

N.B. Each book has been listed under one category only; e.g. a book dealing with farm animals will have been listed either under 'agriculture' or 'animal welfare', but not both. See also publications listed under organisation entries, which do not necessarily appear in this listing.

Agriculture

Bowers, J.K. & Cheshire, Paul, *Agriculture, the Countryside and Land Use: an economic critique*, Methuen, 1983, 192pp.
Carnell, Paul, *Alternatives to Factory Farming: an economic appraisal*, Earth Resources Research, 1983, 130pp.
Gold, Mark, *Assault and Battery: what factory farming means for humans and animals*, Pluto, 1983, 172pp.
Jenkins, David (ed.), *Agriculture and the Environment*, Institute of Terrestrial Ecology, 1984, 195pp.
Pye-Smith, C. & North, R., *Working the Land: a new plan for a healthy agriculture*, Temple Smith, 1984, 138pp.
Shoard, Marion, *The Theft of the Countryside*, Temple Smith, rev.1983, 272pp.
Tranter, R.B. (ed.), *Strategies for Family-Worked Farms in the UK (Proceedings of a symposium organised by the Smallfarmers' Association and the Centre for Agricultural Strategy)*, Centre for Agricultural Strategy, 1983.
WWOOF Directory of Organic Organisations in the UK, 1984, 22pp.

Animal welfare

Duffy, Maureen, *Men and Beasts: an animal rights handbook*, Paladin, 1984, 160pp.
Hall, Rebecca, *Voiceless Victims*, Wildwood House, 1984, 288pp.
Paton, William, *Man and Mouse: animals in medical research*, Oxford Pbks, 1984, 174pp.
Sandys-Winsch, Godfrey, *Animal Law (in England & Wales)*, Shaw & Sons, rev. 1984, 294pp.
Singer, Peter (ed.), *In Defence of Animals*, Blackwell, 1985, 224pp.
Thomas, Richard H., *The Politics of Hunting*, Gower, 1983, 326pp.

Arms/Defence/Peace

Alternative Defence Commission, *Defence Without the Bomb*, Taylor & Francis, 1985, 318pp. [An abridged version is available: *Without the Bomb: non-nuclear defence policies for Britain*, Paladin, 1985, 92pp.]
Baylis, John (ed.), *Alternative Approaches to British Defence Policy*, Macmillan, 1983, 247pp.
Chalmers, Malcolm, *Paying for Defence: military spending and British decline*, Pluto, 1985, 200pp.
Dyson, F., *Weapons and Hope*, Harper & Row, 1984, 340pp.
Farrow, Stephen & Chown, Alex (eds), *The Human Cost of Nuclear War*, Medical Campaign Against Nuclear Weapons, 1983, 164pp.
Galtung, Johan, *There Are Alternatives: four roads to peace and security*, Spokesman, 1984, 221pp.
Glasgow University Media Group, *War and Peace News*, Open U. Press, 1985, 384pp.
Greene, Owen et al., *Nuclear Winter: the evidence and the risks*, Polity Press/Blackwell, 1985, 216pp.
Holroyd, Fred (ed.), *Thinking About Nuclear Weapons: analyses and prescriptions*, Croom Helm, 1985, 432pp.
Johnstone, Diana, *Politics of Euromissiles: Europe's role in America's world*, Verso, 1984, 218pp.
Openshaw, Stan & Steadman, Philip, *Doomsday: Britain after nuclear attack*, Blackwell, 1983, 296pp.
Patterson, Walter C., *The Plutonium Business and the spread of the bomb*, Paladin, 1984, 272pp.
Pugwash, *The Arms Race at a Time of Decision (Annals of Pugwash 1983)*, Macmillan, 1984.
Pugwash, *Nuclear Strategy and World Security (Annals of Pugwash 1984)*, Macmillan, 1985.
Rowan-Robinson, Dr Michael, *Fire and Ice: the Nuclear Winter*, Longman, 1985, 118pp.
Rowe, Dorothy, *Living With the Bomb: can we live without enemies?* Routledge & Kegan Paul, 1985, 243pp.

Schell, Jonathan, *The Abolition,* Picador, 1984, 163pp.
Sheehan, Michael, *The Arms Race,* Martin Robertson, 1983, 242pp.
Stockholm International Peace Research Institute (SIPRI), *SIPRI Yearbook: world armaments and disarmament.* [Abridged version: *The Arms Race and Arms Control.* Taylor & Francis.]
United Nations Organisation, *The United Nations Disarmament Yearbook, vol.7 (1982),* UNO, 1985. [Available from HMSO]

Built environment [*see also* Urban conservation]

Baker, David, *Living With the Past: the historic environment,* privately published, 1984. [3 Oldway, Bletsoe, Bedford MK44 1QG]
Binney, Marcus, *Our Vanishing Heritage,* Arlington, 1984, 256pp.
Clifton-Taylor, Alec & Ireson, A.S., *English Stone Building,* Victor Gollancz, 1983, 288pp.
Gold, John R., *The Urban Vision: Twentieth Century images of the future city,* Croom Helm, 1985, 200pp.

Community enterprise

Jones, Maggie, *Voluntary Organisations and the Media,* Bedford Square Press/NCVO, 1984.
MacShane, Denis, *Using the Media,* Pluto, rev.1983, 218pp.
National Federation of Community Organisations, *Guidelines for a Local Federal Organisation,* 3rd edn. NFCO, 1984, 275pp (loose-leaf).
Pinder Caroline, *Community Start-Up: how to start a community group and keep it going,* National Federation of Community Organisations, 1984, 212pp.
Treweek, Chris *et al., The Alternative Printing Handbook,* Penguin, 1983, 114pp.
Wilson, Des, *Pressure: the A-Z of campaigning in Britain,* Heinemann, 1984, 181pp.

Computerised resources, directories of

Directory of Data Bases and Data Banks, Euronet-Diane.
ENDOC Directory, Commission of the European Communities.
EUSIDIC Database Guide, Learned Information.
Online Bibliographic Databases, Aslib.

Co-operatives

Berry, John & Roberts, Mark, *Co-op Management and Employment,* ICOM, 1984, 83pp.
Cockerton, Peter & Whyatt, Ann, *The Workers Co-operative Handbook,* ICOM, 1984, 128pp.
Co-operative Advisory Group, *Marketing in Worker Co-operatives in the UK,* CAG, 1984. 119pp.
Greater London Enterprise Board, *Survival or Liquidation: a guide for worker co-ops,* GLEB, 1984.
Pearce, John, *Running Your Own Co-operative,* Kogan Page, 1984, 174pp.

Countryside conservation [*see also* Environment: general]

Austin, Vincent, *Rural Project Management: a handbook for students and practitioners,* Batsford Academic & Educational, 1984.
Blunden, John & Turner, Graham, *Critical Countryside,* BBC Pubs, 1985.
Clayden, Paul, *Our Common Land: the law and history of commons and village greens,* Open Spaces Society, 1984, 120pp.
Dasmann, Raymond F., *Environmental Conservation,* Wiley, 1984, 496pp.
Denyer-Green, Barry, *Wildlife & Countryside Act 1981: the practitioner's companion,* Surveyors Pubs, 1983, 265pp.
Green, Bryn H., *Countryside Conservation,* 2nd edn., Allen & Unwin, 1985.
Harte, J.D.C., *Landscape, Land Use and the Law: an introduction to the law relating to the landscape and its use,* E.&.F.N. Spon, 1985.
Lacey, William, (ed.), *Britain's National Parks,* Windward Books, 1984, 192pp.
Muir, Richard & Duffy, Eric, *The Shell Countryside Book,* J.M. Dent, 1984, 318pp.
Parkes, C., *Laws of the Countryside.* [Available from M.Marshall, 2 Causeway Cottages, Middleton, Saxmundham, Suffolk IP17 3NH]
Pye-Smith, C. & Rose, C., *Crisis and Conservation: conflict in the British countryside,* Penguin, 1984, 213pp.

Crafts

Conservation Bureau, *Scottish Conservation Directory 1985–86*, Conservation Bureau (Scottish Development Agency), 1985, 192pp.
Crafts Council. *Conservation Sourcebook*. [updated periodically]
Seymour, John, *The Forgotten Arts: a practical guide to traditional skills*, Dorling Kindersley (in association with the National Trust), 1984.

Development

Albery, Nicholas & Kinzley, Mark, *How to Save the World: a Fourth World guide to the politics of scale*, Turnstone, 1984, 318pp.
Brandt Commission, *Common Crisis: North-South co-operation for world recovery*, Pan, 1983, 192pp.
Council for Education in World Citizenship, *World Studies Resource Guide*, CEWC, 1984, 32pp.
Horberry, John, *Environmental Guidelines Survey: an analysis of environmental procedures and guidelines governing development aid*, International Institute for Environment and Development, 1983.
International Union for Conservation of Nature & Natural Resources, *National Conservation Strategies: a framework for sustainable development*, IUCN, 1984, 52pp.
Redclift, M.R., *Development and the Environmental Crisis: red or green alternatives*, Methuen, 1984.

Ecology

Putnam, R.J. & Wratten, S.D., *Principles of Ecology*, Croom Helm, 1985, 384pp.
Ramade, François, *The Ecology of Natural Resources*, Wiley, 1984.
Roberts, R.D. & T.M., *Planning and Ecology*, Chapman & Hall, 1984.
Smith, Dianne P., *Urban Ecology*, (Practical Ecology Series), Allen & Unwin, 1984.
Vink, A.P.A. (ed. D.A. Davidson), *Landscape Ecology and Land Use*, Longman, 1983.

Energy

Bending, R. & Eden, R. (Cambridge Energy Research Group), *UK Energy: structure, prospects and policies*, Cambridge U. Press, 1985, 320pp.
Croall, Stephen & Sempler, Kaianders, *Nuclear Power for Beginners*, 3rd rev. edn, Writers & Readers, 1985, 176pp.
Dept of Energy, *The Pattern of Energy Use in the UK (1980)*, DEn, 1984, 145pp.
Elkington, John, *Sun Traps*, Penguin, 1984, 400pp.
Evans, N.L. (Cambridge Energy Research Group) & Hope, C.W. (U. of Leeds), *Nuclear Power: futures, costs and benefits*, Cambridge U. Press, 1984, 200pp.
Flood, Michael, *Solar Prospects: the potential for renewable energy*, Wildwood House, 1983.
Ince, Martin, *Sizewell Report: what happened at the Inquiry?*, Pluto, 1984, 212pp.
Littler, John & Thomas, Randall, *Design With Energy: the conservation and use of energy in buildings*, Cambridge U. Press, 1984, 366pp.
Lloyd Jones, Peter, *The Economics of Nuclear Power Programs in the United Kingdom*, Macmillan, 1984.
Ramage, Janet, *Energy: a guide book*, Oxford U. Press, 1983, 366pp.
Schumacher, Diana, *Energy: crisis or opportunity?*, Macmillan, 1985, 352pp.
Valentine, John, *Atomic Crossroads: before and after Sizewell*, Merlin, 1985, 236pp.

Environment: general [*see also* Countryside conservation]

Association of Metropolitan Authorities, *Green Policy*, AMA, 1985.
Baldock, David, *Wetland Drainage in Europe*, International Institute for Environment & Development, 1984, 175pp.
Blunden, John & Curry, Nigel (eds), *The Changing Countryside*, Croom Helm, 1985, 270pp.
[Abridged version: *The Countryside Handbook*, 100pp.]
Channel Four TV/Shell, *Worldwise Environmental Action Pack*, 1985, 62pp.
Civic Trust, *Environmental Directory: national and regional organisations of interest to those concerned with amenity and the environment*, Civic Trust, 1984, 68pp.
Clayden, Paul & Trevelyan, John, *Rights of Way: a guide to law and practice*, Open Spaces Society/Ramblers Association, 1983, 359pp.

Council for Environmental Conservation, *Directory of Environmental Journals and Media Contacts*, CoEnCo, 1984.

Dept of the Environment, *Report on DoE Research and Development April 1982–March 1984*, HMSO, 1985. [First of a new series of biennial reports on the R&D activities of the DoE, covering a great many environmental topics.]

Drabble, Phil, *What Price the Countryside?*, Michael Joseph, 1985.

Haigh, Nigel, *EEC Environmental Policy and Britain*, Environmental Data Services (for International Institute for Environment & Development), 1984.

King, Angela & Clifford, Susan, *Holding Your Ground: an action guide to local conservation*, Temple Smith, 1985, 340pp.

Lee, Brian H., *The British Naturalists' Association Guide to Fields, Farms and Hedgerows*, BNA, 1985, 128pp.

Mabey, Richard, *Second Nature*, Jonathan Cape, 1984, 233pp.

McCormick, John, *The User's Guide to the Environment*, Kogan Page, 1985, 250pp.

Myers, Norman (ed.), *The Gaia Atlas of Planet Management*, Pan, 1985, 272pp.

Ortoland, L., *Environmental Planning and Decision Making*, Wiley, 1984, 448pp.

Pitt, D. (ed.), *Youth, Conservation and Energy: questions and answers on the future of population, resources, environment and development*, International Union for Conservation of Nature & Natural Resources, 1985, 110pp.

Shreeve & Rackman (eds), *Conservation Annual*, Conservation Foundation, 1984, 120pp.

United Nations Environment Programme, *European Environment Yearbook*, UNEP Regional Office for Europe [Geneva Office, Palais des Nations, CH–1211 Geneva, Switzerland]. [Includes address list of European environmental organisations]

Wilson, Des (ed.), *The Environmental Crisis: a handbook for all Friends of the Earth*, Heinemann Educational, 1984, 196pp.

Young, Geoffrey, *The Sunday Times Countryside Companion*, Country Life, 1985.

Environmental education

Barclay, Derrick, *Interpretation of the Environment*, Carnegie Trust, 1984 [bibliography].

Conservation Trust, *Environmental Education Enquiries*, 4th edn, CT, 1985.

Conservation Trust, *Guide to Resources in Environmental Education*, 10th edn, CT, 1985 [annual].

Dept of Education & Science, *Environmental Education: sources of information for teachers*.

Ethics, Philosophy, Political ecology

Attfield, Robin, *The Ethics of Environmental Concern*, Blackwell, 1983, 232pp.

Lowe, Philip & Goyder, Jane, *Environmental Groups in Politics* Allen & Unwin, 1983, 220pp.

Pepper, D.M., *The Roots of Modern Environmentalism*, Croom Helm, 1984, 256pp.

Porritt, Jonathon, *Seeing Green: the politics of ecology explained*, Blackwell, 1985, 249pp.

Robertson, James, *The Sane Alternative*, rev. 1983. Privately published [The Old Bakehouse, Ilges Lane, Cholsey, Wallingford, Oxon. OX10 9NU]

Food and Health

Batt, Eva, *Vegan Cooking: the classic vegan cookbook*, Thorsons, 1985, 144pp.

Cox, Michael & Crockett, Desda, *The New Vegetarian: the complete survival plan for those who have given up meat*, Thorsons/Vegetarian Society, 1985, 160pp.

Fulder, Dr Stephen, *The Handbook of Complementary Medicine*, Coronet, 1984, 368pp.

Gear, Alan, *The Organic Food Guide*, Henry Doubleday Research Association, 1983, 126pp.

Hodgkinson, Neville, *Will to be Well: the real alternative medicine*, Hutchinson, 1984, 281pp.

Howard, Alex, *Finding a Way: a realist's introduction to self-help therapy*, Gateway, 1985, 212pp.

Hulke, M., *Encyclopaedia of Alternative Medicine and Self-Help*, Rider.

Oddy, Derek & Miller, Derek (eds), *Diet and Health in Modern Britain*, Croom Helm, 1984, 224pp.

Tracy, Lisa, *The Gradual Vegetarian: for everyone finally ready to make the change*, Century, 1985, 300pp.

Vegetarian Society, *International Vegetarian Handbook 1985–6*, Thorsons, 1985, 358pp.

Forestry and Trees

Dudley, Nigel, *The Death of Trees*, Pluto, 1985, 133pp.

Grove, Richard, *The Future of Forestry*, British Association of Nature Conservationists, 1984.

Perkins, Benjamin, *Trees*, Century, 1984, 176pp.

Poore, Duncan, *Replenishing the World's Forests: why replenish? – world forests, past, present and future,* International Institute for Environment & Development, 1984.

Nature conservation

Hammond, Nicholas (ed.), *RSPB Nature Reserves,* Croom Helm, 1985, 184pp.
The Macmillan Guide to Britain's Nature Reserves, Macmillan (in co-operation with the Royal Society for Nature Conservation), 1984, 700pp.
Meenan, Audrey, *Directory of Natural History and Related Societies in Britain and Ireland,* British Museum (Natural History), 1983, 410pp.
Nature Conservancy Council (Interpretive Branch), *Nature Conservation in Great Britain,* NCC, 1984, 112pp.
Perring, F.H. & Farrell, L. (compilers), *British Red Data Book 1,* Royal Society for Nature Conservation, 1983.

Plants (inc. herbs)

Bunney, S. (ed.), *The Illustrated Book of Herbs,* Octopus, 1984.
Huxley, Anthony, *Green Inheritance: the World Wildlife Fund Book of Plants,* Collins, 1985, 192pp.
IUCN Conservation Monitoring Centre (Threatened Plants Unit), *Plants in Danger: what do we know?,* IUCN, 1984.
Perring, F.H., *RSNC Guide to British Wild Flowers,* Country Life Books, 1984.

Pollution

Control of Pollution Encyclopaedia, 2 vols (loose-leaf), Butterworths, [regularly updated].
Elsworth, Steve, *Acid Rain in the UK and Europe,* Pluto, 1984, 160pp.
Environment Committee (House of Commons), *Fourth Report: Acid Rain* (HC446), HMSO, 1984, 76pp.
Fry, G.L.A. & Cooke, A.S., *Acid Deposition and its Implications for Nature Conservation in Britain,* Nature Conservancy Council, 1984, 59pp.
Graham & Trotman (for the Commission of the European Communities), *Acid Rain: a review of the phenomenon in the EEC and Europe,* Environmental Resources Ltd, 1983, 150pp.
Hawkins, Keith, *Environment and Enforcement: regulation and the social definition of pollution,* Oxford U. Press, 1984, 268pp.
Hazardous Waste Inspectorate, *Hazardous Waste Management: an overview* [First Report], DoE, DoE (NI), Scottish Office & Welsh Office, 1985, 59pp.
International Register of Potentially Toxic Chemicals, *IRPTC Legal File,* 2 vols, United Nations Organisation, 900pp. [Available from HMSO.]
Landown, Richard & Yule, William (eds), *The Lead Debate: the environment, toxicology and child health,* Croom Helm, 1985, 250pp.
Lean, Mary, *Pollution and the Environment,* Macdonald, 1985, 64pp.
McCormick, John, *Acid Earth: the global threat of acid pollution,* Earthscan, 1985, 190pp.
National Society for Clean Air, *NSCA Reference Book,* 2nd edn, NSCA, 1984, 306pp.
Royal Commission on Environmental Pollution, *Tackling Pollution: experience and prospects* [Tenth Report], HMSO, 1984.
Wilson, Des, *The Lead Scandal,* Heinemann, 1983, 192pp.

Population

Gould, W.T.S. & Lawton, R. (eds), *Planning for Population Change,* Croom Helm, 1985, 256pp.

Resource management

Cloke, Paul & Park, Chris, *Rural Resource Management: a geographical perspective,* Croom Helm, 1985, 352pp.
International Institute for Environment & Development, *World Resources Report,* IIED/World Resources Institute, 1985.

Rural living and self-sufficiency

Kitto, Dick (ed.), *Rural Resettlement Handbook,* rev. 3rd edn, Rural Resettlement Group/Prism Alpha/Lighthouse, 1984, 300pp.

Sweeney, Sedley, *The Challenge of Smallholding*, Oxford U. Press, 1985.

Safety

Advisory Committee on Major Hazards, *The Control of Major Hazards* [Third Report], HMSO, 1984.
Cliff, Kenneth S., *Accidents: causes, prevention and services*, Croom Helm, 1984, 320pp.

Self-employment

Barrow, C., *Small Business Guide*, rev. edn, BBC Pubs, 1984, 254pp.
Bollard, Alan, *Just For Starters: a handbook of small-scale business opportunities*, Intermediate
    Technology Pubs, 1984, 208pp.

Technology

Bertell, Dr Rosalie, *No Immediate Danger: prognosis for a radioactive Earth*, The Women's Press,
    1985, 352pp.
Carr, Marilyn, *The AT Reader: theory and practice in Appropriate Technology*, Intermediate
    Technology Pubs, 1985, 488pp.
Intermediate Technology Development Group, *Appropriate Technology Institutions: a directory*,
    rev. edn, ITDG, 1985, 38pp.
Sinclair, Angela, *A Guide to Appropriate Technology Institutions*, Intermediate Technology Pubs,
    1985, 124pp.

Transport

Bagwell, Philip, *End of the Line? The fate of public transport under Thatcher*, Verso, 1984, 218pp.
Bell, G.J. *et al.*, *The Economics and Planning of Transport*, Heinemann, 1983.
Civic Trust, *Bypasses and the Juggernaut: fact and fiction*, CT, 1983, 75pp.
McRobie, G. *et al.*, *Setting the Wheels in Motion: towards a national cycling policy*, Bristol U., 1983,
    74pp.
Taplin, M.R. *et al.*, *Light Rail Transit Today*, Light Rail Transit Association, 1984, 64pp.
Wistrich, Enid, *The Politics of Transport*, Longman, 1983, 186pp.

Urban conservation [*see also* Built environment]

Aldous, Tony, *Tackling Dereliction*, Fed. of Civil Engineering Contractors, 1984.
Eley, Peter & Worthington, John, *Industrial Rehabilitation: the use of redundant buildings for small
    enterprises*, Architectural Press, 1984.
Mynors, Charles (ed.), *Urban Conservation and Historic Buildings: a guide to legislation*, Architec-
    tural Press, 1984, 96pp.
URBED (Urban & Economic Development Group), *Development Agencies for Wasteland*, URBED,
    1983, 100pp.

Wildlife

Baines, Chris, *How to Make a Wildlife Garden*, H. Hamilton, 1985, 192pp.
Baines, Chris, *Wildlife Conservation in Towns*, Croom Helm, 1984, 96pp.
Lewis, Gill & Williams, Gwyn, *Rivers and Wildlife Handbook: a guide to practices which further
    the conservation of wildlife on rivers*, Royal Society for the Protection of Birds, 1984.
Martin, Richard M. *First Aid and Care of Wildlife*, David & Charles, 1984, 288pp.
Myers, Norman, *A Wealth of Wild Species*, Bowker, 1984.
Wilson, Ronald, *The Urban Dweller's Wildlife Companion*, Blandford, 1983, 143pp.
World Wildlife Fund Yearbook [annual], WWF, c. 500pp.

SUBJECT INDEX

Nottinghamshire Environment Advisory
  Council
Offa's Dyke Association
Oldham and Rochdale Groundwork Trust
Open Spaces Society
Opencast Mining Intelligence Group
Orkney Heritage Society
Peak and Northern Footpaths Society
Peak National Park Centre
Peak Park Joint Planning Board
Pembrokeshire Coast National Park Committee
Pennine Way Council
Prince of Wales' Committee
Ramblers' Association
Rossendale Groundwork Trust
Royal Institution of Chartered Surveyors
Royal Society of Arts
Scottish Conservation Projects Trust
Scottish Countryside Rangers Association
Scottish Rights of Way Society
Scottish Wild Land Group
Scottish Youth Hostels Association
Seal Sands Conservation Group
Shell Better Britain Campaign
Snowdonia National Park Authority
Society of Sussex Downsmen
South West Way Association
Suffolk Countryside Campaign
Suffolk Preservation Society
Town and Country Planning Association
Ulster Countryside Committee
Ulster Society for the Preservation of the
  Countryside
West Midlands Think Green Network
Wild Flower Society
Wildlife and Countryside Services
Yorkshire Dales National Park Authority
Youth Environmental Action
Youth Hostel Association of Northern Ireland
Youth Hostels Association

Crafts
Association of Conservation Officers
Association of Designer/Leatherworkers
Basketmakers' Association
British Wood Turners Association
Building Conservation Trust
Crafts Commission
Crafts Council
Craftsmen Potters Association of Great Britain
Dry Stone Walling Association
Federation of British Craft Societies
Institute of Antiquarian Craftsmén
Men of the Stones
Mocrafts
National Federation of Young Farmers' Club
National Society of Master Thatchers
Skills Exchange Network for a Stable Economy

Cycling see also Transport
Bicycle Association of Great Britain
British Cycling Federation
Cyclebag

Cyclists' Association
Cyclists' Touring Club
Fellowship of Cycling Old-Timers
Friends of the Earth (Scotland)
London Cycling Campaign
Northern Ireland Cycling Federation
Tandem Club

Dairying see Agriculture
Defence see Arms control/peace movement

Development
Appropriate Health Resources and Techno-
  logies Action Group
Catholic Fund for Overseas Development
Centre for Economic and Environmental
  Development
Centre for Urban and Regional Development
  Studies
Centre for World Development Education
Commonwealth Human Ecology Council
Council for Education in World Citizenship
Council for Small Industries in Rural Areas
Development Commission
Earthlife
Ecoculture
Economic and Social Research Council
Environmental Conservation and Development
  Group
Fourth World Movement
Green Deserts
Heritage Holidays
Highlands and Island Development Board
Institute of Development Studies
Intermediate Technology Development Group
Intermediate Technology Power
Intermediate Technology Transport
Intermediate Technology Workshops
International Centre for Conservation
  Education
International Institute for Environment and
  Development
International Planned Parenthood Federation
Land Resources Development Centre
National Association of Development Education
  Centres
Overseas Development Administration
Quaker Peace and Service
Scottish Development Agency
Scottish Development Department
Scottish Education and Action for Development
Survival International
The Other Economic Summit
Third World First
Tools For Self-Reliance
United World Education and Research Trust
War on Want
WaterAid
Welsh Development Agency
World Development Movement
World Food Assembly

Entomology see Insects; Nature conservation

Environment: international agencies

Environment: planning & policy

Environmental consultants

Environmental education

Bedfordshire & Huntingdonshire Naturalists' Trust
Berkshire, Buckinghamshire & Oxfordshire Naturalists' Trust
Berwickshire Naturalists'Club
Brecknock Naturalists' Trust
British Arachnological Society
British Association of Nature Conservationists
British Butterfly Conservation Society
British Entomological and Natural History Society
British Herpetological Society
British Naturalists' Association
Cambridgeshire & Isle of Ely Naturalists' Trust
Cheshire Conservation Trust
City Wildlife Project
Cleveland Nature Conservation Trust
Committee for Nature Conservation (NI)
Cornwall Trust for Nature Conservation
Council for Environmental Conservation
Council for National Parks
Council for the Protection of Rural England
Council for the Protection of Rural Wales
Cumbria Trust for Nature Conservation
Department of the Environment for Northern Ireland
Derbyshire Naturalists' Trust
Devon Trust for Nature Conservation
Dorset Naturalists' Trust
Durham County Conservation Trust
Essex Naturalists' Trust
Fauna and Flora Preservation Society
Glamorgan Nature Conservation Trust
Gloucestershire Trust for Nature Conservation
Gwent Trust for Nature Conservation
Hampshire & Isle of Wight Naturalists' Trust
Herefordshire & Radnorshire Nature Trust
Hertfordshire & Middlesex Trust for Nature Conservation
IUCN Conservation Monitoring Centre
Joint Committee for the Conservation of British Insects
Kent Trust for Nature Conservation
Lancashire Trust for Nature Conservation
Leicestershire & Rutland Trust for Nature Conservation
Lincolnshire & South Humberside Trust for Nature Conservation
London Wildlife Trust
Mammal Society
Manx Nature Conservation Trust
Montgomery Trust for Nature Conservation
Nature Conservancy Council
Nature Reserves Committee (NI)
Norfolk Naturalists' Trust
North Wales Naturalists' Trust
North Western Naturalists' Union
Northamptonshire Trust for Nature Conservation
Northumberland Wildlife Trust
Nottinghamshire Trust for Nature Conservation
Plymouth Urban Wildlife Group

Protection and Conservation of Animals and Plant Life
Royal Entomological Society
Royal Society for Nature Conservation
Scottish Wildlife Trust
Shropshire Trust for Nature Conservation
Somerset Trust for Nature Conservation
Staffordshire Nature Conservation Trust
Suffolk Trust for Nature Conservation
Surrey Trust for Nature Conservation
Sussex Trust for Nature Conservation
Ulster Trust for Nature Conservation
Urban Wildlife Group
Warwickshire Nature Conservation Trust
WATCH Trust for Environmental Education
West Wales Trust for Nature Conservation
Wildlife and Countryside Services
Wiltshire Trust for Nature Conservation
Worcestershire Nature Conservation Trust
World Wildlife Fund
Yorkshire Wildlife Trust

Nature reserves see Nature conservation/study
Nature study see Nature conservation/study

Naturopathy see also Natural therapies
British College of Naturopathy and Osteopathy
British Naturopathic and Osteopathic Association
Incorporated Society of Registered Naturopaths
Osteopathic and Naturopathic Guild

Noise see Pollution: noise
Nuclear power see Energy: nuclear
Nuclear weapons see Arms control/peace movement
Nutrition see Food; Health: personal

Ocean thermal energy conversion (OTEC) see Energy: ocean thermal energy conversion
Oceanography see Earth sciences
Oil see Energy: fossil fuels
Open spaces see Countryside conservation; Environment: planning; Urban conservation
Organic farming/gardening see Agriculture; Horticulture

Organisations not based in the UK or Ireland
CONCAWE (Conservation of Clean Air and Water in Western Europe)
ECHO (European Commission Host Organisation)
Environment Liaison Centre
EURATOM (European Atomic Energy Community)
European Atomic Energy Society
European Environmental Bureau
European Information Centre for Nature Conservation
European Nuclear Society

Food and Agriculture Organisation
Friends of the Earth (International Secretariat)
Institute for European Environmental Policy
International Atomic Energy Agency
International Energy Agency
International Nuclear Law Association
International Radiation Protection Association
International Research Center on Environment
  and Development
International Union for Conservation of Nature
  and Natural Resources
OECD (Organisation for European Co-oper-
  ation and Development)
OECD Nuclear Energy Agency
Pugwash Conferences on Science and World
  Affairs (Executive Office)
SATIS (Socially Appropriate Technology Infor-
  mation Service)
SIPRI (Stockholm International Peace Research
  Institute)
UNESCO (UN Educational, Scientific and
  Cultural Organisation)
United Nations Environment Programme
World Commission on Environment and
  Development
World Health Organisation

Ornithology see Birds
Osteopathy see Manipulative medicine
Otters see Wildlife

Peace see Arms control/peace movement

Permaculture
Appropriate Technology Group
Lifestyle 2000
Permaculture Association (Britain)
Practical Alternatives

Personal development & human potential
Association for Self-Help and Community
  Groups
Association of Humanistic Psychology
  Practitioners
Centre for Alternative Education and Research
Centre for Transpersonal Psychology
Dharma Therapy Trust
Dunamis
Eigenwelt Studies
Findhorn Foundation
Foundation for Holistic Consciousness
Future in Our Hands
Institute of Psychosynthesis
Interhelp
Interskill
Mediating Network
Morpeth Centre for Psychotherapy
Morpeth Meditation
New Era Centre
Northumbria Seekers
Open Centre
Progressive League
Psychotherapy Centre

Teilhard Centre
Theosophical Society
Wrekin Trust

Pesticides see Agriculture; Pollution:
  foodstuffs
Petroleum see Energy: fossil fuels
Pets see Animal welfare
Planning see Environment: planning & policy

Plants & plant science see also Horticulture;
  Nature conservation
Botanical Society of the British Isles
Botanical Society of Edinburgh
British Lichen Society
Commonwealth Bureau of Plant Breeding and
  Genetics
Commonwealth Mycological Institute
Fauna and Flora Preservation Society
Garden History Society
Institute of Terrestrial Ecology
IUCN Conservation Monitoring Centre
National Council for the Conservation of Plants
  and Gardens
National Institute of Agricultural Botany
Protection and Conservation of Animals and
  Plant Life
Royal Botanic Gardens, Kew
Royal Botanical and Horticultural Society
Royal Horticultural Society
Royal Horticultural Society of Ireland
Seed Bank & Exchange
Unit of Comparative Plant Ecology
Weed Research Organisation
Welsh Plant Breeding Station
Wild Flower Society

Poisonous wastes see Health: environmental;
  Pollution

Political ecology see also Ethics/philosophy
Conservative Ecology Group
Council for Education in World Citizenship
Ecology Party
Ecoropa
Fellowship Party
Fourth World Movement
Green Alliance
Green Alliance (RI)
Green Collective
Huntingdon Greens
Liberal Ecology Group
SDP Greens
SERA (Socialist Environment and Resources
  Association)
Socialist Countryside Group
Student Green Network

Pollution see specific, below
see also Health: environmental

Pollution: atmospheric
ASH (Action on Smoking and Health)

Pollution: coastal/marine

Pollution: foodstuffs/land contamination

Pollution: inland water